Ross Richie	CEO & Founder
Matt Gagnon	Editor-In-Chief
Filip Sablik	President of Publishing & Marketing
Stephen Christy	President of Development
Lance Kreiter	VP of Licensing & Merchandising
Phil Barbaro	VP of Finance
Bryce Carlson	Managing Editor
Mel Caylo	Marketing Manager
Scott Newman	Production Design Manager
Irene Bradish	Operations Manager
Sierra Hahn	Senior Editor
Dafna Pleban	Editor
Shannon Watters	Editor
Eric Harburn	Editor
Whitney Leopard	Associate Editor
Jasmine Amiri	Associate Editor
Chris Rosa	Associate Editor
Alex Galer	Assistant Editor
Cameron Chittock	Assistant Editor
Mary Gumport	Assistant Editor
Matthew Levine	Assistant Editor
Kelsey Dieterich	Production Designer
Jillian Crab	Production Designer
Michelle Ankley	Production Design Assistant
Grace Park	Production Design Assistant
Aaron Ferrara	Operations Coordinator
Elizabeth Loughridge	Accounting Coordinator
José Meza	Sales Assistant
James Arriola	Mailroom Assistant
Holly Aitchison	Operations Assistant
Stephanie Hocutt	Marketing Assistant
Sam Kusek	Direct Market Representative

TOIL AND TROUBLE, September 2016. Published by Archaia, a division of Boom Entertainment, Inc. Toil and Trouble is ™ & © 2016 Mairghread Scott. All rights reserved. Archaia™ and the Archaia logo are trademarks of Boom Entertainment, Inc., registered in various countries and categories. All characters, events, and institutions depicted herein are fictional. Any similarity between any of the names, characters, persons, events, and/or institutions in this publications to actual names, characters, and persons, whether living or dead, events, and/or institutions is unintended and purely coincidental.

BOOM! Studios, 5670 Wilshire Boulevard, Suite 450, Los Angeles, CA 90036-5679. Printed in China. First Printing.

ISBN: 978-1-60886-878-0, eISBN: 978-1-61398-549-6

Created & Written by
Mairghread Scott

Illustrated by
Kelly & Nichole Matthews

Lettered by
Warren Montgomery

Cover by
Sarah Stone

Character Designs by
Sarah Stone & Kyla Vanderklugt

Designer
Jillian Crab

Associate Editor
Whitney Leopard

Editor
Sierra Hahn

Special Thanks to Rebecca Taylor, Eliza Frye,
The Comic Book Women, my wonderful family,
and of course, William Shakespeare.

Act One

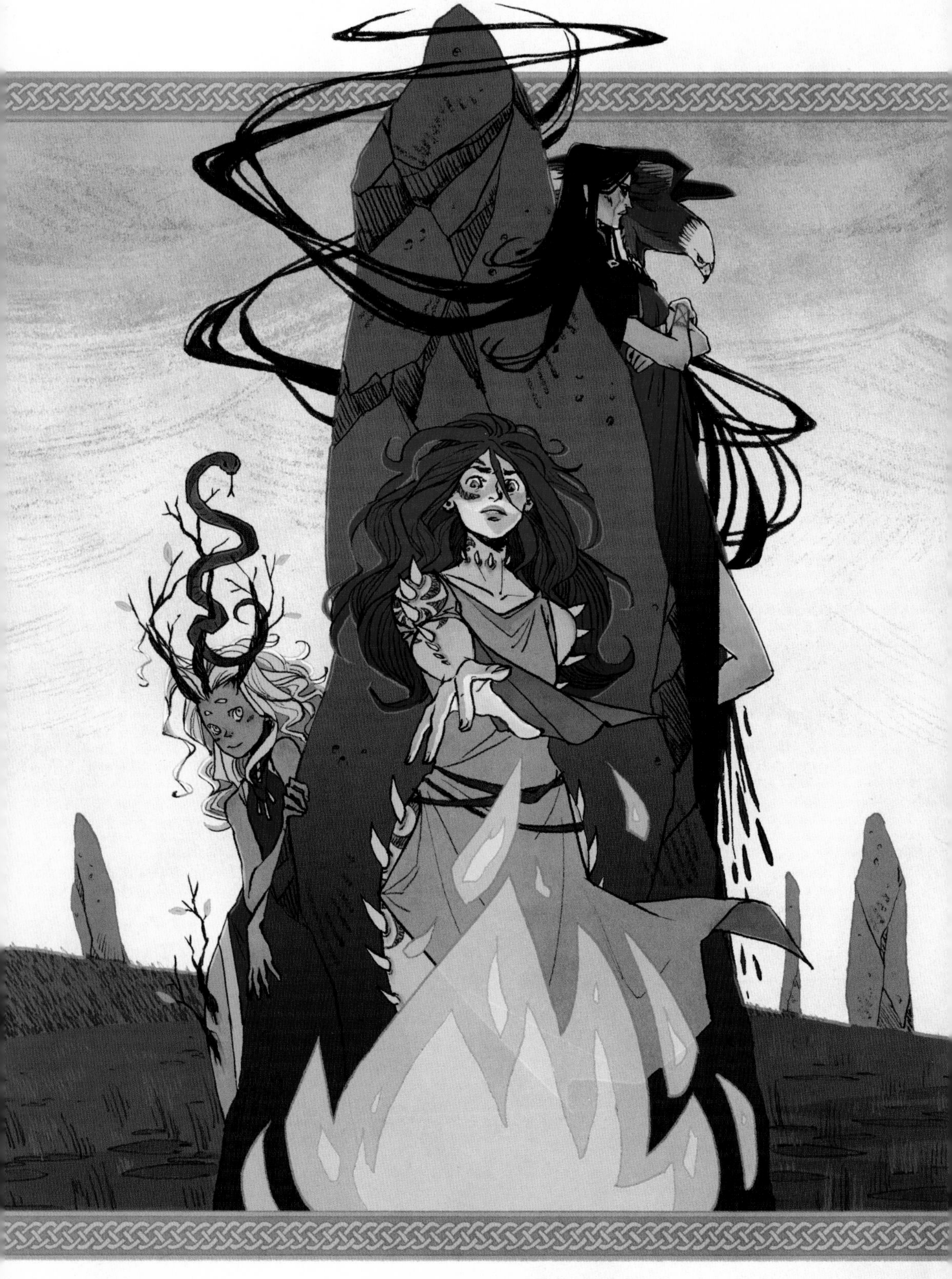

Issue One Cover by Kyla Vanderklugt

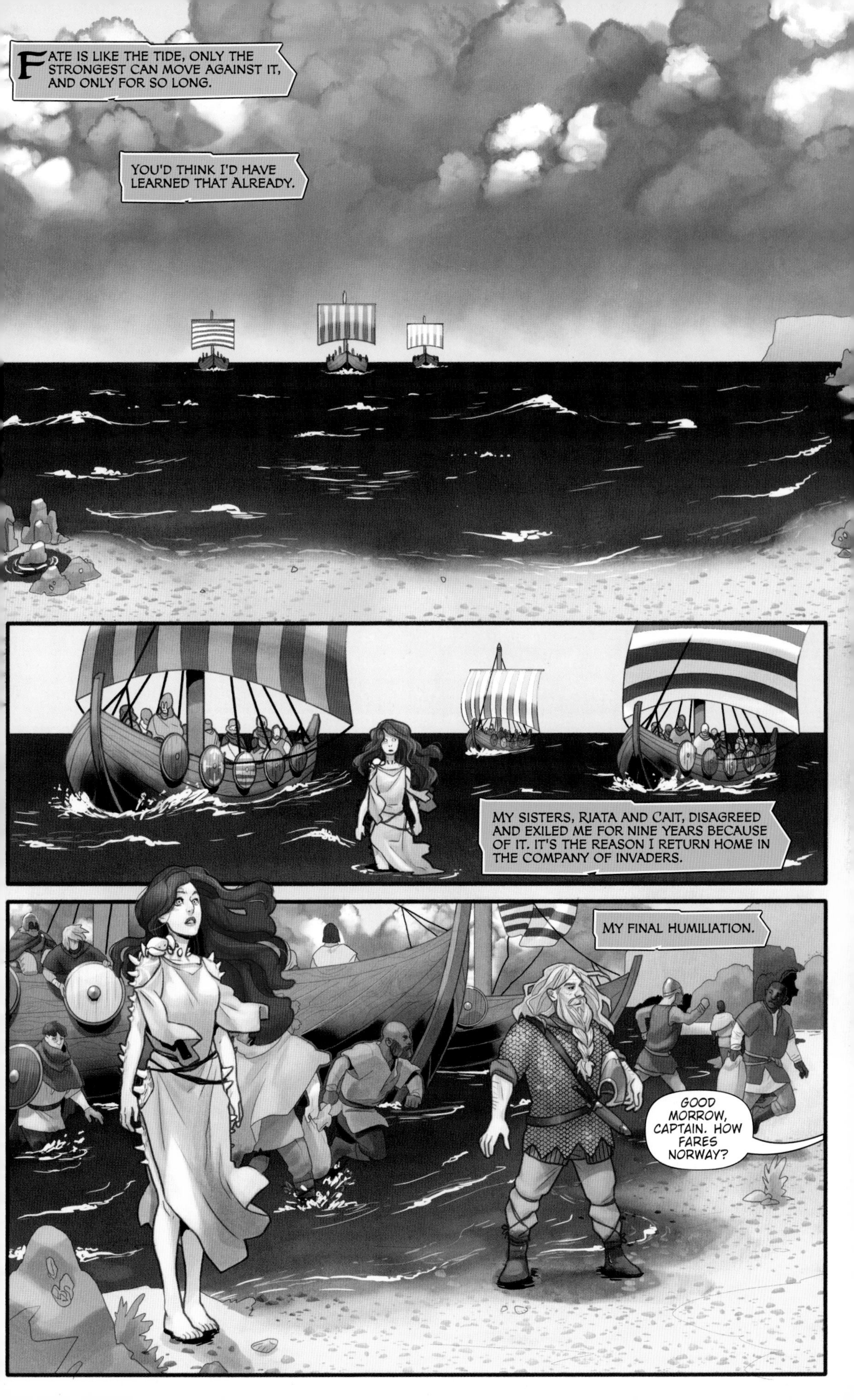
FATE IS LIKE THE TIDE, ONLY THE STRONGEST CAN MOVE AGAINST IT, AND ONLY FOR SO LONG.
YOU'D THINK I'D HAVE LEARNED THAT ALREADY.
MY SISTERS, RIATA AND CAIT, DISAGREED AND EXILED ME FOR NINE YEARS BECAUSE OF IT. IT'S THE REASON I RETURN HOME IN THE COMPANY OF INVADERS.
MY FINAL HUMILIATION.
GOOD MORROW, CAPTAIN. HOW FARES NORWAY?

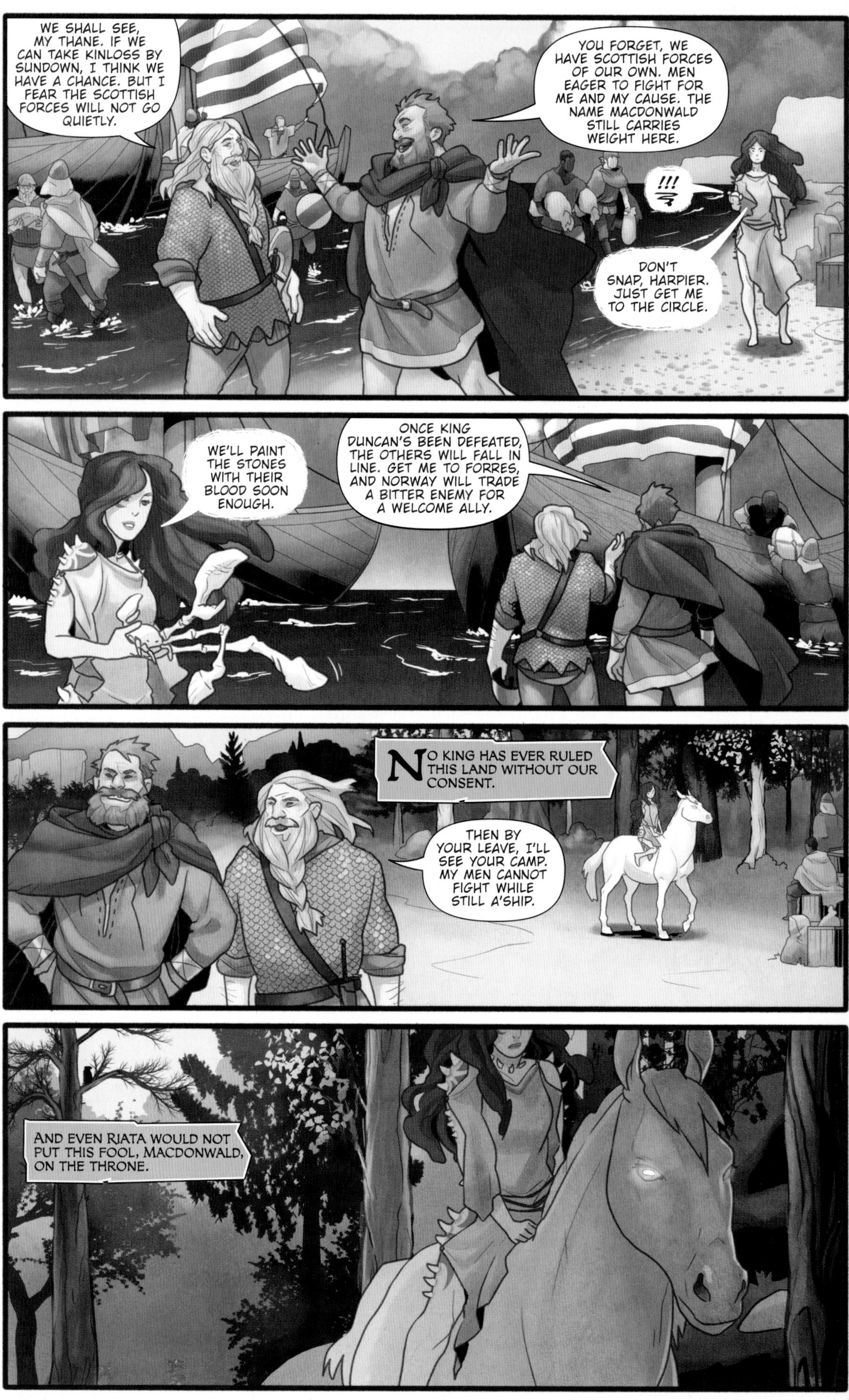

WE SHALL SEE, MY THANE. IF WE CAN TAKE KINLOSS BY SUNDOWN, I THINK WE HAVE A CHANCE. BUT I FEAR THE SCOTTISH FORCES WILL NOT GO QUIETLY.
YOU FORGET, WE HAVE SCOTTISH FORCES OF OUR OWN. MEN EAGER TO FIGHT FOR ME AND MY CAUSE. THE NAME MACDONWALD STILL CARRIES WEIGHT HERE.
!!!
DON'T SNAP, HARPIER. JUST GET ME TO THE CIRCLE.
WE'LL PAINT THE STONES WITH THEIR BLOOD SOON ENOUGH.
ONCE KING DUNCAN'S BEEN DEFEATED, THE OTHERS WILL FALL IN LINE. GET ME TO FORRES, AND NORWAY WILL TRADE A BITTER ENEMY FOR A WELCOME ALLY.
NO KING HAS EVER RULED THIS LAND WITHOUT OUR CONSENT.
THEN BY YOUR LEAVE, I'LL SEE YOUR CAMP. MY MEN CANNOT FIGHT WHILE STILL A'SHIP.
AND EVEN RIATA WOULD NOT PUT THIS FOOL, MACDONWALD, ON THE THRONE.

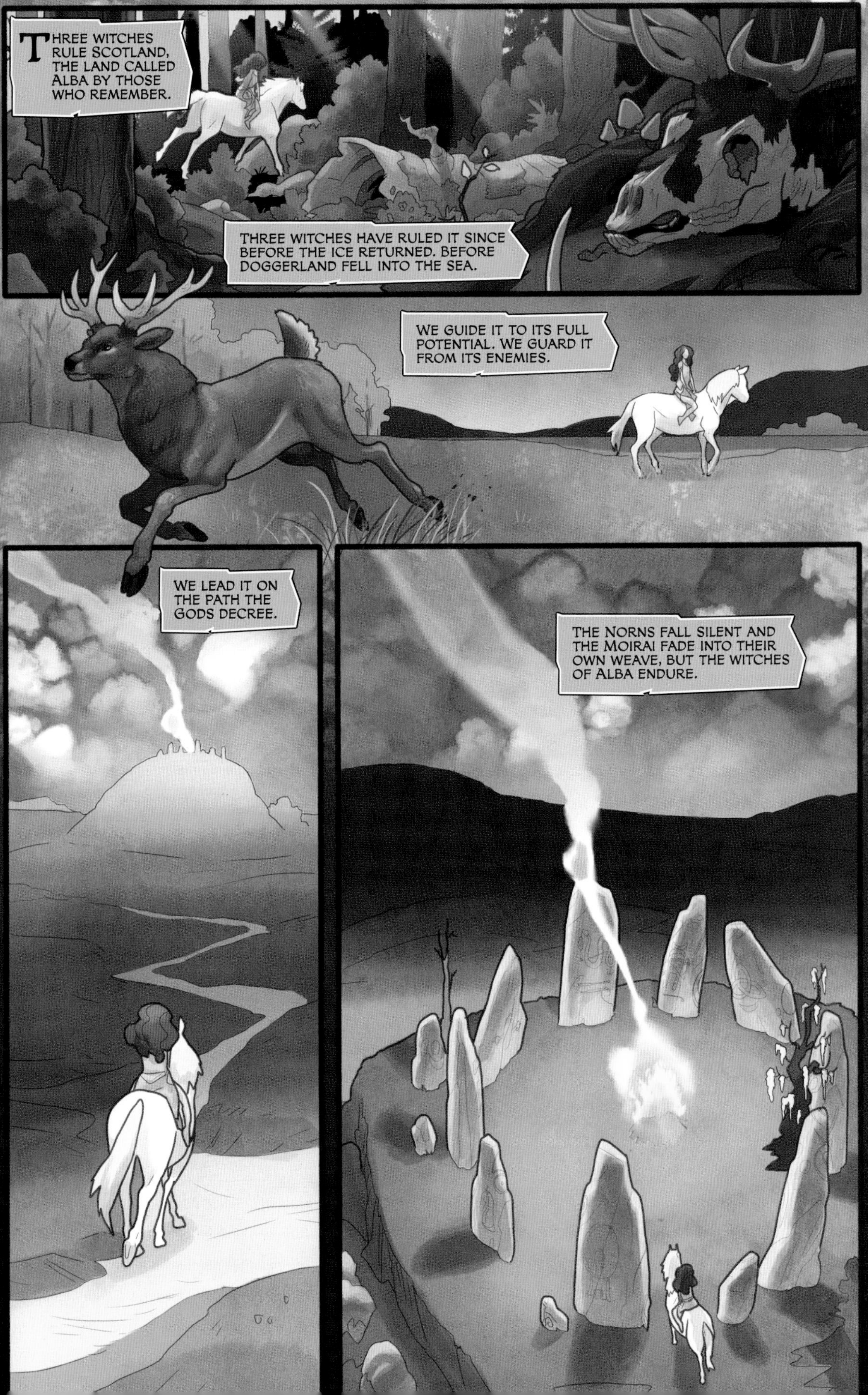
THREE WITCHES RULE SCOTLAND, THE LAND CALLED ALBA BY THOSE WHO REMEMBER.
THREE WITCHES HAVE RULED IT SINCE BEFORE THE ICE RETURNED. BEFORE DOGGERLAND FELL INTO THE SEA.
WE GUIDE IT TO ITS FULL POTENTIAL. WE GUARD IT FROM ITS ENEMIES.
WE LEAD IT ON THE PATH THE GODS DECREE.
THE NORNS FALL SILENT AND THE MOIRAI FADE INTO THEIR OWN WEAVE, BUT THE WITCHES OF ALBA ENDURE.

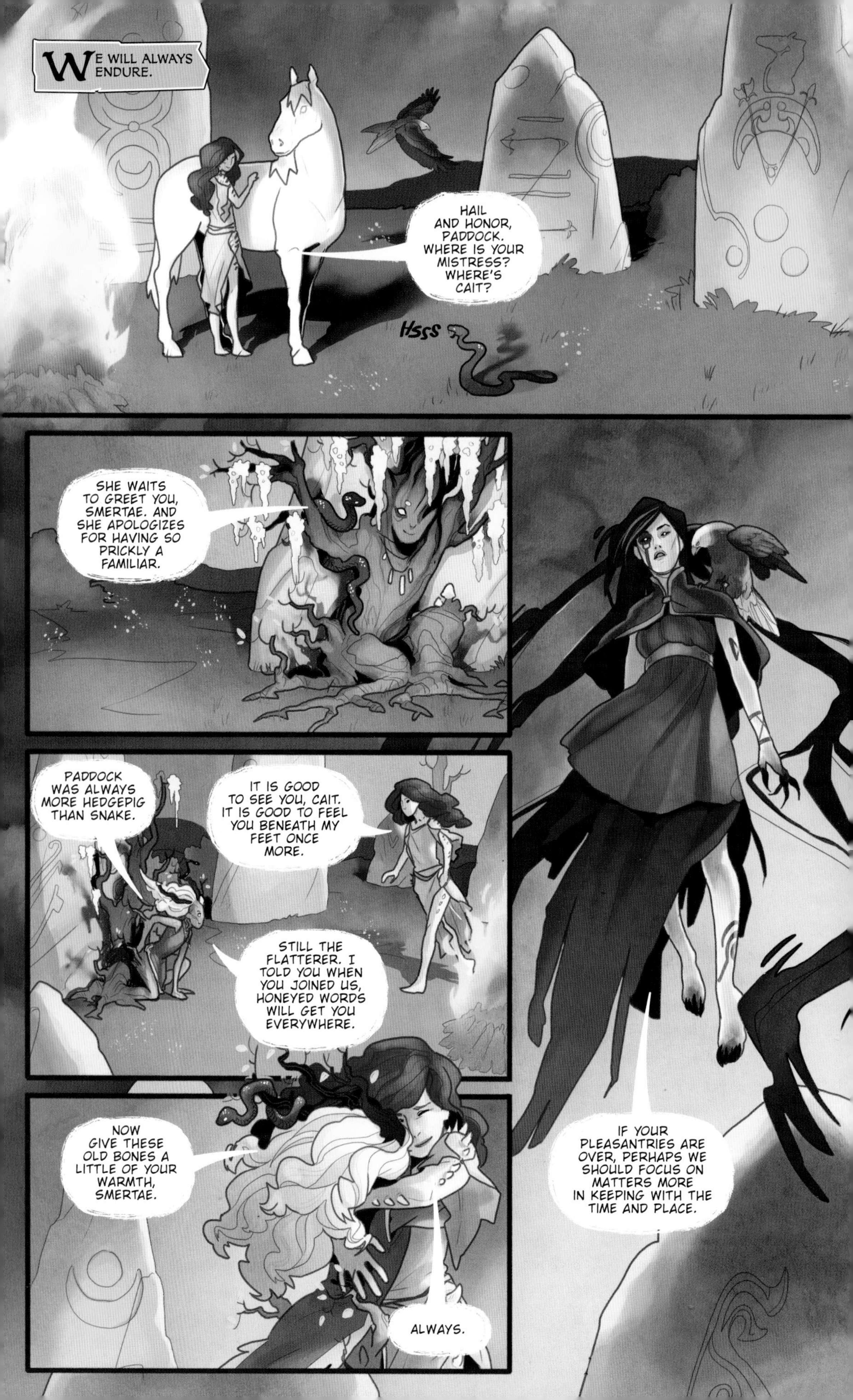
WE WILL ALWAYS ENDURE.
HAIL AND HONOR, PADDOCK. WHERE IS YOUR MISTRESS? WHERE'S CAIT?
HSSS
SHE WAITS TO GREET YOU, SMERTAE. AND SHE APOLOGIZES FOR HAVING SO PRICKLY A FAMILIAR.
PADDOCK WAS ALWAYS MORE HEDGEPIG THAN SNAKE.
IT IS GOOD TO SEE YOU, CAIT. IT IS GOOD TO FEEL YOU BENEATH MY FEET ONCE MORE.
STILL THE FLATTERER. I TOLD YOU WHEN YOU JOINED US, HONEYED WORDS WILL GET YOU EVERYWHERE.
NOW GIVE THESE OLD BONES A LITTLE OF YOUR WARMTH, SMERTAE.
ALWAYS.
IF YOUR PLEASANTRIES ARE OVER, PERHAPS WE SHOULD FOCUS ON MATTERS MORE IN KEEPING WITH THE TIME AND PLACE.

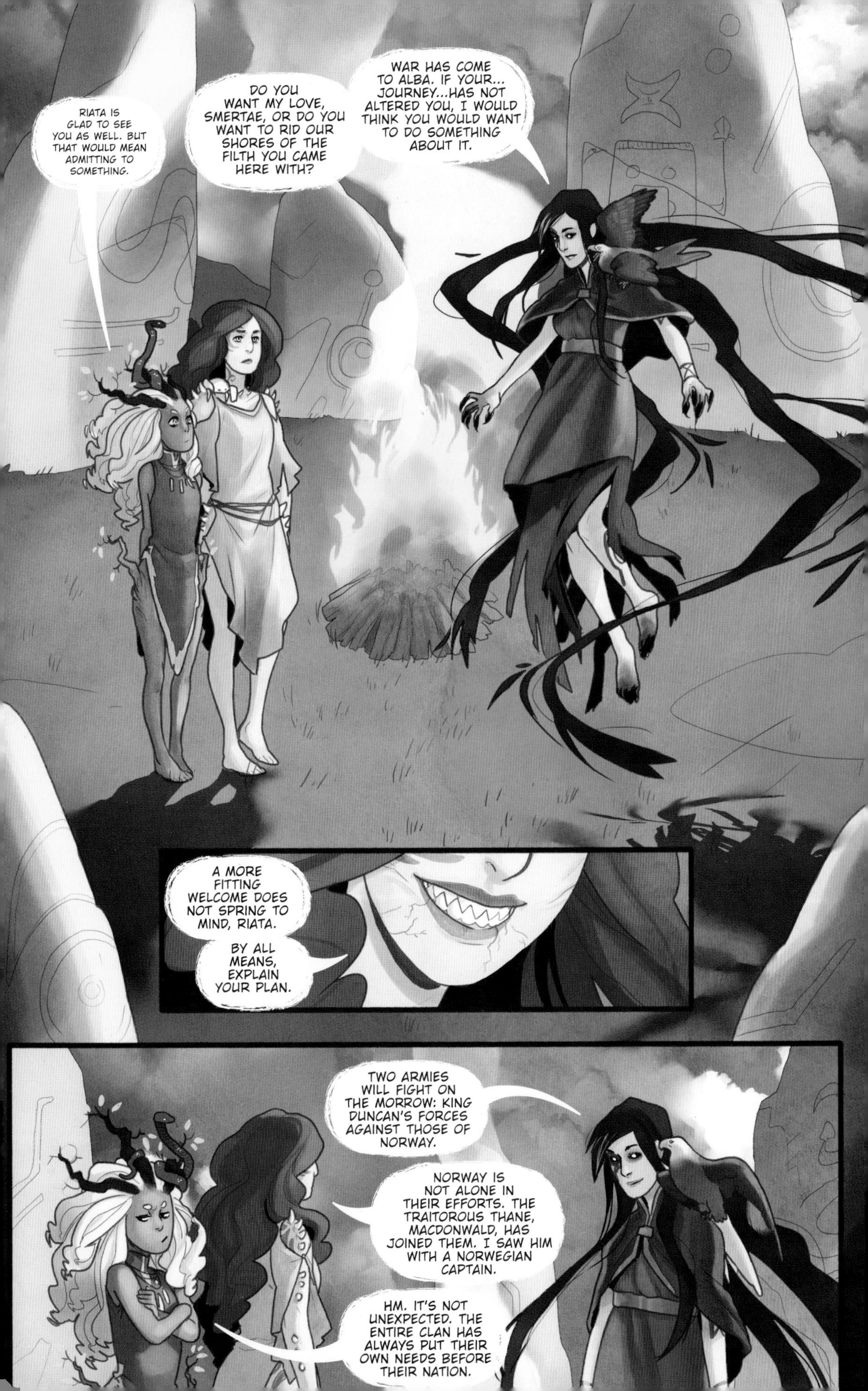
RIATA IS GLAD TO SEE YOU AS WELL. BUT THAT WOULD MEAN ADMITTING TO SOMETHING.
DO YOU WANT MY LOVE, SMERTAE, OR DO YOU WANT TO RID OUR SHORES OF THE FILTH YOU CAME HERE WITH?
WAR HAS COME TO ALBA. IF YOUR... JOURNEY...HAS NOT ALTERED YOU, I WOULD THINK YOU WOULD WANT TO DO SOMETHING ABOUT IT.
A MORE FITTING WELCOME DOES NOT SPRING TO MIND, RIATA.
BY ALL MEANS, EXPLAIN YOUR PLAN.
TWO ARMIES WILL FIGHT ON THE MORROW: KING DUNCAN'S FORCES AGAINST THOSE OF NORWAY.
NORWAY IS NOT ALONE IN THEIR EFFORTS. THE TRAITOROUS THANE, MACDONWALD, HAS JOINED THEM. I SAW HIM WITH A NORWEGIAN CAPTAIN.
HM. IT'S NOT UNEXPECTED. THE ENTIRE CLAN HAS ALWAYS PUT THEIR OWN NEEDS BEFORE THEIR NATION.

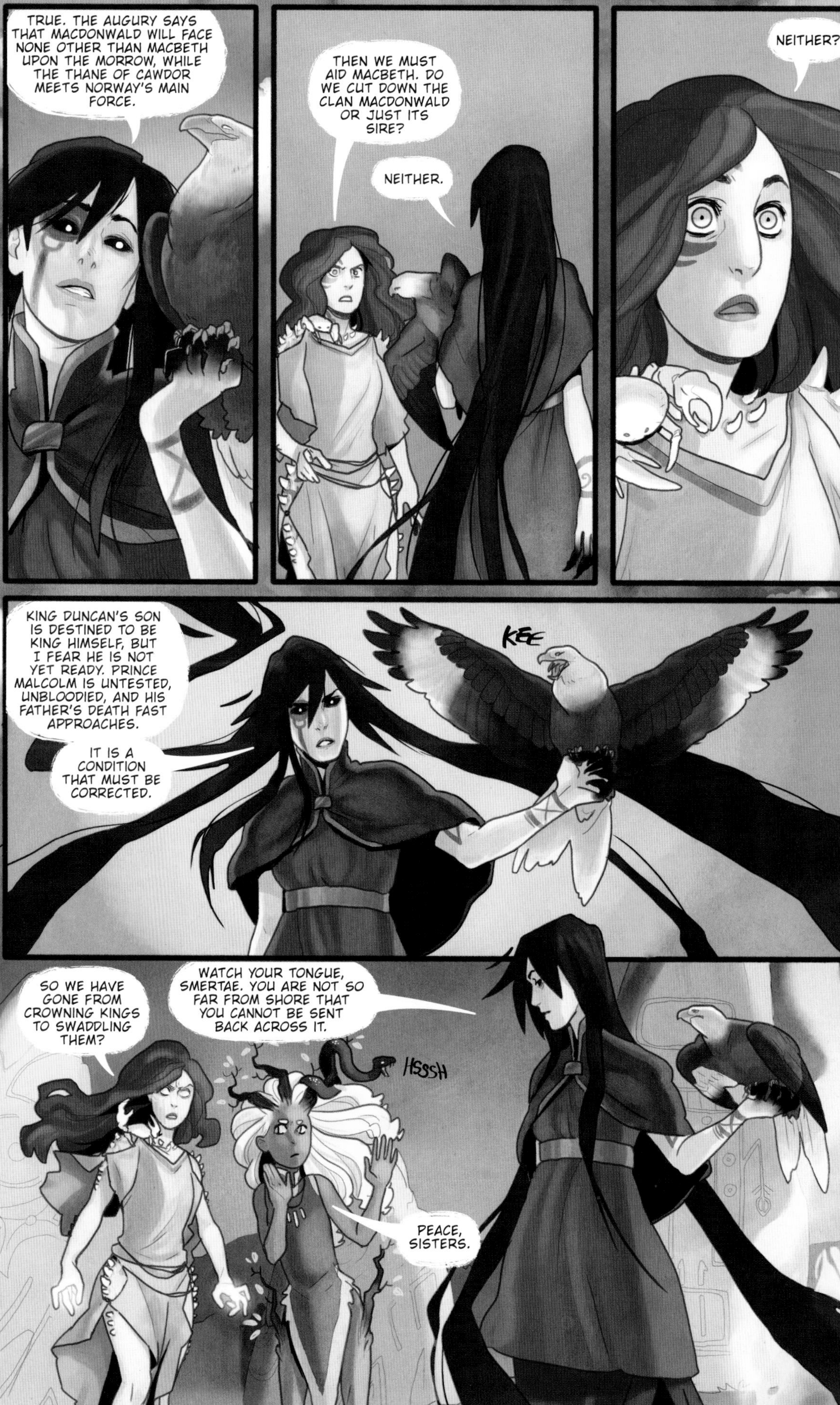
TRUE. THE AUGURY SAYS THAT MACDONWALD WILL FACE NONE OTHER THAN MACBETH UPON THE MORROW, WHILE THE THANE OF CAWDOR MEETS NORWAY'S MAIN FORCE.
THEN WE MUST AID MACBETH. DO WE CUT DOWN THE CLAN MACDONWALD OR JUST ITS SIRE?
NEITHER.
NEITHER?
KING DUNCAN'S SON IS DESTINED TO BE KING HIMSELF, BUT I FEAR HE IS NOT YET READY. PRINCE MALCOLM IS UNTESTED, UNBLOODIED, AND HIS FATHER'S DEATH FAST APPROACHES.
IT IS A CONDITION THAT MUST BE CORRECTED.
KEE
SO WE HAVE GONE FROM CROWNING KINGS TO SWADDLING THEM?
WATCH YOUR TONGUE, SMERTAE. YOU ARE NOT SO FAR FROM SHORE THAT YOU CANNOT BE SENT BACK ACROSS IT.
HSSSH
PEACE, SISTERS.

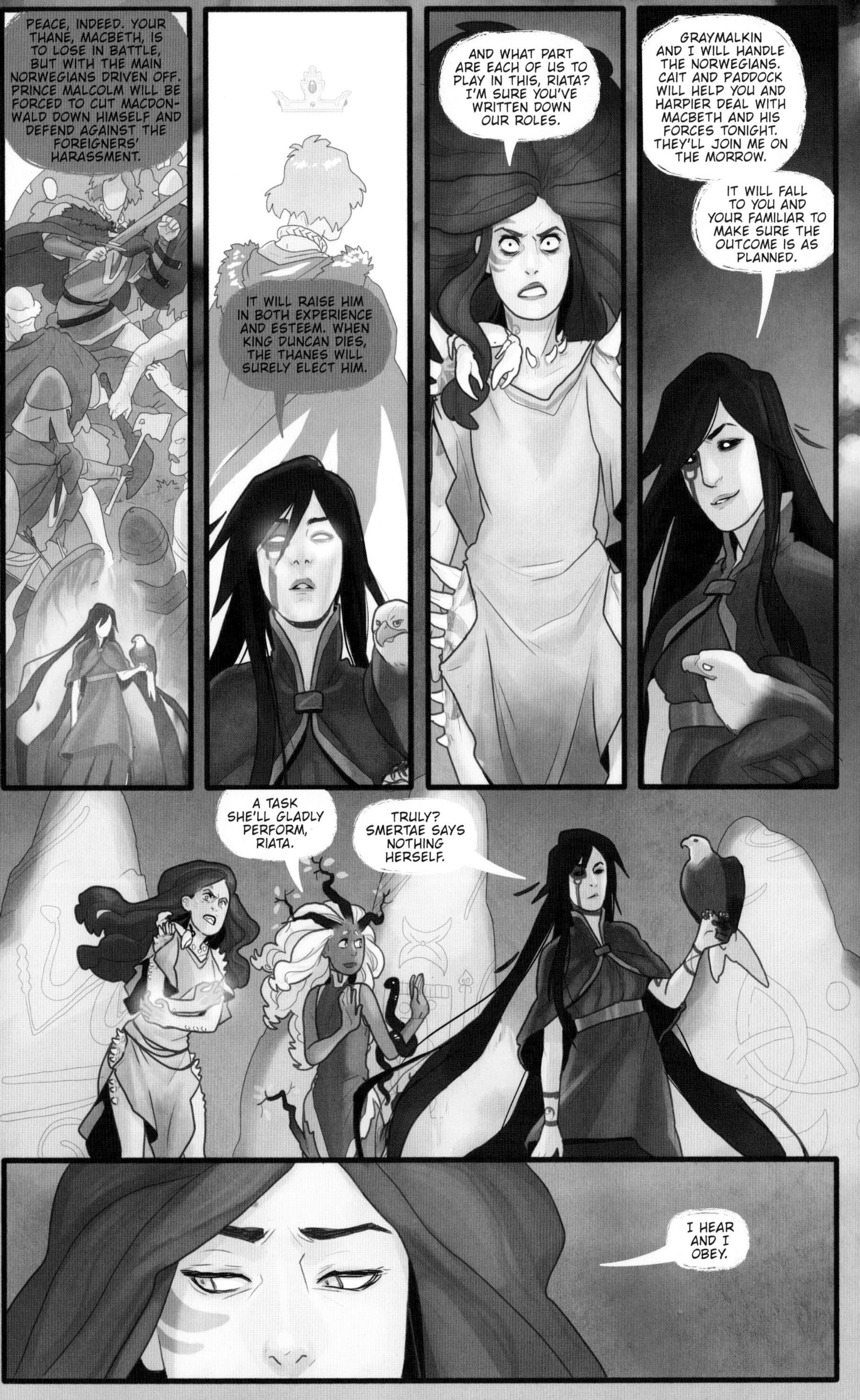
PEACE, INDEED. YOUR THANE, MACBETH, IS TO LOSE IN BATTLE, BUT WITH THE MAIN NORWEGIANS DRIVEN OFF. PRINCE MALCOLM WILL BE FORCED TO CUT MACDON-WALD DOWN HIMSELF AND DEFEND AGAINST THE FOREIGNERS' HARASSMENT.
IT WILL RAISE HIM IN BOTH EXPERIENCE AND ESTEEM. WHEN KING DUNCAN DIES, THE THANES WILL SURELY ELECT HIM.
AND WHAT PART ARE EACH OF US TO PLAY IN THIS, RIATA? I'M SURE YOU'VE WRITTEN DOWN OUR ROLES.
GRAYMALKIN AND I WILL HANDLE THE NORWEGIANS. CAIT AND PADDOCK WILL HELP YOU AND HARPIER DEAL WITH MACBETH AND HIS FORCES TONIGHT. THEY'LL JOIN ME ON THE MORROW.
IT WILL FALL TO YOU AND YOUR FAMILIAR TO MAKE SURE THE OUTCOME IS AS PLANNED.
A TASK SHE'LL GLADLY PERFORM, RIATA.
TRULY? SMERTAE SAYS NOTHING HERSELF.
I HEAR AND I OBEY.

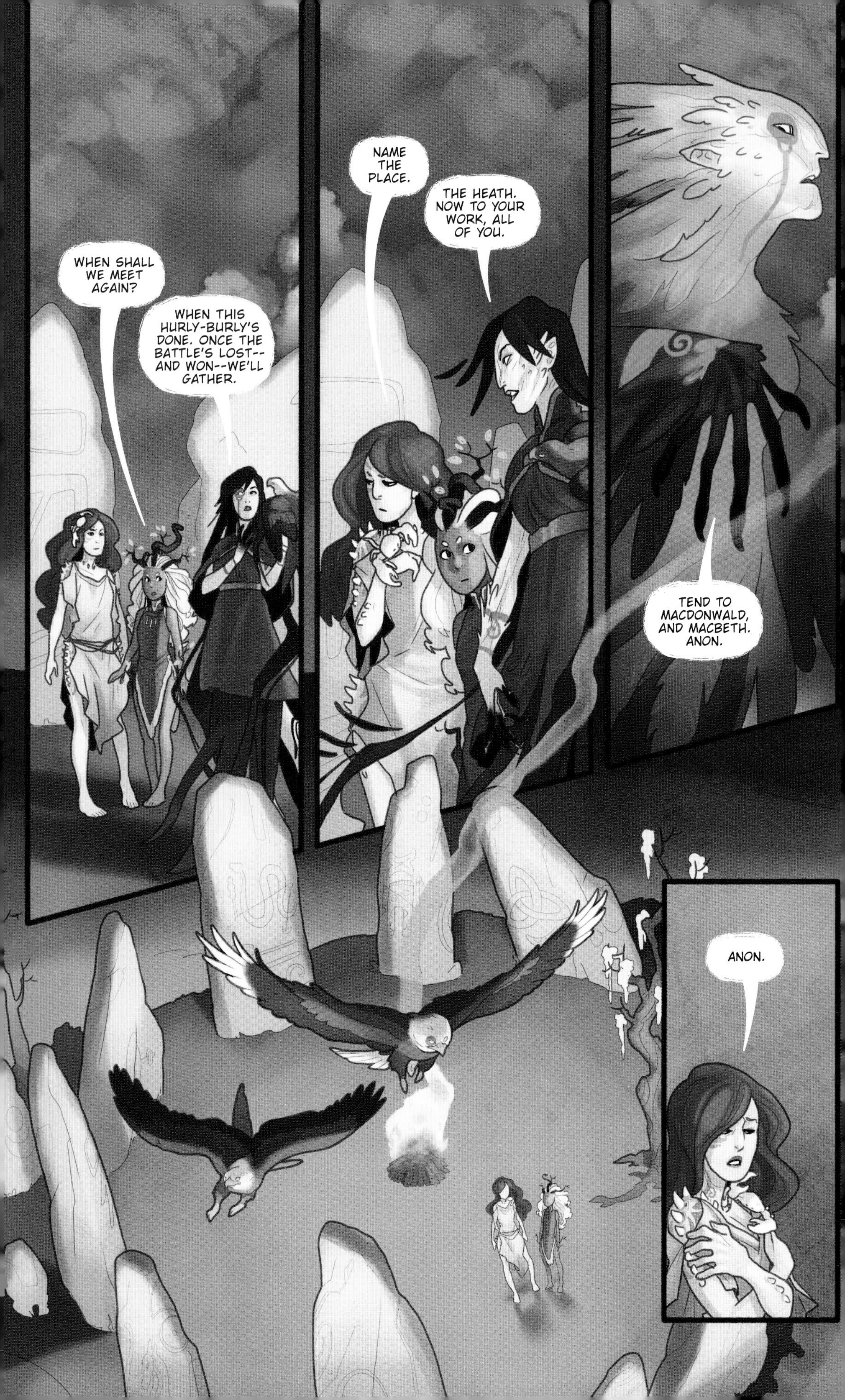
WHEN SHALL WE MEET AGAIN?
WHEN THIS HURLY-BURLY'S DONE. ONCE THE BATTLE'S LOST--AND WON--WE'LL GATHER.
NAME THE PLACE.
THE HEATH. NOW TO YOUR WORK, ALL OF YOU.
TEND TO MACDONWALD, AND MACBETH. ANON.
ANON.

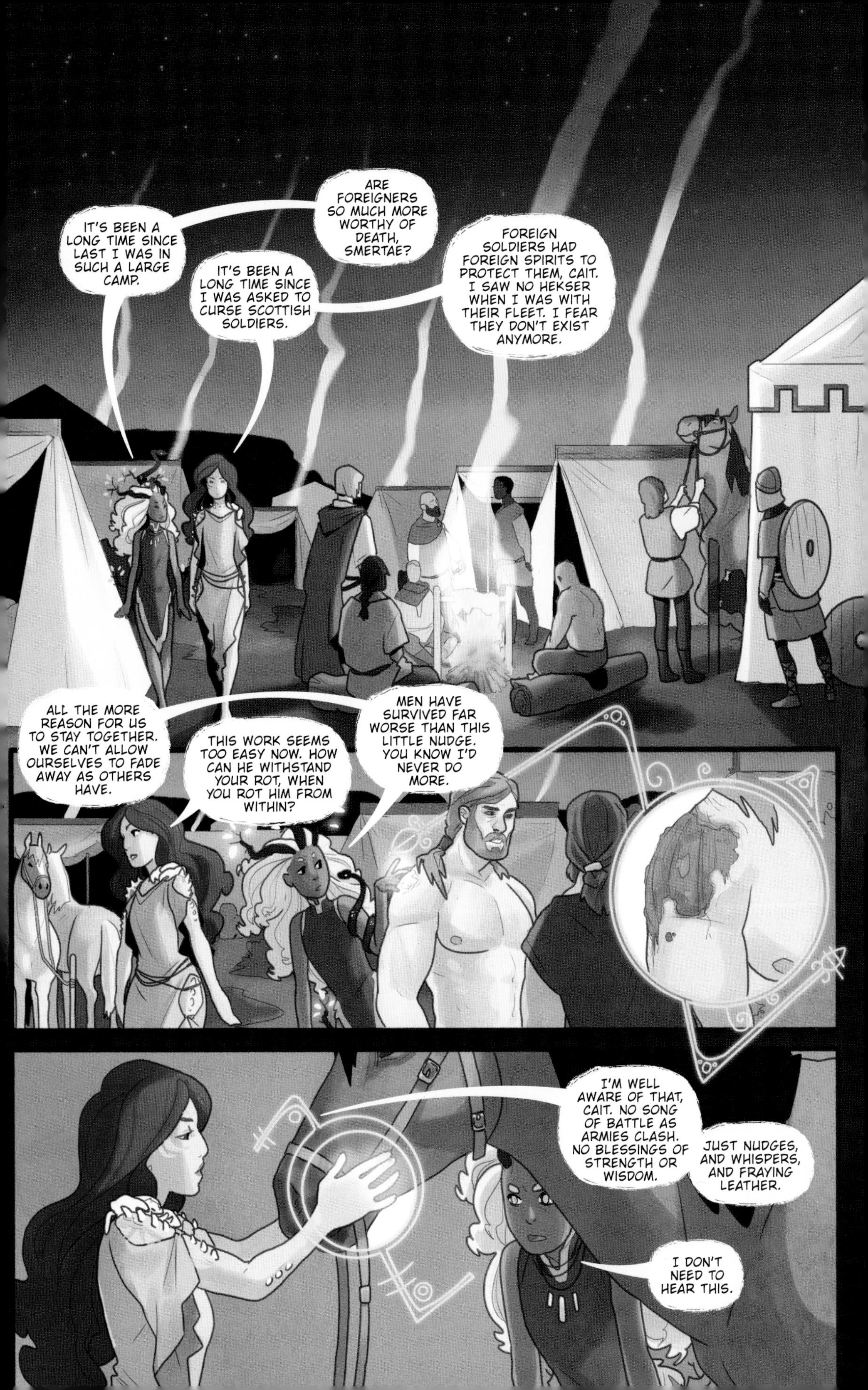
IT'S BEEN A LONG TIME SINCE LAST I WAS IN SUCH A LARGE CAMP.
ARE FOREIGNERS SO MUCH MORE WORTHY OF DEATH, SMERTAE?
IT'S BEEN A LONG TIME SINCE I WAS ASKED TO CURSE SCOTTISH SOLDIERS.
FOREIGN SOLDIERS HAD FOREIGN SPIRITS TO PROTECT THEM, CAIT. I SAW NO HEKSER WHEN I WAS WITH THEIR FLEET. I FEAR THEY DON'T EXIST ANYMORE.
ALL THE MORE REASON FOR US TO STAY TOGETHER. WE CAN'T ALLOW OURSELVES TO FADE AWAY AS OTHERS HAVE.
THIS WORK SEEMS TOO EASY NOW. HOW CAN HE WITHSTAND YOUR ROT, WHEN YOU ROT HIM FROM WITHIN?
MEN HAVE SURVIVED FAR WORSE THAN THIS LITTLE NUDGE. YOU KNOW I'D NEVER DO MORE.
I'M WELL AWARE OF THAT, CAIT. NO SONG OF BATTLE AS ARMIES CLASH. NO BLESSINGS OF STRENGTH OR WISDOM.
JUST NUDGES, AND WHISPERS, AND FRAYING LEATHER.
I DON'T NEED TO HEAR THIS.

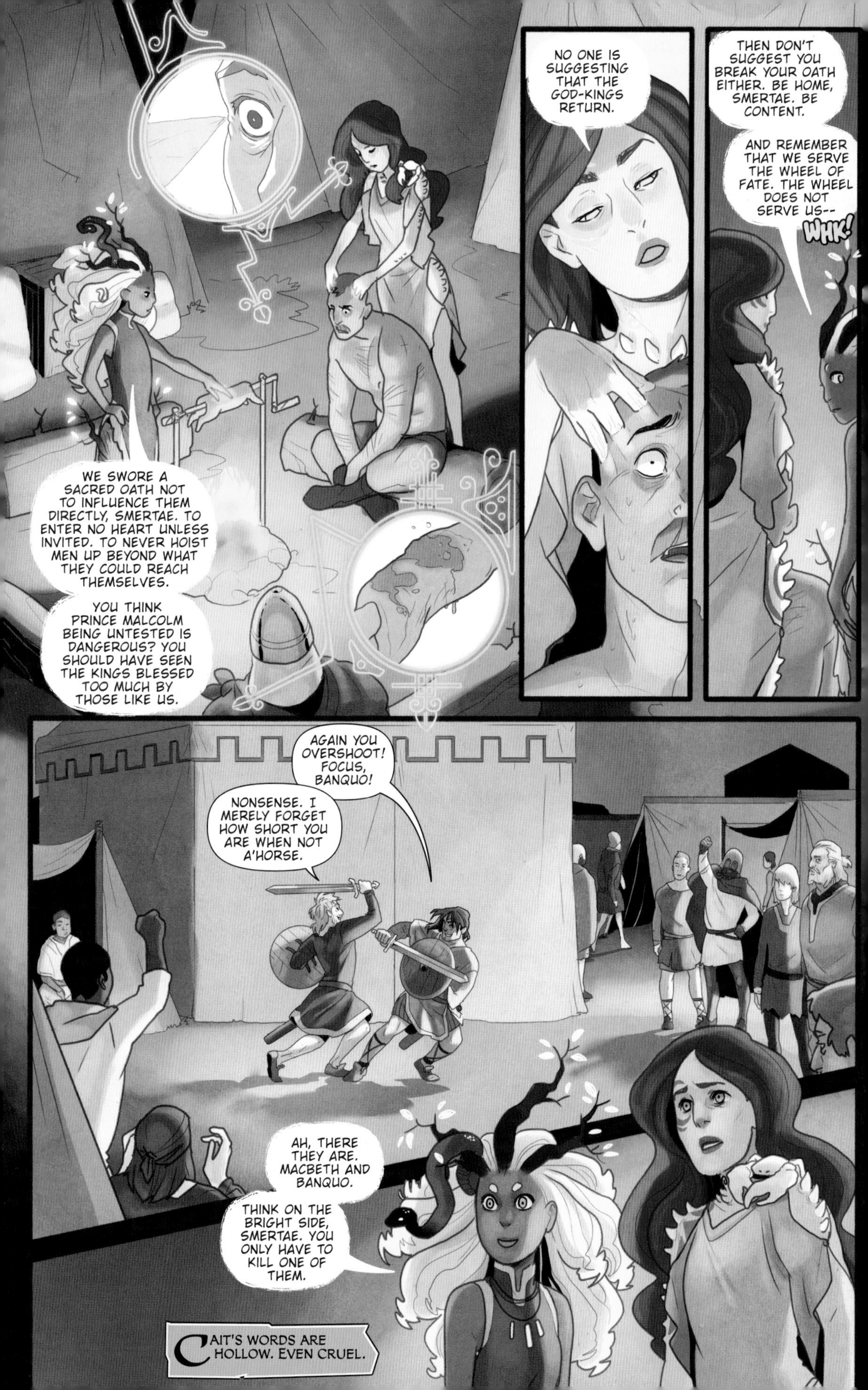
WE SWORE A SACRED OATH NOT TO INFLUENCE THEM DIRECTLY, SMERTAE. TO ENTER NO HEART UNLESS INVITED. TO NEVER HOIST MEN UP BEYOND WHAT THEY COULD REACH THEMSELVES.
YOU THINK PRINCE MALCOLM BEING UNTESTED IS DANGEROUS? YOU SHOULD HAVE SEEN THE KINGS BLESSED TOO MUCH BY THOSE LIKE US.
NO ONE IS SUGGESTING THAT THE GOD-KINGS RETURN.
THEN DON'T SUGGEST YOU BREAK YOUR OATH EITHER. BE HOME, SMERTAE. BE CONTENT.
AND REMEMBER THAT WE SERVE THE WHEEL OF FATE. THE WHEEL DOES NOT SERVE US--
WHK!
AGAIN YOU OVERSHOOT! FOCUS, BANQUO!
NONSENSE. I MERELY FORGET HOW SHORT YOU ARE WHEN NOT A'HORSE.
AH, THERE THEY ARE. MACBETH AND BANQUO.
THINK ON THE BRIGHT SIDE, SMERTAE. YOU ONLY HAVE TO KILL ONE OF THEM.
CAIT'S WORDS ARE HOLLOW. EVEN CRUEL.

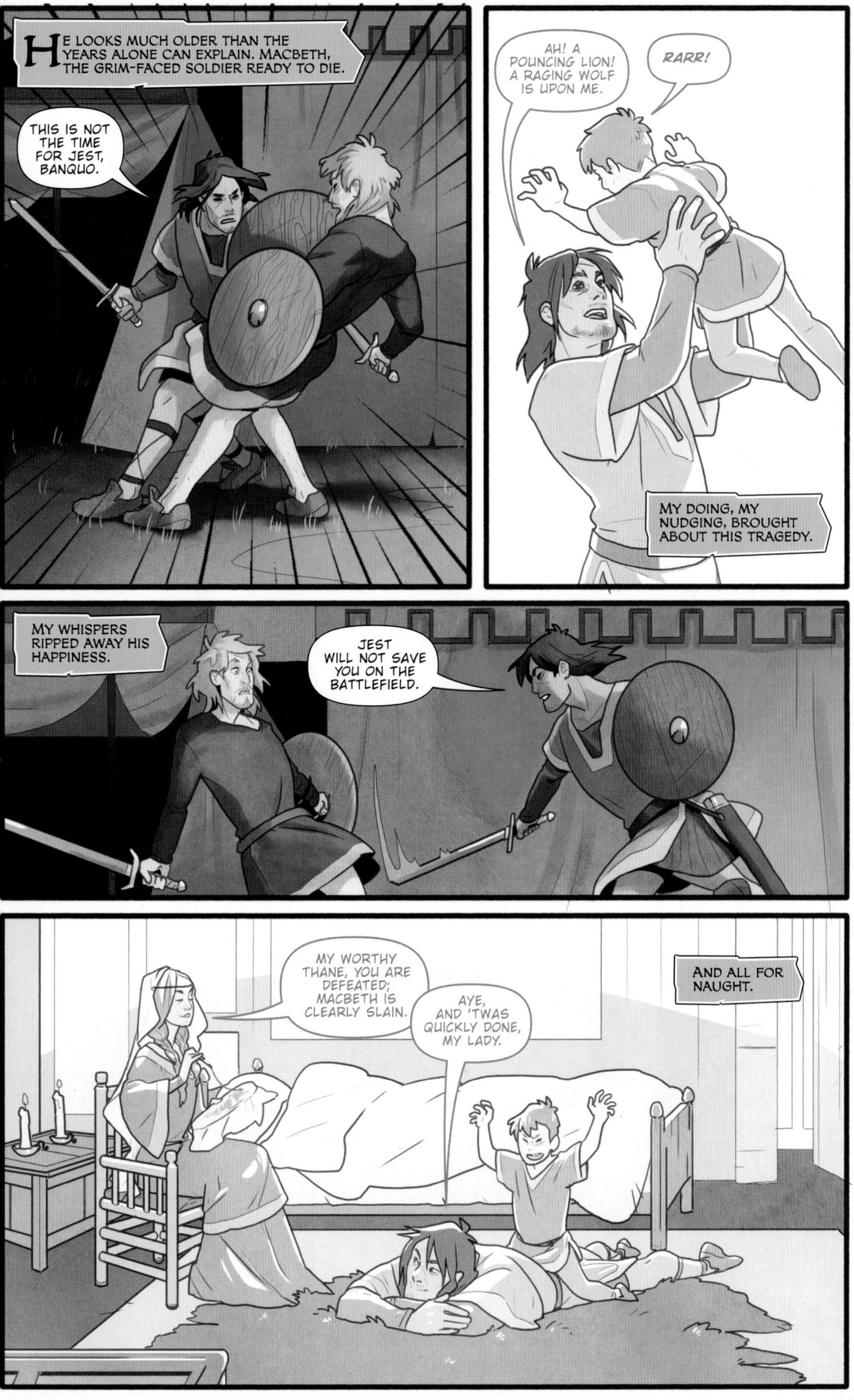
HE LOOKS MUCH OLDER THAN THE YEARS ALONE CAN EXPLAIN. MACBETH, THE GRIM-FACED SOLDIER READY TO DIE.
THIS IS NOT THE TIME FOR JEST, BANQUO.
AH! A POUNCING LION! A RAGING WOLF IS UPON ME.
RARR!
MY DOING, MY NUDGING, BROUGHT ABOUT THIS TRAGEDY.
MY WHISPERS RIPPED AWAY HIS HAPPINESS.
JEST WILL NOT SAVE YOU ON THE BATTLEFIELD.
MY WORTHY THANE, YOU ARE DEFEATED; MACBETH IS CLEARLY SLAIN.
AYE, AND 'TWAS QUICKLY DONE, MY LADY.
AND ALL FOR NAUGHT.

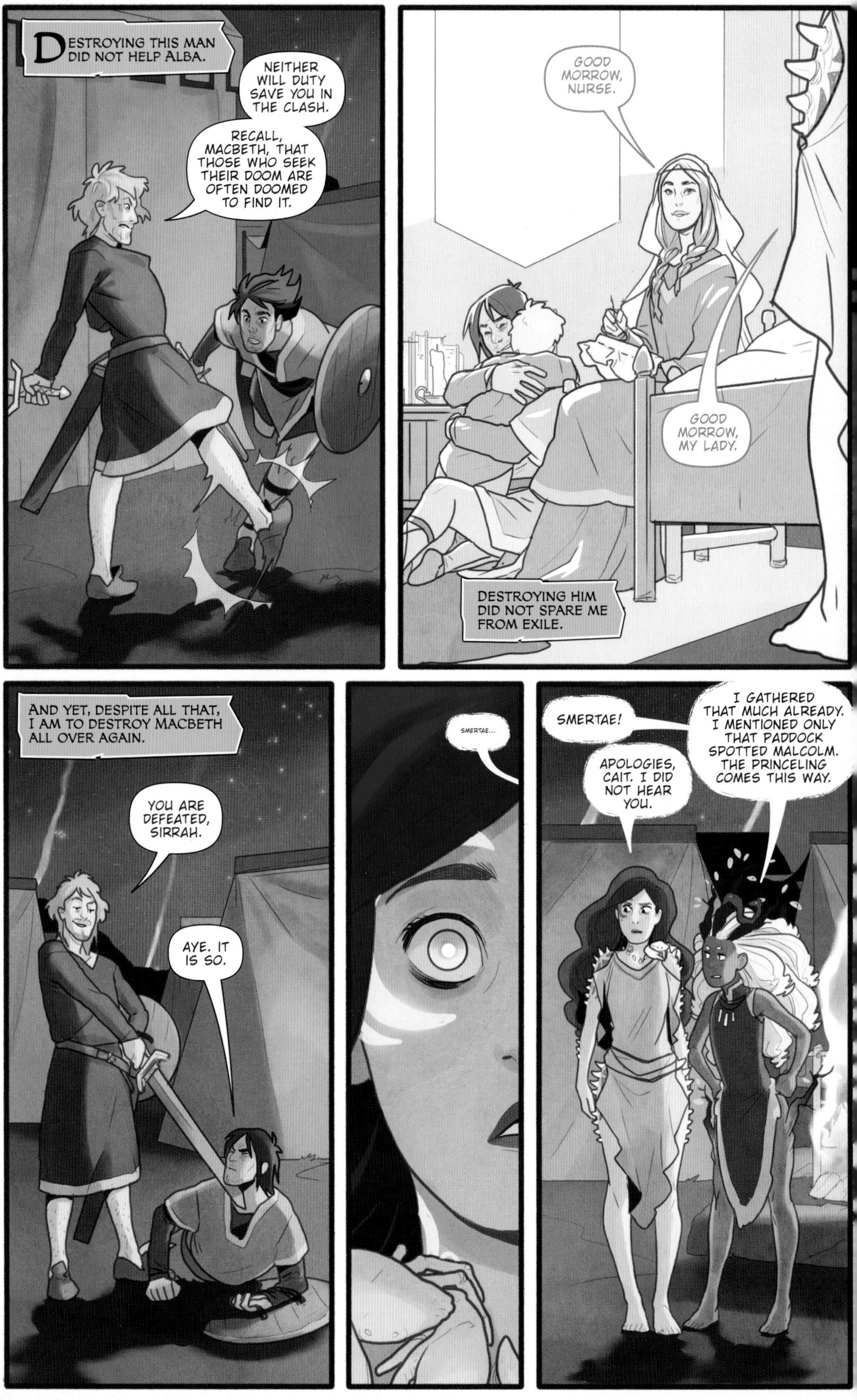
DESTROYING THIS MAN DID NOT HELP ALBA.
NEITHER WILL DUTY SAVE YOU IN THE CLASH.
RECALL, MACBETH, THAT THOSE WHO SEEK THEIR DOOM ARE OFTEN DOOMED TO FIND IT.
GOOD MORROW, NURSE.
GOOD MORROW, MY LADY.
DESTROYING HIM DID NOT SPARE ME FROM EXILE.
AND YET, DESPITE ALL THAT, I AM TO DESTROY MACBETH ALL OVER AGAIN.
YOU ARE DEFEATED, SIRRAH.
AYE. IT IS SO.
SMERTAE...
SMERTAE!
I GATHERED THAT MUCH ALREADY. I MENTIONED ONLY THAT PADDOCK SPOTTED MALCOLM. THE PRINCELING COMES THIS WAY.
APOLOGIES, CAIT. I DID NOT HEAR YOU.

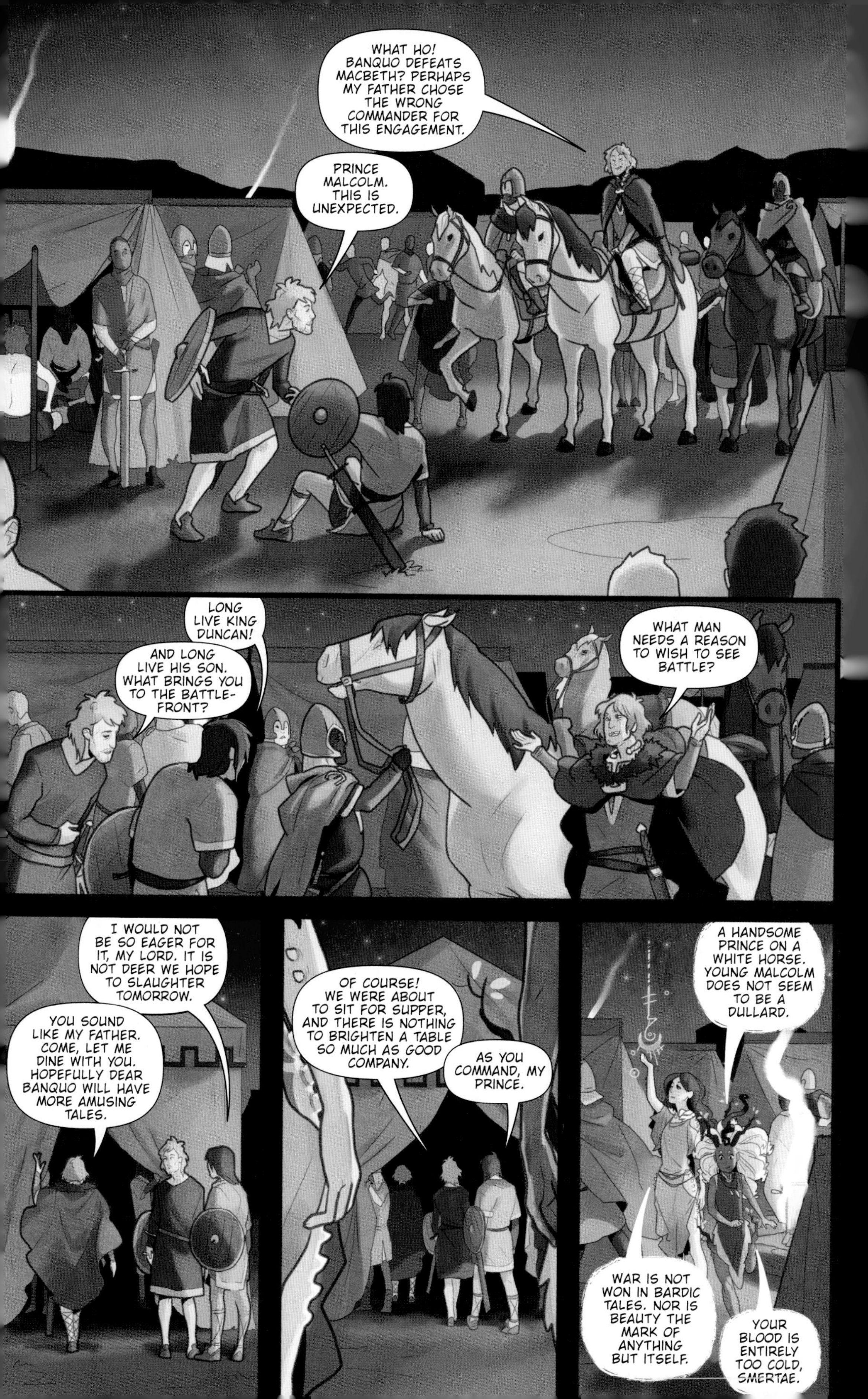
WHAT HO! BANQUO DEFEATS MACBETH? PERHAPS MY FATHER CHOSE THE WRONG COMMANDER FOR THIS ENGAGEMENT.
PRINCE MALCOLM. THIS IS UNEXPECTED.
LONG LIVE KING DUNCAN!
AND LONG LIVE HIS SON. WHAT BRINGS YOU TO THE BATTLE-FRONT?
WHAT MAN NEEDS A REASON TO WISH TO SEE BATTLE?
I WOULD NOT BE SO EAGER FOR IT, MY LORD. IT IS NOT DEER WE HOPE TO SLAUGHTER TOMORROW.
YOU SOUND LIKE MY FATHER. COME, LET ME DINE WITH YOU. HOPEFULLY DEAR BANQUO WILL HAVE MORE AMUSING TALES.
OF COURSE! WE WERE ABOUT TO SIT FOR SUPPER, AND THERE IS NOTHING TO BRIGHTEN A TABLE SO MUCH AS GOOD COMPANY.
AS YOU COMMAND, MY PRINCE.
A HANDSOME PRINCE ON A WHITE HORSE. YOUNG MALCOLM DOES NOT SEEM TO BE A DULLARD.
WAR IS NOT WON IN BARDIC TALES. NOR IS BEAUTY THE MARK OF ANYTHING BUT ITSELF.
YOUR BLOOD IS ENTIRELY TOO COLD, SMERTAE.

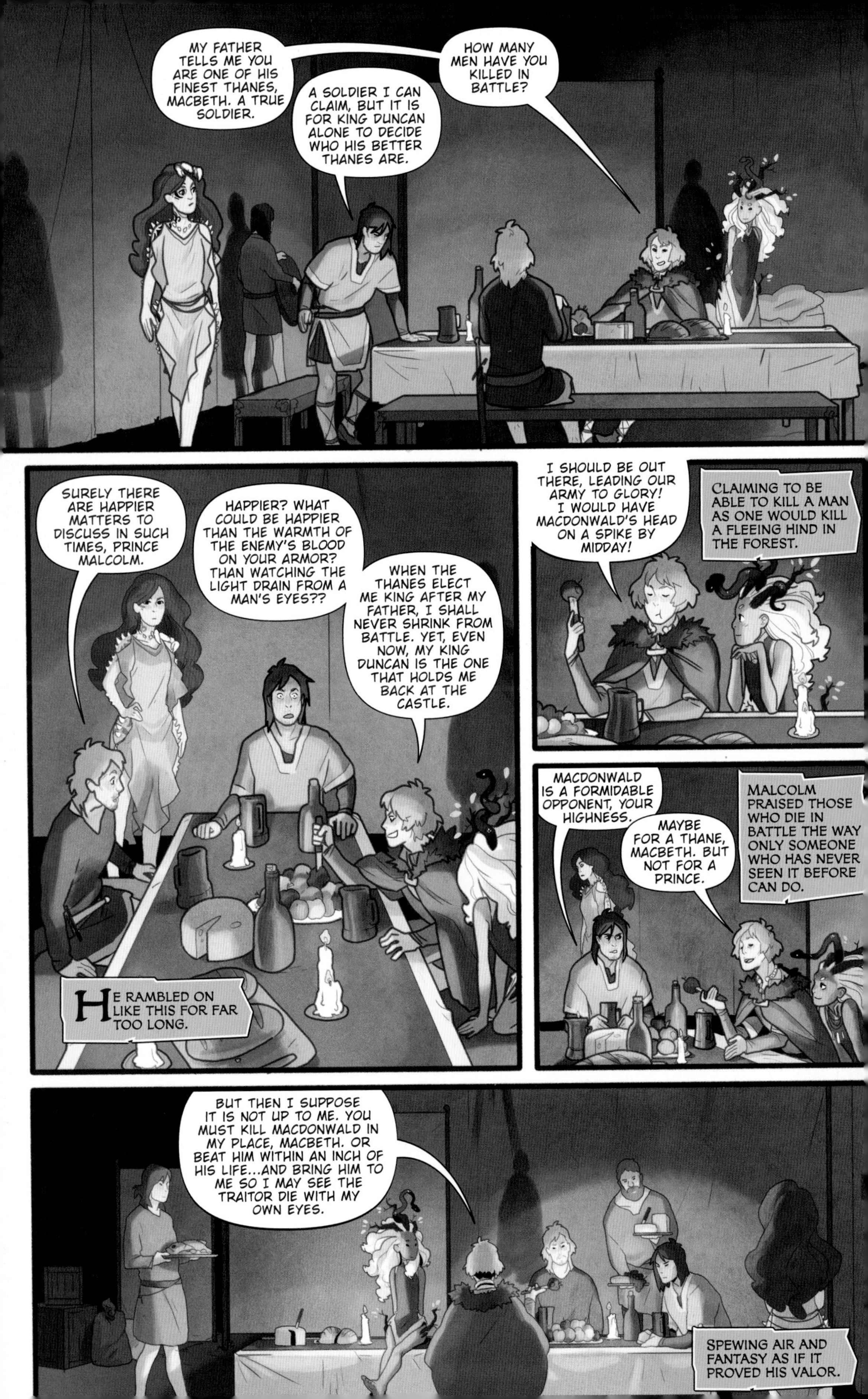
MY FATHER TELLS ME YOU ARE ONE OF HIS FINEST THANES, MACBETH. A TRUE SOLDIER.
A SOLDIER I CAN CLAIM, BUT IT IS FOR KING DUNCAN ALONE TO DECIDE WHO HIS BETTER THANES ARE.
HOW MANY MEN HAVE YOU KILLED IN BATTLE?
SURELY THERE ARE HAPPIER MATTERS TO DISCUSS IN SUCH TIMES, PRINCE MALCOLM.
HAPPIER? WHAT COULD BE HAPPIER THAN THE WARMTH OF THE ENEMY'S BLOOD ON YOUR ARMOR? THAN WATCHING THE LIGHT DRAIN FROM A MAN'S EYES??
WHEN THE THANES ELECT ME KING AFTER MY FATHER, I SHALL NEVER SHRINK FROM BATTLE. YET, EVEN NOW, MY KING DUNCAN IS THE ONE THAT HOLDS ME BACK AT THE CASTLE.
HE RAMBLED ON LIKE THIS FOR FAR TOO LONG.
I SHOULD BE OUT THERE, LEADING OUR ARMY TO GLORY! I WOULD HAVE MACDONWALD'S HEAD ON A SPIKE BY MIDDAY!
CLAIMING TO BE ABLE TO KILL A MAN AS ONE WOULD KILL A FLEEING HIND IN THE FOREST.
MACDONWALD IS A FORMIDABLE OPPONENT, YOUR HIGHNESS.
MAYBE FOR A THANE, MACBETH. BUT NOT FOR A PRINCE.
MALCOLM PRAISED THOSE WHO DIE IN BATTLE THE WAY ONLY SOMEONE WHO HAS NEVER SEEN IT BEFORE CAN DO.
BUT THEN I SUPPOSE IT IS NOT UP TO ME. YOU MUST KILL MACDONWALD IN MY PLACE, MACBETH. OR BEAT HIM WITHIN AN INCH OF HIS LIFE...AND BRING HIM TO ME SO I MAY SEE THE TRAITOR DIE WITH MY OWN EYES.
SPEWING AIR AND FANTASY AS IF IT PROVED HIS VALOR.

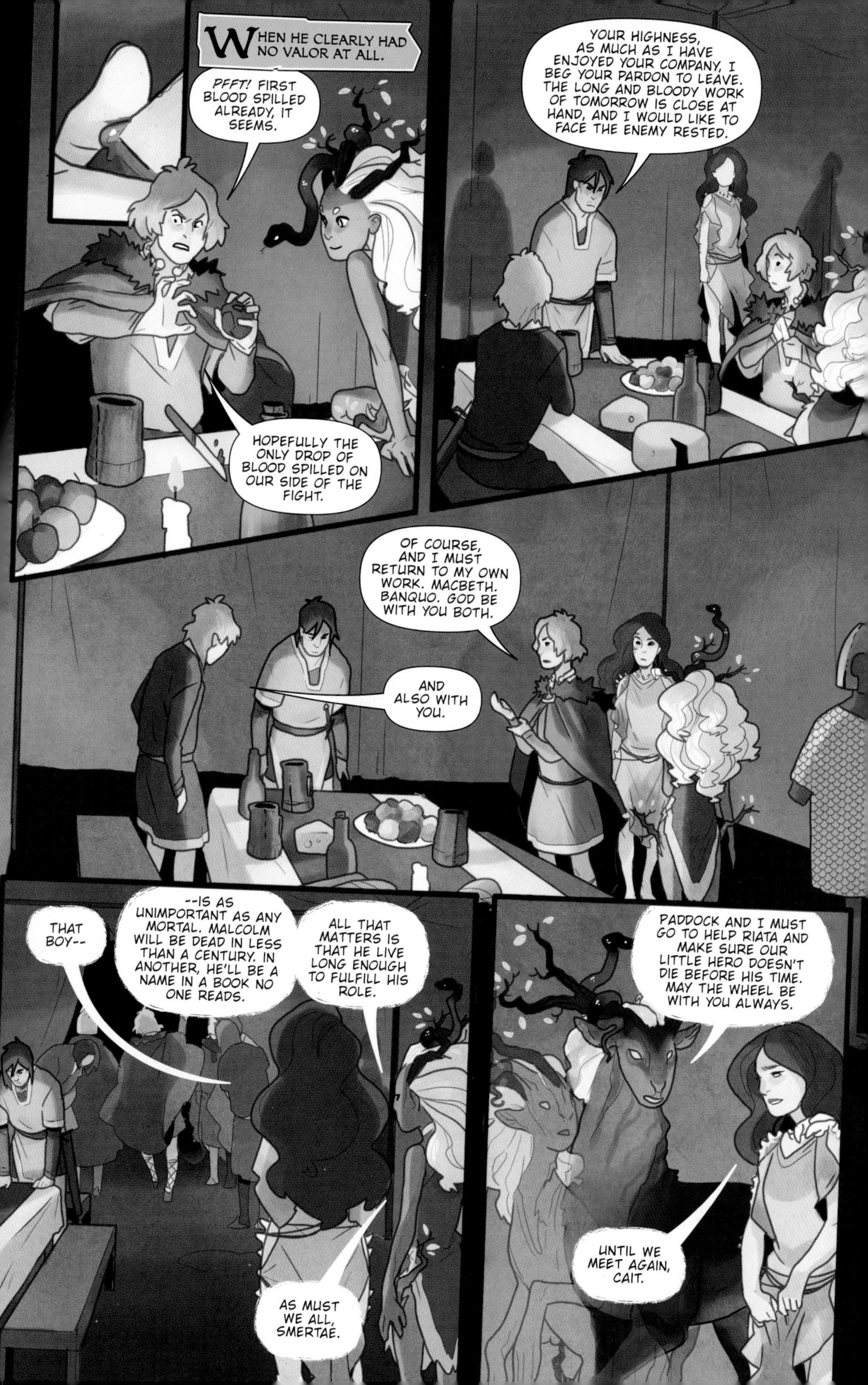
WHEN HE CLEARLY HAD NO VALOR AT ALL.
PFFT! FIRST BLOOD SPILLED ALREADY, IT SEEMS.
HOPEFULLY THE ONLY DROP OF BLOOD SPILLED ON OUR SIDE OF THE FIGHT.
YOUR HIGHNESS, AS MUCH AS I HAVE ENJOYED YOUR COMPANY, I BEG YOUR PARDON TO LEAVE. THE LONG AND BLOODY WORK OF TOMORROW IS CLOSE AT HAND, AND I WOULD LIKE TO FACE THE ENEMY RESTED.
OF COURSE, AND I MUST RETURN TO MY OWN WORK. MACBETH. BANQUO. GOD BE WITH YOU BOTH.
AND ALSO WITH YOU.
THAT BOY--
--IS AS UNIMPORTANT AS ANY MORTAL. MALCOLM WILL BE DEAD IN LESS THAN A CENTURY. IN ANOTHER, HE'LL BE A NAME IN A BOOK NO ONE READS.
ALL THAT MATTERS IS THAT HE LIVE LONG ENOUGH TO FULFILL HIS ROLE.
AS MUST WE ALL, SMERTAE.
PADDOCK AND I MUST GO TO HELP RIATA AND MAKE SURE OUR LITTLE HERO DOESN'T DIE BEFORE HIS TIME. MAY THE WHEEL BE WITH YOU ALWAYS.
UNTIL WE MEET AGAIN, CAIT.

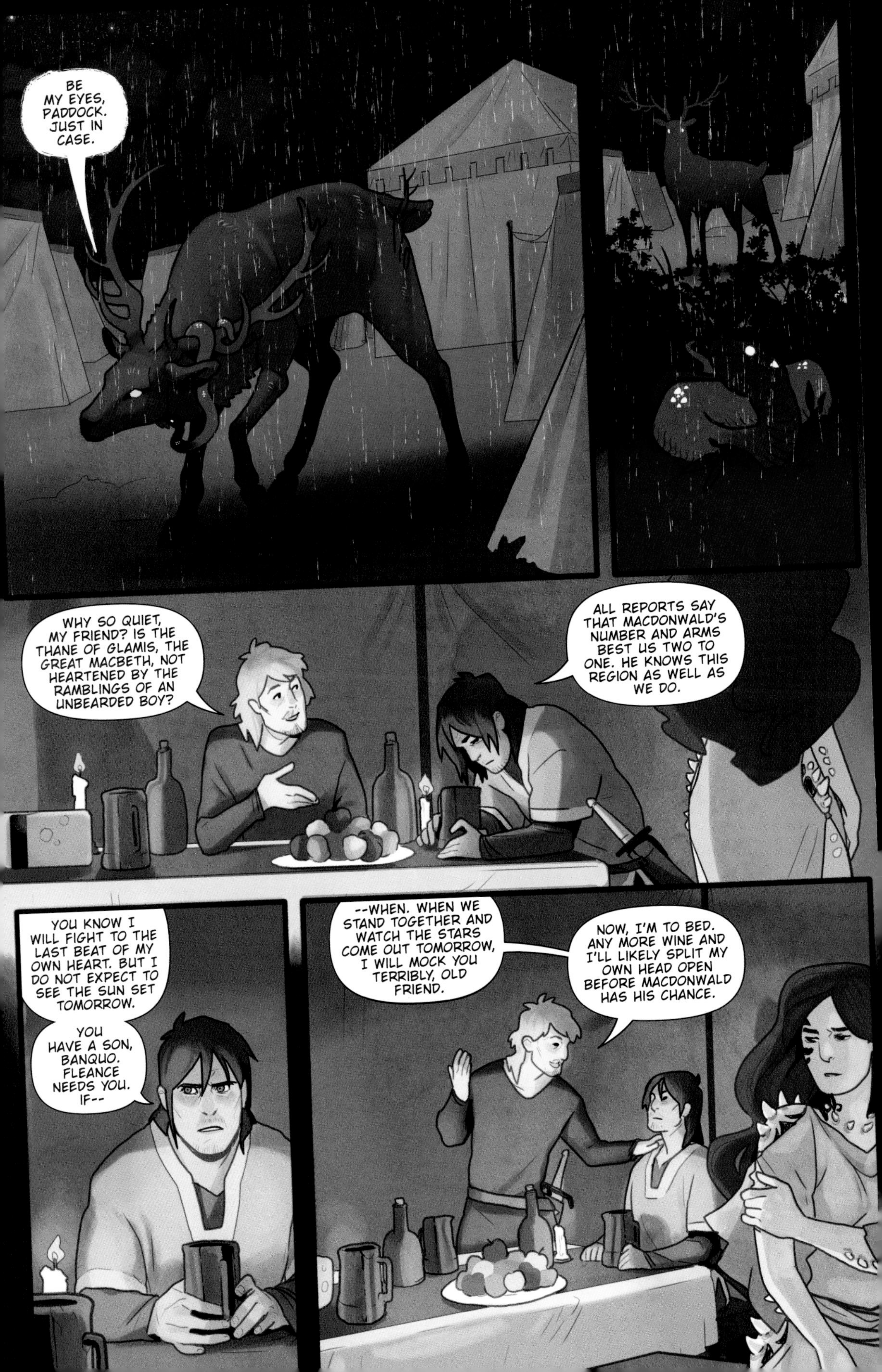
BE MY EYES, PADDOCK. JUST IN CASE.
WHY SO QUIET, MY FRIEND? IS THE THANE OF GLAMIS, THE GREAT MACBETH, NOT HEARTENED BY THE RAMBLINGS OF AN UNBEARDED BOY?
ALL REPORTS SAY THAT MACDONWALD'S NUMBER AND ARMS BEST US TWO TO ONE. HE KNOWS THIS REGION AS WELL AS WE DO.
YOU KNOW I WILL FIGHT TO THE LAST BEAT OF MY OWN HEART. BUT I DO NOT EXPECT TO SEE THE SUN SET TOMORROW.
YOU HAVE A SON, BANQUO. FLEANCE NEEDS YOU. IF--
--WHEN. WHEN WE STAND TOGETHER AND WATCH THE STARS COME OUT TOMORROW, I WILL MOCK YOU TERRIBLY, OLD FRIEND.
NOW, I'M TO BED. ANY MORE WINE AND I'LL LIKELY SPLIT MY OWN HEAD OPEN BEFORE MACDONWALD HAS HIS CHANCE.

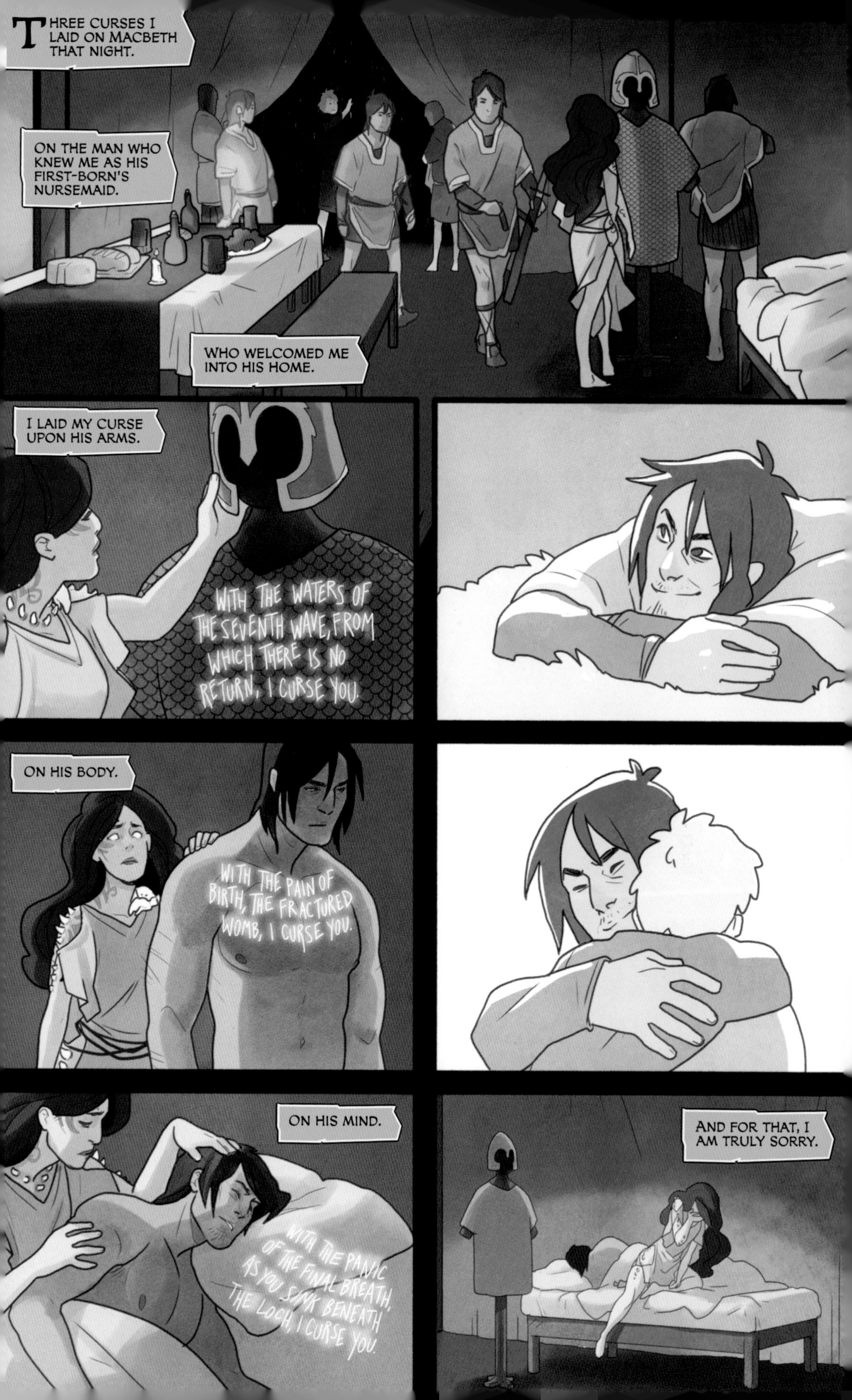
THREE CURSES I LAID ON MACBETH THAT NIGHT.
ON THE MAN WHO KNEW ME AS HIS FIRST-BORN'S NURSEMAID.
WHO WELCOMED ME INTO HIS HOME.
I LAID MY CURSE UPON HIS ARMS.
WITH THE WATERS OF THE SEVENTH WAVE, FROM WHICH THERE IS NO RETURN, I CURSE YOU.
ON HIS BODY.
WITH THE PAIN OF BIRTH, THE FRACTURED WOMB, I CURSE YOU.
ON HIS MIND.
WITH THE PANIC OF THE FINAL BREATH, AS YOU SINK BENEATH THE LOCH, I CURSE YOU.
AND FOR THAT, I AM TRULY SORRY.

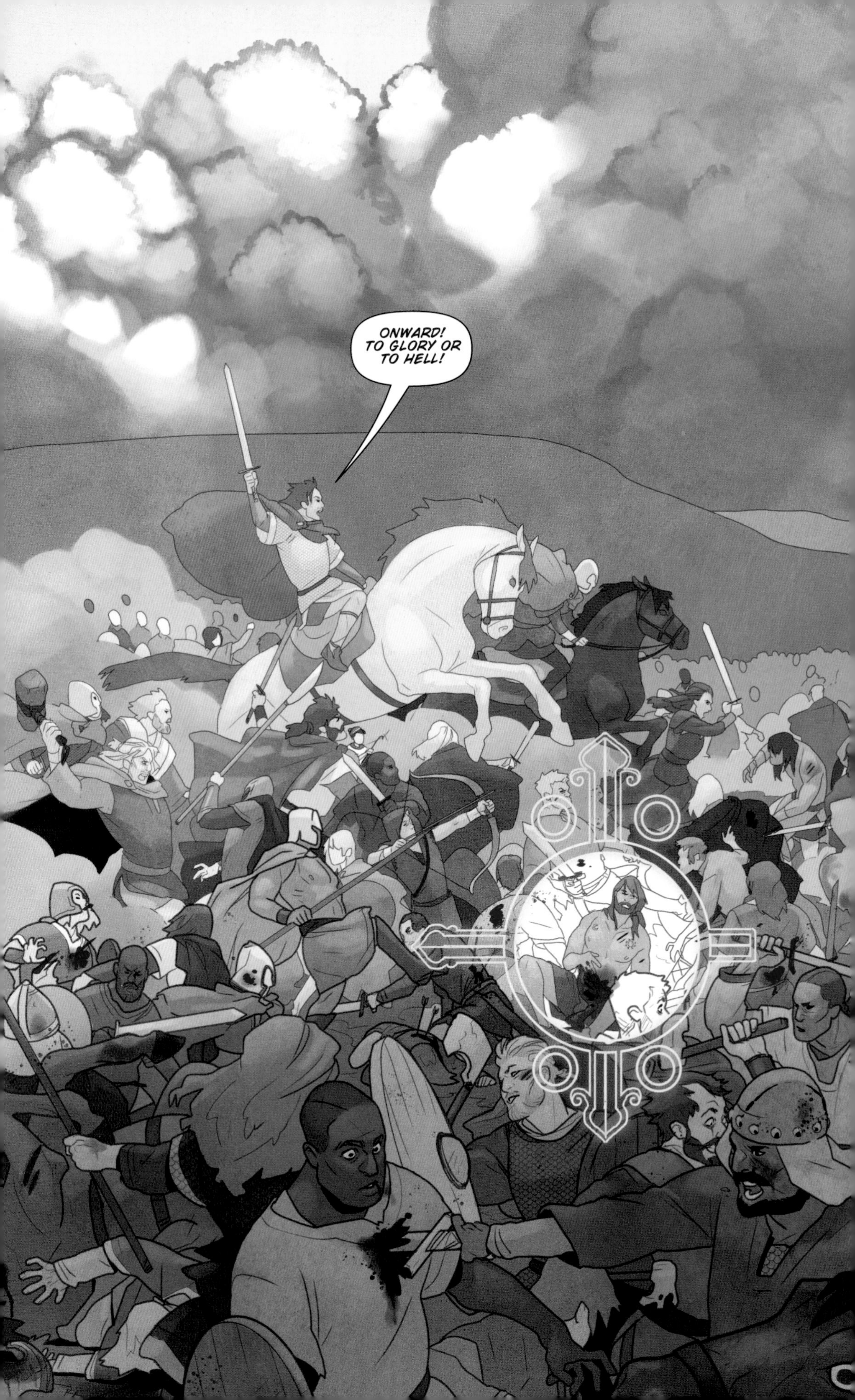
ONWARD! TO GLORY OR TO HELL!

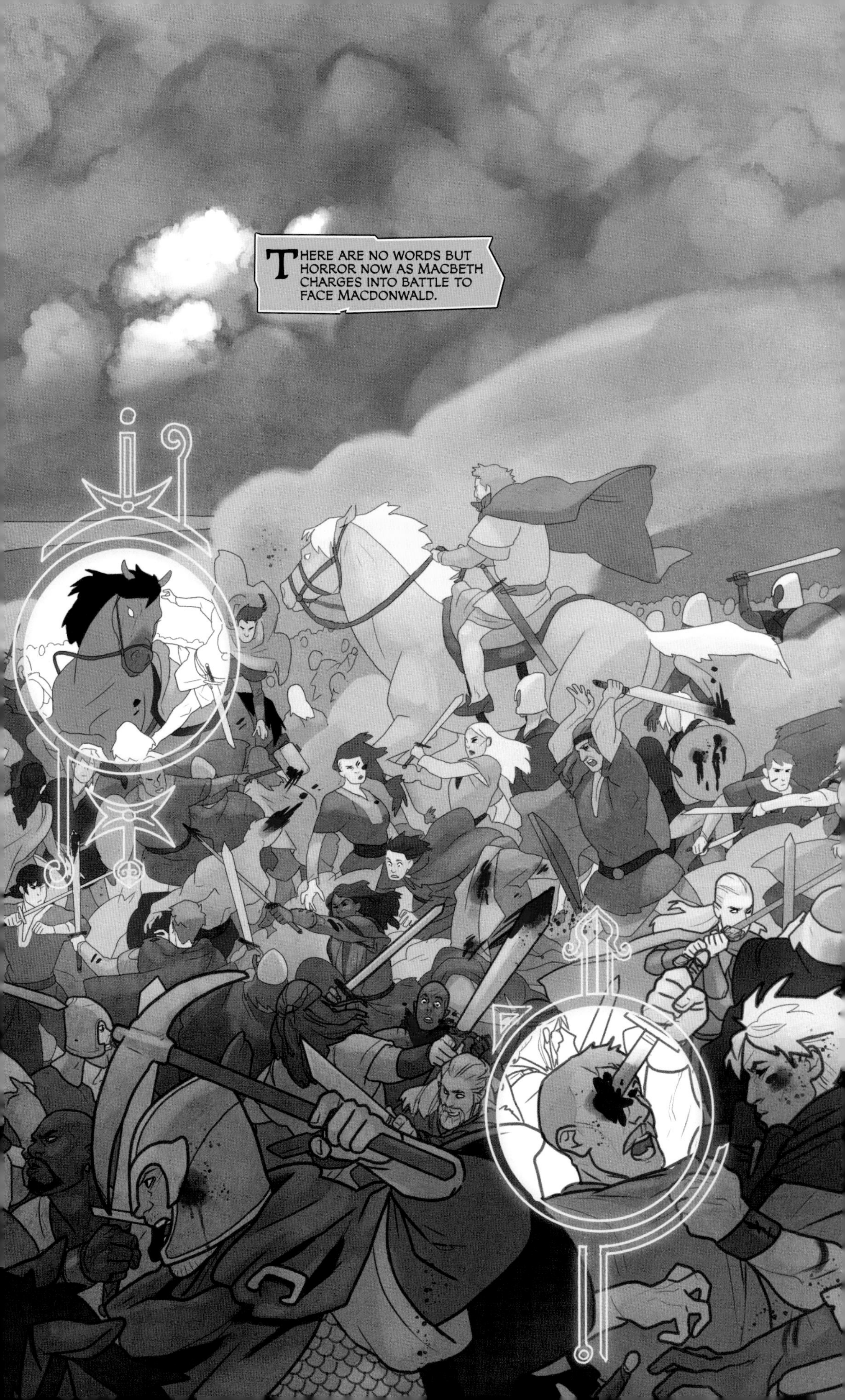
THERE ARE NO WORDS BUT HORROR NOW AS MACBETH CHARGES INTO BATTLE TO FACE MACDONWALD.

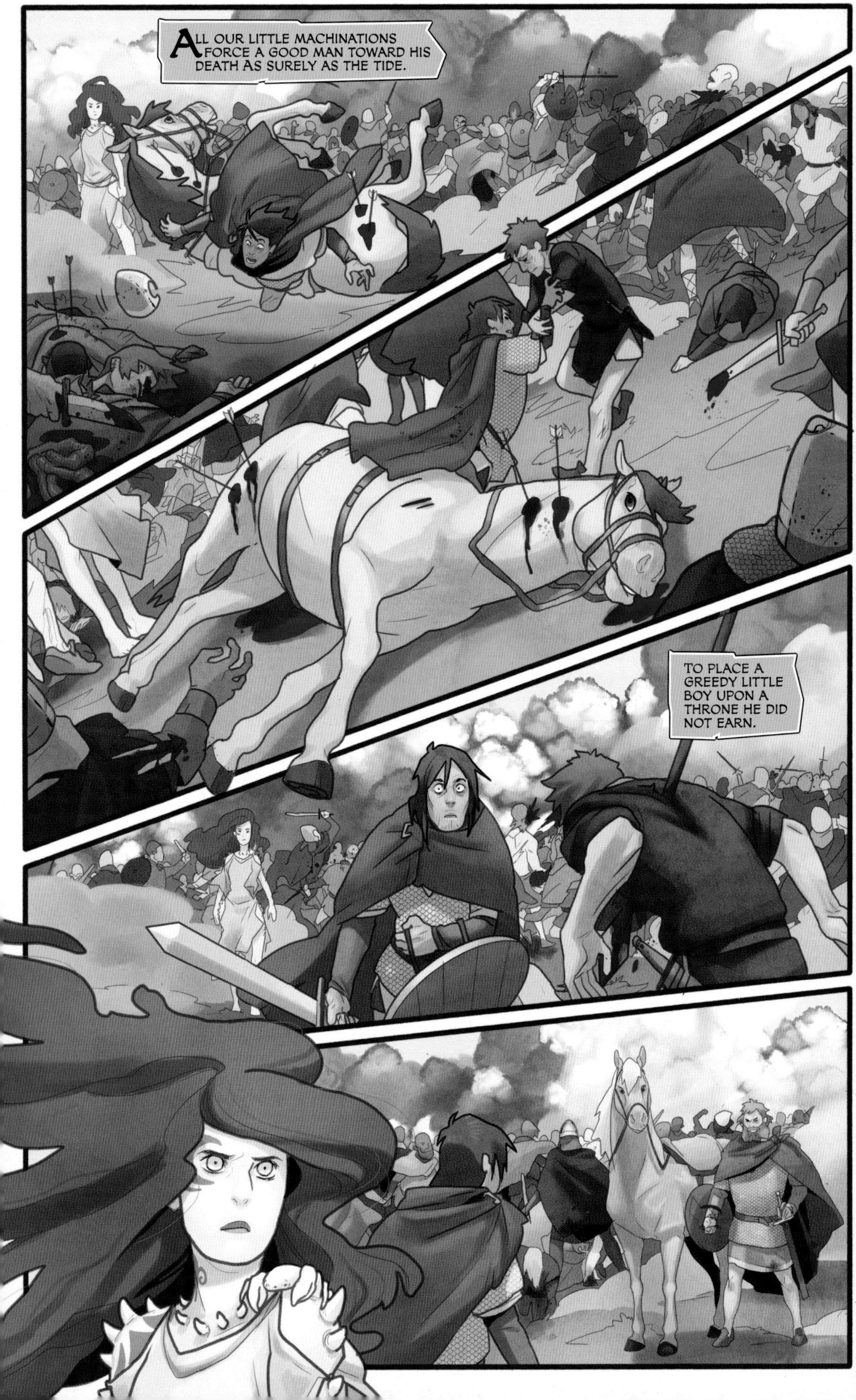

ALL OUR LITTLE MACHINATIONS FORCE A GOOD MAN TOWARD HIS DEATH AS SURELY AS THE TIDE.
TO PLACE A GREEDY LITTLE BOY UPON A THRONE HE DID NOT EARN.

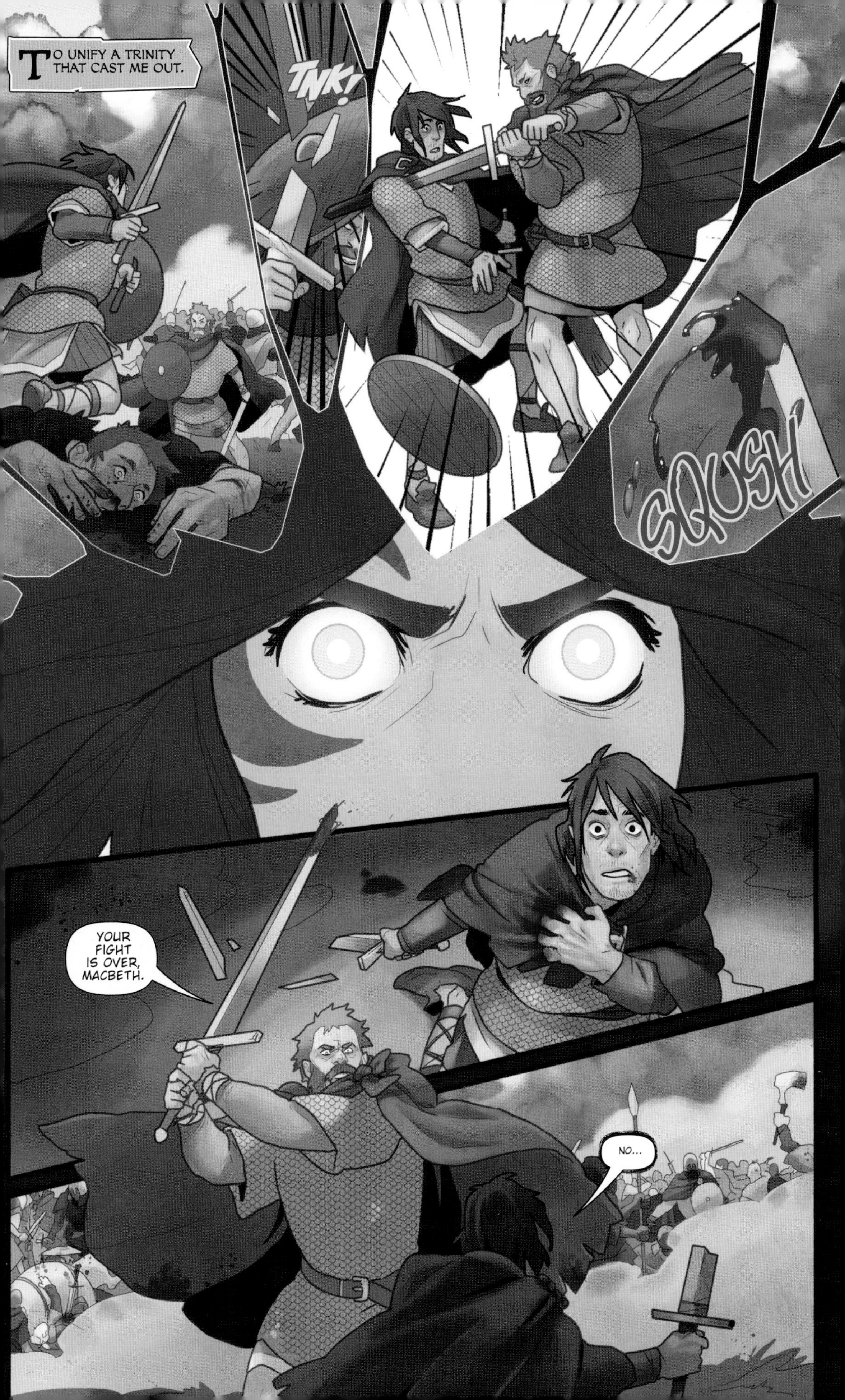
TO UNIFY A TRINITY THAT CAST ME OUT.
TNK!
SQUSH
YOUR FIGHT IS OVER, MACBETH.
NO...

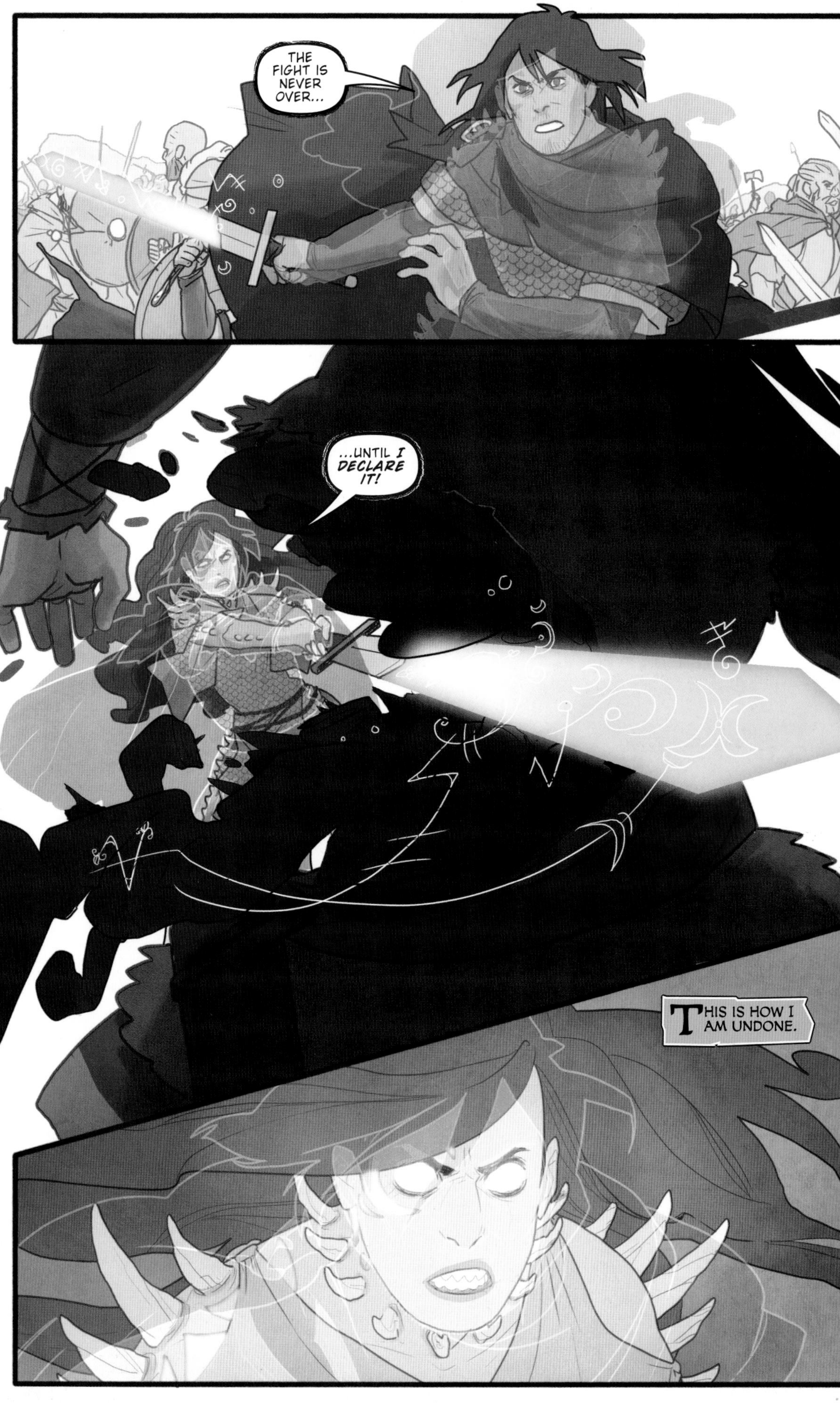
THE FIGHT IS NEVER OVER...
...UNTIL I DECLARE IT!
THIS IS HOW I AM UNDONE.

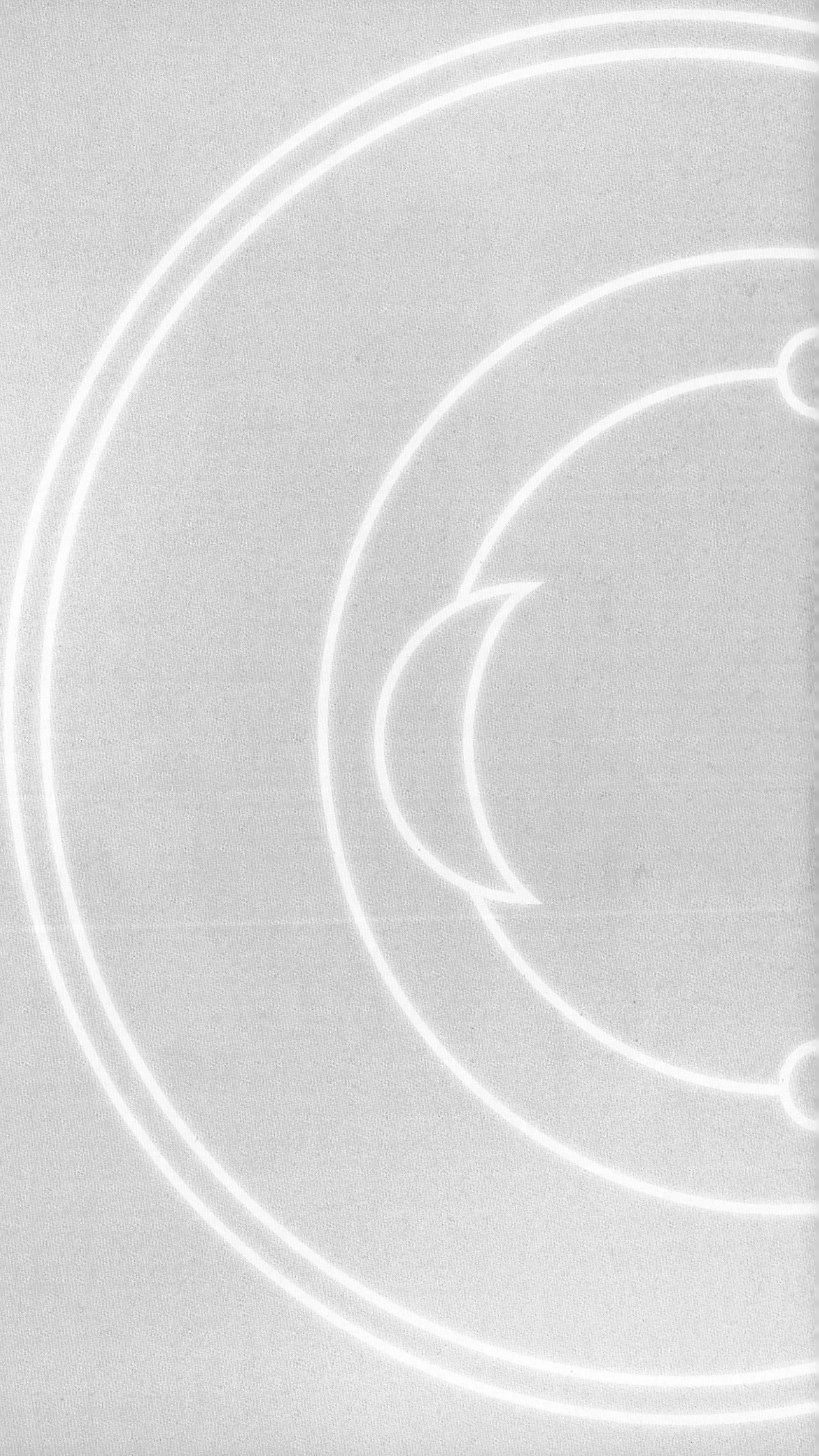

Act Two

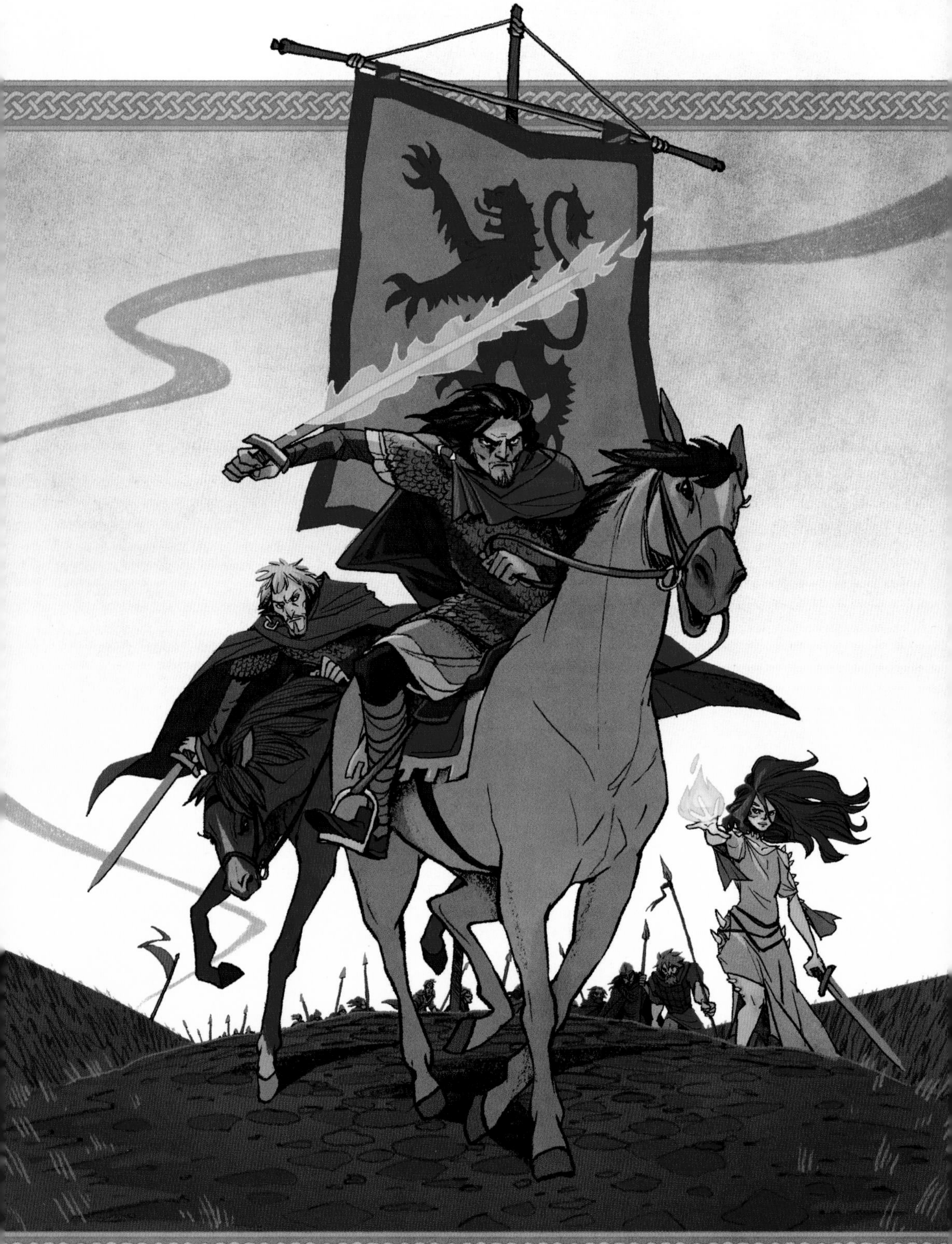

Issue Two Cover by Kyla Vanderklugt

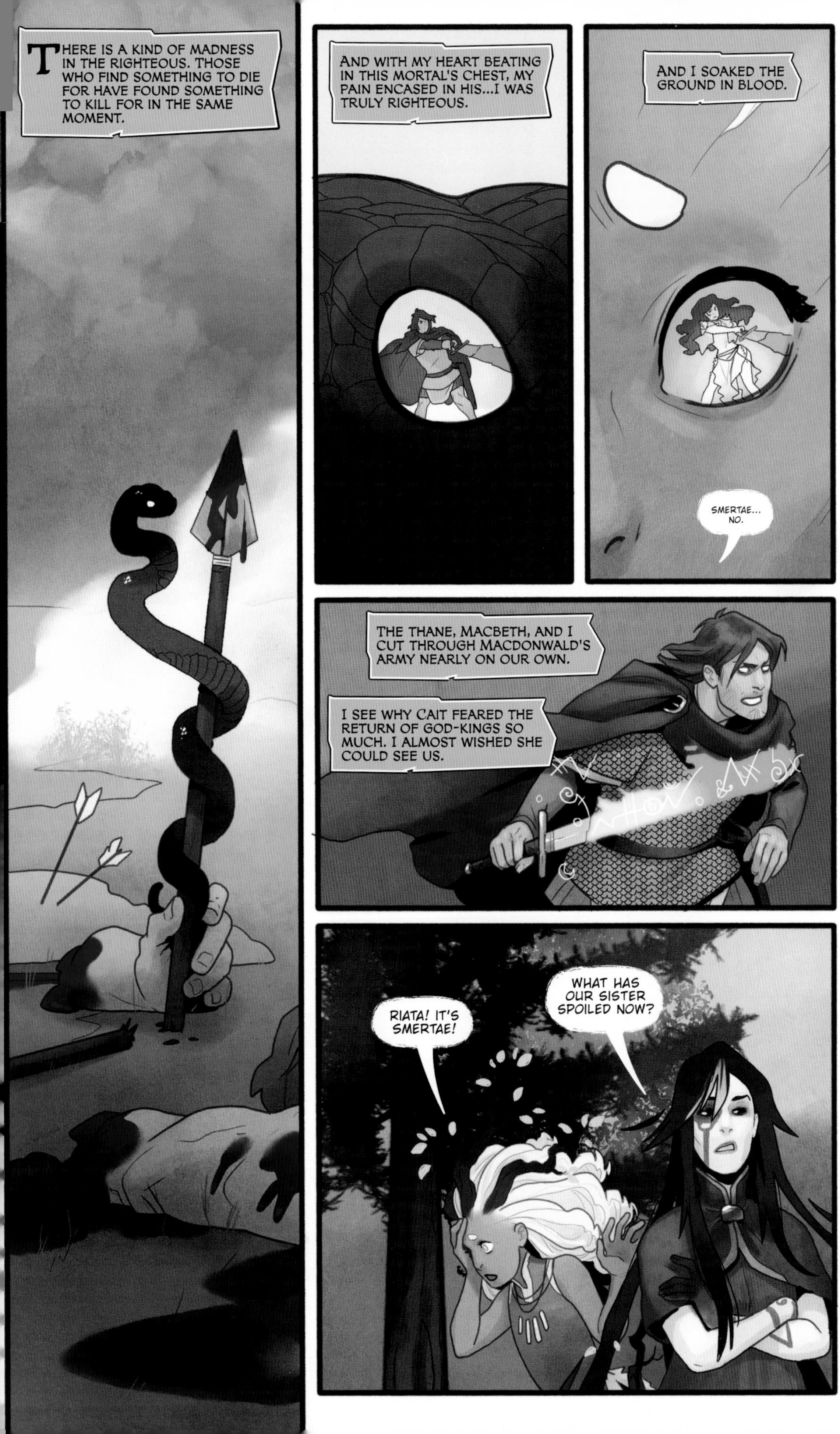
THERE IS A KIND OF MADNESS IN THE RIGHTEOUS. THOSE WHO FIND SOMETHING TO DIE FOR HAVE FOUND SOMETHING TO KILL FOR IN THE SAME MOMENT.
AND WITH MY HEART BEATING IN THIS MORTAL'S CHEST, MY PAIN ENCASED IN HIS...I WAS TRULY RIGHTEOUS.
AND I SOAKED THE GROUND IN BLOOD.
SMERTAE... NO.
THE THANE, MACBETH, AND I CUT THROUGH MACDONWALD'S ARMY NEARLY ON OUR OWN.
I SEE WHY CAIT FEARED THE RETURN OF GOD-KINGS SO MUCH. I ALMOST WISHED SHE COULD SEE US.
RIATA! IT'S SMERTAE!
WHAT HAS OUR SISTER SPOILED NOW?

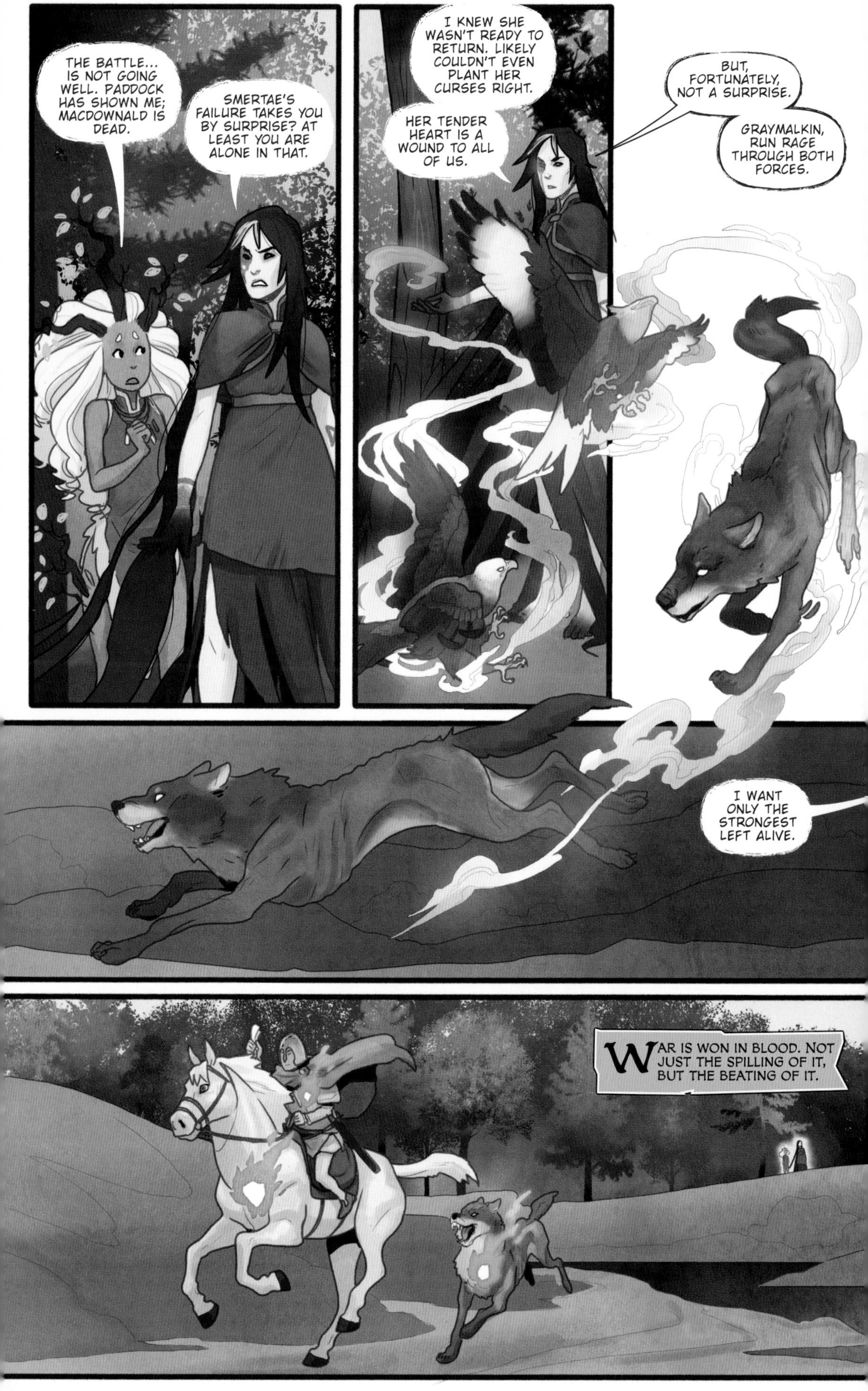
THE BATTLE... IS NOT GOING WELL. PADDOCK HAS SHOWN ME; MACDOWNALD IS DEAD.
SMERTAE'S FAILURE TAKES YOU BY SURPRISE? AT LEAST YOU ARE ALONE IN THAT.
I KNEW SHE WASN'T READY TO RETURN. LIKELY COULDN'T EVEN PLANT HER CURSES RIGHT.
HER TENDER HEART IS A WOUND TO ALL OF US.
BUT, FORTUNATELY, NOT A SURPRISE.
GRAYMALKIN, RUN RAGE THROUGH BOTH FORCES.
I WANT ONLY THE STRONGEST LEFT ALIVE.
WAR IS WON IN BLOOD. NOT JUST THE SPILLING OF IT, BUT THE BEATING OF IT.

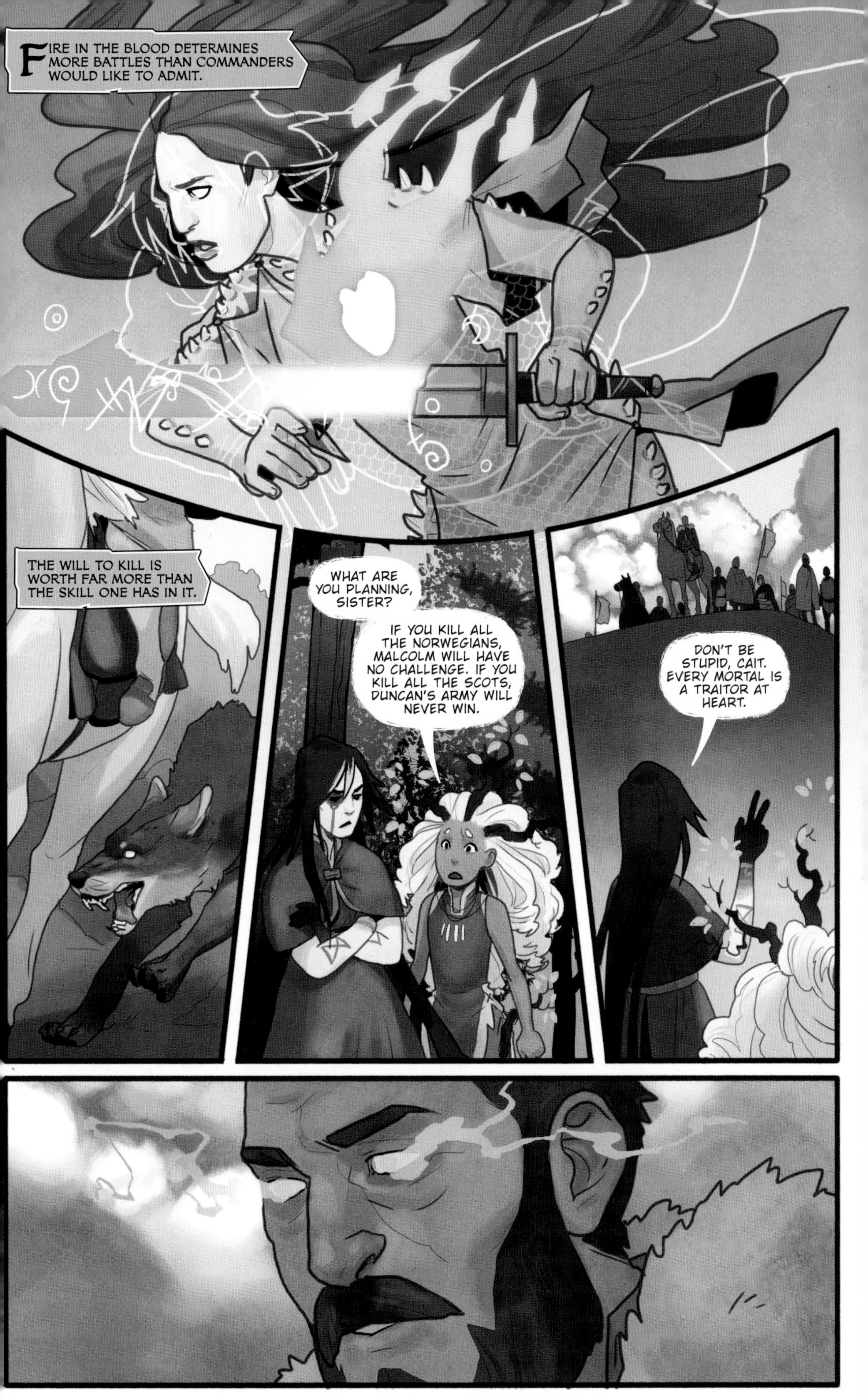
FIRE IN THE BLOOD DETERMINES MORE BATTLES THAN COMMANDERS WOULD LIKE TO ADMIT.
THE WILL TO KILL IS WORTH FAR MORE THAN THE SKILL ONE HAS IN IT.
WHAT ARE YOU PLANNING, SISTER?
IF YOU KILL ALL THE NORWEGIANS, MALCOLM WILL HAVE NO CHALLENGE. IF YOU KILL ALL THE SCOTS, DUNCAN'S ARMY WILL NEVER WIN.
DON'T BE STUPID, CAIT. EVERY MORTAL IS A TRAITOR AT HEART.

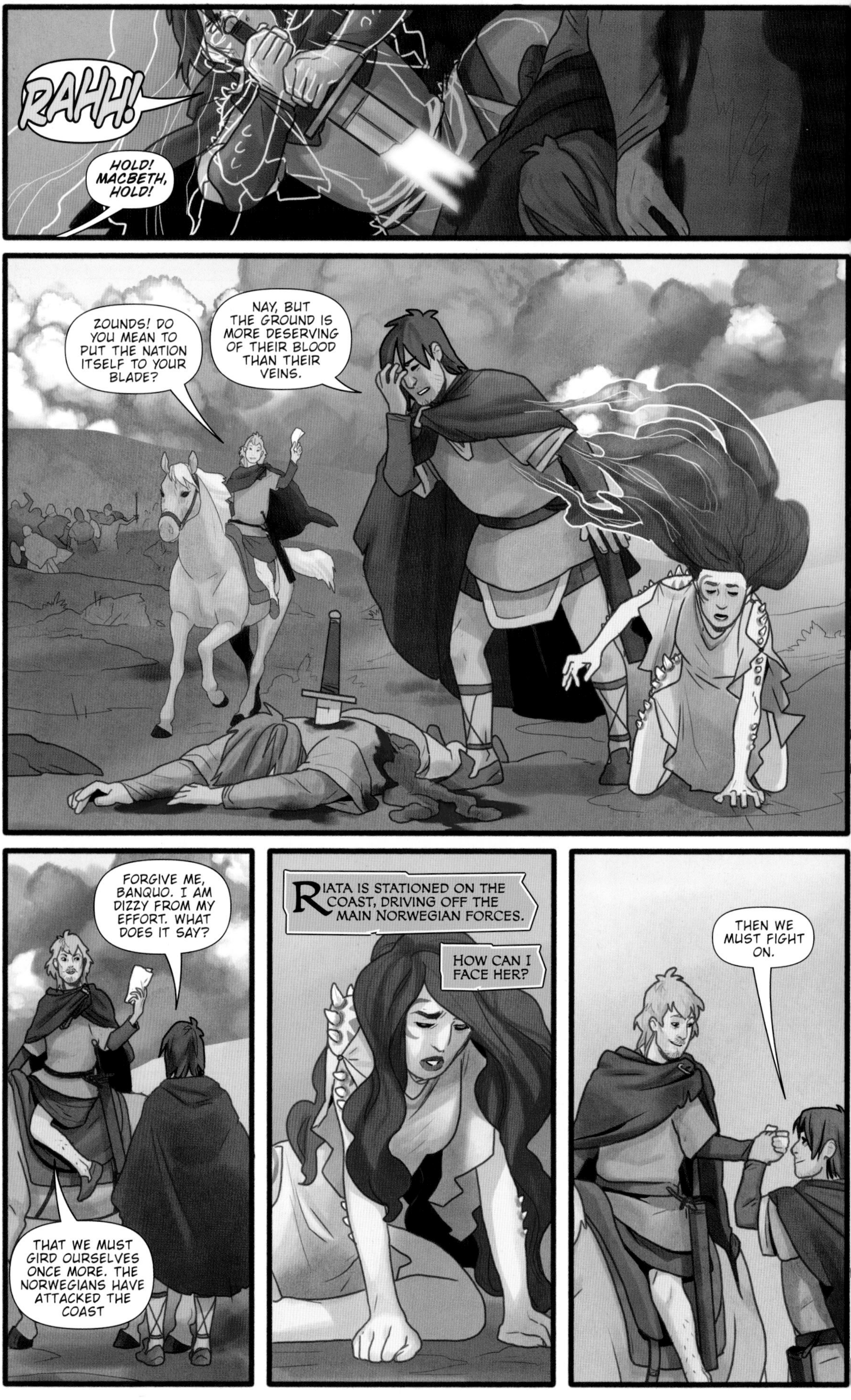
RAHH!
HOLD! MACBETH, HOLD!
ZOUNDS! DO YOU MEAN TO PUT THE NATION ITSELF TO YOUR BLADE?
NAY, BUT THE GROUND IS MORE DESERVING OF THEIR BLOOD THAN THEIR VEINS.
FORGIVE ME, BANQUO. I AM DIZZY FROM MY EFFORT. WHAT DOES IT SAY?
THAT WE MUST GIRD OURSELVES ONCE MORE. THE NORWEGIANS HAVE ATTACKED THE COAST
RIATA IS STATIONED ON THE COAST, DRIVING OFF THE MAIN NORWEGIAN FORCES.
HOW CAN I FACE HER?
THEN WE MUST FIGHT ON.

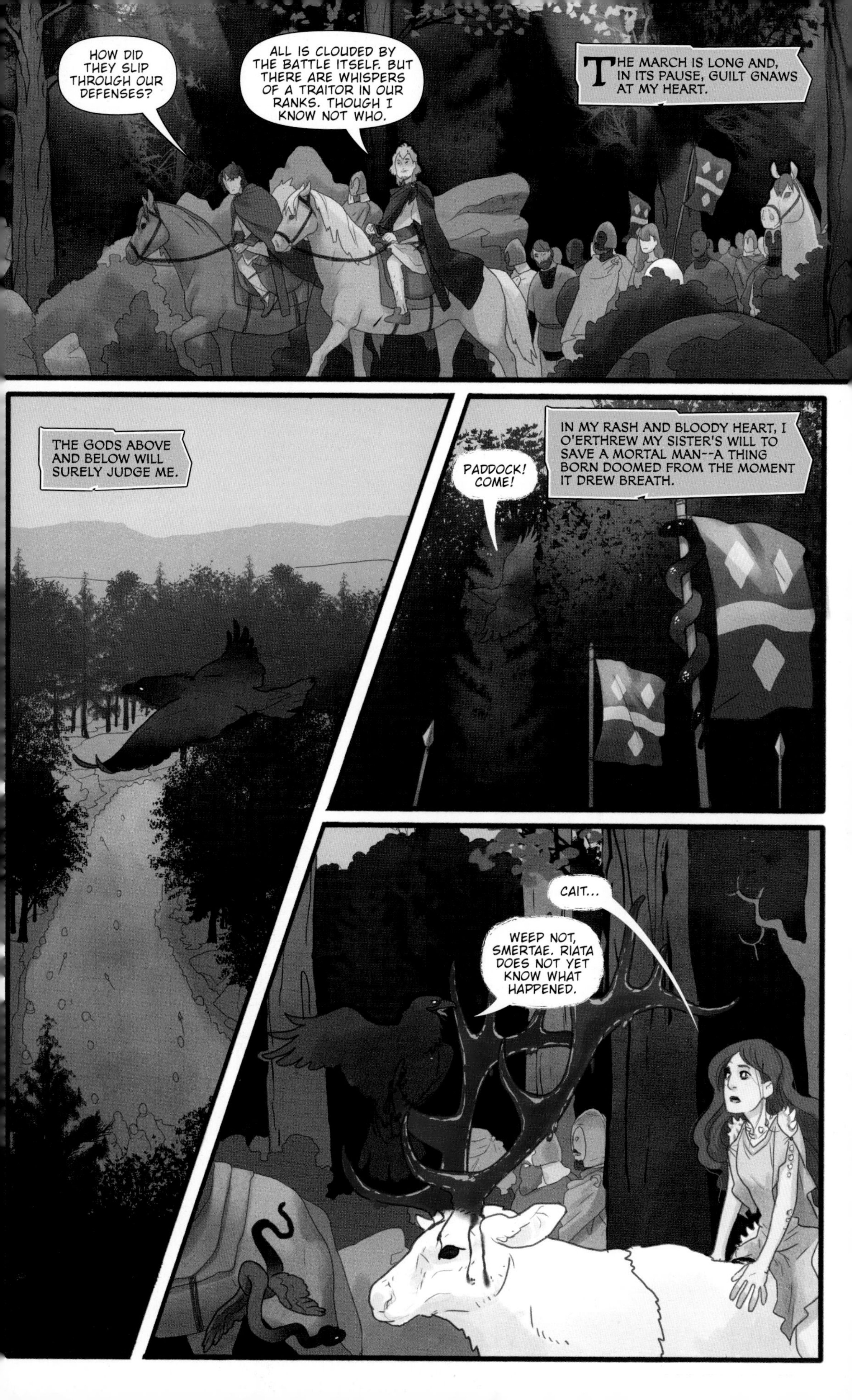
HOW DID THEY SLIP THROUGH OUR DEFENSES?
ALL IS CLOUDED BY THE BATTLE ITSELF. BUT THERE ARE WHISPERS OF A TRAITOR IN OUR RANKS. THOUGH I KNOW NOT WHO.
THE MARCH IS LONG AND, IN ITS PAUSE, GUILT GNAWS AT MY HEART.
THE GODS ABOVE AND BELOW WILL SURELY JUDGE ME.
IN MY RASH AND BLOODY HEART, I O'ERTHREW MY SISTER'S WILL TO SAVE A MORTAL MAN--A THING BORN DOOMED FROM THE MOMENT IT DREW BREATH.
PADDOCK! COME!
CAIT...
WEEP NOT, SMERTAE. RIATA DOES NOT YET KNOW WHAT HAPPENED.

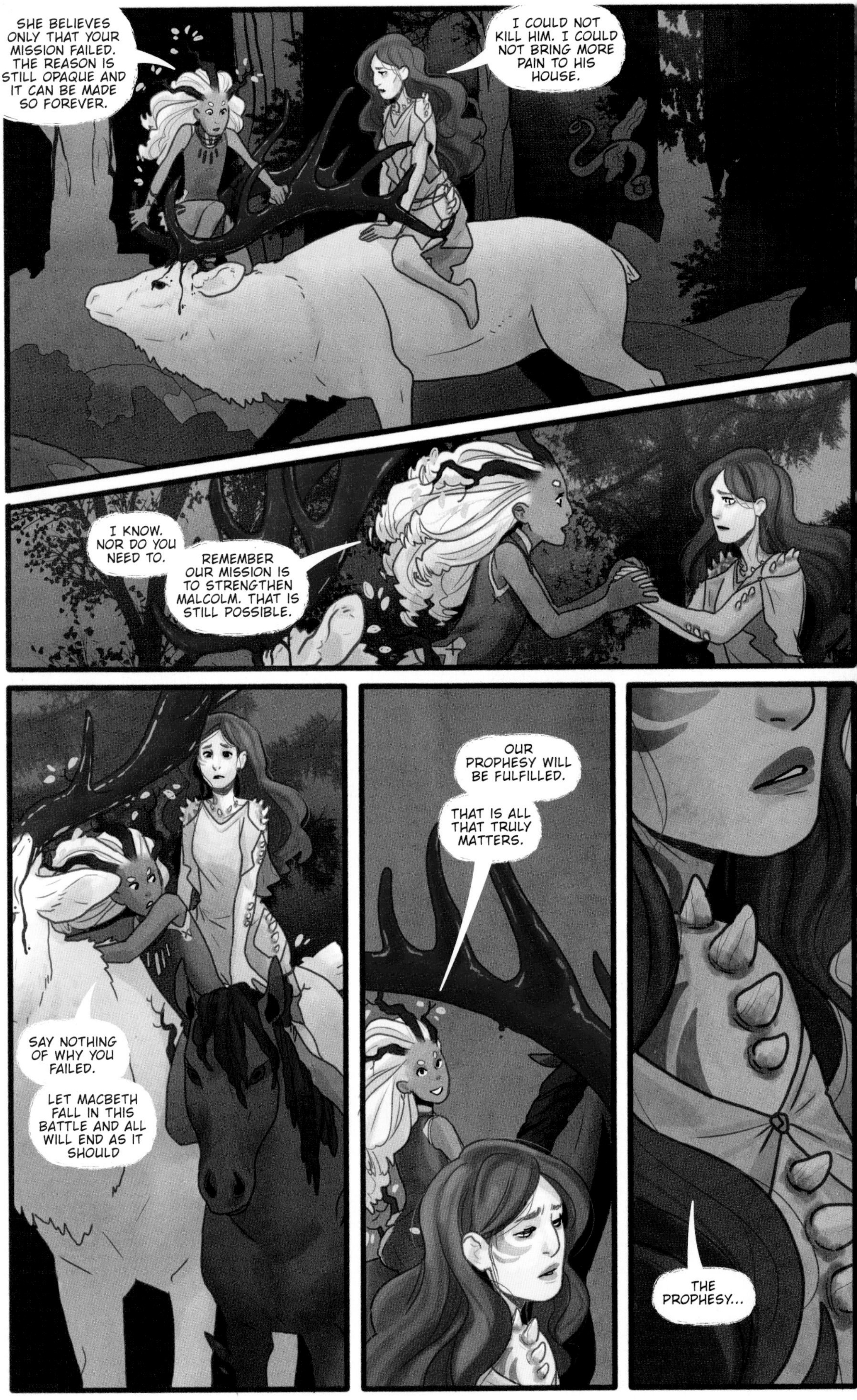
SHE BELIEVES ONLY THAT YOUR MISSION FAILED. THE REASON IS STILL OPAQUE AND IT CAN BE MADE SO FOREVER.
I COULD NOT KILL HIM. I COULD NOT BRING MORE PAIN TO HIS HOUSE.
I KNOW. NOR DO YOU NEED TO.
REMEMBER OUR MISSION IS TO STRENGTHEN MALCOLM. THAT IS STILL POSSIBLE.
SAY NOTHING OF WHY YOU FAILED.
LET MACBETH FALL IN THIS BATTLE AND ALL WILL END AS IT SHOULD
OUR PROPHESY WILL BE FULFILLED.
THAT IS ALL THAT TRULY MATTERS.
THE PROPHESY...

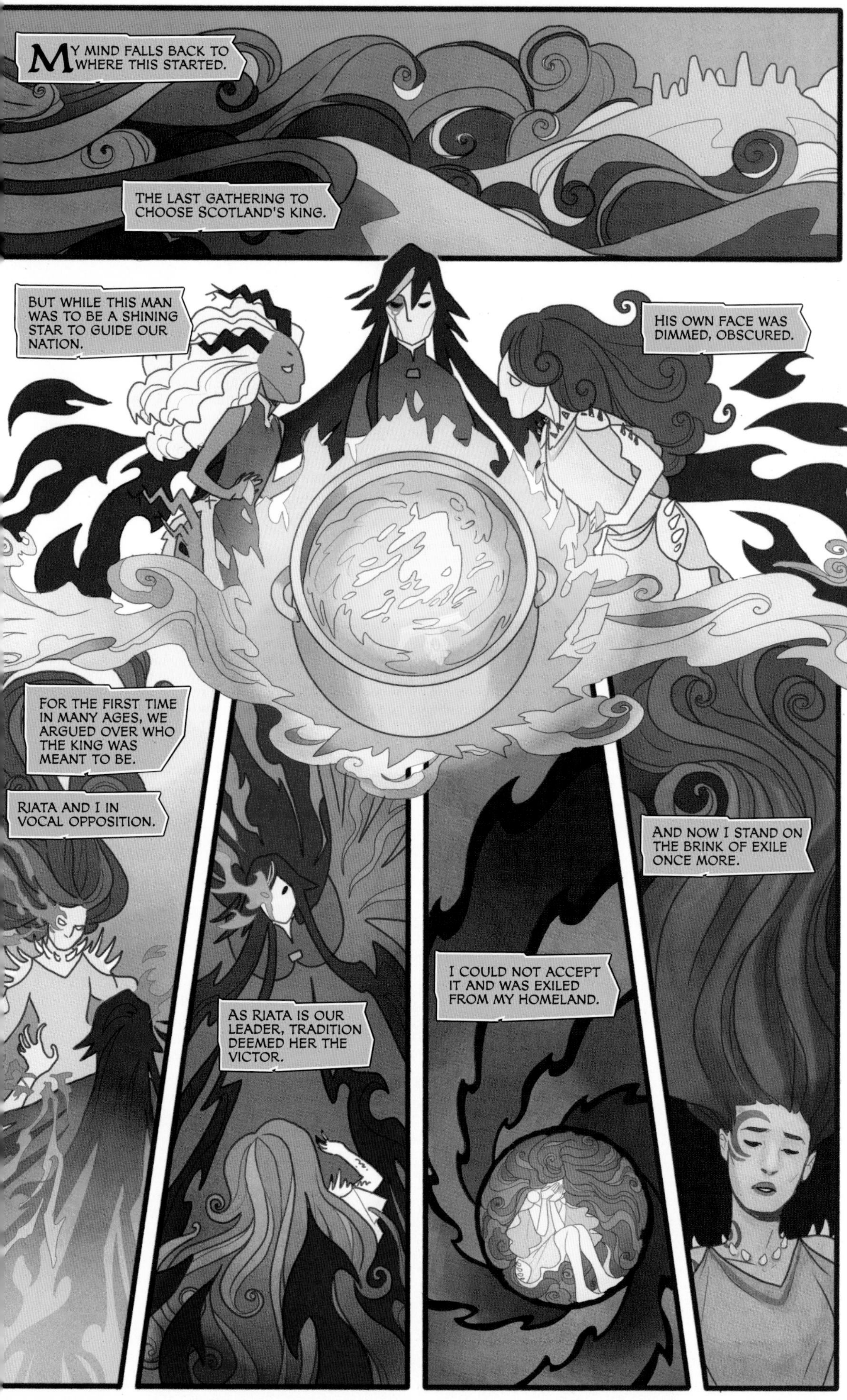
MY MIND FALLS BACK TO WHERE THIS STARTED.
THE LAST GATHERING TO CHOOSE SCOTLAND'S KING.
BUT WHILE THIS MAN WAS TO BE A SHINING STAR TO GUIDE OUR NATION.
HIS OWN FACE WAS DIMMED, OBSCURED.
FOR THE FIRST TIME IN MANY AGES, WE ARGUED OVER WHO THE KING WAS MEANT TO BE.
RIATA AND I IN VOCAL OPPOSITION.
AS RIATA IS OUR LEADER, TRADITION DEEMED HER THE VICTOR.
I COULD NOT ACCEPT IT AND WAS EXILED FROM MY HOMELAND.
AND NOW I STAND ON THE BRINK OF EXILE ONCE MORE.

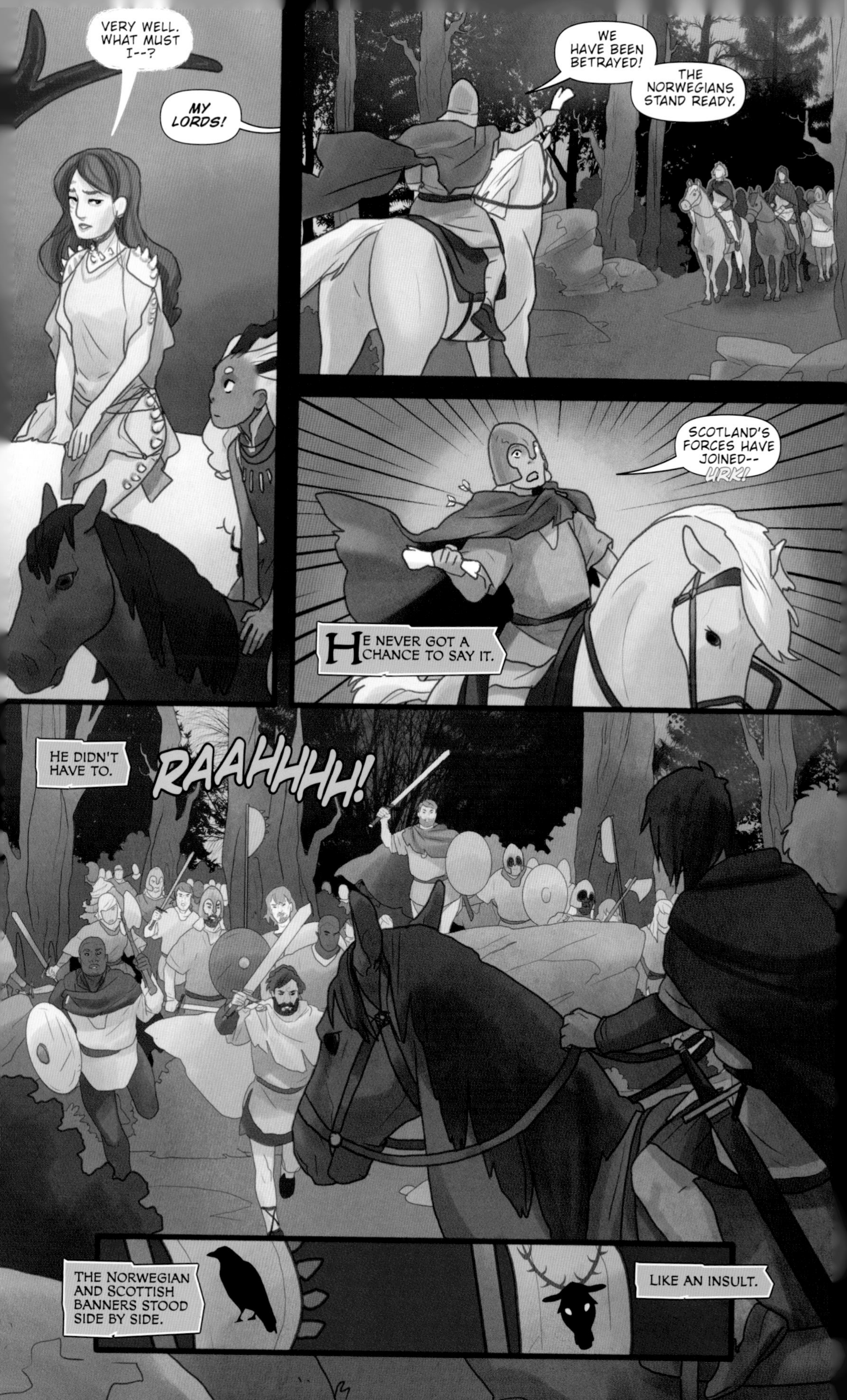
VERY WELL. WHAT MUST I--?
MY LORDS!
WE HAVE BEEN BETRAYED!
THE NORWEGIANS STAND READY.
SCOTLAND'S FORCES HAVE JOINED--
URK!
HE NEVER GOT A CHANCE TO SAY IT.
HE DIDN'T HAVE TO.
RAAHHHH!
THE NORWEGIAN AND SCOTTISH BANNERS STOOD SIDE BY SIDE.
LIKE AN INSULT.

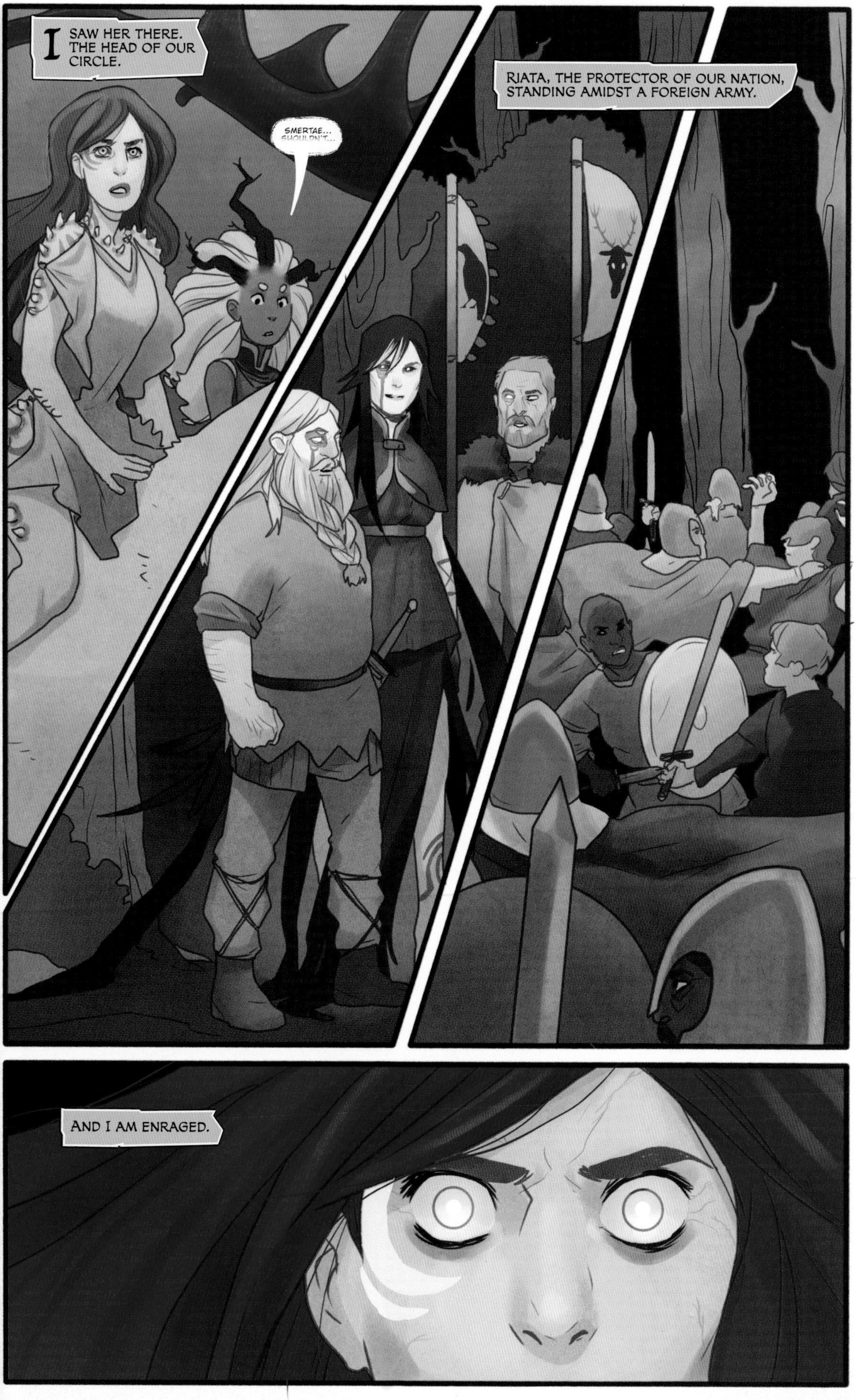
I SAW HER THERE. THE HEAD OF OUR CIRCLE.
SMERTAE... SHOULDN'T...
RIATA, THE PROTECTOR OF OUR NATION, STANDING AMIDST A FOREIGN ARMY.
AND I AM ENRAGED.

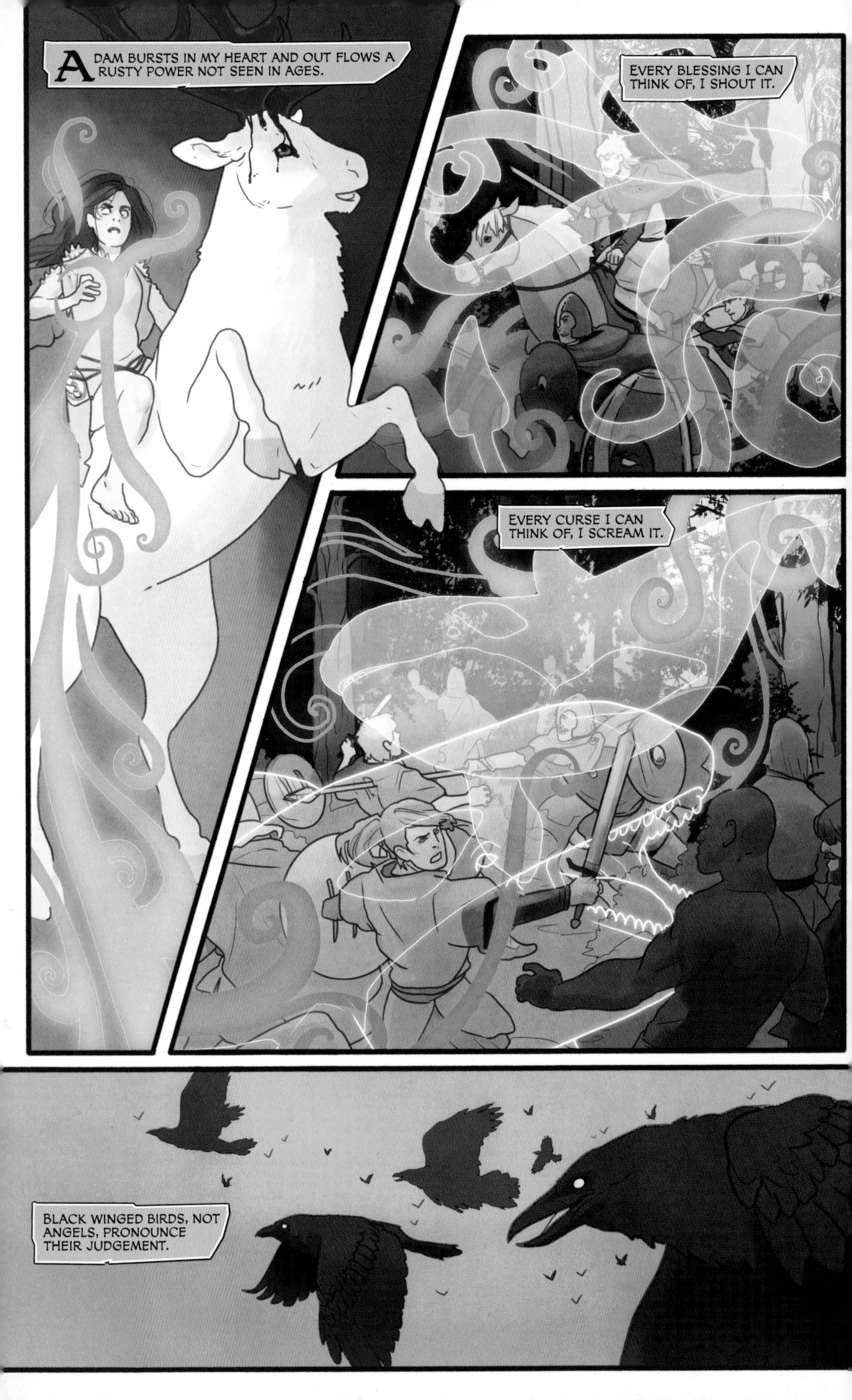
A DAM BURSTS IN MY HEART AND OUT FLOWS A RUSTY POWER NOT SEEN IN AGES.
EVERY BLESSING I CAN THINK OF, I SHOUT IT.
EVERY CURSE I CAN THINK OF, I SCREAM IT.
BLACK WINGED BIRDS, NOT ANGELS, PRONOUNCE THEIR JUDGEMENT.

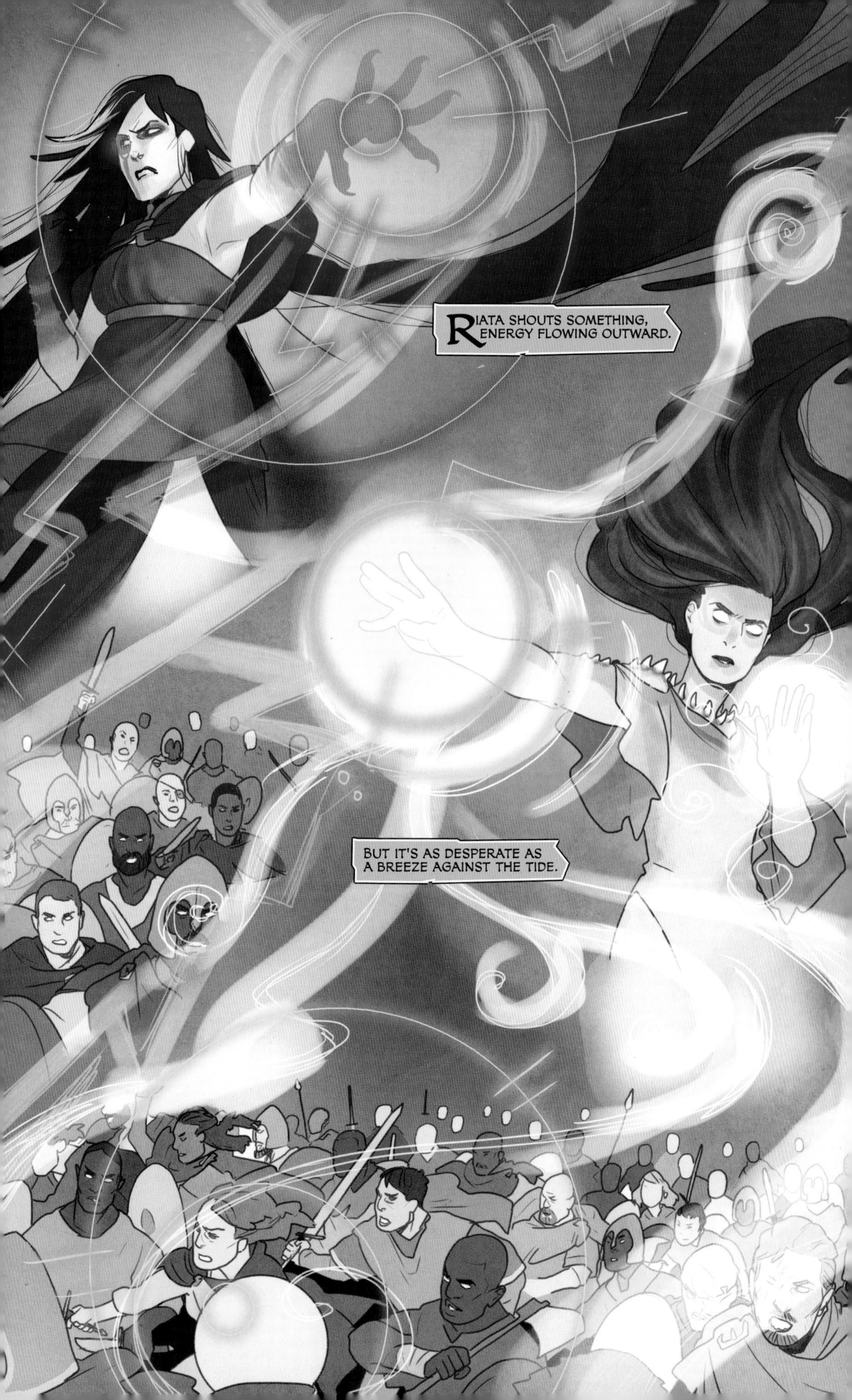
RIATA SHOUTS SOMETHING, ENERGY FLOWING OUTWARD.
BUT IT'S AS DESPERATE AS A BREEZE AGAINST THE TIDE.

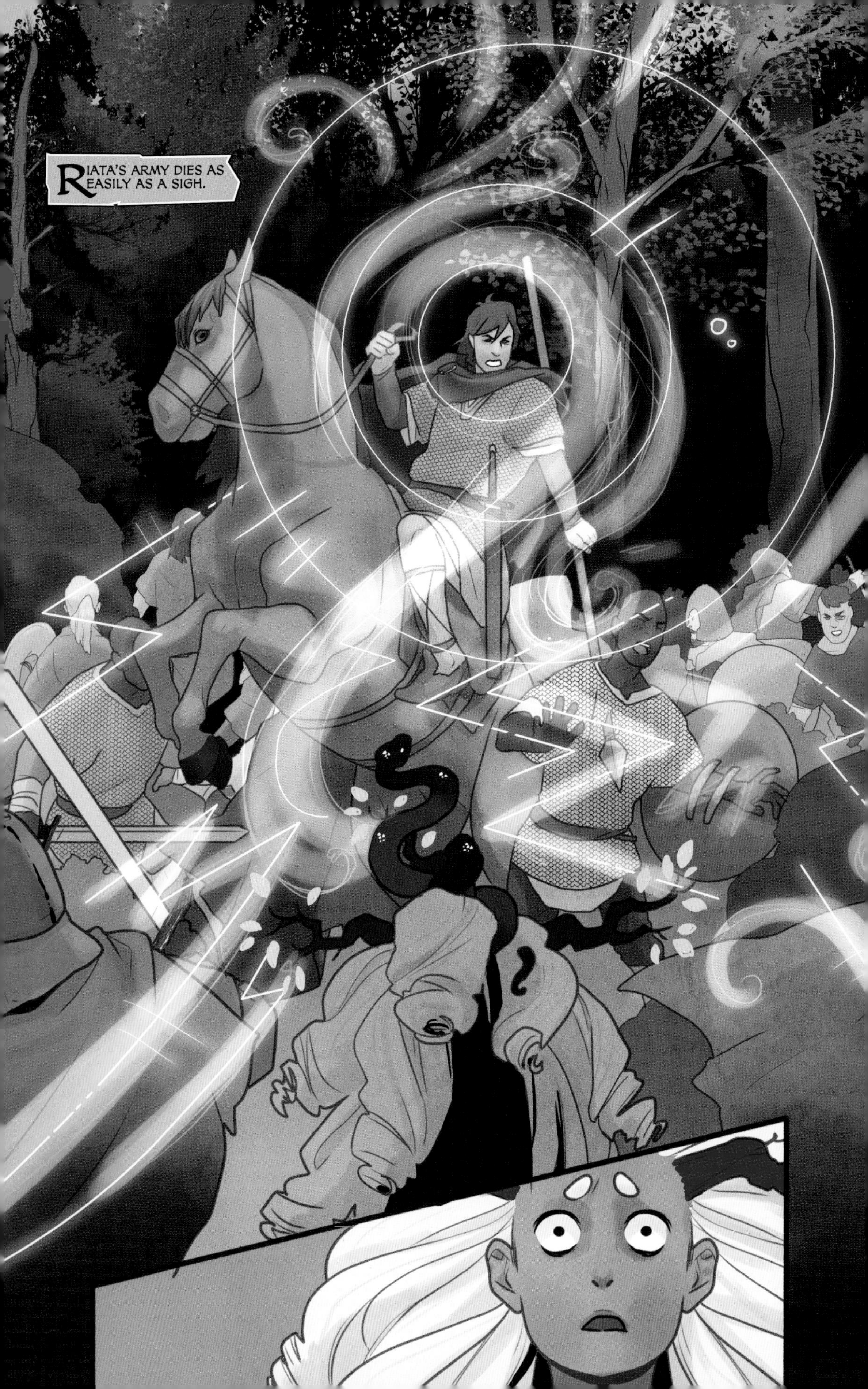
RIATA'S ARMY DIES AS EASILY AS A SIGH.

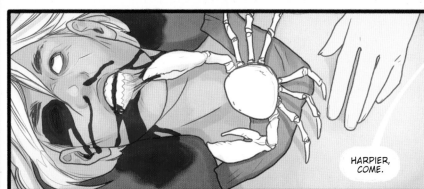

AND ALL THAT'S LEFT IS RUIN.

HARPIER, COME.

I DON'T KNOW. I'VE BARED MY SWORD, HARPIER.

!!!

TELL ME, SMERTAE. DID YOU ALWAYS INTEND TO BETRAY US?

THE REST IS UP TO HER.

OR DID YOU CRAFT THIS "MORAL STANDING" TO COVER UP YOUR FAILURE?

I STAND WITH SCOTLAND. IT'S YOU WHO CRIES OVER A FOREIGN CORPSE.

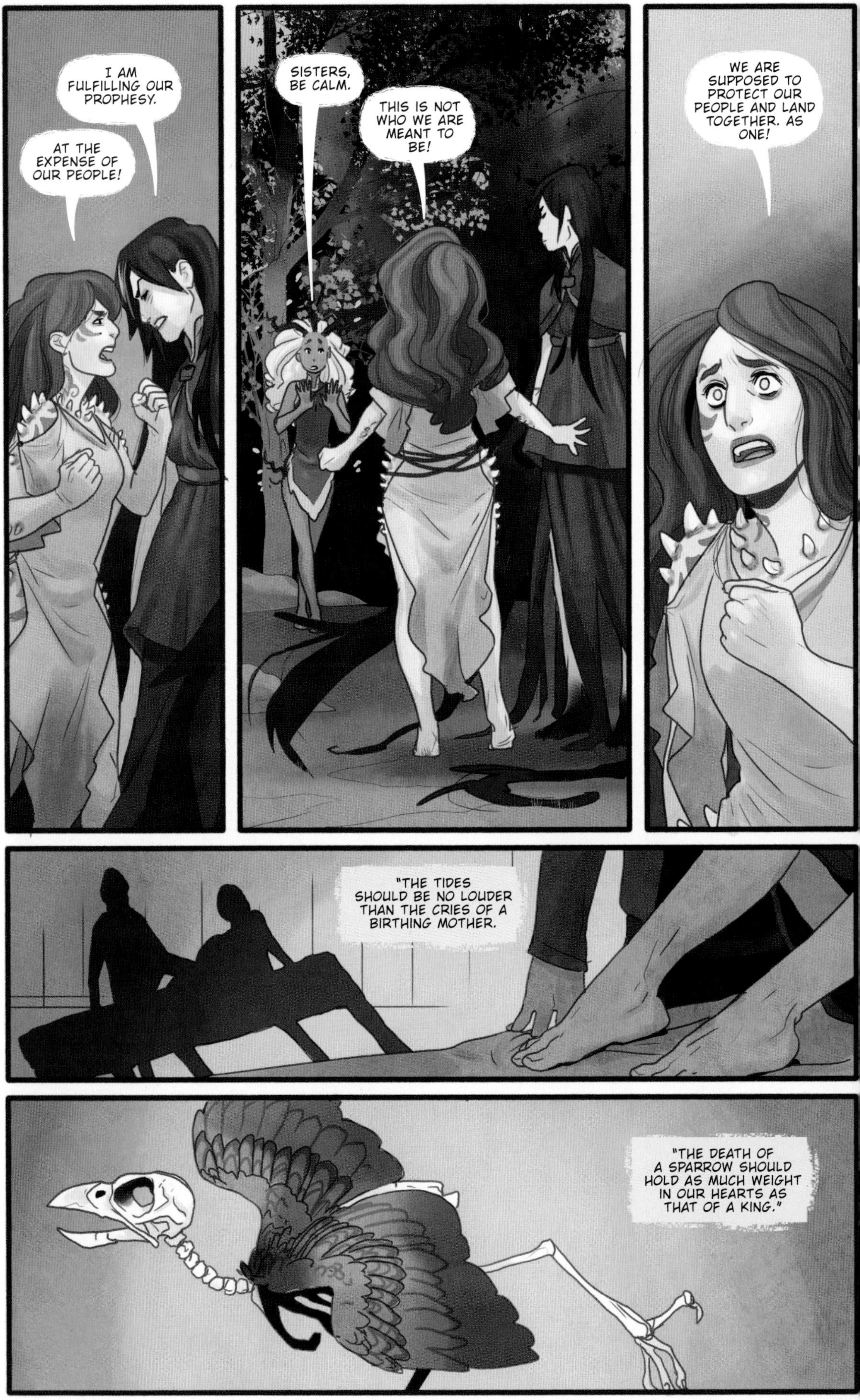
I AM FULFILLING OUR PROPHESY.
AT THE EXPENSE OF OUR PEOPLE!
SISTERS, BE CALM.
THIS IS NOT WHO WE ARE MEANT TO BE!
WE ARE SUPPOSED TO PROTECT OUR PEOPLE AND LAND TOGETHER. AS ONE!
"THE TIDES SHOULD BE NO LOUDER THAN THE CRIES OF A BIRTHING MOTHER.
"THE DEATH OF A SPARROW SHOULD HOLD AS MUCH WEIGHT IN OUR HEARTS AS THAT OF A KING."

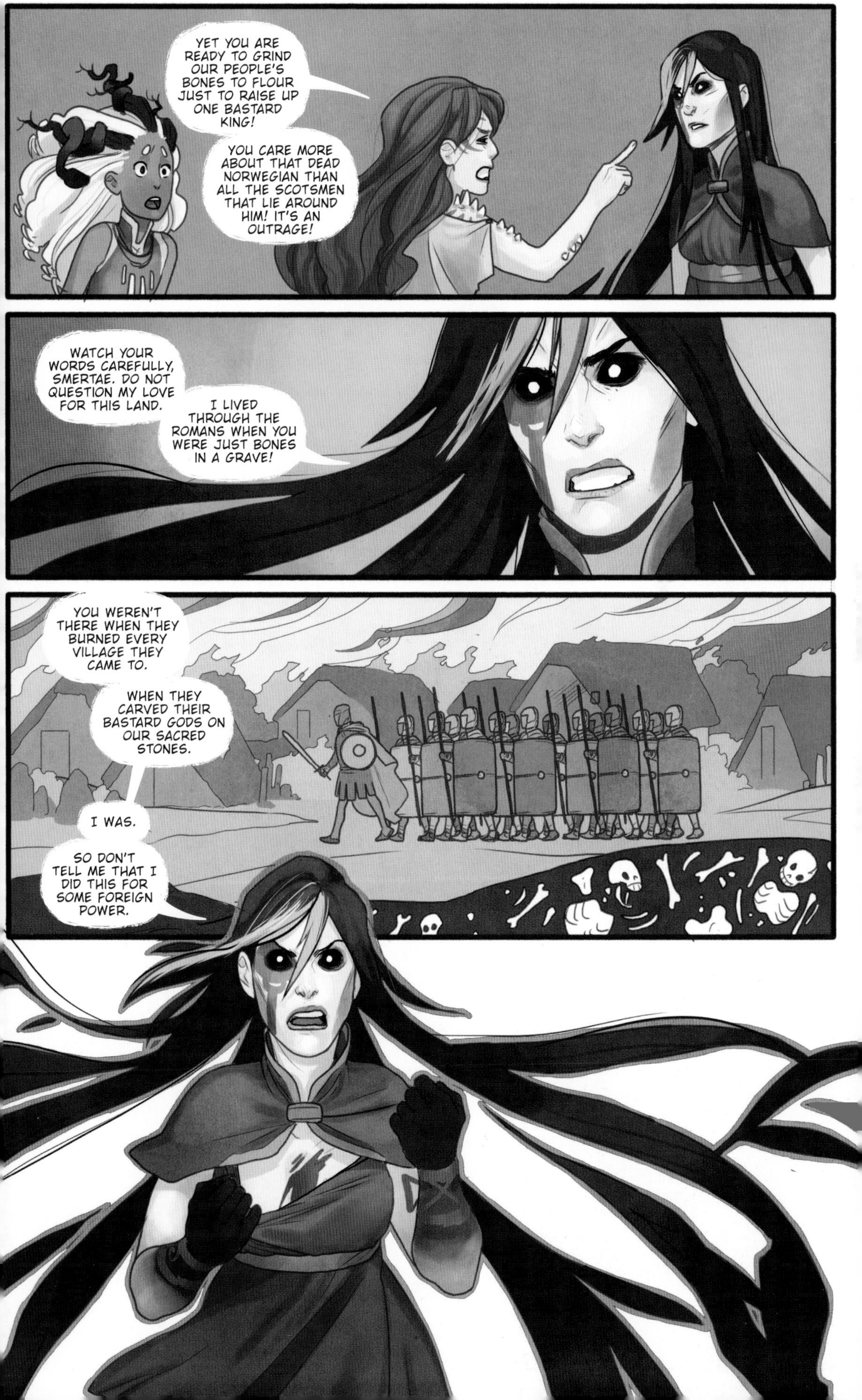
YET YOU ARE READY TO GRIND OUR PEOPLE'S BONES TO FLOUR JUST TO RAISE UP ONE BASTARD KING!
YOU CARE MORE ABOUT THAT DEAD NORWEGIAN THAN ALL THE SCOTSMEN THAT LIE AROUND HIM! IT'S AN OUTRAGE!
WATCH YOUR WORDS CAREFULLY, SMERTAE. DO NOT QUESTION MY LOVE FOR THIS LAND.
I LIVED THROUGH THE ROMANS WHEN YOU WERE JUST BONES IN A GRAVE!
YOU WEREN'T THERE WHEN THEY BURNED EVERY VILLAGE THEY CAME TO.
WHEN THEY CARVED THEIR BASTARD GODS ON OUR SACRED STONES.
I WAS.
SO DON'T TELL ME THAT I DID THIS FOR SOME FOREIGN POWER.

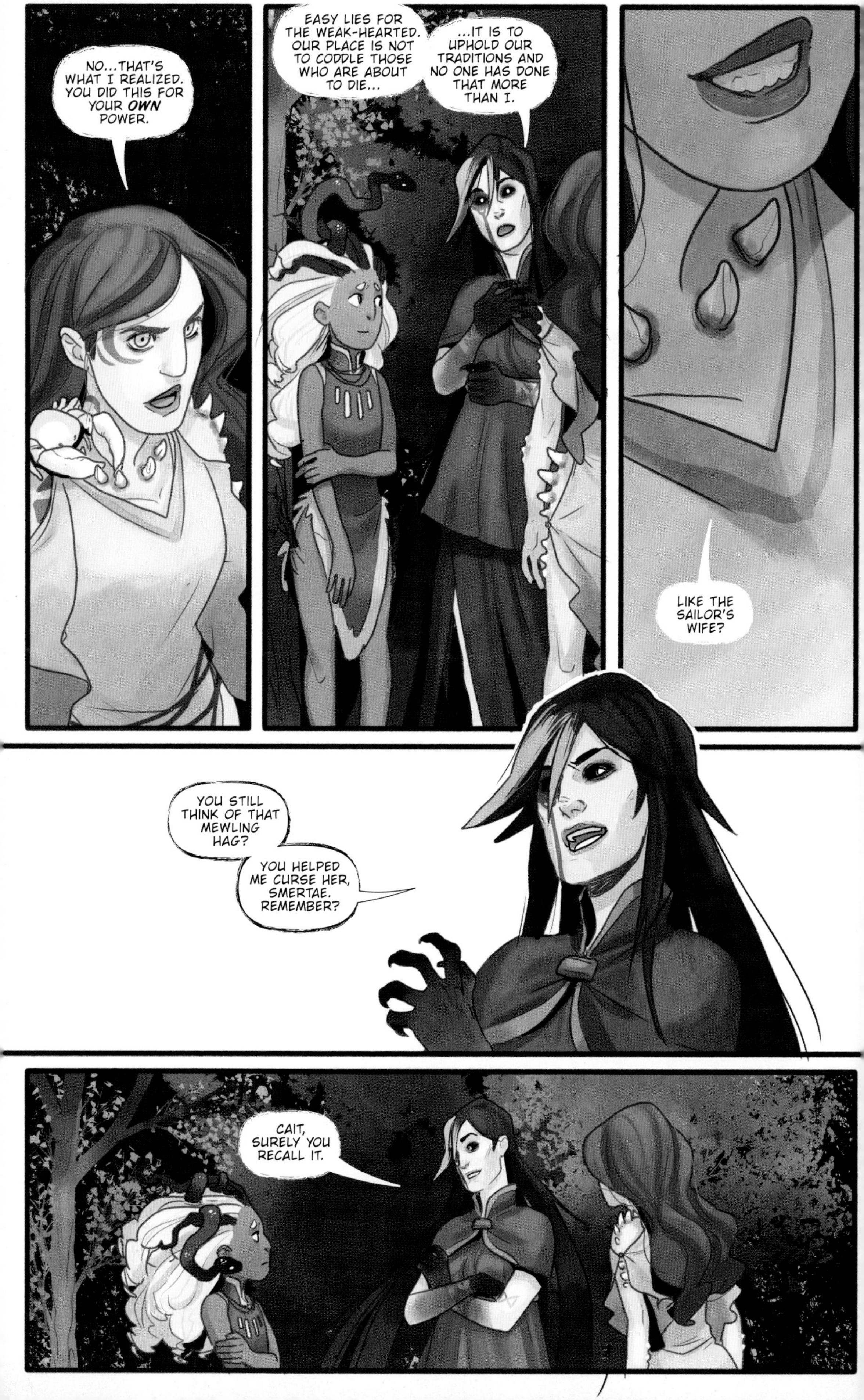

NO...THAT'S WHAT I REALIZED. YOU DID THIS FOR YOUR OWN POWER.
EASY LIES FOR THE WEAK-HEARTED. OUR PLACE IS NOT TO CODDLE THOSE WHO ARE ABOUT TO DIE...
...IT IS TO UPHOLD OUR TRADITIONS AND NO ONE HAS DONE THAT MORE THAN I.
LIKE THE SAILOR'S WIFE?
YOU STILL THINK OF THAT MEWLING HAG?
YOU HELPED ME CURSE HER, SMERTAE. REMEMBER?
CAIT, SURELY YOU RECALL IT.

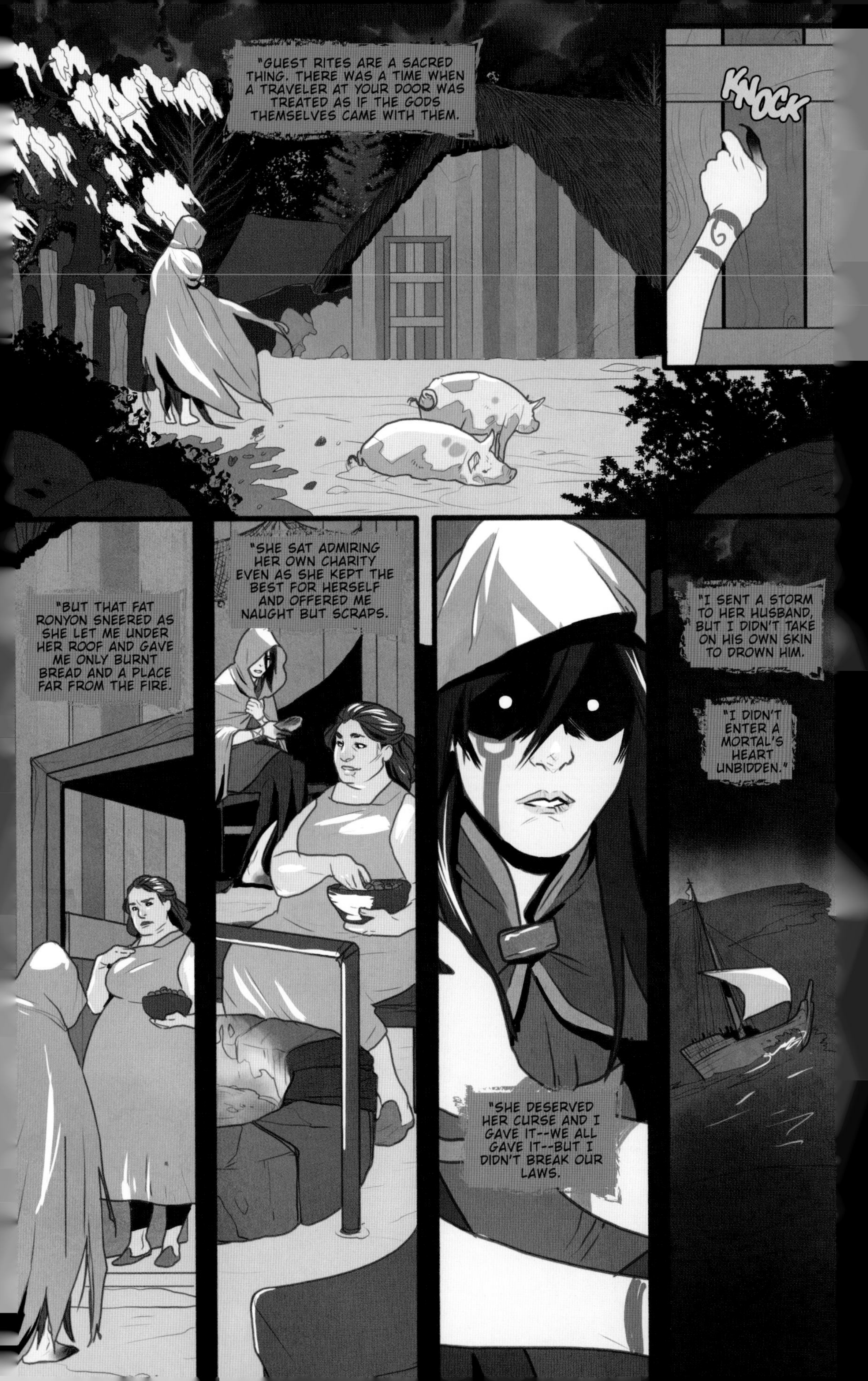
"GUEST RITES ARE A SACRED THING. THERE WAS A TIME WHEN A TRAVELER AT YOUR DOOR WAS TREATED AS IF THE GODS THEMSELVES CAME WITH THEM.
KNOCK
"BUT THAT FAT RONYON SNEERED AS SHE LET ME UNDER HER ROOF AND GAVE ME ONLY BURNT BREAD AND A PLACE FAR FROM THE FIRE.
"SHE SAT ADMIRING HER OWN CHARITY EVEN AS SHE KEPT THE BEST FOR HERSELF AND OFFERED ME NAUGHT BUT SCRAPS.
"SHE DESERVED HER CURSE AND I GAVE IT--WE ALL GAVE IT--BUT I DIDN'T BREAK OUR LAWS.
"I SENT A STORM TO HER HUSBAND, BUT I DIDN'T TAKE ON HIS OWN SKIN TO DROWN HIM.
"I DIDN'T ENTER A MORTAL'S HEART UNBIDDEN."

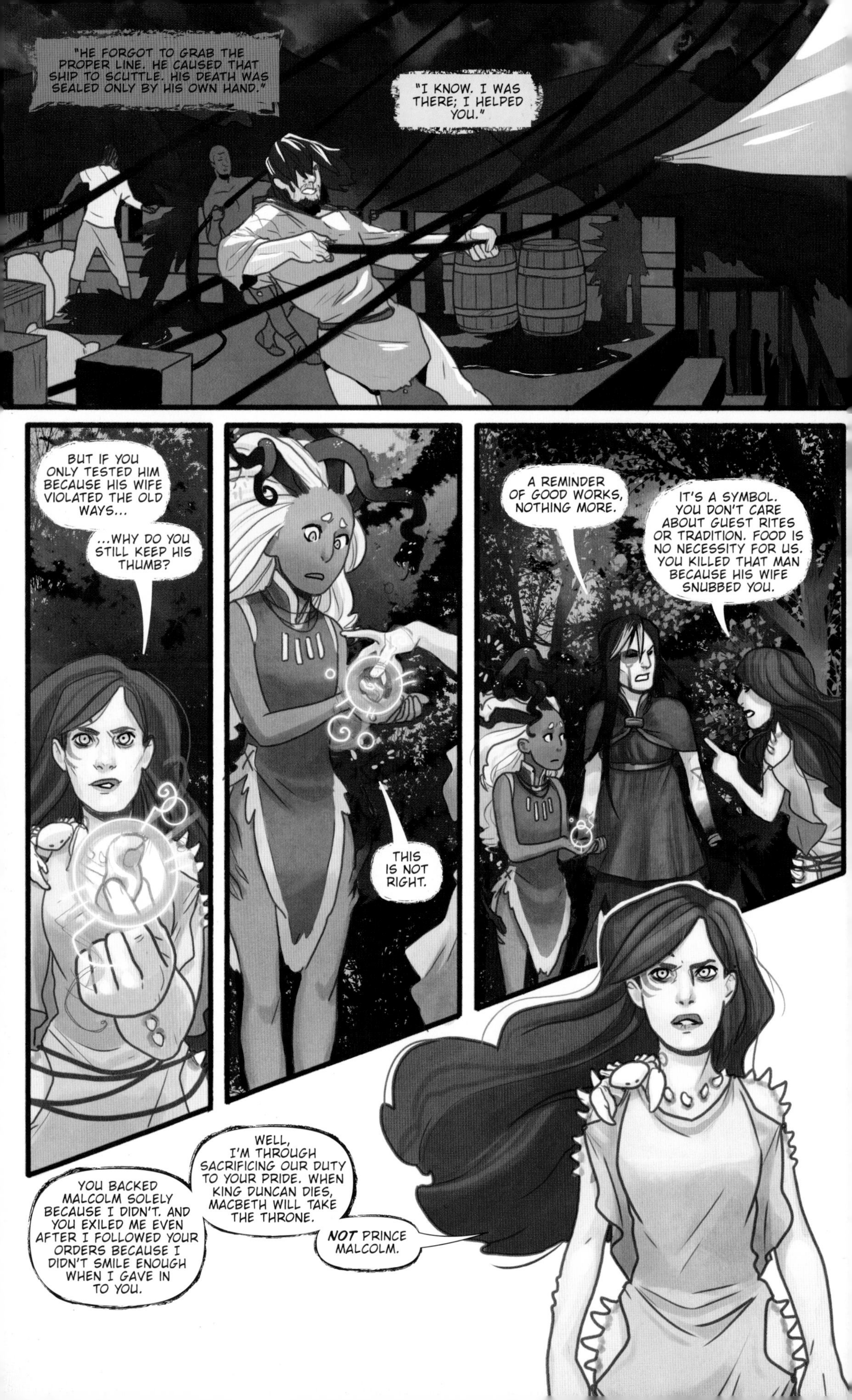

"HE FORGOT TO GRAB THE PROPER LINE. HE CAUSED THAT SHIP TO SCUTTLE. HIS DEATH WAS SEALED ONLY BY HIS OWN HAND."
"I KNOW. I WAS THERE; I HELPED YOU."
BUT IF YOU ONLY TESTED HIM BECAUSE HIS WIFE VIOLATED THE OLD WAYS...
...WHY DO YOU STILL KEEP HIS THUMB?
THIS IS NOT RIGHT.
A REMINDER OF GOOD WORKS, NOTHING MORE.
IT'S A SYMBOL. YOU DON'T CARE ABOUT GUEST RITES OR TRADITION. FOOD IS NO NECESSITY FOR US. YOU KILLED THAT MAN BECAUSE HIS WIFE SNUBBED YOU.
YOU BACKED MALCOLM SOLELY BECAUSE I DIDN'T. AND YOU EXILED ME EVEN AFTER I FOLLOWED YOUR ORDERS BECAUSE I DIDN'T SMILE ENOUGH WHEN I GAVE IN TO YOU.
WELL, I'M THROUGH SACRIFICING OUR DUTY TO YOUR PRIDE. WHEN KING DUNCAN DIES, MACBETH WILL TAKE THE THRONE.
NOT PRINCE MALCOLM.

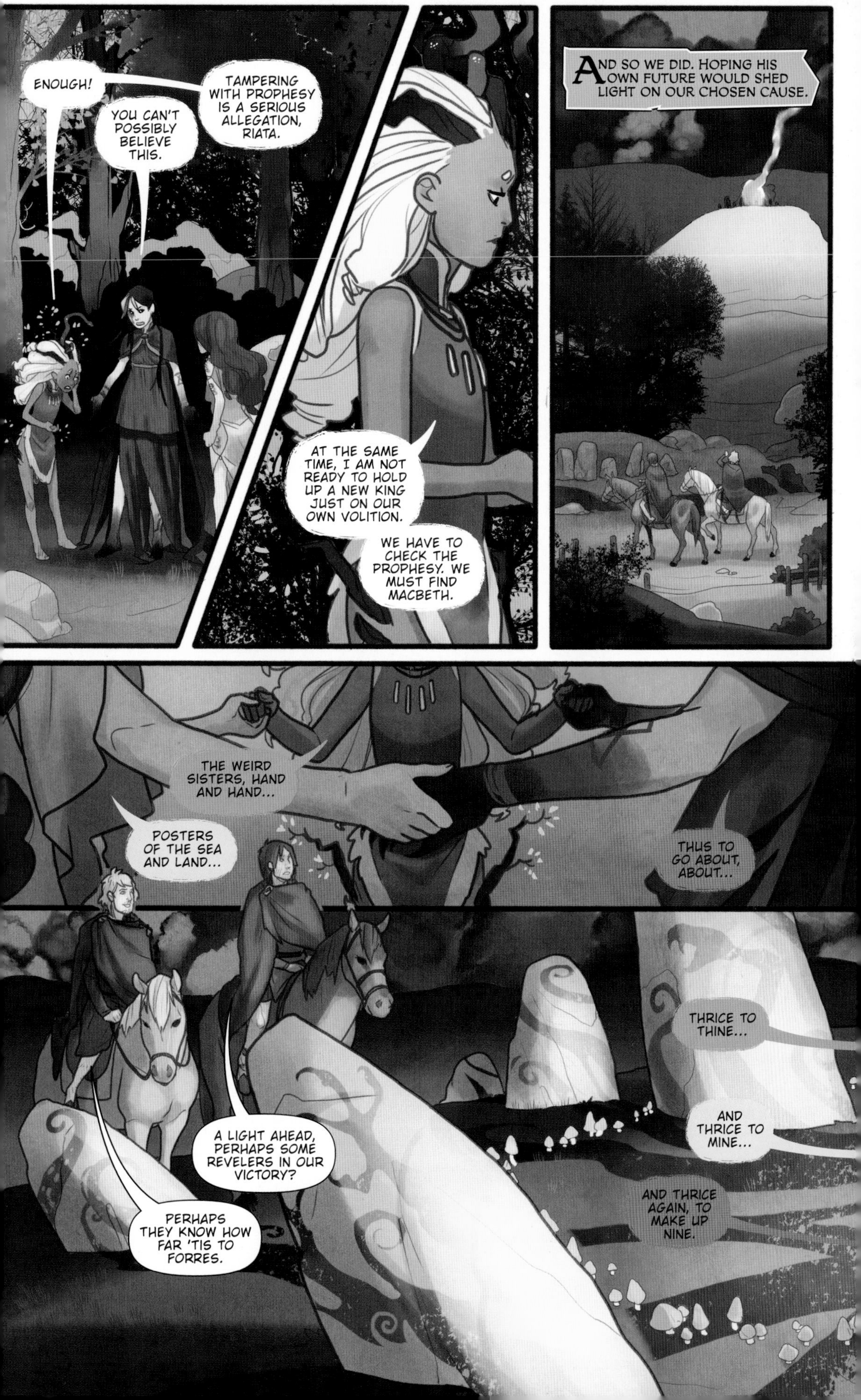

ENOUGH!
YOU CAN'T POSSIBLY BELIEVE THIS.
TAMPERING WITH PROPHESY IS A SERIOUS ALLEGATION, RIATA.
AT THE SAME TIME, I AM NOT READY TO HOLD UP A NEW KING JUST ON OUR OWN VOLITION.
WE HAVE TO CHECK THE PROPHESY. WE MUST FIND MACBETH.
AND SO WE DID. HOPING HIS OWN FUTURE WOULD SHED LIGHT ON OUR CHOSEN CAUSE.
THE WEIRD SISTERS, HAND AND HAND...
POSTERS OF THE SEA AND LAND...
THUS TO GO ABOUT, ABOUT...
THRICE TO THINE...
AND THRICE TO MINE...
AND THRICE AGAIN, TO MAKE UP NINE.
A LIGHT AHEAD, PERHAPS SOME REVELERS IN OUR VICTORY?
PERHAPS THEY KNOW HOW FAR 'TIS TO FORRES.

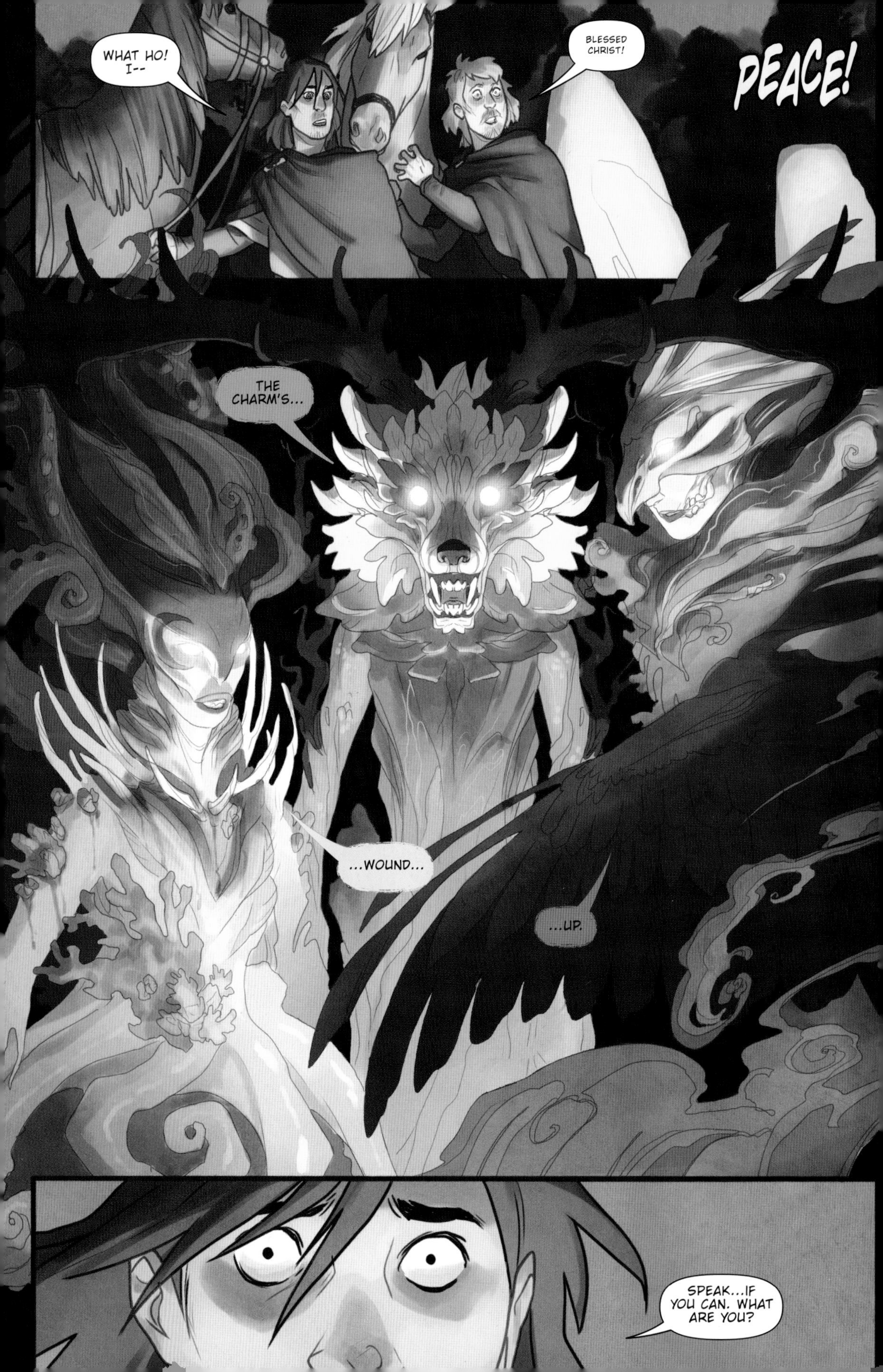
WHAT HO! I--
BLESSED CHRIST!
PEACE!
THE CHARM'S...
...WOUND...
...UP.
SPEAK...IF YOU CAN. WHAT ARE YOU?

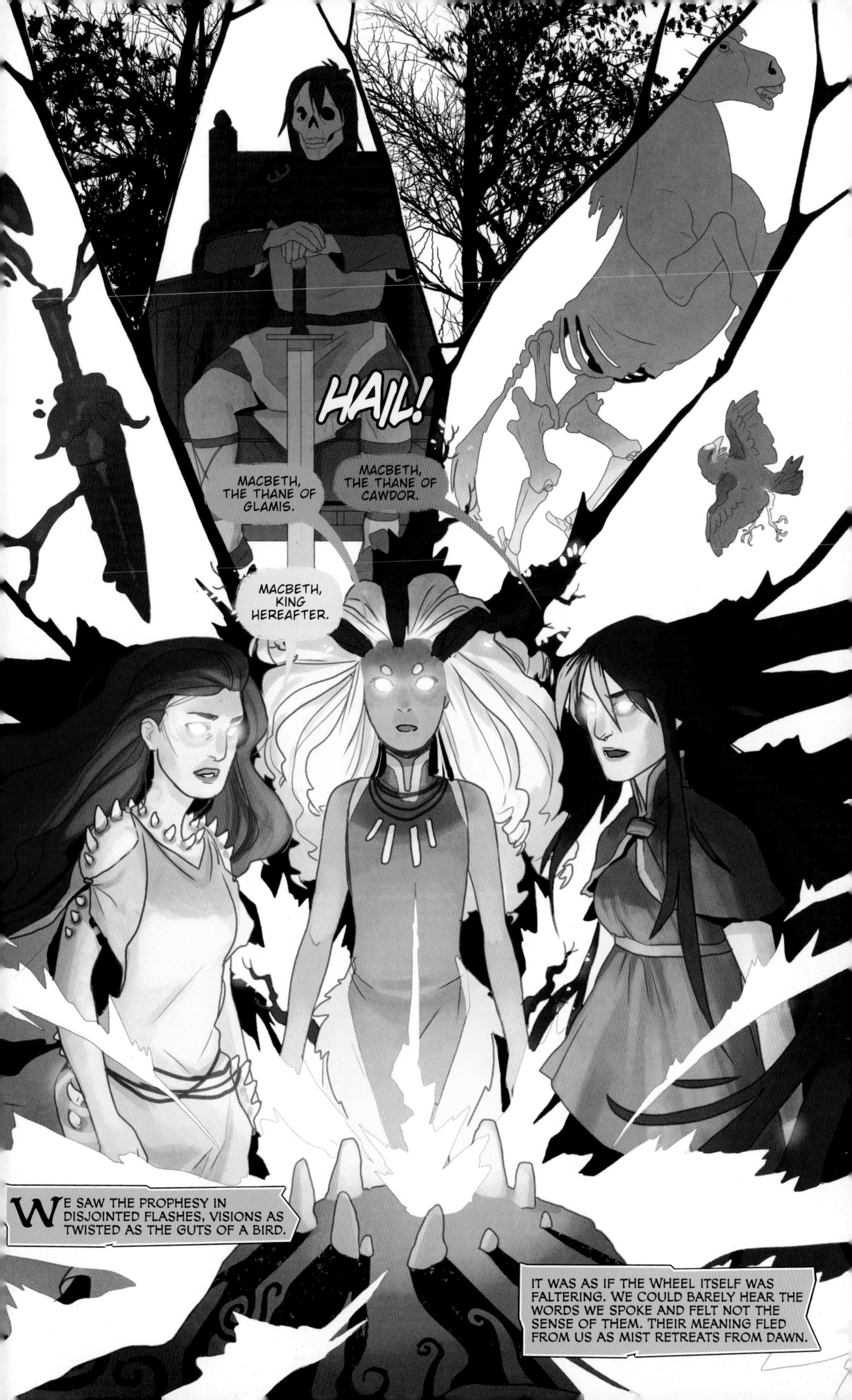
HAIL!
MACBETH, THE THANE OF GLAMIS.
MACBETH, THE THANE OF CAWDOR.
MACBETH, KING HEREAFTER.
WE SAW THE PROPHESY IN DISJOINTED FLASHES, VISIONS AS TWISTED AS THE GUTS OF A BIRD.
IT WAS AS IF THE WHEEL ITSELF WAS FALTERING. WE COULD BARELY HEAR THE WORDS WE SPOKE AND FELT NOT THE SENSE OF THEM. THEIR MEANING FLED FROM US AS MIST RETREATS FROM DAWN.

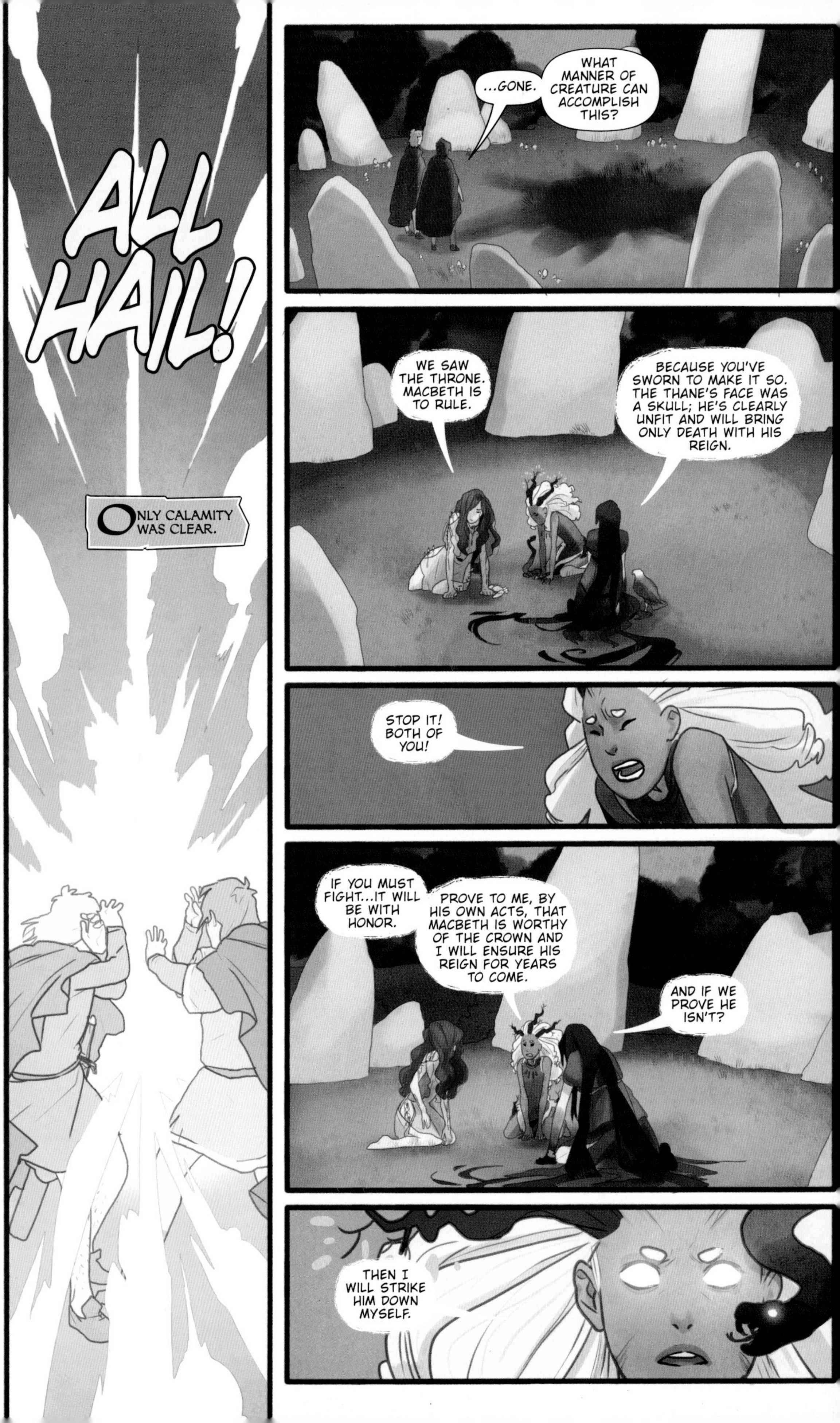
ALL HAIL!
ONLY CALAMITY WAS CLEAR.
...GONE.
WHAT MANNER OF CREATURE CAN ACCOMPLISH THIS?
WE SAW THE THRONE. MACBETH IS TO RULE.
BECAUSE YOU'VE SWORN TO MAKE IT SO. THE THANE'S FACE WAS A SKULL; HE'S CLEARLY UNFIT AND WILL BRING ONLY DEATH WITH HIS REIGN.
STOP IT! BOTH OF YOU!
IF YOU MUST FIGHT...IT WILL BE WITH HONOR.
PROVE TO ME, BY HIS OWN ACTS, THAT MACBETH IS WORTHY OF THE CROWN AND I WILL ENSURE HIS REIGN FOR YEARS TO COME.
AND IF WE PROVE HE ISN'T?
THEN I WILL STRIKE HIM DOWN MYSELF.

Act Three

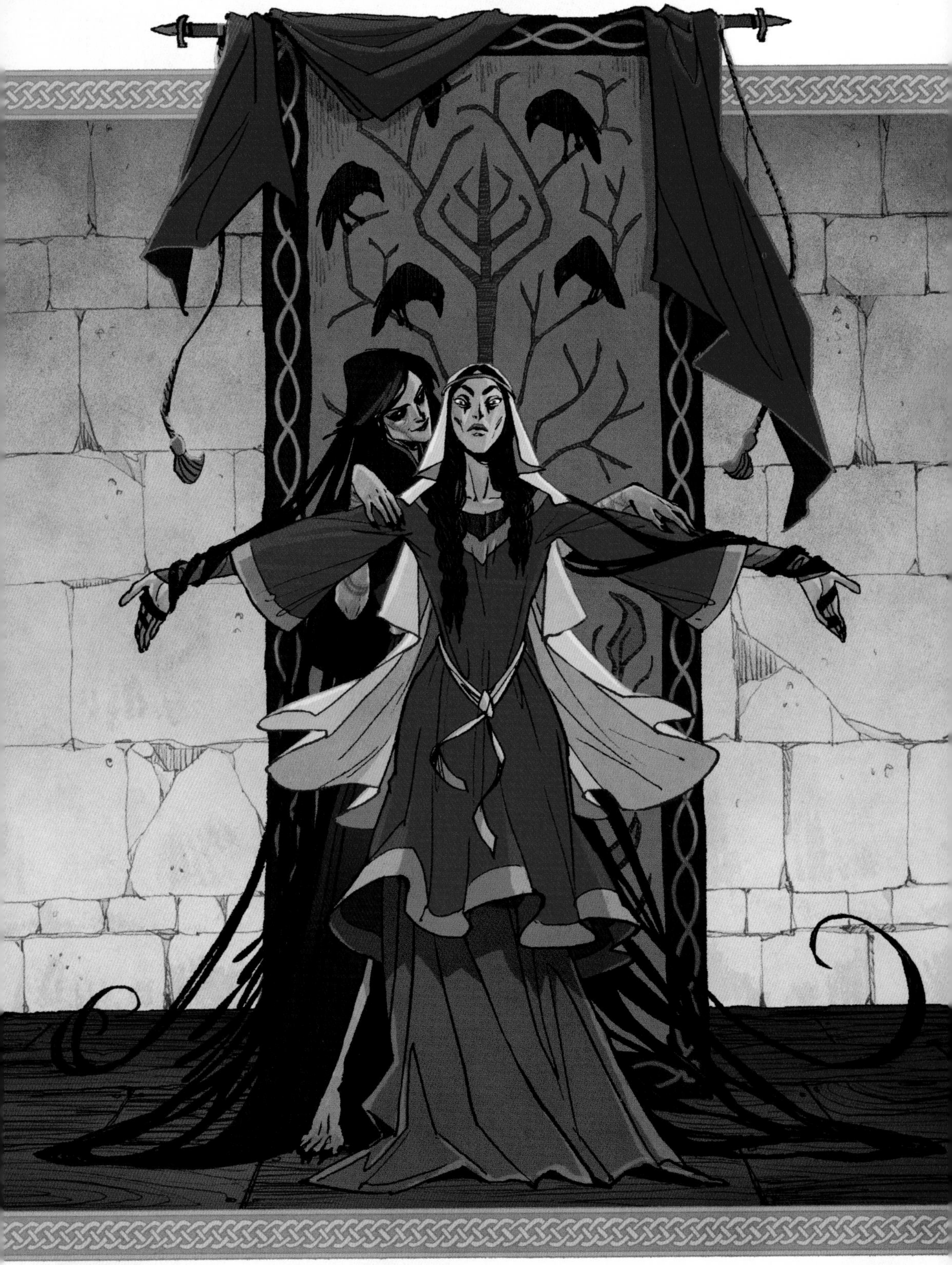

Issue Three Cover by Kyla Vanderklugt

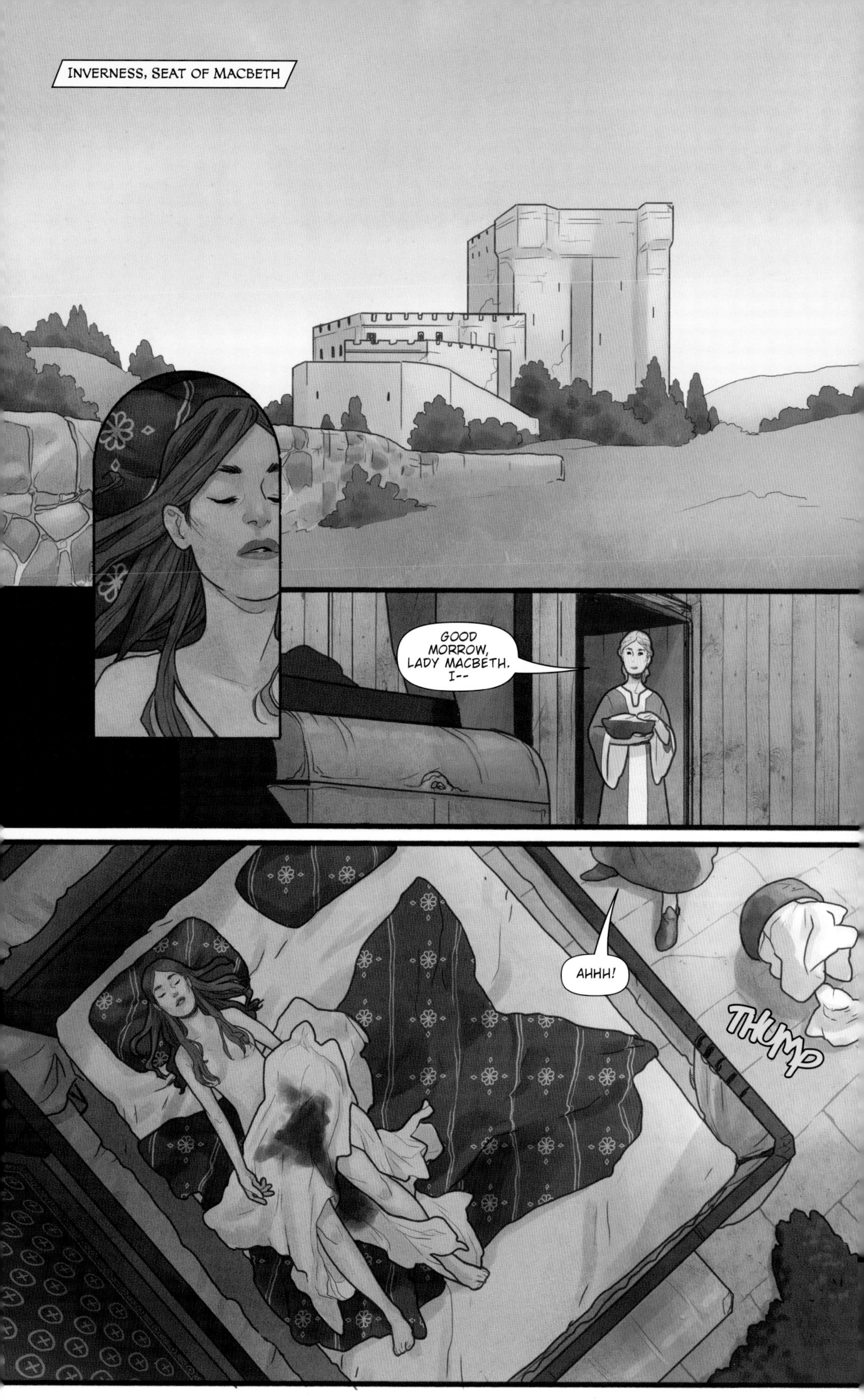
INVERNESS, SEAT OF MACBETH
GOOD MORROW, LADY MACBETH. I--
AHHH!
THUMP

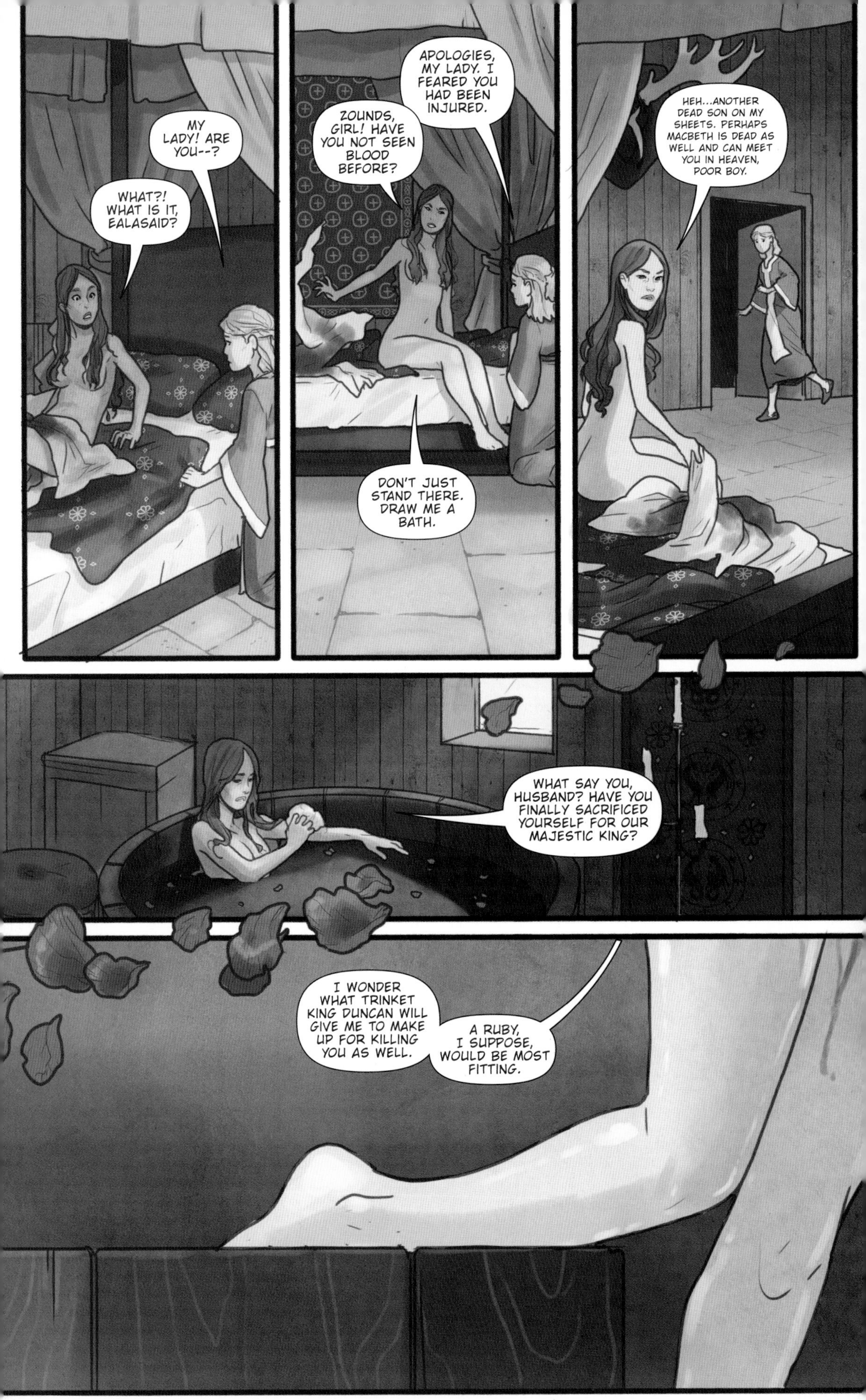
MY LADY! ARE YOU--?
WHAT?! WHAT IS IT, EALASAID?
ZOUNDS, GIRL! HAVE YOU NOT SEEN BLOOD BEFORE?
APOLOGIES, MY LADY. I FEARED YOU HAD BEEN INJURED.
DON'T JUST STAND THERE. DRAW ME A BATH.
HEH...ANOTHER DEAD SON ON MY SHEETS. PERHAPS MACBETH IS DEAD AS WELL AND CAN MEET YOU IN HEAVEN, POOR BOY.
WHAT SAY YOU, HUSBAND? HAVE YOU FINALLY SACRIFICED YOURSELF FOR OUR MAJESTIC KING?
I WONDER WHAT TRINKET KING DUNCAN WILL GIVE ME TO MAKE UP FOR KILLING YOU AS WELL.
A RUBY, I SUPPOSE, WOULD BE MOST FITTING.

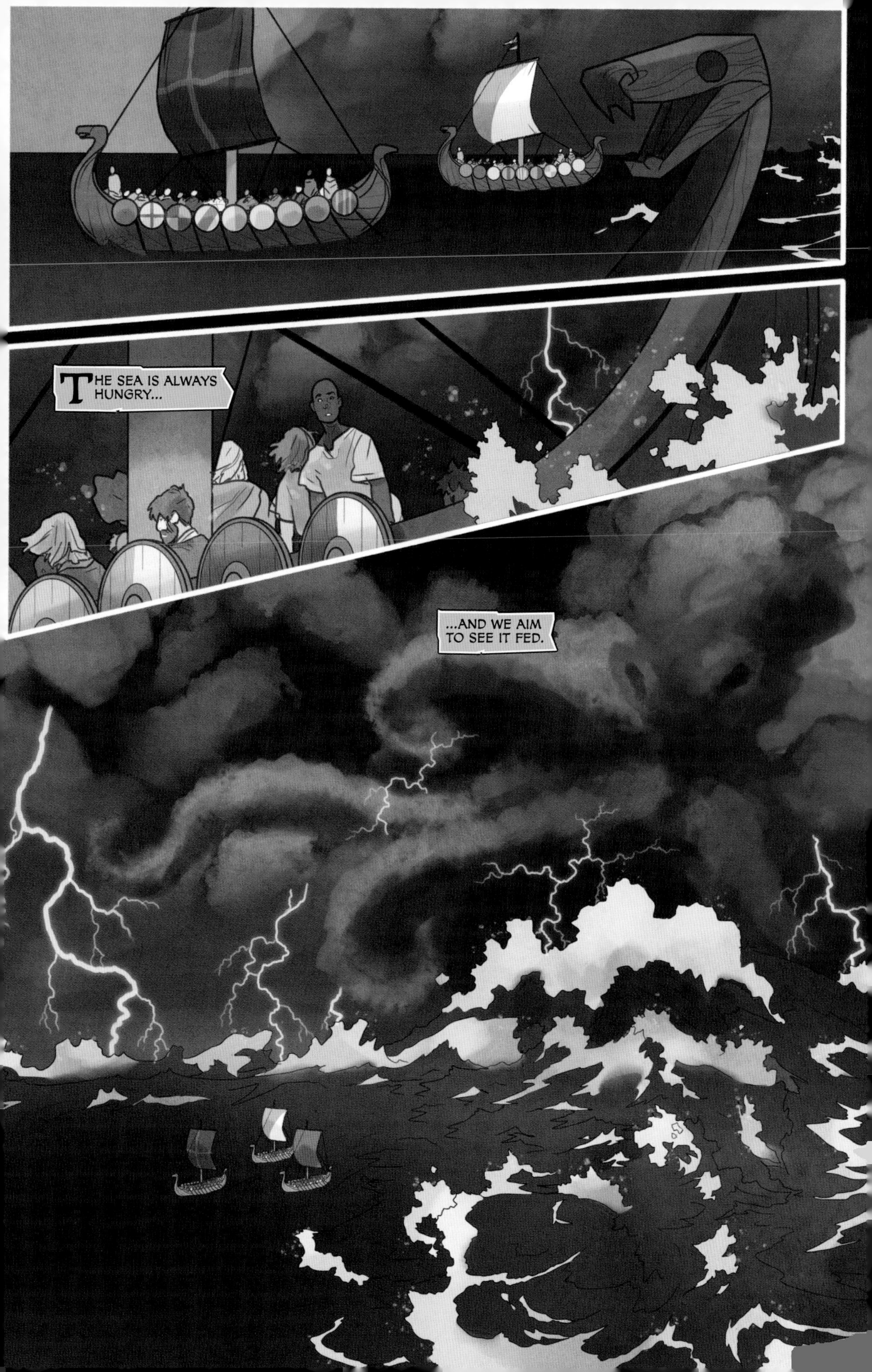
THE SEA IS ALWAYS HUNGRY...
...AND WE AIM TO SEE IT FED.

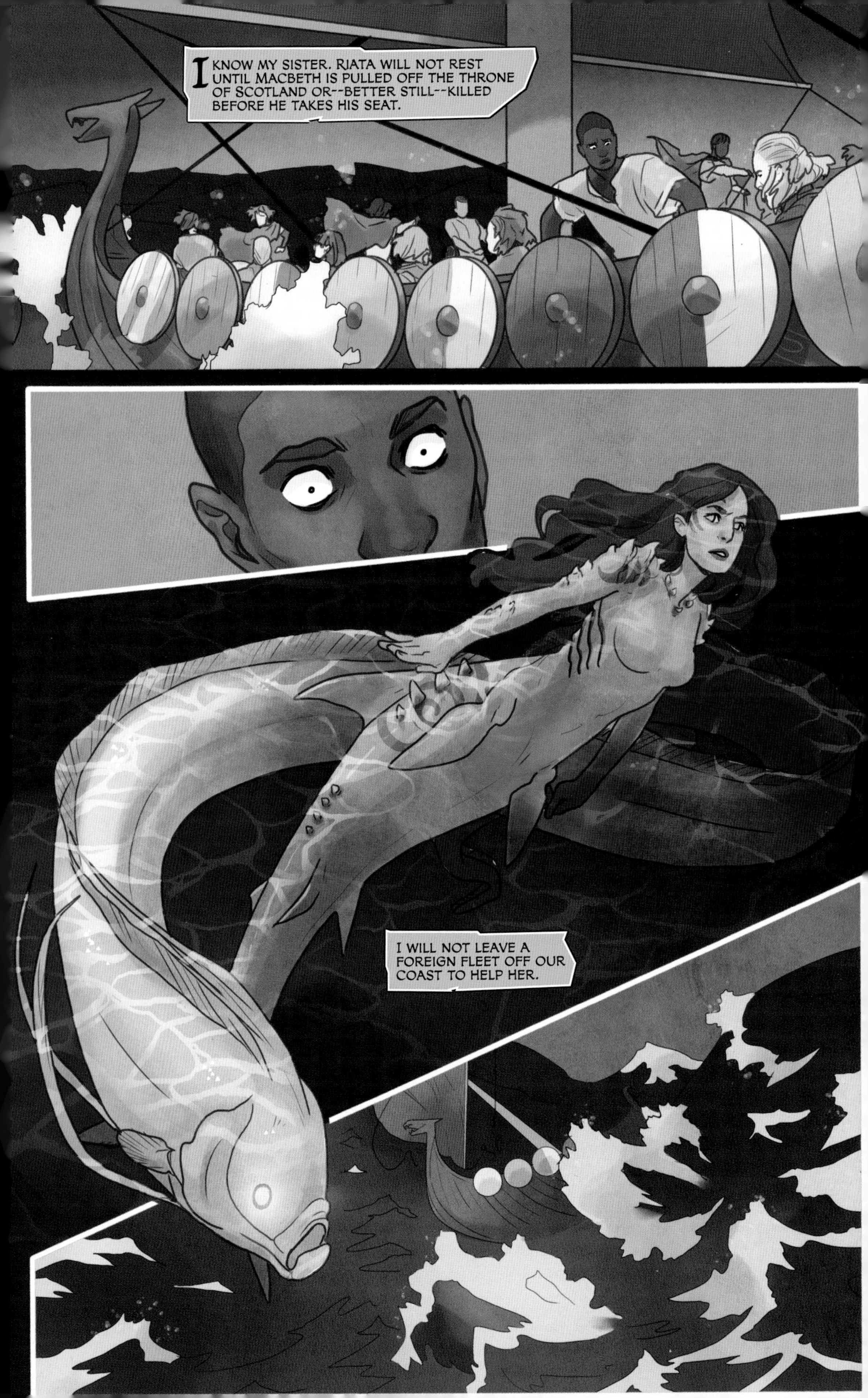
I KNOW MY SISTER. RIATA WILL NOT REST UNTIL MACBETH IS PULLED OFF THE THRONE OF SCOTLAND OR--BETTER STILL--KILLED BEFORE HE TAKES HIS SEAT.
I WILL NOT LEAVE A FOREIGN FLEET OFF OUR COAST TO HELP HER.

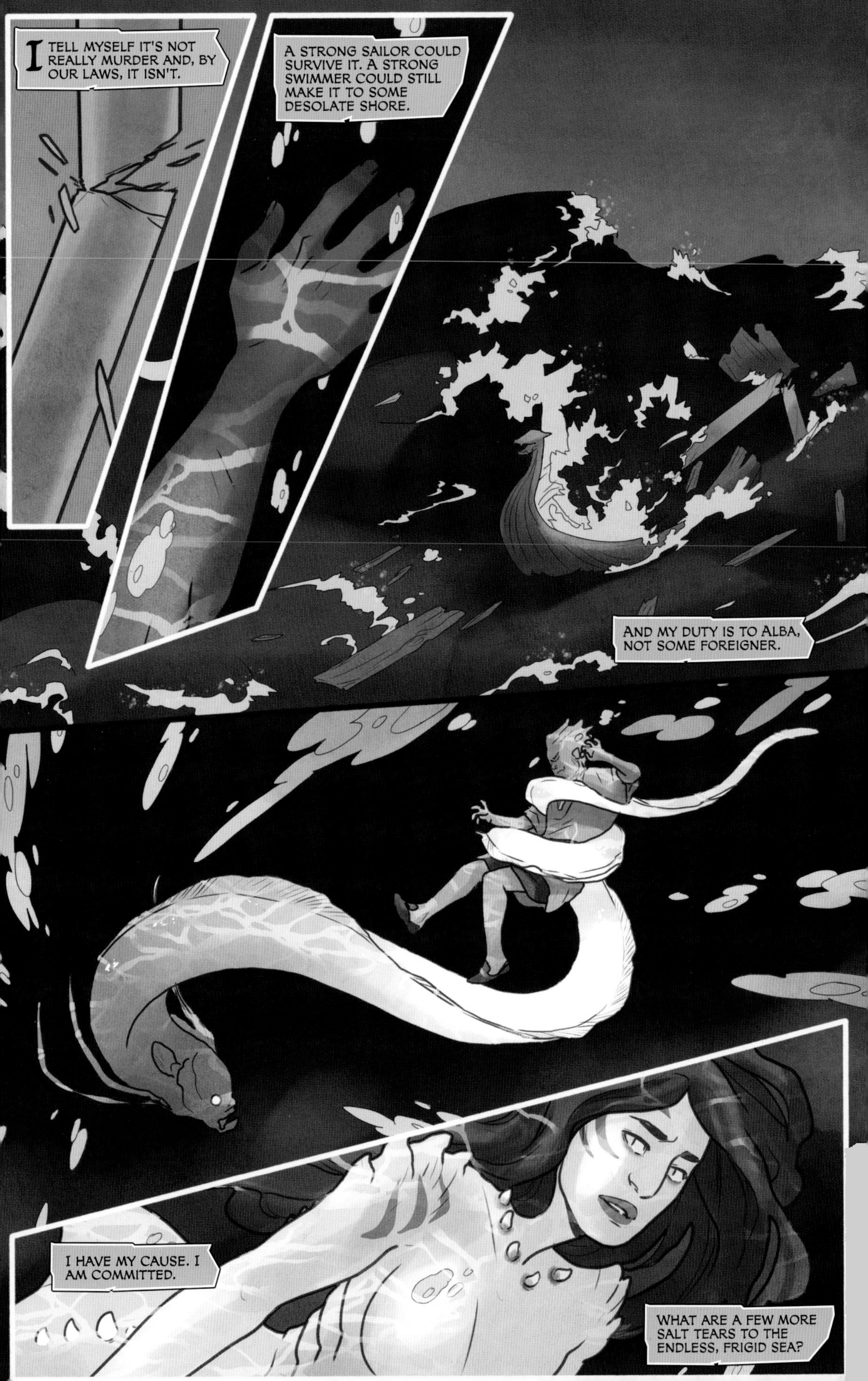
I TELL MYSELF IT'S NOT REALLY MURDER AND, BY OUR LAWS, IT ISN'T.
A STRONG SAILOR COULD SURVIVE IT. A STRONG SWIMMER COULD STILL MAKE IT TO SOME DESOLATE SHORE.
AND MY DUTY IS TO ALBA, NOT SOME FOREIGNER.
I HAVE MY CAUSE. I AM COMMITTED.
WHAT ARE A FEW MORE SALT TEARS TO THE ENDLESS, FRIGID SEA?

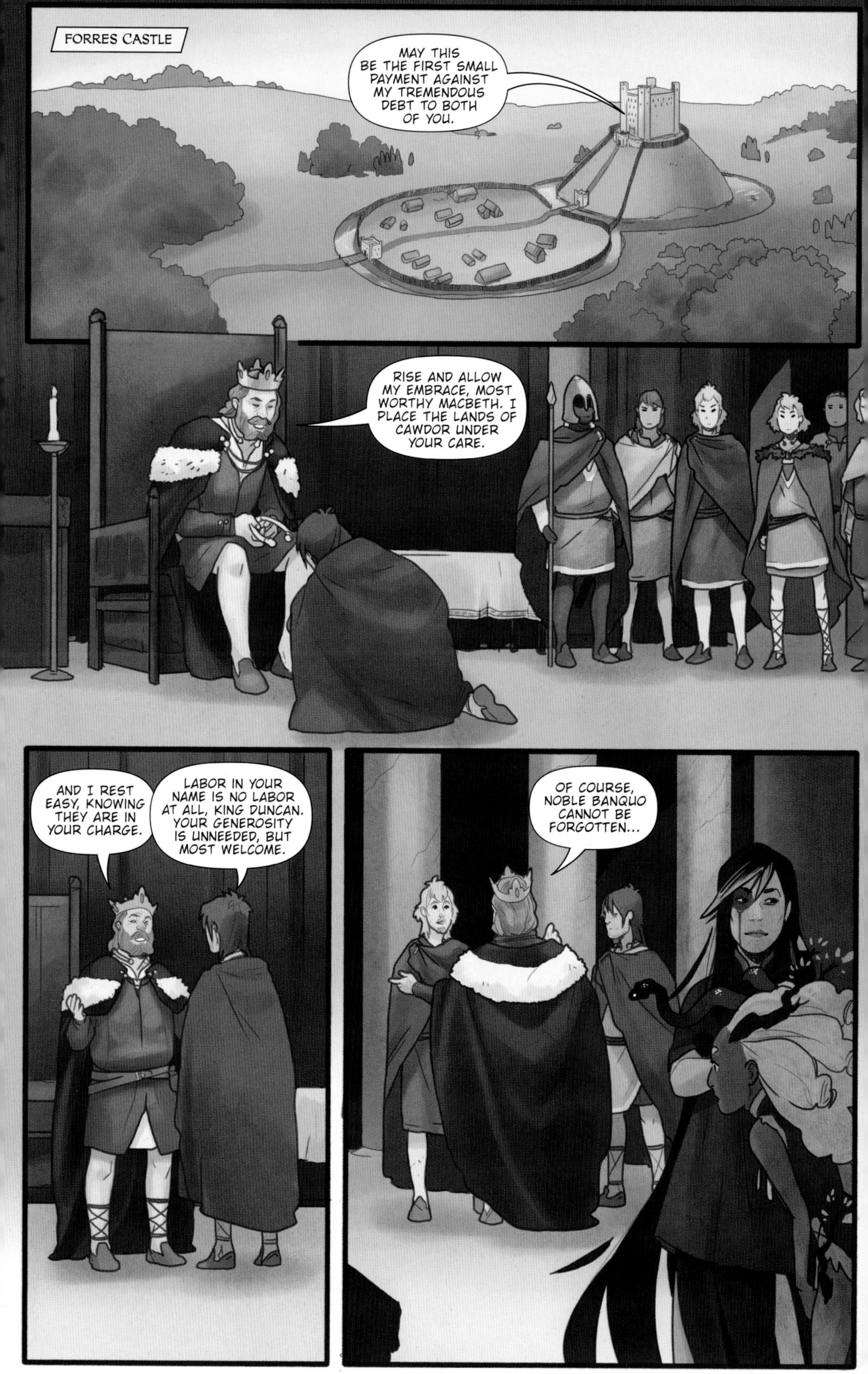
FORRES CASTLE
MAY THIS BE THE FIRST SMALL PAYMENT AGAINST MY TREMENDOUS DEBT TO BOTH OF YOU.
RISE AND ALLOW MY EMBRACE, MOST WORTHY MACBETH. I PLACE THE LANDS OF CAWDOR UNDER YOUR CARE.
AND I REST EASY, KNOWING THEY ARE IN YOUR CHARGE.
LABOR IN YOUR NAME IS NO LABOR AT ALL, KING DUNCAN. YOUR GENEROSITY IS UNNEEDED, BUT MOST WELCOME.
OF COURSE, NOBLE BANQUO CANNOT BE FORGOTTEN...

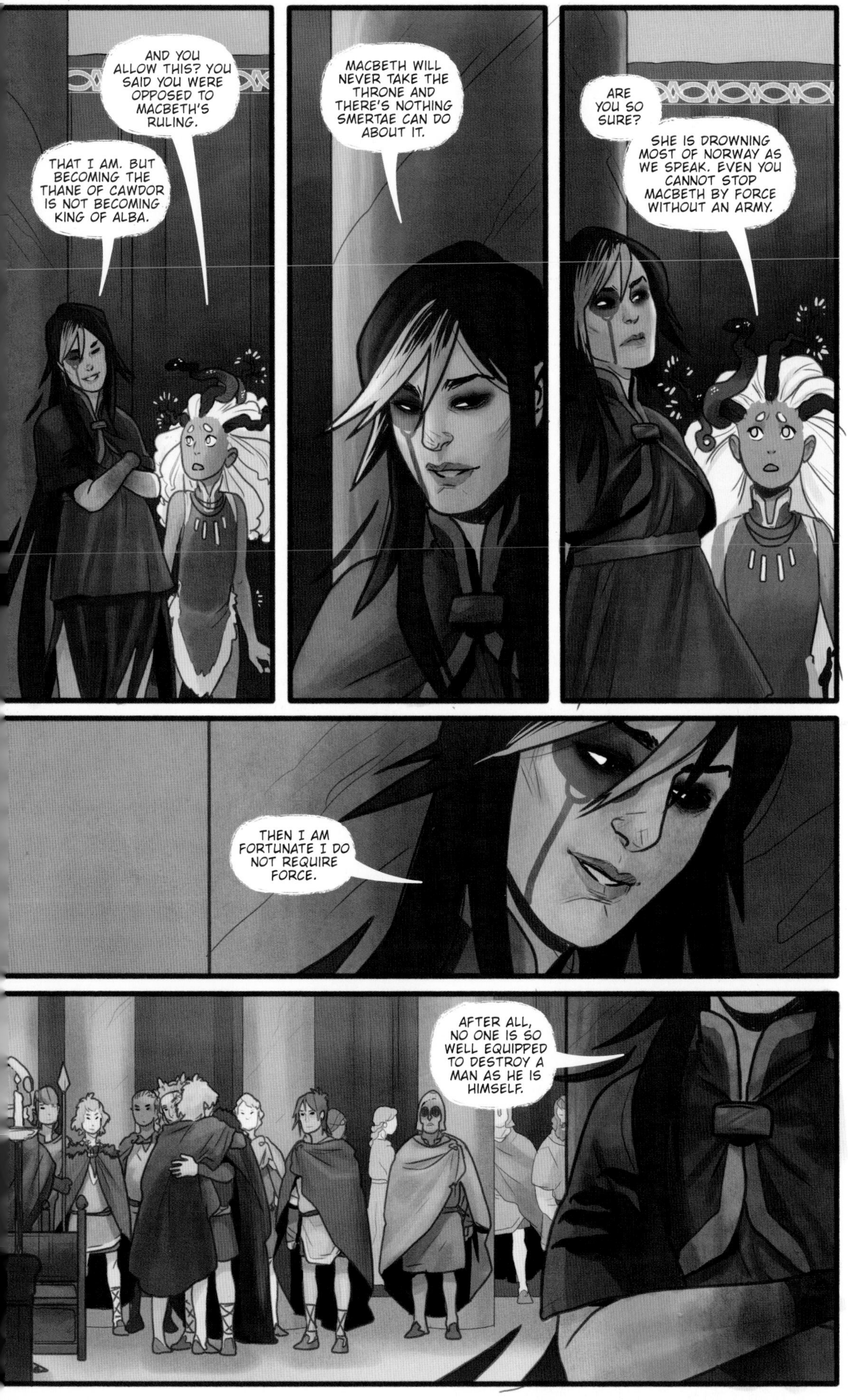
AND YOU ALLOW THIS? YOU SAID YOU WERE OPPOSED TO MACBETH'S RULING.
THAT I AM. BUT BECOMING THE THANE OF CAWDOR IS NOT BECOMING KING OF ALBA.
MACBETH WILL NEVER TAKE THE THRONE AND THERE'S NOTHING SMERTAE CAN DO ABOUT IT.
ARE YOU SO SURE?
SHE IS DROWNING MOST OF NORWAY AS WE SPEAK. EVEN YOU CANNOT STOP MACBETH BY FORCE WITHOUT AN ARMY.
THEN I AM FORTUNATE I DO NOT REQUIRE FORCE.
AFTER ALL, NO ONE IS SO WELL EQUIPPED TO DESTROY A MAN AS HE IS HIMSELF.

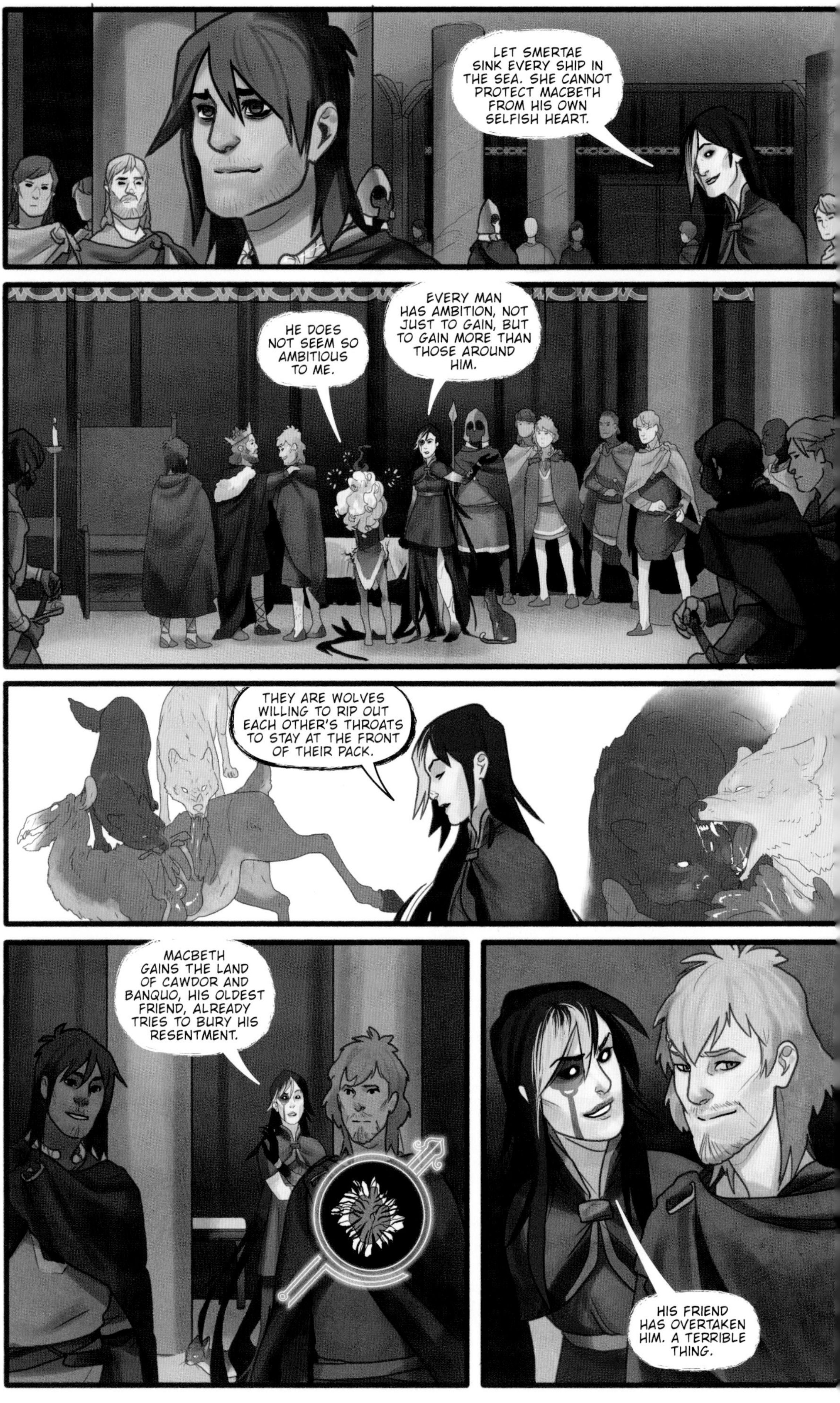
LET SMERTAE SINK EVERY SHIP IN THE SEA. SHE CANNOT PROTECT MACBETH FROM HIS OWN SELFISH HEART.
HE DOES NOT SEEM SO AMBITIOUS TO ME.
EVERY MAN HAS AMBITION, NOT JUST TO GAIN, BUT TO GAIN MORE THAN THOSE AROUND HIM.
THEY ARE WOLVES WILLING TO RIP OUT EACH OTHER'S THROATS TO STAY AT THE FRONT OF THEIR PACK.
MACBETH GAINS THE LAND OF CAWDOR AND BANQUO, HIS OLDEST FRIEND, ALREADY TRIES TO BURY HIS RESENTMENT.
HIS FRIEND HAS OVERTAKEN HIM. A TERRIBLE THING.

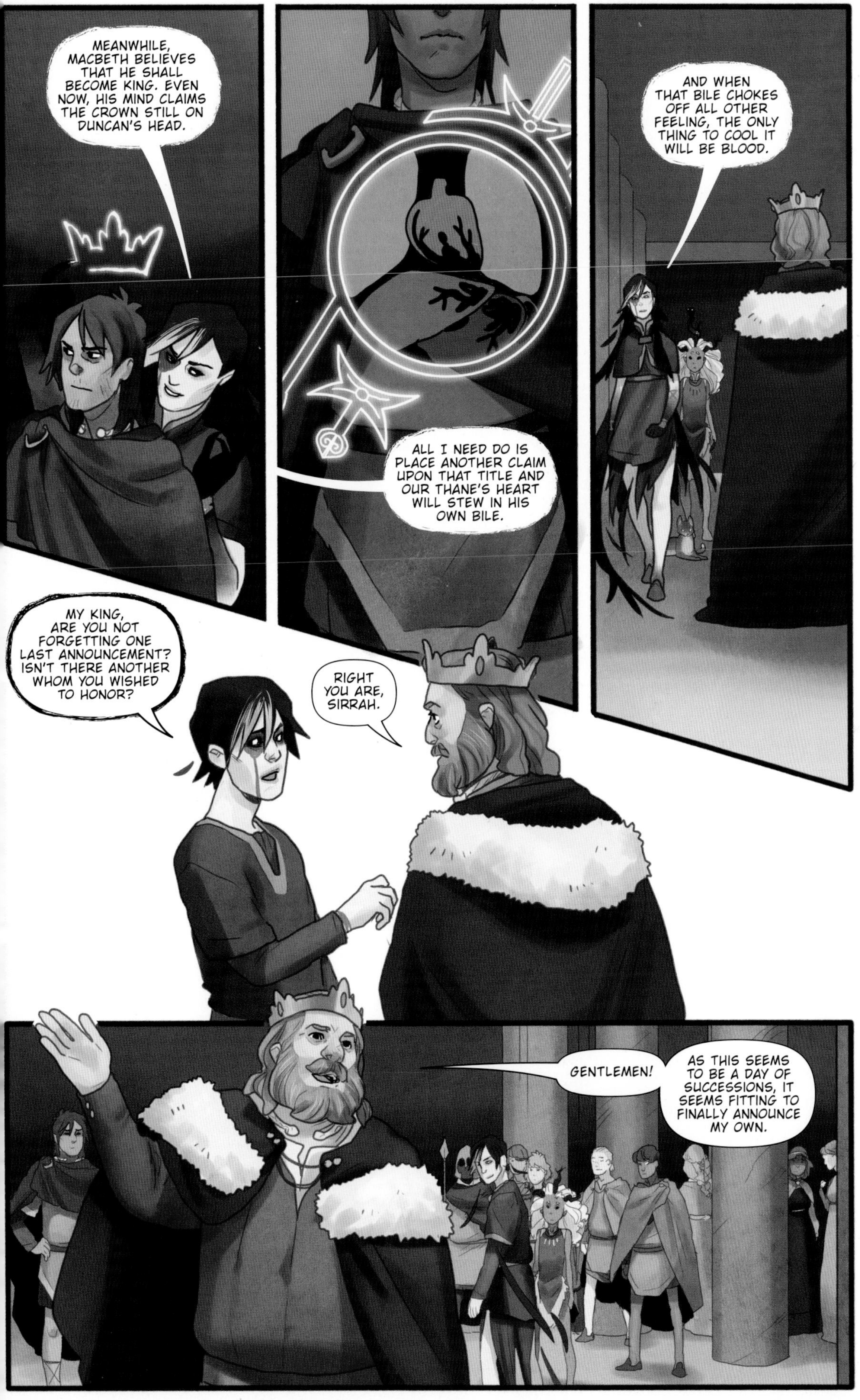

MEANWHILE, MACBETH BELIEVES THAT HE SHALL BECOME KING. EVEN NOW, HIS MIND CLAIMS THE CROWN STILL ON DUNCAN'S HEAD.
ALL I NEED DO IS PLACE ANOTHER CLAIM UPON THAT TITLE AND OUR THANE'S HEART WILL STEW IN HIS OWN BILE.
AND WHEN THAT BILE CHOKES OFF ALL OTHER FEELING, THE ONLY THING TO COOL IT WILL BE BLOOD.
MY KING, ARE YOU NOT FORGETTING ONE LAST ANNOUNCEMENT? ISN'T THERE ANOTHER WHOM YOU WISHED TO HONOR?
RIGHT YOU ARE, SIRRAH.
GENTLEMEN!
AS THIS SEEMS TO BE A DAY OF SUCCESSIONS, IT SEEMS FITTING TO FINALLY ANNOUNCE MY OWN.

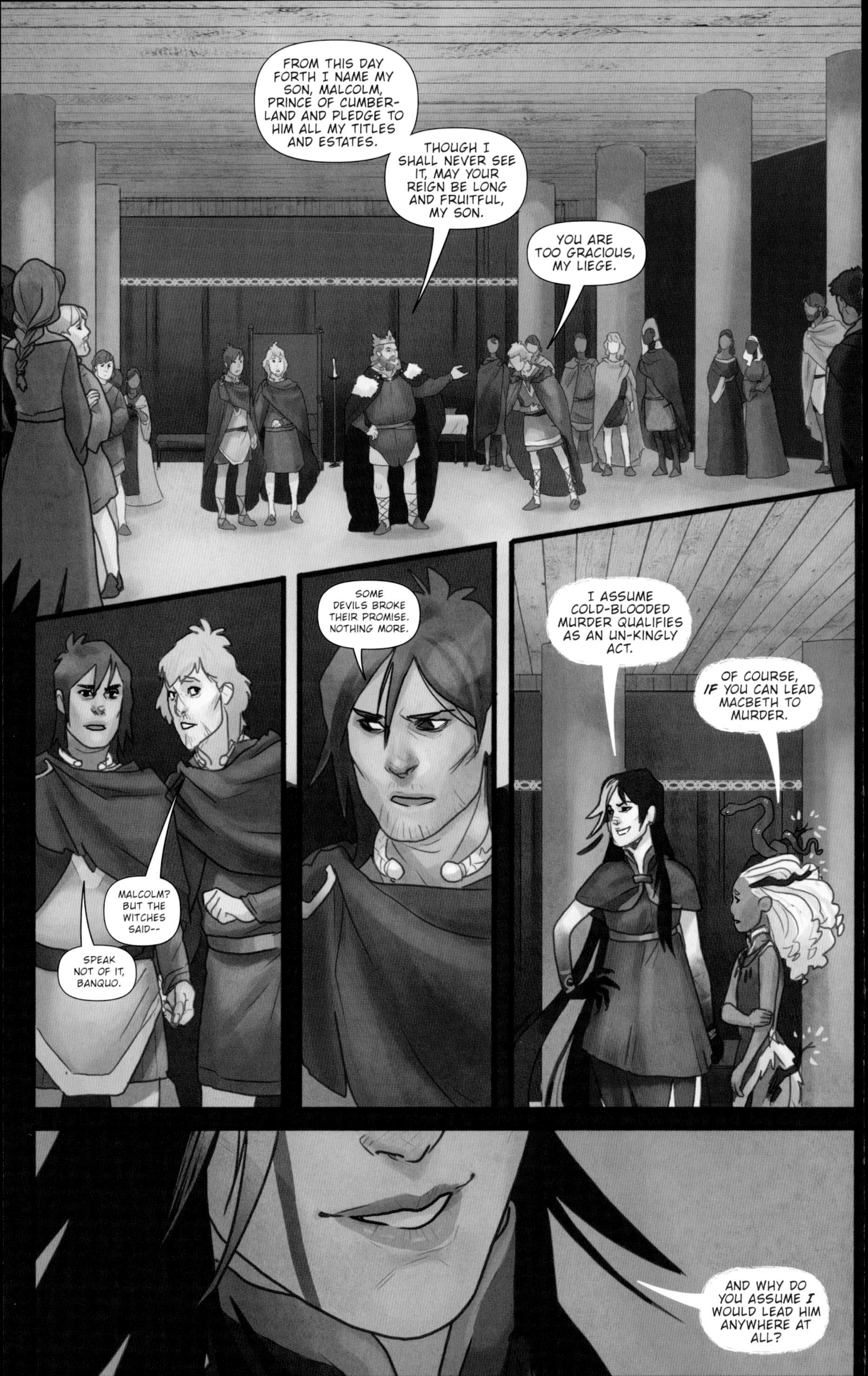
FROM THIS DAY FORTH I NAME MY SON, MALCOLM, PRINCE OF CUMBER-LAND AND PLEDGE TO HIM ALL MY TITLES AND ESTATES.
THOUGH I SHALL NEVER SEE IT, MAY YOUR REIGN BE LONG AND FRUITFUL, MY SON.
YOU ARE TOO GRACIOUS, MY LIEGE.
MALCOLM? BUT THE WITCHES SAID--
SPEAK NOT OF IT, BANQUO.
SOME DEVILS BROKE THEIR PROMISE. NOTHING MORE.
I ASSUME COLD-BLOODED MURDER QUALIFIES AS AN UN-KINGLY ACT.
OF COURSE, *IF* YOU CAN LEAD MACBETH TO MURDER.
AND WHY DO YOU ASSUME *I* WOULD LEAD HIM ANYWHERE AT ALL?

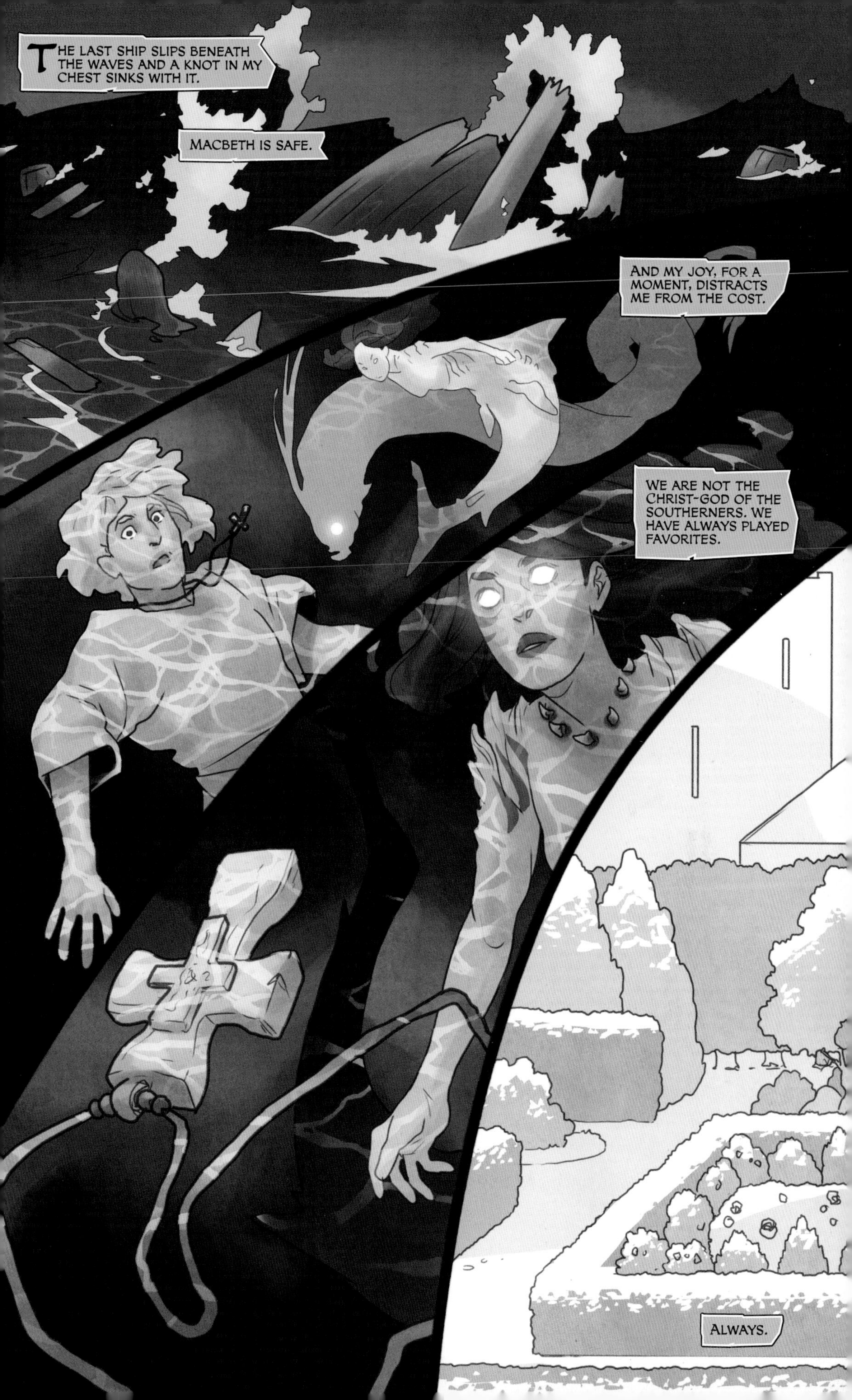
THE LAST SHIP SLIPS BENEATH THE WAVES AND A KNOT IN MY CHEST SINKS WITH IT.
MACBETH IS SAFE.
AND MY JOY, FOR A MOMENT, DISTRACTS ME FROM THE COST.
WE ARE NOT THE CHRIST-GOD OF THE SOUTHERNERS. WE HAVE ALWAYS PLAYED FAVORITES.
ALWAYS.

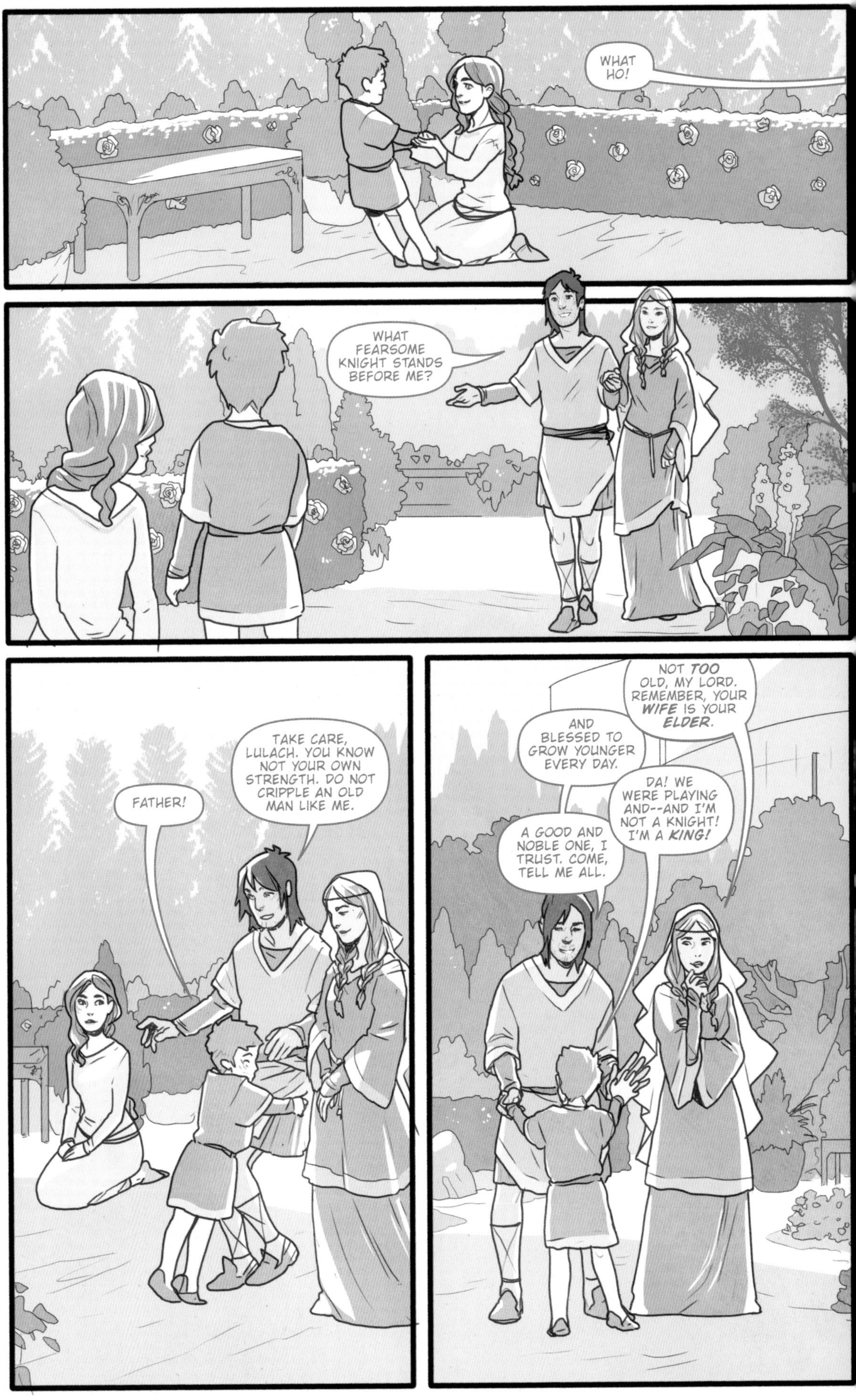
WHAT HO!
WHAT FEARSOME KNIGHT STANDS BEFORE ME?
FATHER!
TAKE CARE, LULACH. YOU KNOW NOT YOUR OWN STRENGTH. DO NOT CRIPPLE AN OLD MAN LIKE ME.
NOT TOO OLD, MY LORD. REMEMBER, YOUR WIFE IS YOUR ELDER.
AND BLESSED TO GROW YOUNGER EVERY DAY.
DA! WE WERE PLAYING AND--AND I'M NOT A KNIGHT! I'M A KING!
A GOOD AND NOBLE ONE, I TRUST. COME, TELL ME ALL.

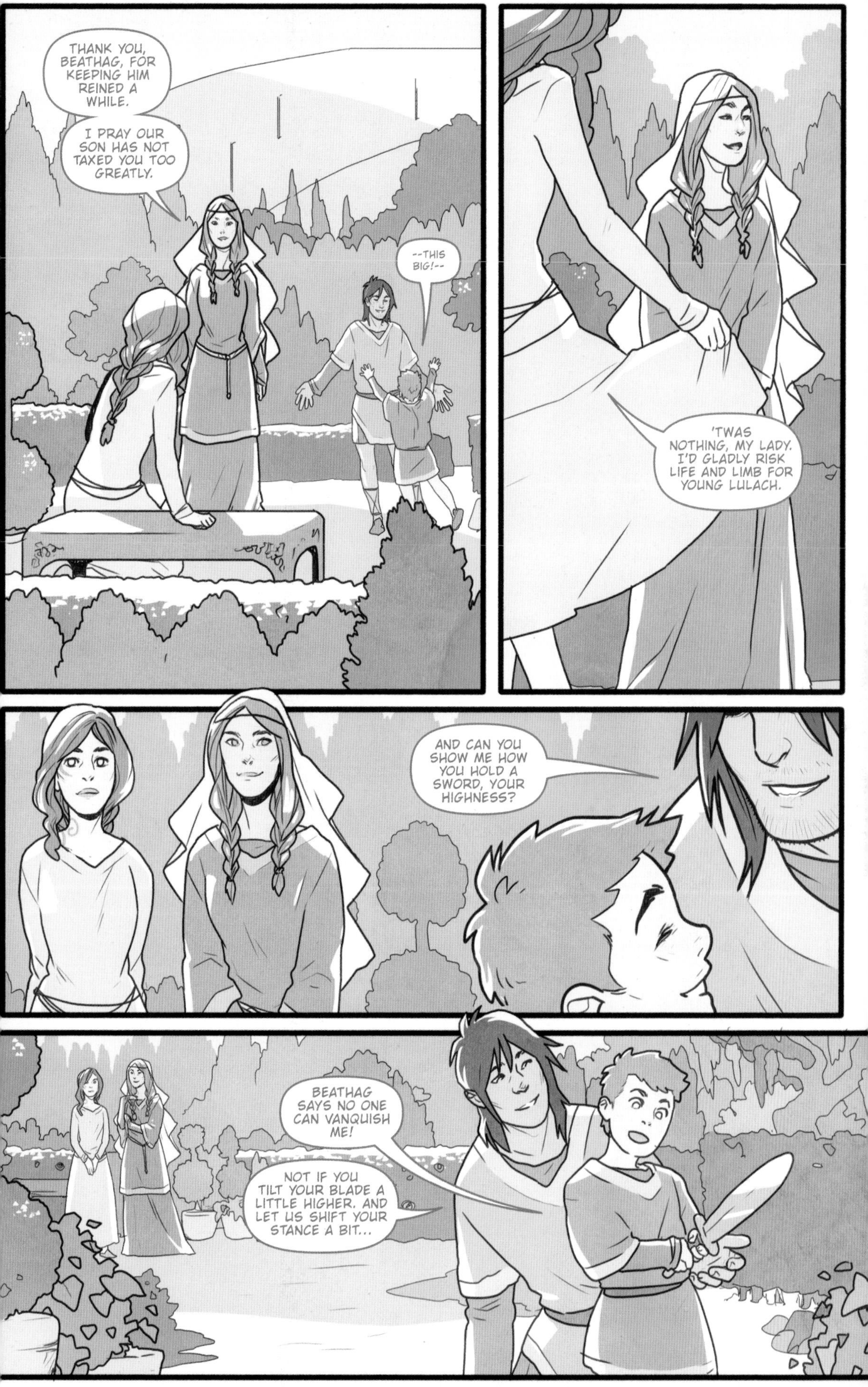
THANK YOU, BEATHAG, FOR KEEPING HIM REINED A WHILE.
I PRAY OUR SON HAS NOT TAXED YOU TOO GREATLY.
--THIS BIG!--
'TWAS NOTHING, MY LADY. I'D GLADLY RISK LIFE AND LIMB FOR YOUNG LULACH.
AND CAN YOU SHOW ME HOW YOU HOLD A SWORD, YOUR HIGHNESS?
BEATHAG SAYS NO ONE CAN VANQUISH ME!
NOT IF YOU TILT YOUR BLADE A LITTLE HIGHER. AND LET US SHIFT YOUR STANCE A BIT...

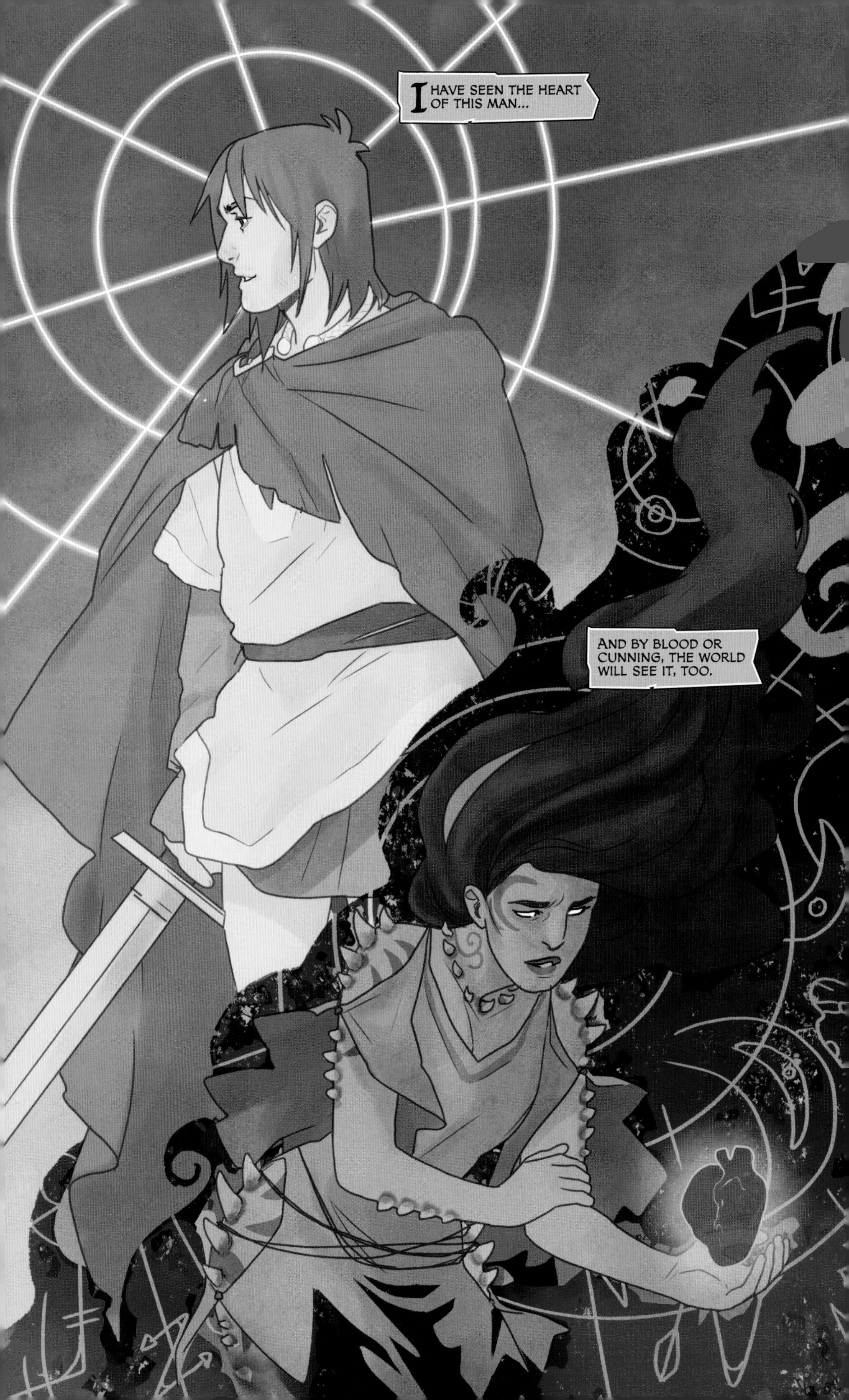
I HAVE SEEN THE HEART OF THIS MAN...
AND BY BLOOD OR CUNNING, THE WORLD WILL SEE IT, TOO.

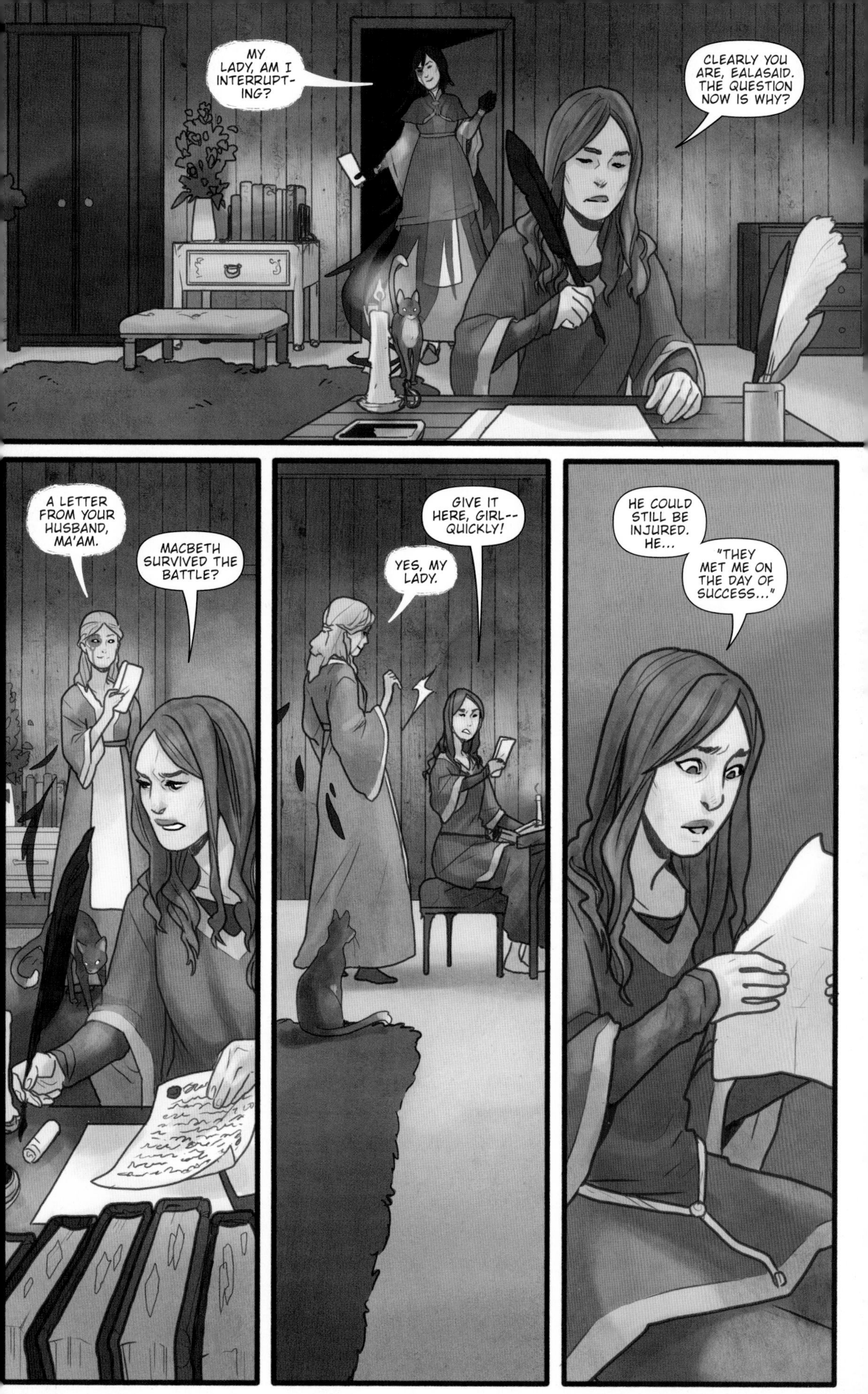
MY LADY, AM I INTERRUPTING?
CLEARLY YOU ARE, EALASAID. THE QUESTION NOW IS WHY?
A LETTER FROM YOUR HUSBAND, MA'AM.
MACBETH SURVIVED THE BATTLE?
GIVE IT HERE, GIRL--QUICKLY!
YES, MY LADY.
HE COULD STILL BE INJURED. HE...
"THEY MET ME ON THE DAY OF SUCCESS..."

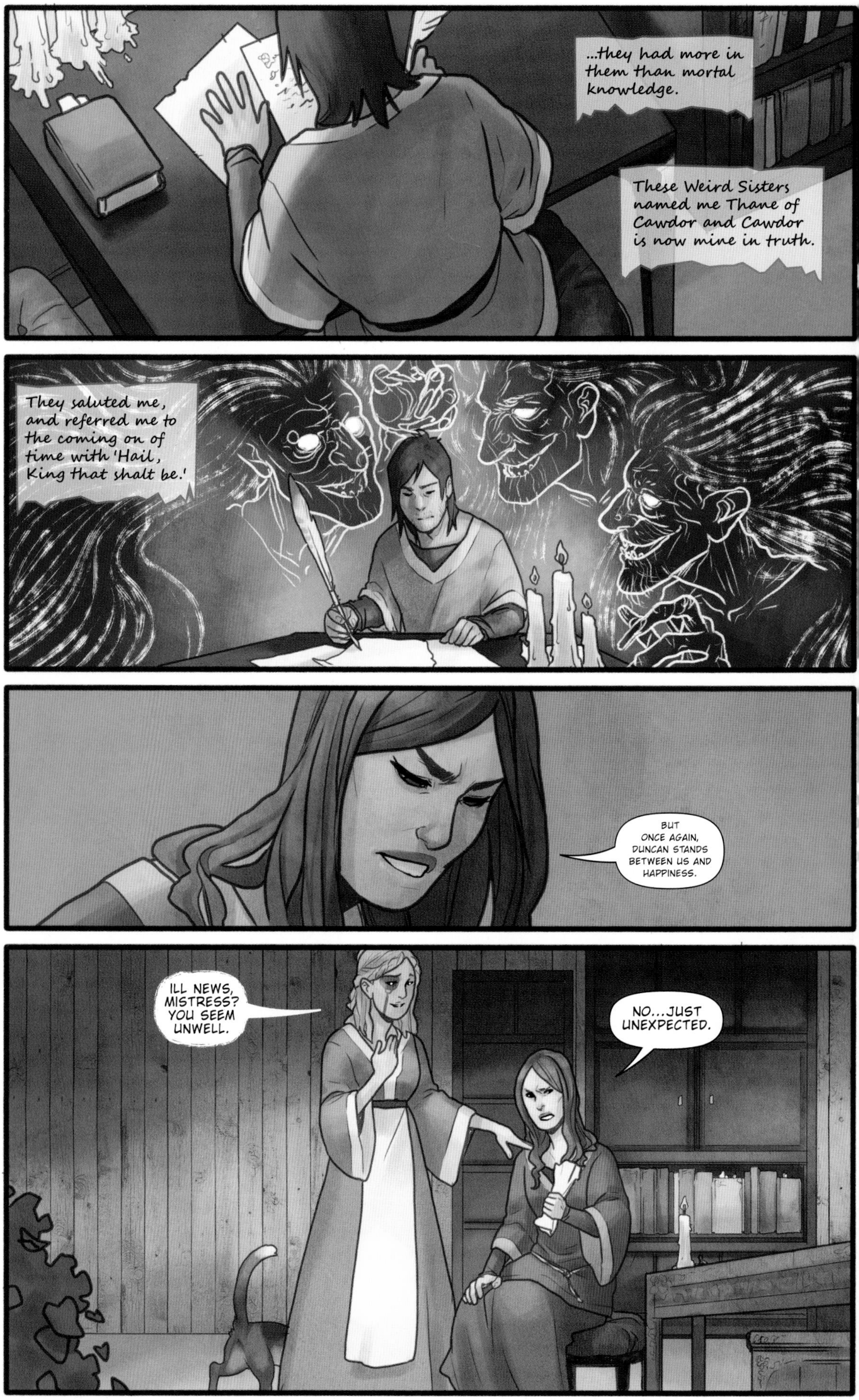
...they had more in them than mortal knowledge.
These Weird Sisters named me Thane of Cawdor and Cawdor is now mine in truth.
They saluted me, and referred me to the coming on of time with 'Hail, King that shalt be.'
BUT ONCE AGAIN, DUNCAN STANDS BETWEEN US AND HAPPINESS.
ILL NEWS, MISTRESS? YOU SEEM UNWELL.
NO...JUST UNEXPECTED.

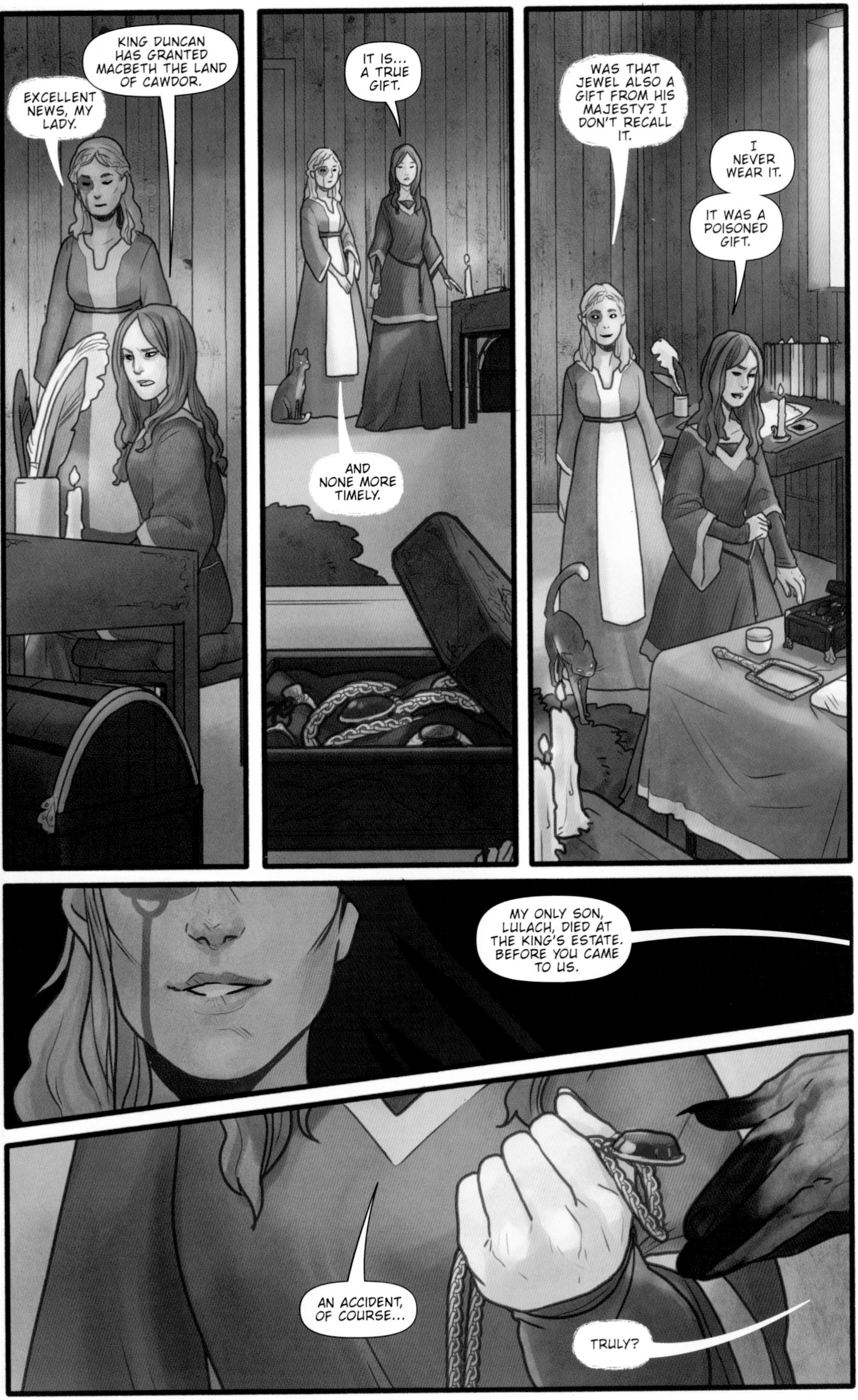
KING DUNCAN HAS GRANTED MACBETH THE LAND OF CAWDOR.
EXCELLENT NEWS, MY LADY.
IT IS... A TRUE GIFT.
AND NONE MORE TIMELY.
WAS THAT JEWEL ALSO A GIFT FROM HIS MAJESTY? I DON'T RECALL IT.
I NEVER WEAR IT.
IT WAS A POISONED GIFT.
MY ONLY SON, LULACH, DIED AT THE KING'S ESTATE. BEFORE YOU CAME TO US.
AN ACCIDENT, OF COURSE...
TRULY?

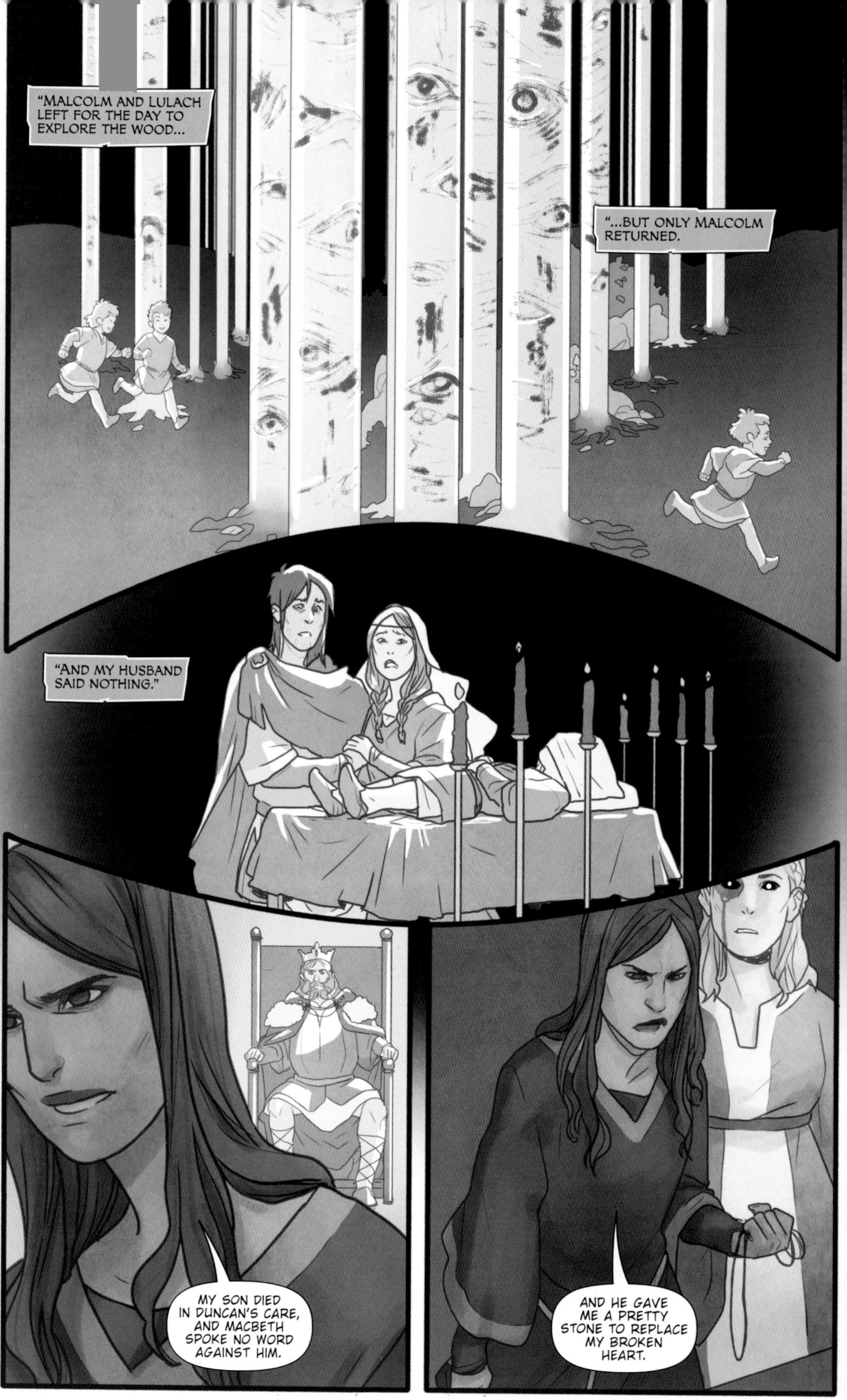
"MALCOLM AND LULACH LEFT FOR THE DAY TO EXPLORE THE WOOD...
"...BUT ONLY MALCOLM RETURNED.
"AND MY HUSBAND SAID NOTHING."
MY SON DIED IN DUNCAN'S CARE, AND MACBETH SPOKE NO WORD AGAINST HIM.
AND HE GAVE ME A PRETTY STONE TO REPLACE MY BROKEN HEART.

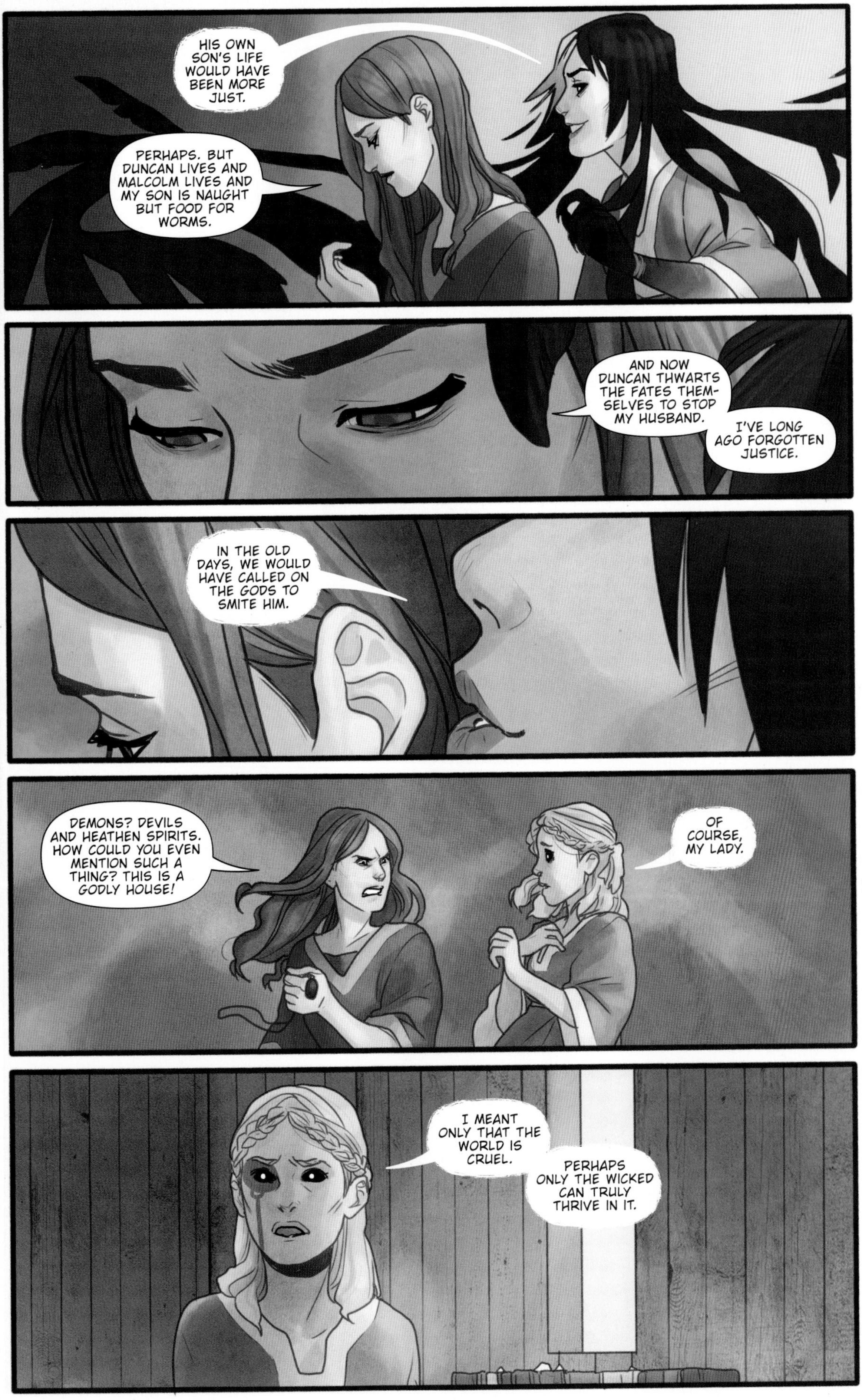
HIS OWN SON'S LIFE WOULD HAVE BEEN MORE JUST.
PERHAPS. BUT DUNCAN LIVES AND MALCOLM LIVES AND MY SON IS NAUGHT BUT FOOD FOR WORMS.
AND NOW DUNCAN THWARTS THE FATES THEM-SELVES TO STOP MY HUSBAND.
I'VE LONG AGO FORGOTTEN JUSTICE.
IN THE OLD DAYS, WE WOULD HAVE CALLED ON THE GODS TO SMITE HIM.
DEMONS? DEVILS AND HEATHEN SPIRITS. HOW COULD YOU EVEN MENTION SUCH A THING? THIS IS A GODLY HOUSE!
OF COURSE, MY LADY.
I MEANT ONLY THAT THE WORLD IS CRUEL.
PERHAPS ONLY THE WICKED CAN TRULY THRIVE IN IT.

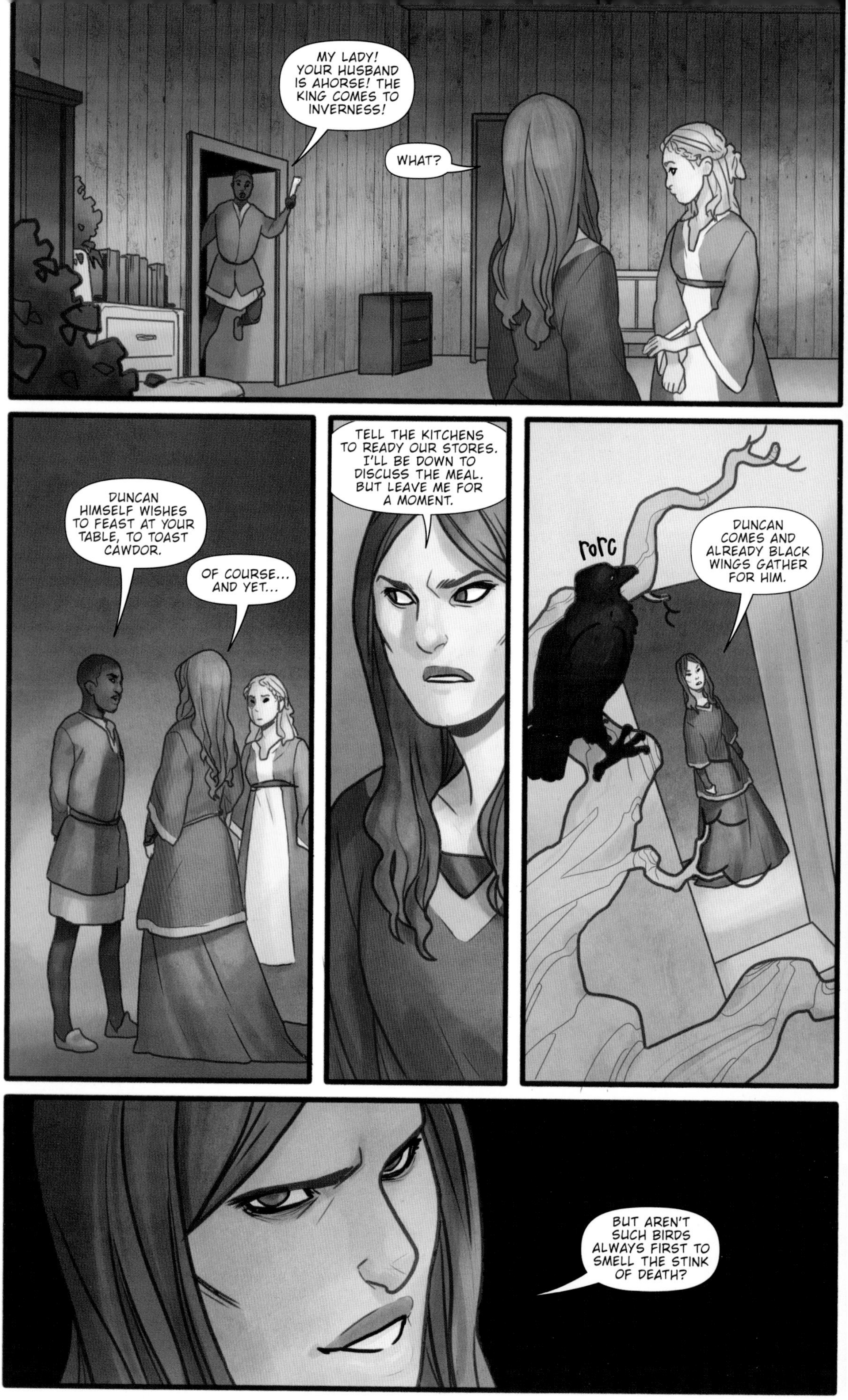
MY LADY! YOUR HUSBAND IS AHORSE! THE KING COMES TO INVERNESS!
WHAT?
DUNCAN HIMSELF WISHES TO FEAST AT YOUR TABLE, TO TOAST CAWDOR.
OF COURSE... AND YET...
TELL THE KITCHENS TO READY OUR STORES. I'LL BE DOWN TO DISCUSS THE MEAL. BUT LEAVE ME FOR A MOMENT.
RORC
DUNCAN COMES AND ALREADY BLACK WINGS GATHER FOR HIM.
BUT AREN'T SUCH BIRDS ALWAYS FIRST TO SMELL THE STINK OF DEATH?

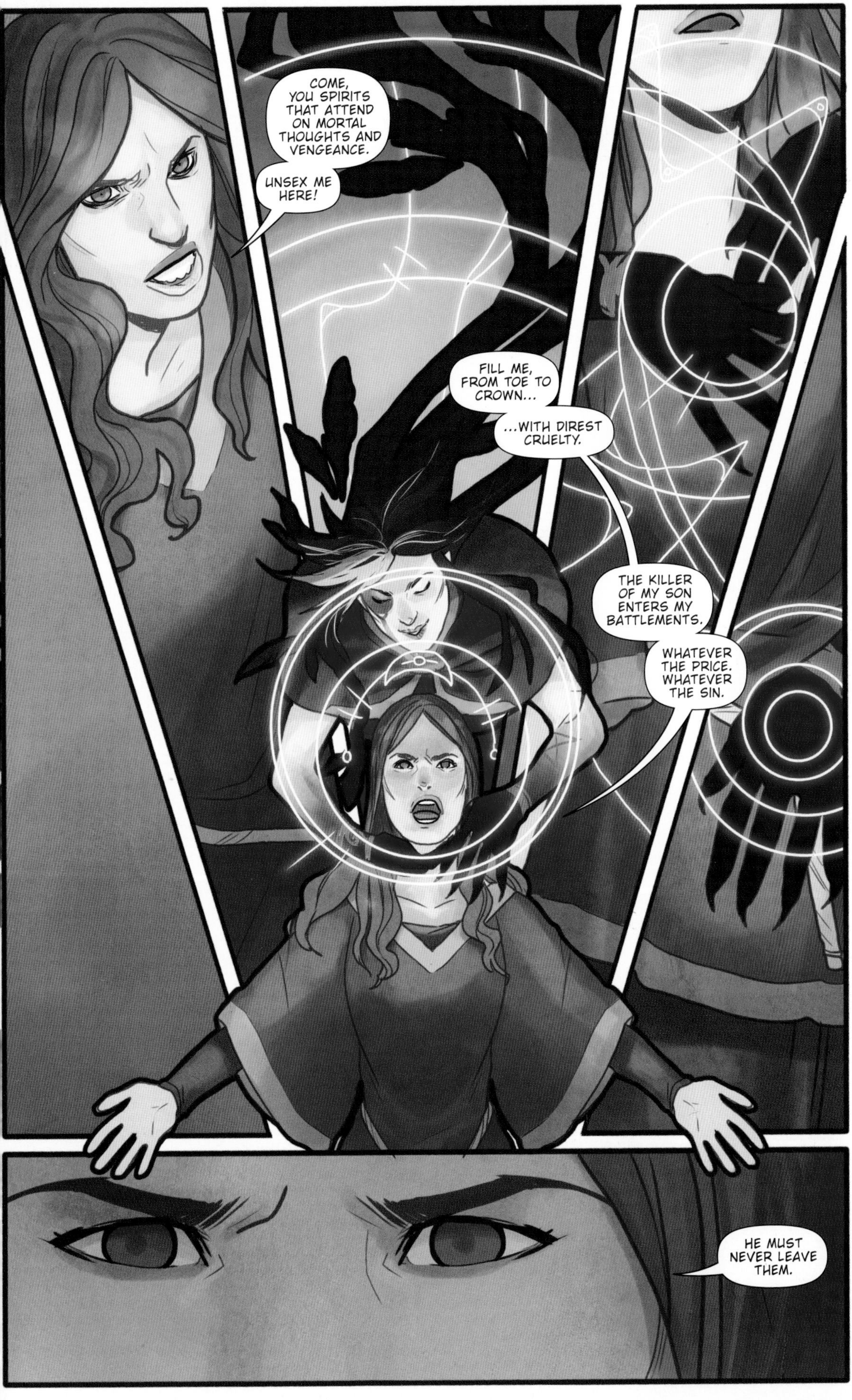
COME, YOU SPIRITS THAT ATTEND ON MORTAL THOUGHTS AND VENGEANCE.
UNSEX ME HERE!
FILL ME, FROM TOE TO CROWN...
...WITH DIREST CRUELTY.
THE KILLER OF MY SON ENTERS MY BATTLEMENTS.
WHATEVER THE PRICE. WHATEVER THE SIN.
HE MUST NEVER LEAVE THEM.

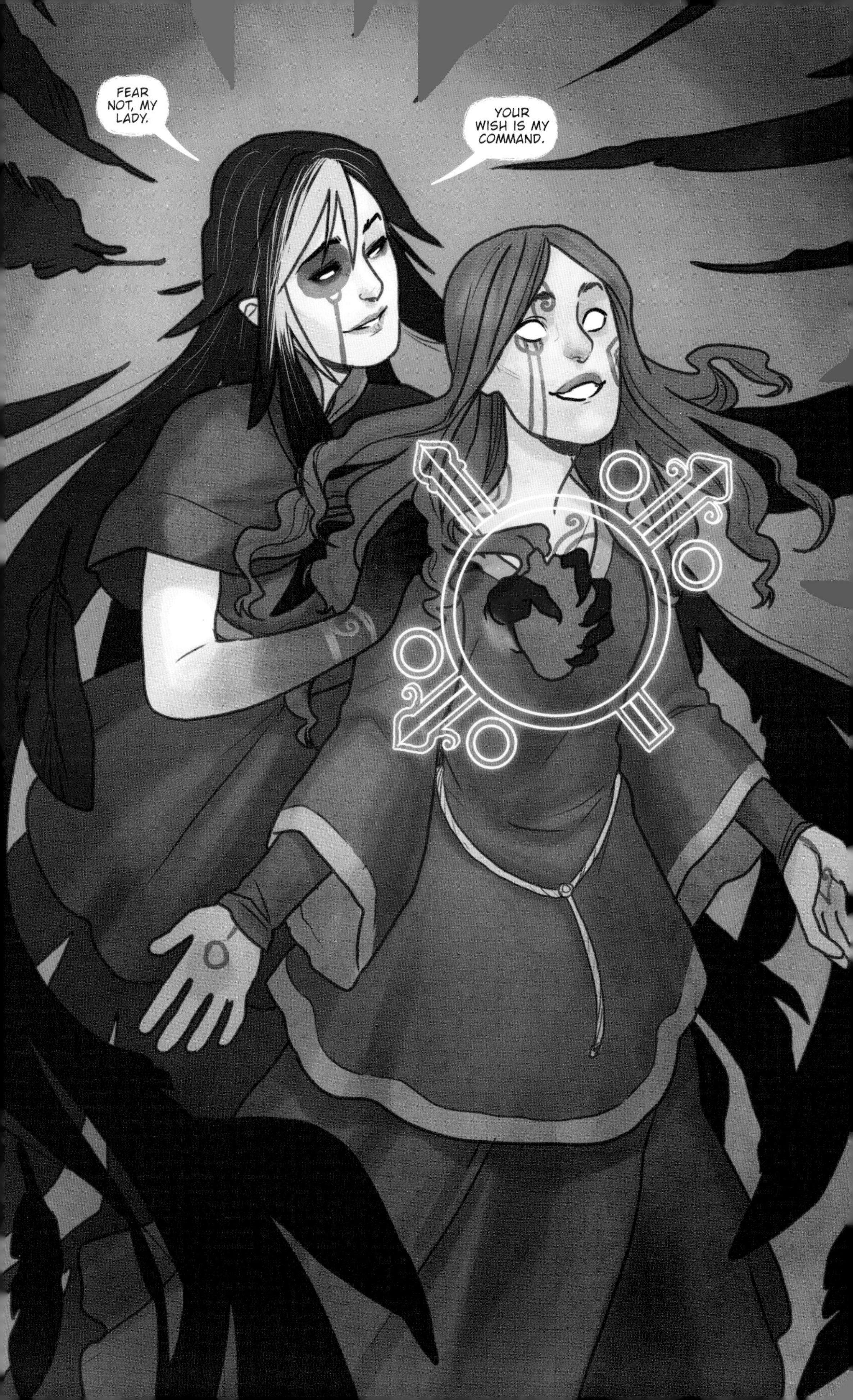
FEAR NOT, MY LADY.
YOUR WISH IS MY COMMAND.

Act Four

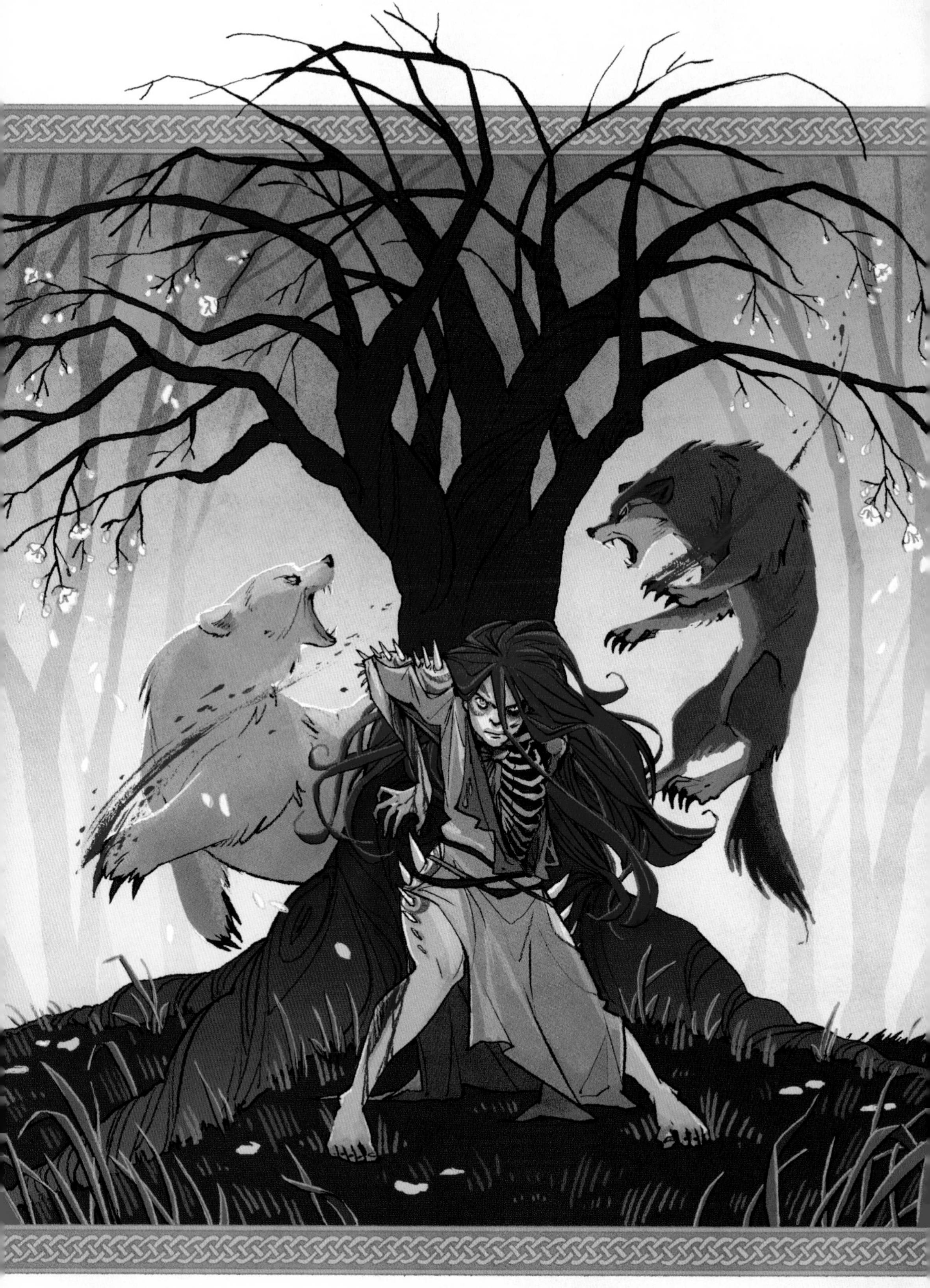

Issue Four Cover by Kyla Vanderklugt

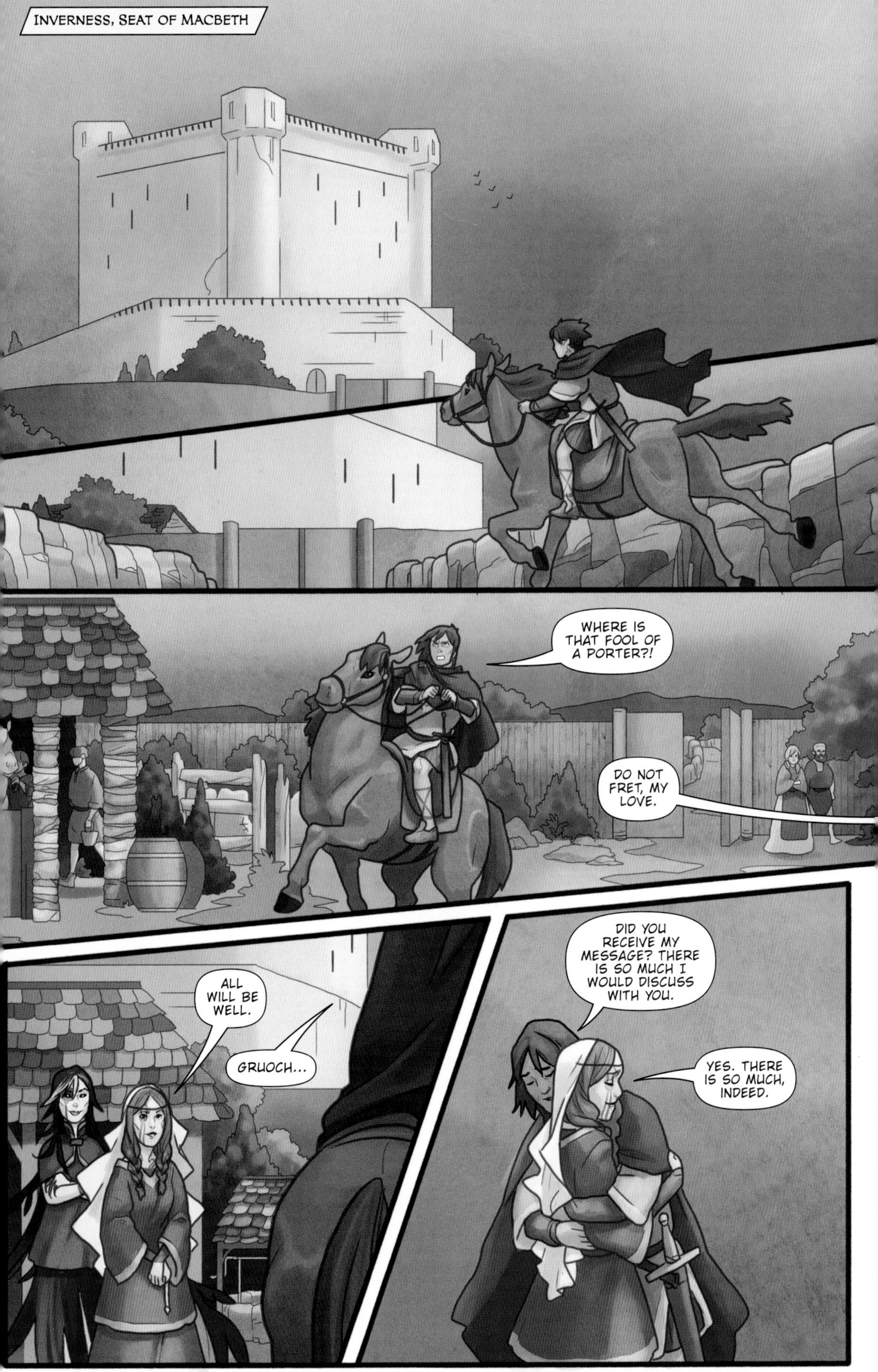
INVERNESS, SEAT OF MACBETH
WHERE IS THAT FOOL OF A PORTER?!
DO NOT FRET, MY LOVE.
ALL WILL BE WELL.
GRUOCH...
DID YOU RECEIVE MY MESSAGE? THERE IS SO MUCH I WOULD DISCUSS WITH YOU.
YES. THERE IS SO MUCH, INDEED.

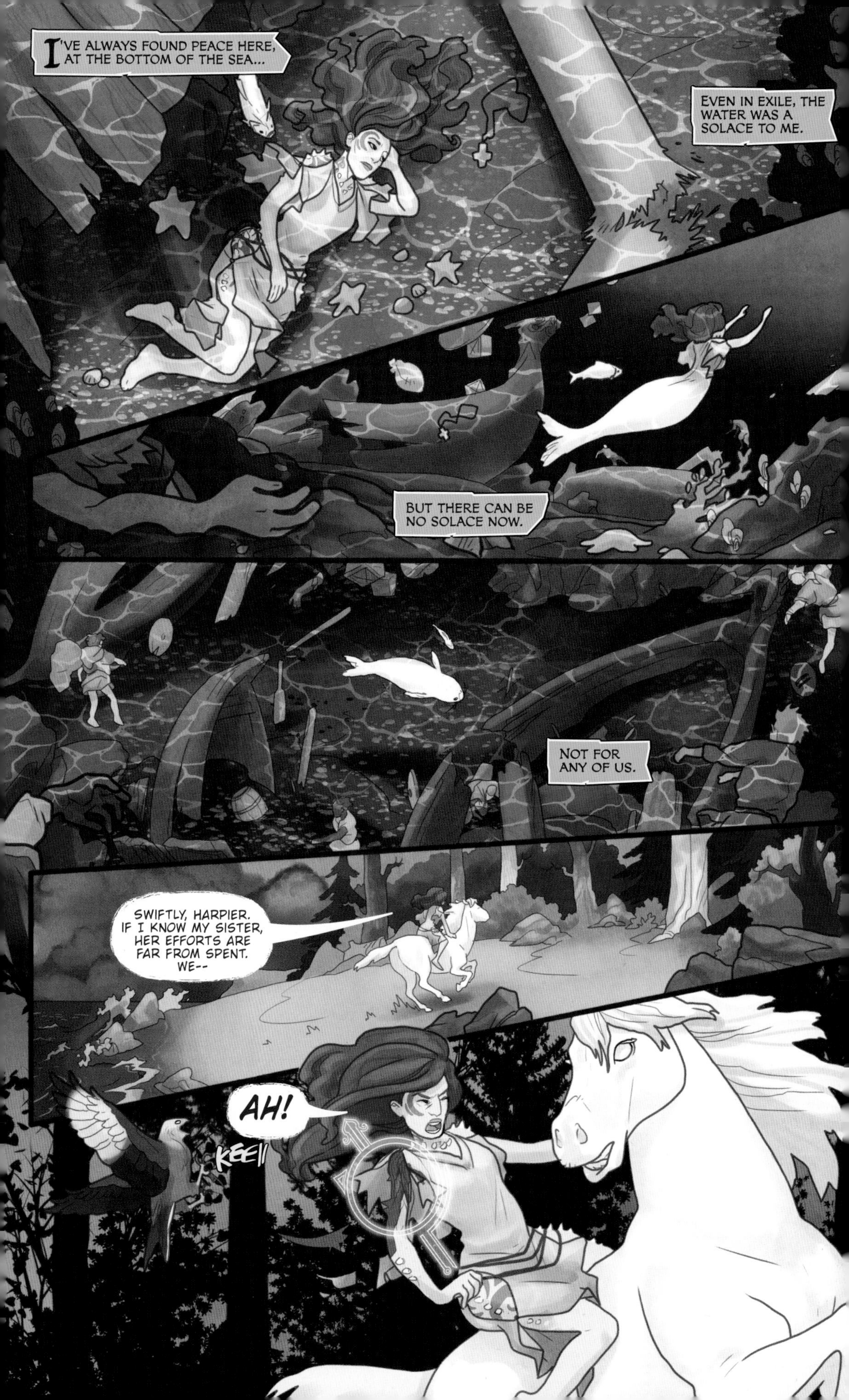
I'VE ALWAYS FOUND PEACE HERE, AT THE BOTTOM OF THE SEA...
EVEN IN EXILE, THE WATER WAS A SOLACE TO ME.
BUT THERE CAN BE NO SOLACE NOW.
NOT FOR ANY OF US.
SWIFTLY, HARPIER. IF I KNOW MY SISTER, HER EFFORTS ARE FAR FROM SPENT. WE--
AH!
KEE!!

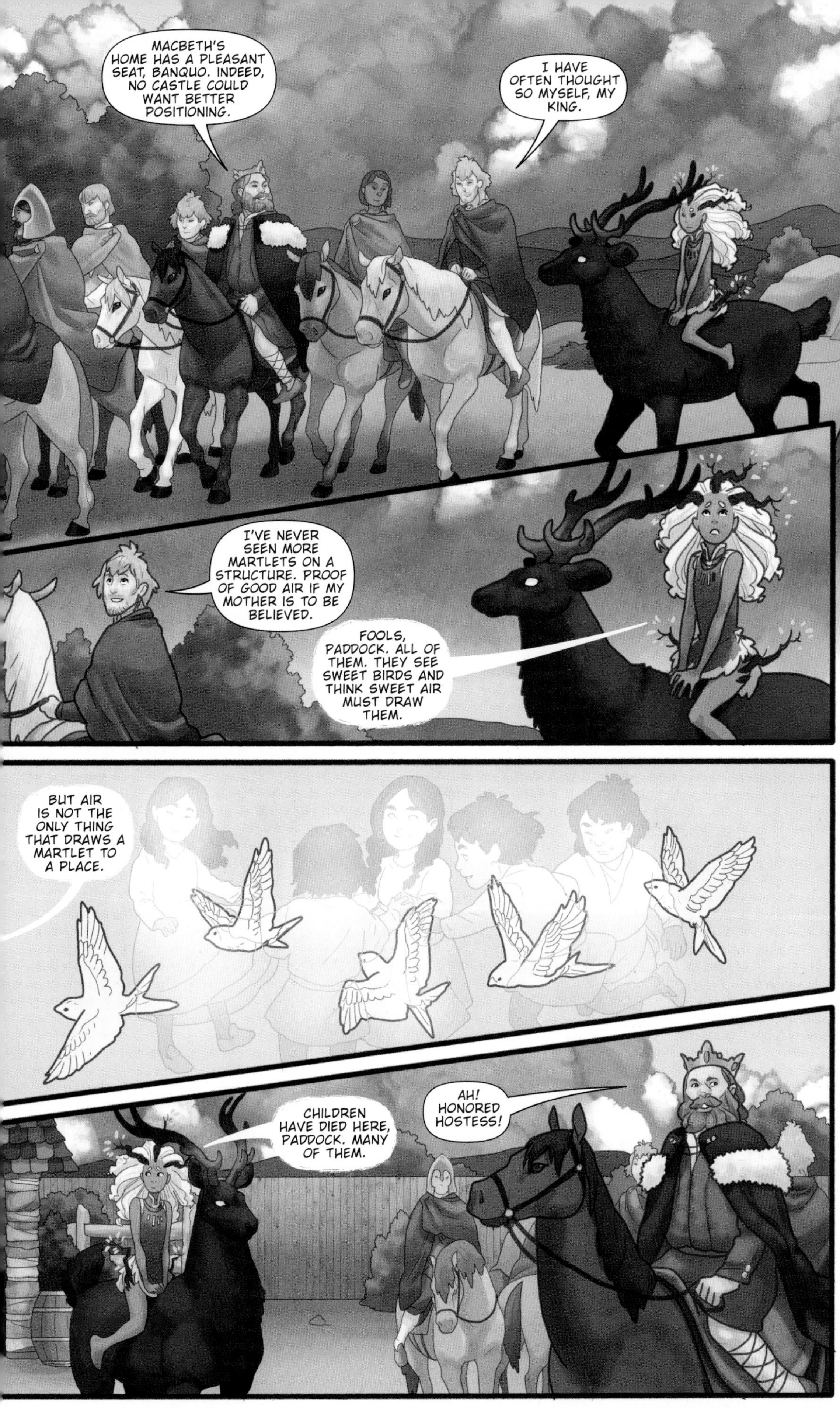
MACBETH'S HOME HAS A PLEASANT SEAT, BANQUO. INDEED, NO CASTLE COULD WANT BETTER POSITIONING.
I HAVE OFTEN THOUGHT SO MYSELF, MY KING.
I'VE NEVER SEEN MORE MARTLETS ON A STRUCTURE. PROOF OF GOOD AIR IF MY MOTHER IS TO BE BELIEVED.
FOOLS, PADDOCK. ALL OF THEM. THEY SEE SWEET BIRDS AND THINK SWEET AIR MUST DRAW THEM.
BUT AIR IS NOT THE ONLY THING THAT DRAWS A MARTLET TO A PLACE.
CHILDREN HAVE DIED HERE, PADDOCK. MANY OF THEM.
AH! HONORED HOSTESS!

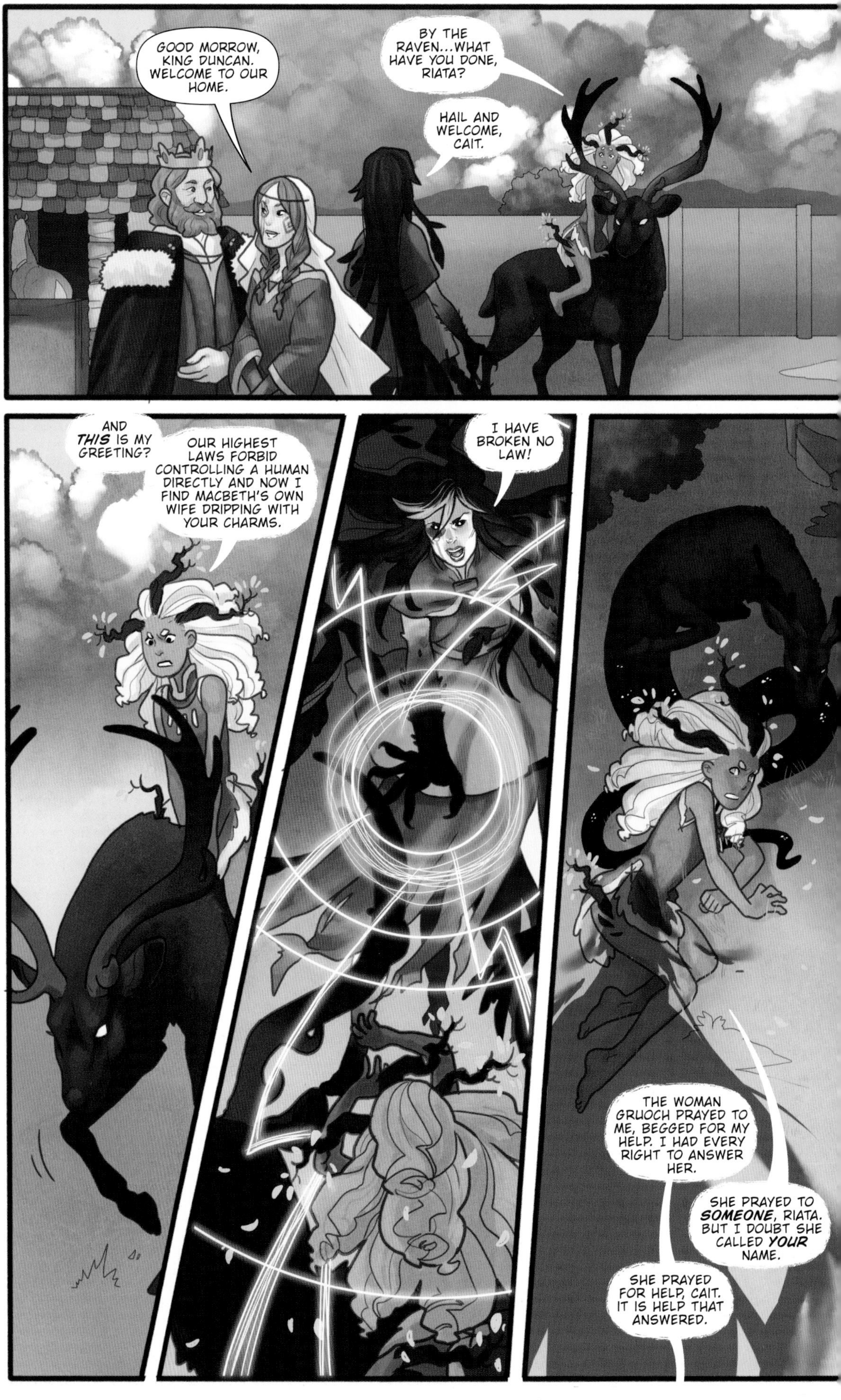
GOOD MORROW, KING DUNCAN. WELCOME TO OUR HOME.
BY THE RAVEN...WHAT HAVE YOU DONE, RIATA?
HAIL AND WELCOME, CAIT.
AND *THIS* IS MY GREETING?
OUR HIGHEST LAWS FORBID CONTROLLING A HUMAN DIRECTLY AND NOW I FIND MACBETH'S OWN WIFE DRIPPING WITH YOUR CHARMS.
I HAVE BROKEN NO LAW!
THE WOMAN GRUOCH PRAYED TO ME, BEGGED FOR MY HELP. I HAD EVERY RIGHT TO ANSWER HER.
SHE PRAYED TO *SOMEONE*, RIATA. BUT I DOUBT SHE CALLED *YOUR* NAME.
SHE PRAYED FOR HELP, CAIT. IT IS HELP THAT ANSWERED.

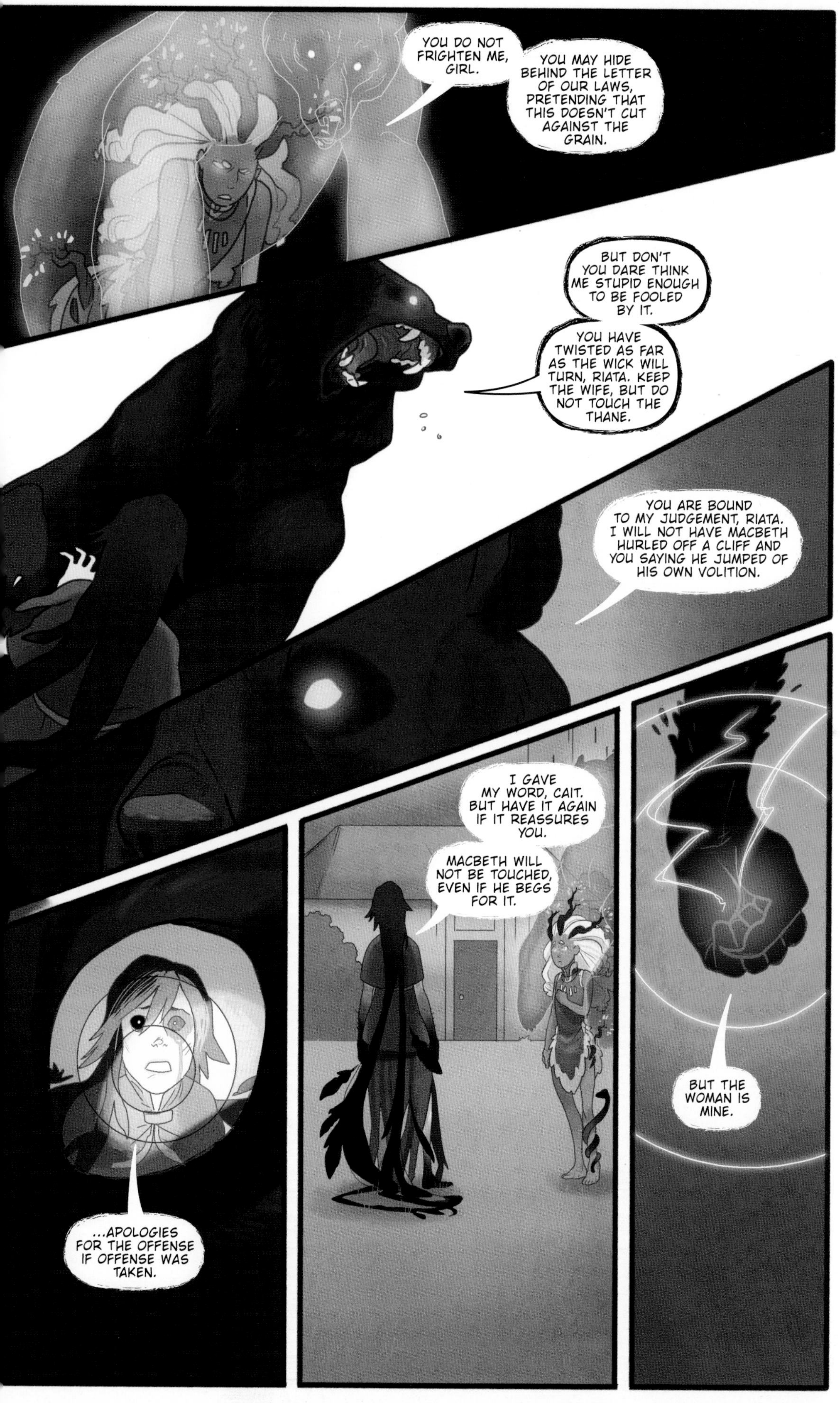

YOU DO NOT FRIGHTEN ME, GIRL.
YOU MAY HIDE BEHIND THE LETTER OF OUR LAWS, PRETENDING THAT THIS DOESN'T CUT AGAINST THE GRAIN.
BUT DON'T YOU DARE THINK ME STUPID ENOUGH TO BE FOOLED BY IT.
YOU HAVE TWISTED AS FAR AS THE WICK WILL TURN, RIATA. KEEP THE WIFE, BUT DO NOT TOUCH THE THANE.
YOU ARE BOUND TO MY JUDGEMENT, RIATA. I WILL NOT HAVE MACBETH HURLED OFF A CLIFF AND YOU SAYING HE JUMPED OF HIS OWN VOLITION.
...APOLOGIES FOR THE OFFENSE IF OFFENSE WAS TAKEN.
I GAVE MY WORD, CAIT. BUT HAVE IT AGAIN IF IT REASSURES YOU.
MACBETH WILL NOT BE TOUCHED, EVEN IF HE BEGS FOR IT.
BUT THE WOMAN IS MINE.

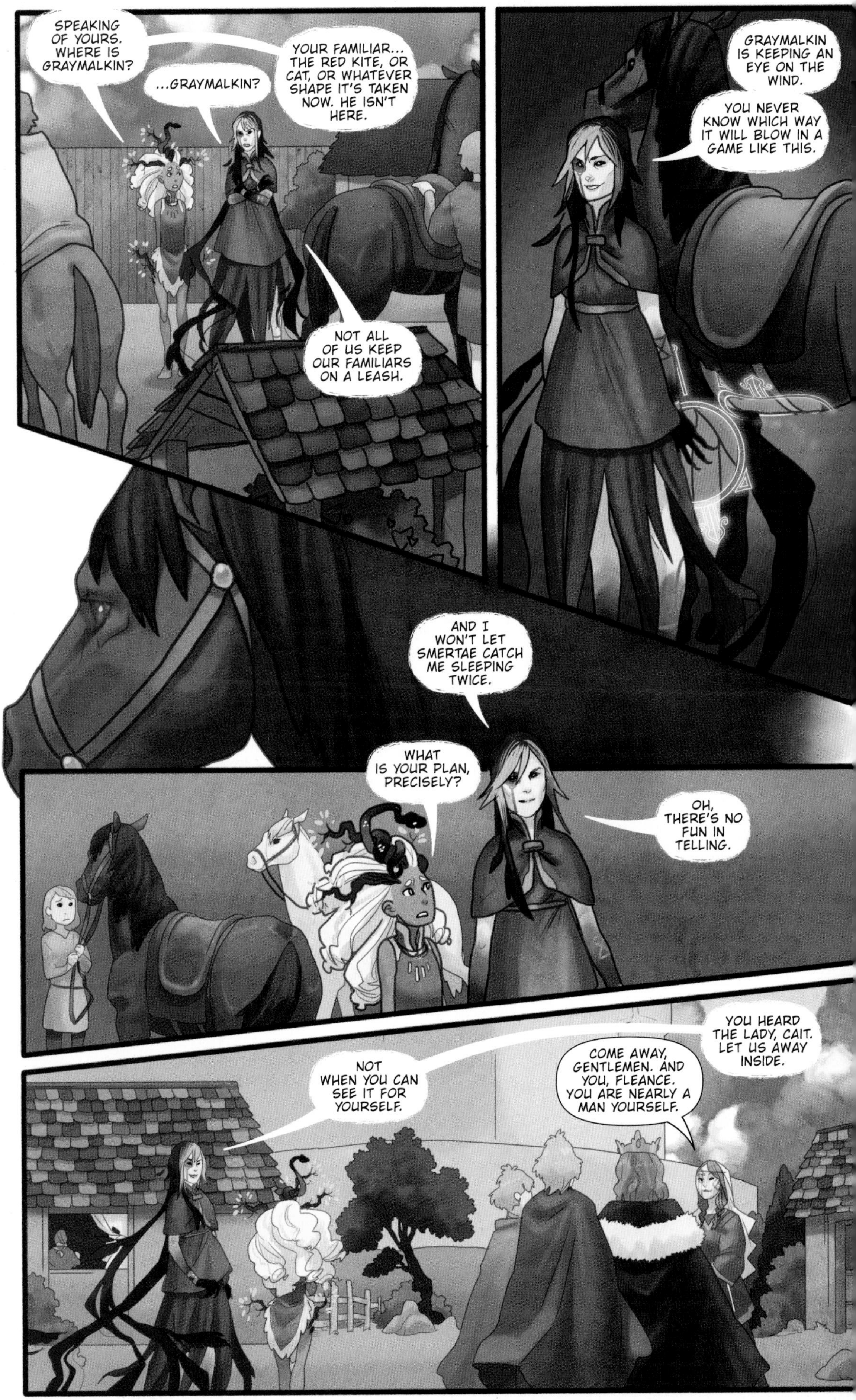
SPEAKING OF YOURS. WHERE IS GRAYMALKIN?
...GRAYMALKIN?
YOUR FAMILIAR... THE RED KITE, OR CAT, OR WHATEVER SHAPE IT'S TAKEN NOW. HE ISN'T HERE.
NOT ALL OF US KEEP OUR FAMILIARS ON A LEASH.
GRAYMALKIN IS KEEPING AN EYE ON THE WIND.
YOU NEVER KNOW WHICH WAY IT WILL BLOW IN A GAME LIKE THIS.
AND I WON'T LET SMERTAE CATCH ME SLEEPING TWICE.
WHAT IS YOUR PLAN, PRECISELY?
OH, THERE'S NO FUN IN TELLING.
NOT WHEN YOU CAN SEE IT FOR YOURSELF.
YOU HEARD THE LADY, CAIT. LET US AWAY INSIDE.
COME AWAY, GENTLEMEN. AND YOU, FLEANCE. YOU ARE NEARLY A MAN YOURSELF.

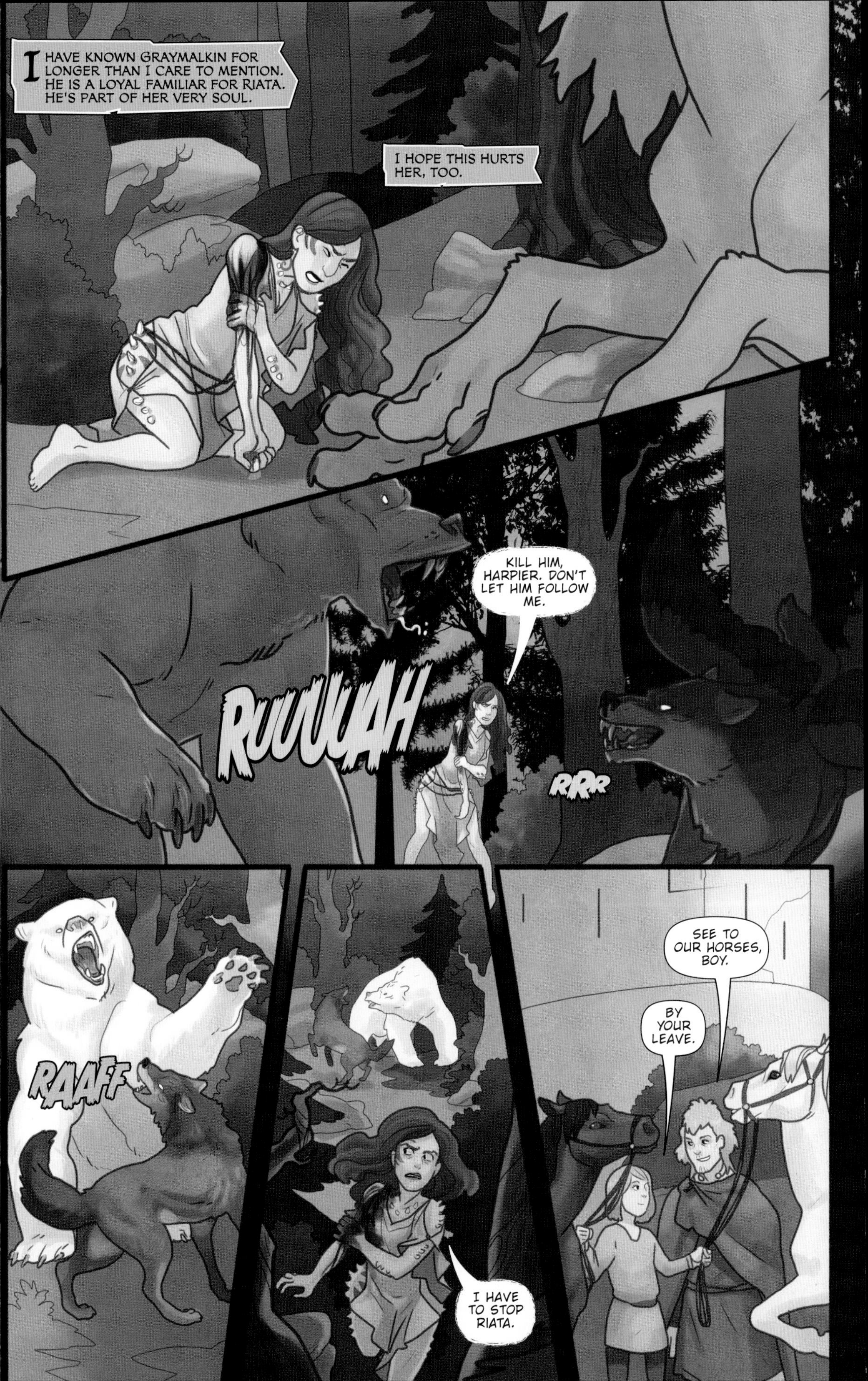
I HAVE KNOWN GRAYMALKIN FOR LONGER THAN I CARE TO MENTION. HE IS A LOYAL FAMILIAR FOR RIATA. HE'S PART OF HER VERY SOUL.
I HOPE THIS HURTS HER, TOO.
KILL HIM, HARPIER. DON'T LET HIM FOLLOW ME.
RUUUUAH
RRR
RAAFF
I HAVE TO STOP RIATA.
SEE TO OUR HORSES, BOY.
BY YOUR LEAVE.

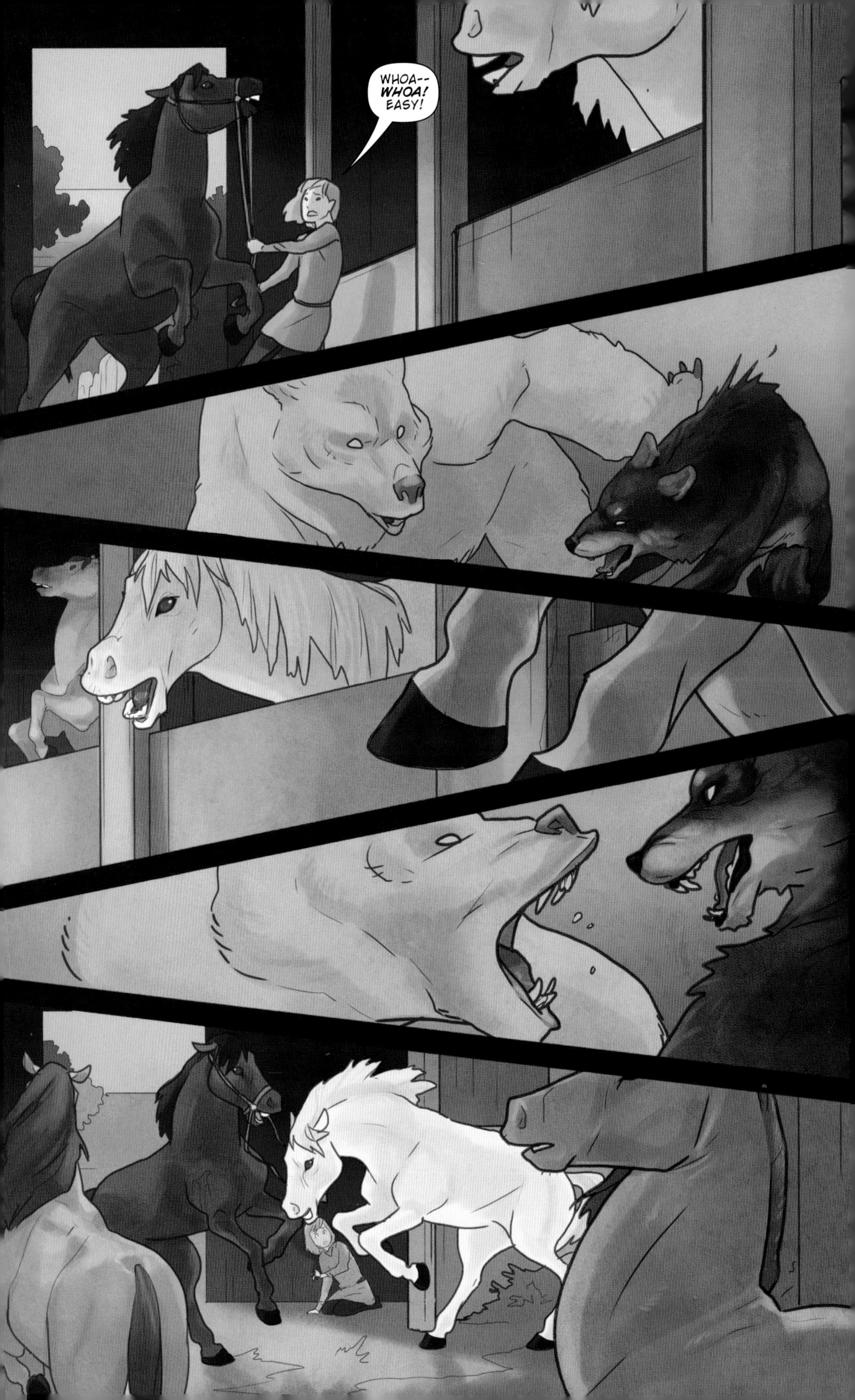
WHOA--
WHOA!
EASY!

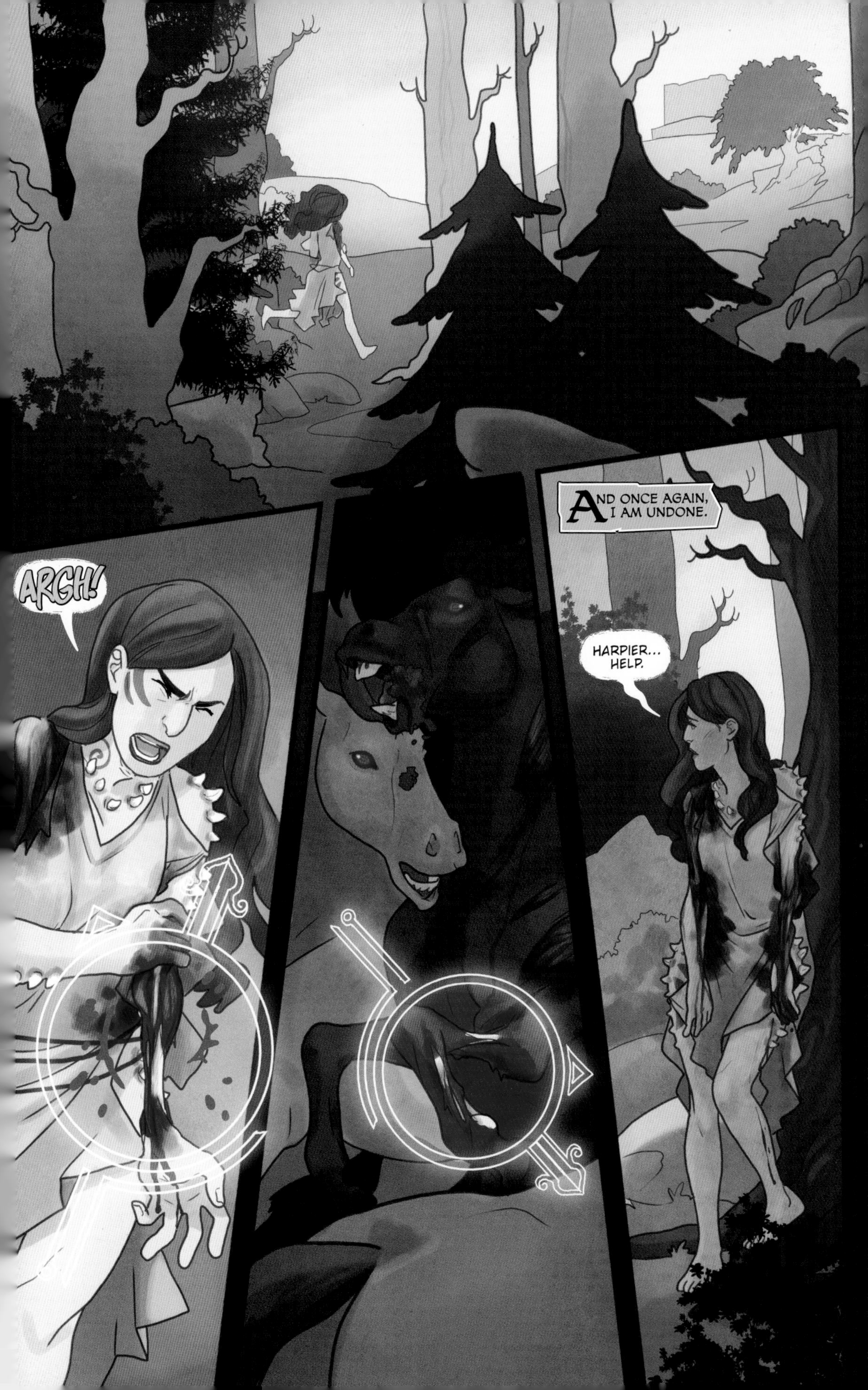
AND ONCE AGAIN, I AM UNDONE.
ARGH!
HARPIER... HELP.

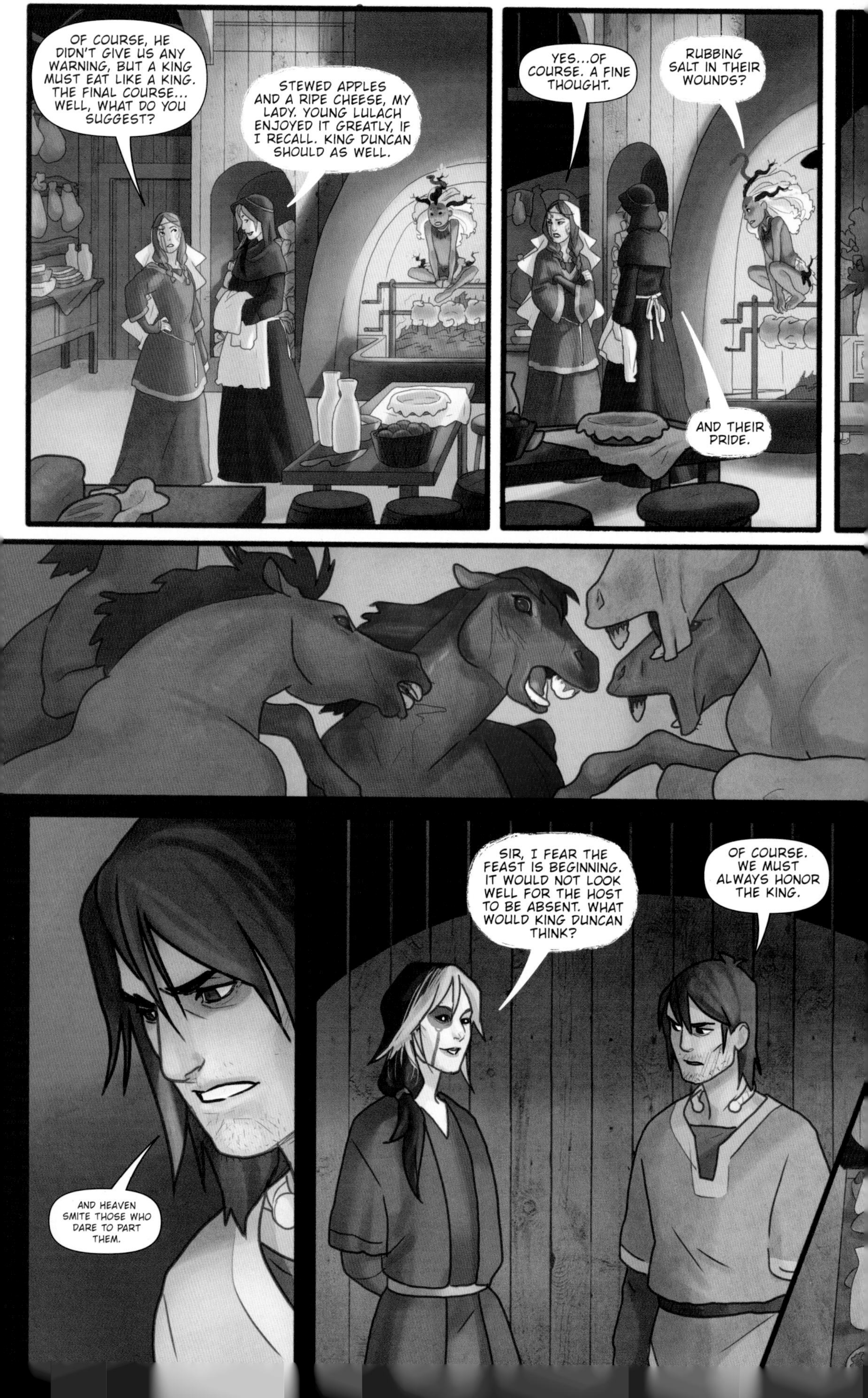
OF COURSE, HE DIDN'T GIVE US ANY WARNING, BUT A KING MUST EAT LIKE A KING. THE FINAL COURSE... WELL, WHAT DO YOU SUGGEST?
STEWED APPLES AND A RIPE CHEESE, MY LADY. YOUNG LULACH ENJOYED IT GREATLY, IF I RECALL. KING DUNCAN SHOULD AS WELL.
YES...OF COURSE. A FINE THOUGHT.
RUBBING SALT IN THEIR WOUNDS?
AND THEIR PRIDE.
SIR, I FEAR THE FEAST IS BEGINNING. IT WOULD NOT LOOK WELL FOR THE HOST TO BE ABSENT. WHAT WOULD KING DUNCAN THINK?
OF COURSE. WE MUST ALWAYS HONOR THE KING.
AND HEAVEN SMITE THOSE WHO DARE TO PART THEM.

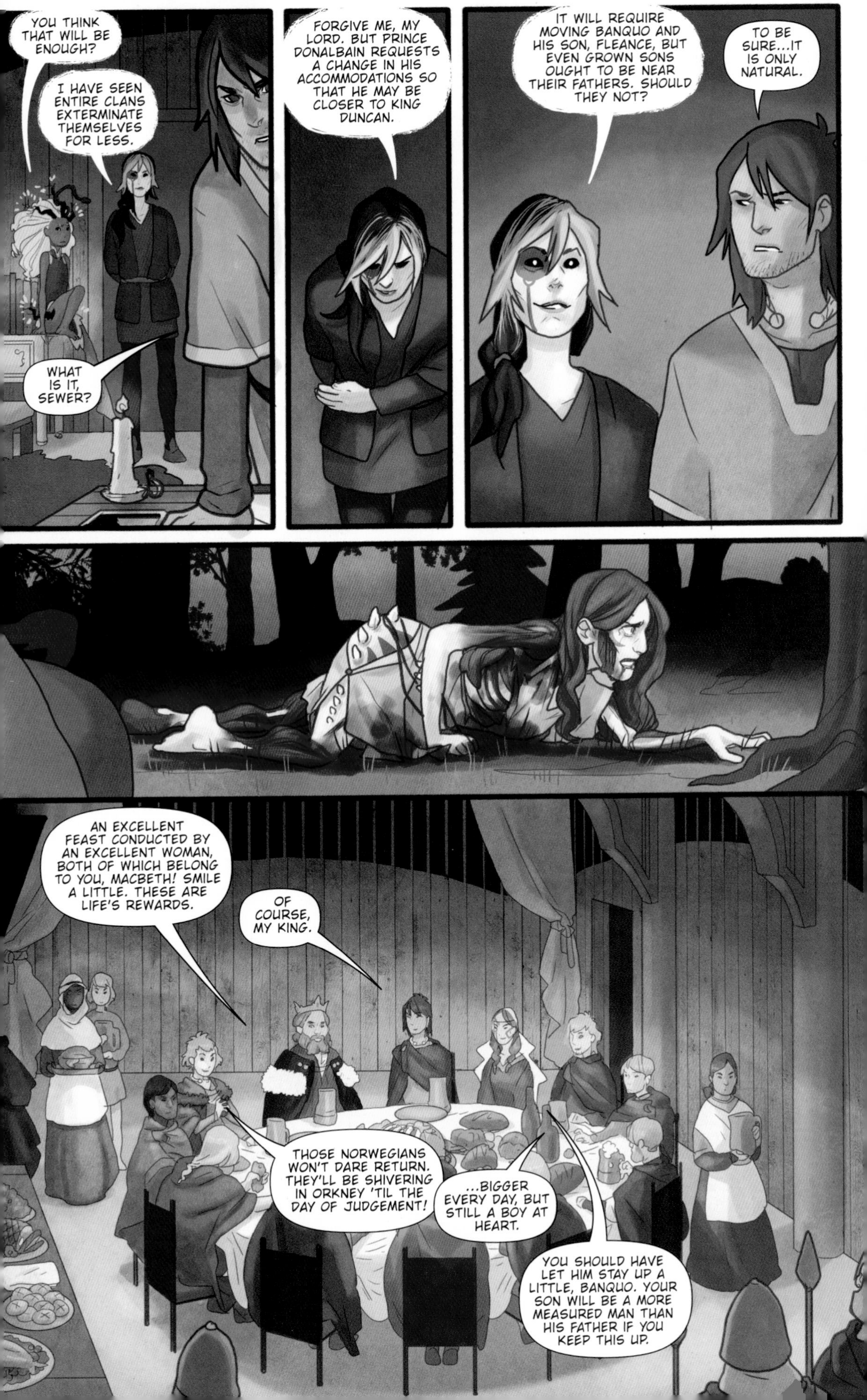
YOU THINK THAT WILL BE ENOUGH?
I HAVE SEEN ENTIRE CLANS EXTERMINATE THEMSELVES FOR LESS.
WHAT IS IT, SEWER?
FORGIVE ME, MY LORD. BUT PRINCE DONALBAIN REQUESTS A CHANGE IN HIS ACCOMMODATIONS SO THAT HE MAY BE CLOSER TO KING DUNCAN.
IT WILL REQUIRE MOVING BANQUO AND HIS SON, FLEANCE, BUT EVEN GROWN SONS OUGHT TO BE NEAR THEIR FATHERS. SHOULD THEY NOT?
TO BE SURE...IT IS ONLY NATURAL.
AN EXCELLENT FEAST CONDUCTED BY AN EXCELLENT WOMAN, BOTH OF WHICH BELONG TO YOU, MACBETH! SMILE A LITTLE. THESE ARE LIFE'S REWARDS.
OF COURSE, MY KING.
THOSE NORWEGIANS WON'T DARE RETURN. THEY'LL BE SHIVERING IN ORKNEY 'TIL THE DAY OF JUDGEMENT!
...BIGGER EVERY DAY, BUT STILL A BOY AT HEART.
YOU SHOULD HAVE LET HIM STAY UP A LITTLE, BANQUO. YOUR SON WILL BE A MORE MEASURED MAN THAN HIS FATHER IF YOU KEEP THIS UP.

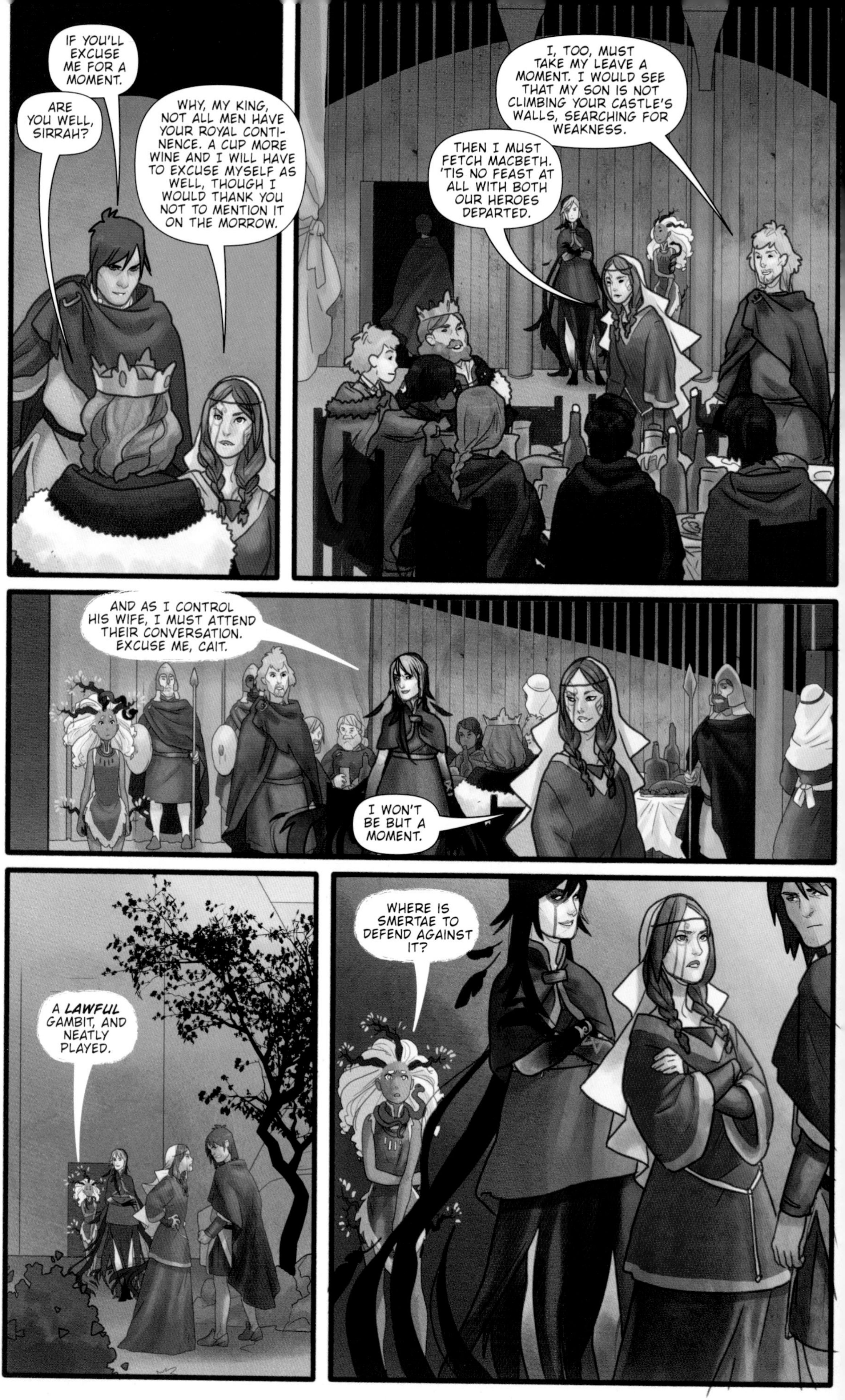
IF YOU'LL EXCUSE ME FOR A MOMENT.
ARE YOU WELL, SIRRAH?
WHY, MY KING, NOT ALL MEN HAVE YOUR ROYAL CONTI-NENCE. A CUP MORE WINE AND I WILL HAVE TO EXCUSE MYSELF AS WELL, THOUGH I WOULD THANK YOU NOT TO MENTION IT ON THE MORROW.
I, TOO, MUST TAKE MY LEAVE A MOMENT. I WOULD SEE THAT MY SON IS NOT CLIMBING YOUR CASTLE'S WALLS, SEARCHING FOR WEAKNESS.
THEN I MUST FETCH MACBETH. 'TIS NO FEAST AT ALL WITH BOTH OUR HEROES DEPARTED.
AND AS I CONTROL HIS WIFE, I MUST ATTEND THEIR CONVERSATION. EXCUSE ME, CAIT.
I WON'T BE BUT A MOMENT.
A ***LAWFUL*** GAMBIT, AND NEATLY PLAYED.
WHERE IS SMERTAE TO DEFEND AGAINST IT?

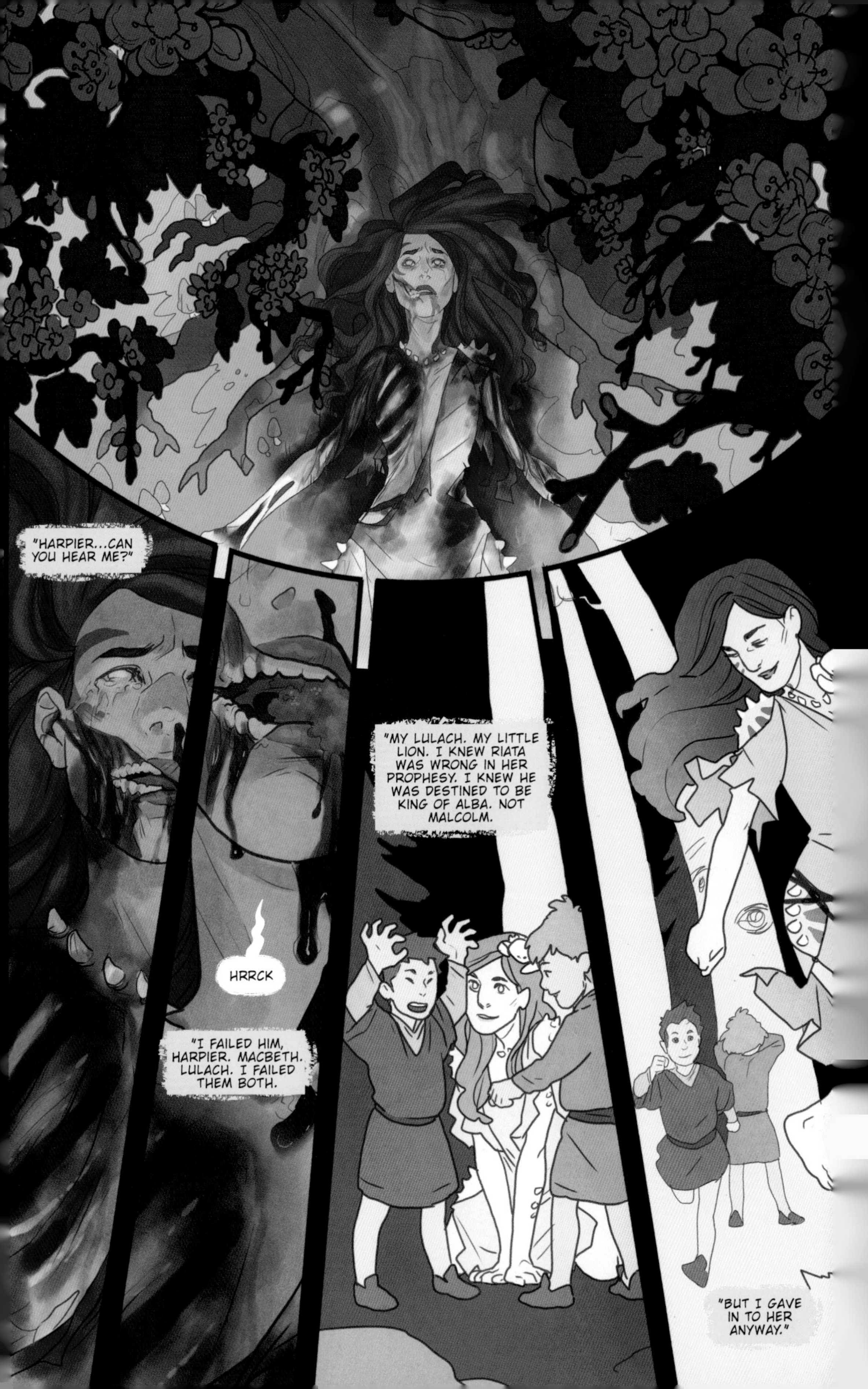
"HARPIER...CAN YOU HEAR ME?"
HRRCK
"I FAILED HIM, HARPIER. MACBETH. LULACH. I FAILED THEM BOTH.
"MY LULACH. MY LITTLE LION. I KNEW RIATA WAS WRONG IN HER PROPHESY. I KNEW HE WAS DESTINED TO BE KING OF ALBA. NOT MALCOLM.
"BUT I GAVE IN TO HER ANYWAY."

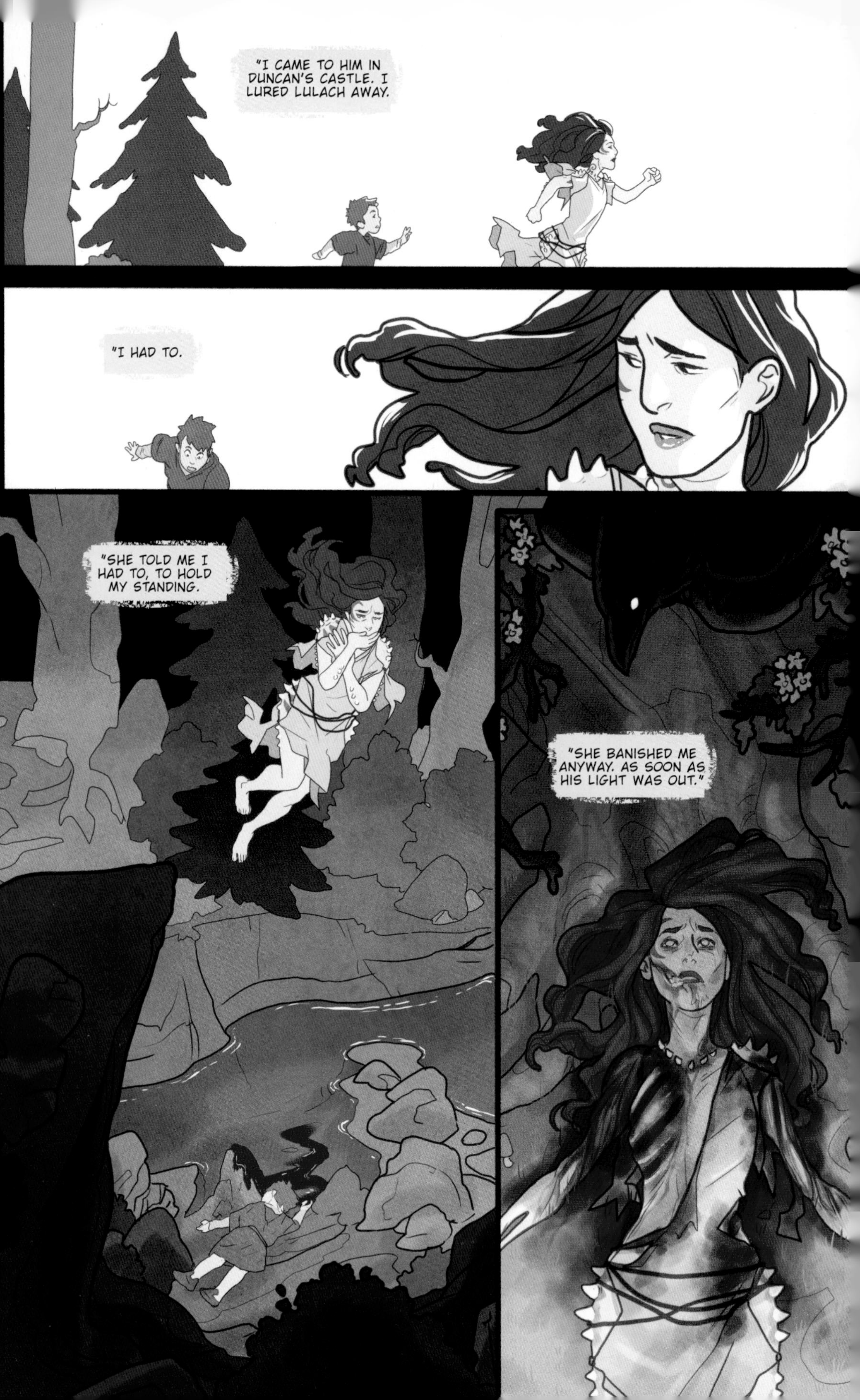
"I CAME TO HIM IN DUNCAN'S CASTLE. I LURED LULACH AWAY.
"I HAD TO.
"SHE TOLD ME I HAD TO, TO HOLD MY STANDING.
"SHE BANISHED ME ANYWAY. AS SOON AS HIS LIGHT WAS OUT."

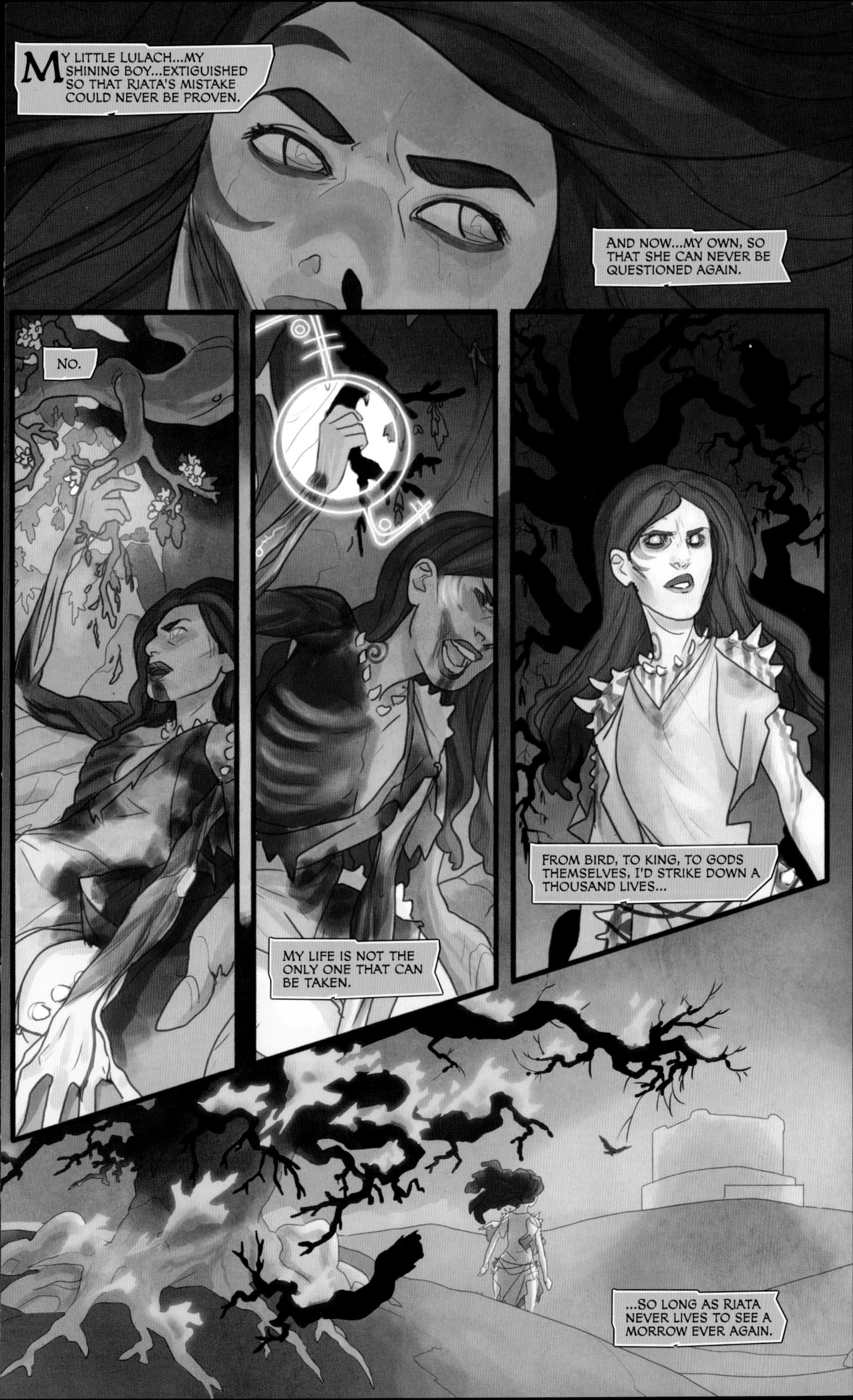
MY LITTLE LULACH...MY SHINING BOY...EXTIGUISHED SO THAT RIATA'S MISTAKE COULD NEVER BE PROVEN.
AND NOW...MY OWN, SO THAT SHE CAN NEVER BE QUESTIONED AGAIN.
NO.
MY LIFE IS NOT THE ONLY ONE THAT CAN BE TAKEN.
FROM BIRD, TO KING, TO GODS THEMSELVES, I'D STRIKE DOWN A THOUSAND LIVES...
...SO LONG AS RIATA NEVER LIVES TO SEE A MORROW EVER AGAIN.

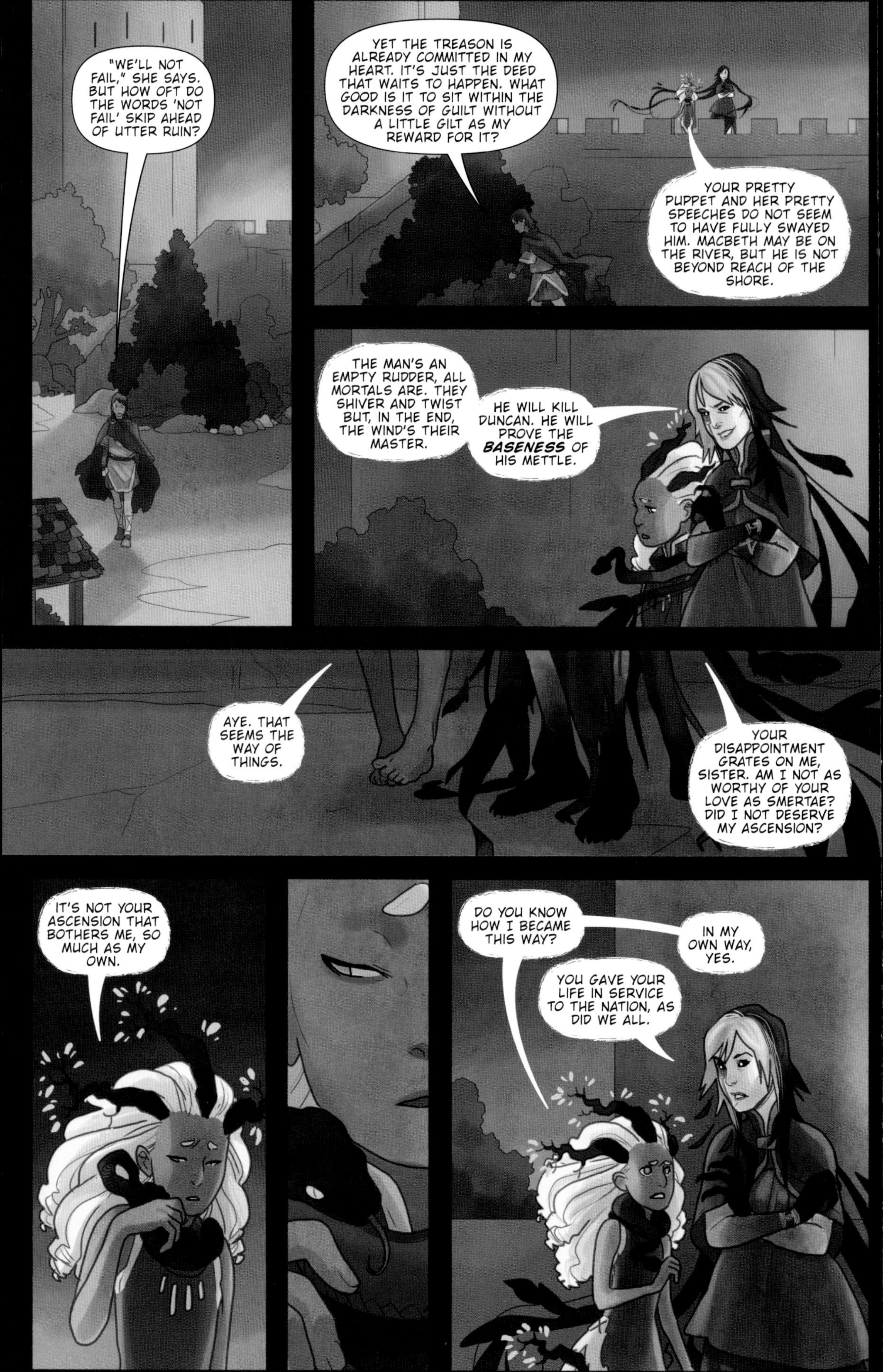
"WE'LL NOT FAIL," SHE SAYS. BUT HOW OFT DO THE WORDS 'NOT FAIL' SKIP AHEAD OF UTTER RUIN?
YET THE TREASON IS ALREADY COMMITTED IN MY HEART. IT'S JUST THE DEED THAT WAITS TO HAPPEN. WHAT GOOD IS IT TO SIT WITHIN THE DARKNESS OF GUILT WITHOUT A LITTLE GILT AS MY REWARD FOR IT?
YOUR PRETTY PUPPET AND HER PRETTY SPEECHES DO NOT SEEM TO HAVE FULLY SWAYED HIM. MACBETH MAY BE ON THE RIVER, BUT HE IS NOT BEYOND REACH OF THE SHORE.
THE MAN'S AN EMPTY RUDDER, ALL MORTALS ARE. THEY SHIVER AND TWIST BUT, IN THE END, THE WIND'S THEIR MASTER.
HE WILL KILL DUNCAN. HE WILL PROVE THE ***BASENESS*** OF HIS METTLE.
AYE. THAT SEEMS THE WAY OF THINGS.
YOUR DISAPPOINTMENT GRATES ON ME, SISTER. AM I NOT AS WORTHY OF YOUR LOVE AS SMERTAE? DID I NOT DESERVE MY ASCENSION?
IT'S NOT YOUR ASCENSION THAT BOTHERS ME, SO MUCH AS MY OWN.
DO YOU KNOW HOW I BECAME THIS WAY?
IN MY OWN WAY, YES.
YOU GAVE YOUR LIFE IN SERVICE TO THE NATION, AS DID WE ALL.

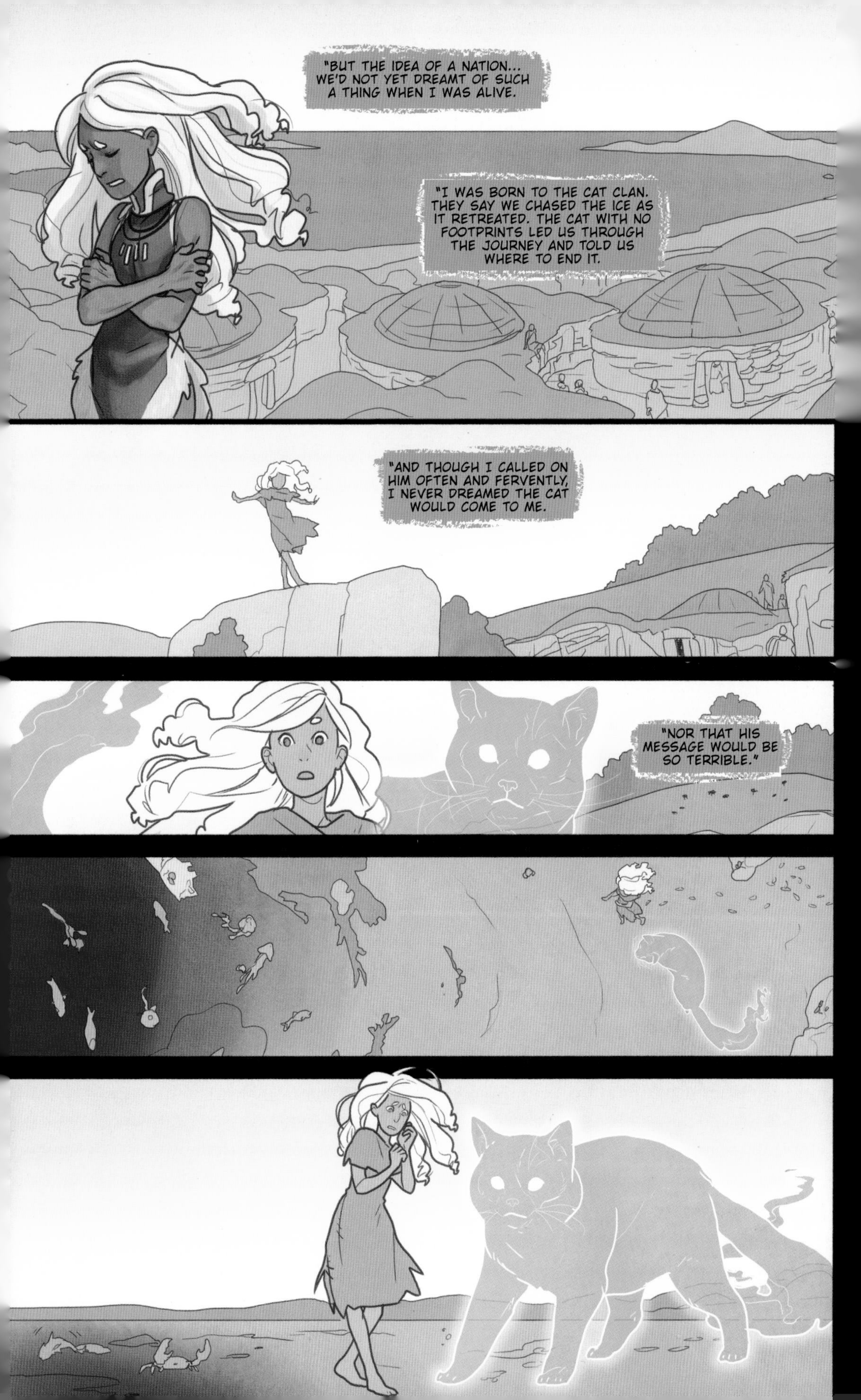
"BUT THE IDEA OF A NATION... WE'D NOT YET DREAMT OF SUCH A THING WHEN I WAS ALIVE.
"I WAS BORN TO THE CAT CLAN. THEY SAY WE CHASED THE ICE AS IT RETREATED. THE CAT WITH NO FOOTPRINTS LED US THROUGH THE JOURNEY AND TOLD US WHERE TO END IT.
"AND THOUGH I CALLED ON HIM OFTEN AND FERVENTLY, I NEVER DREAMED THE CAT WOULD COME TO ME.
"NOR THAT HIS MESSAGE WOULD BE SO TERRIBLE."

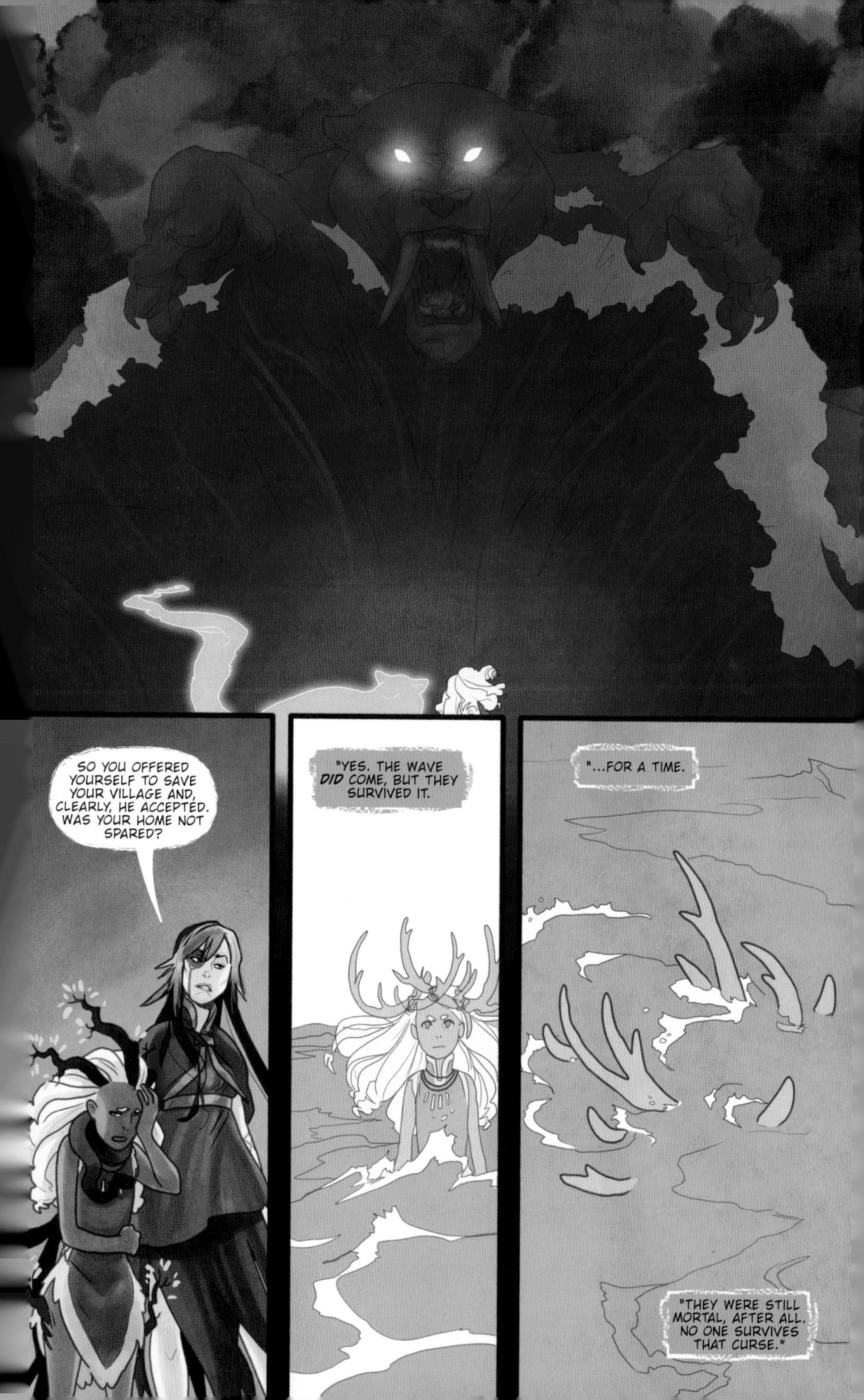
SO YOU OFFERED YOURSELF TO SAVE YOUR VILLAGE AND, CLEARLY, HE ACCEPTED. WAS YOUR HOME NOT SPARED?
"YES. THE WAVE *DID* COME, BUT THEY SURVIVED IT.
"...FOR A TIME.
"THEY WERE STILL MORTAL, AFTER ALL. NO ONE SURVIVES THAT CURSE."

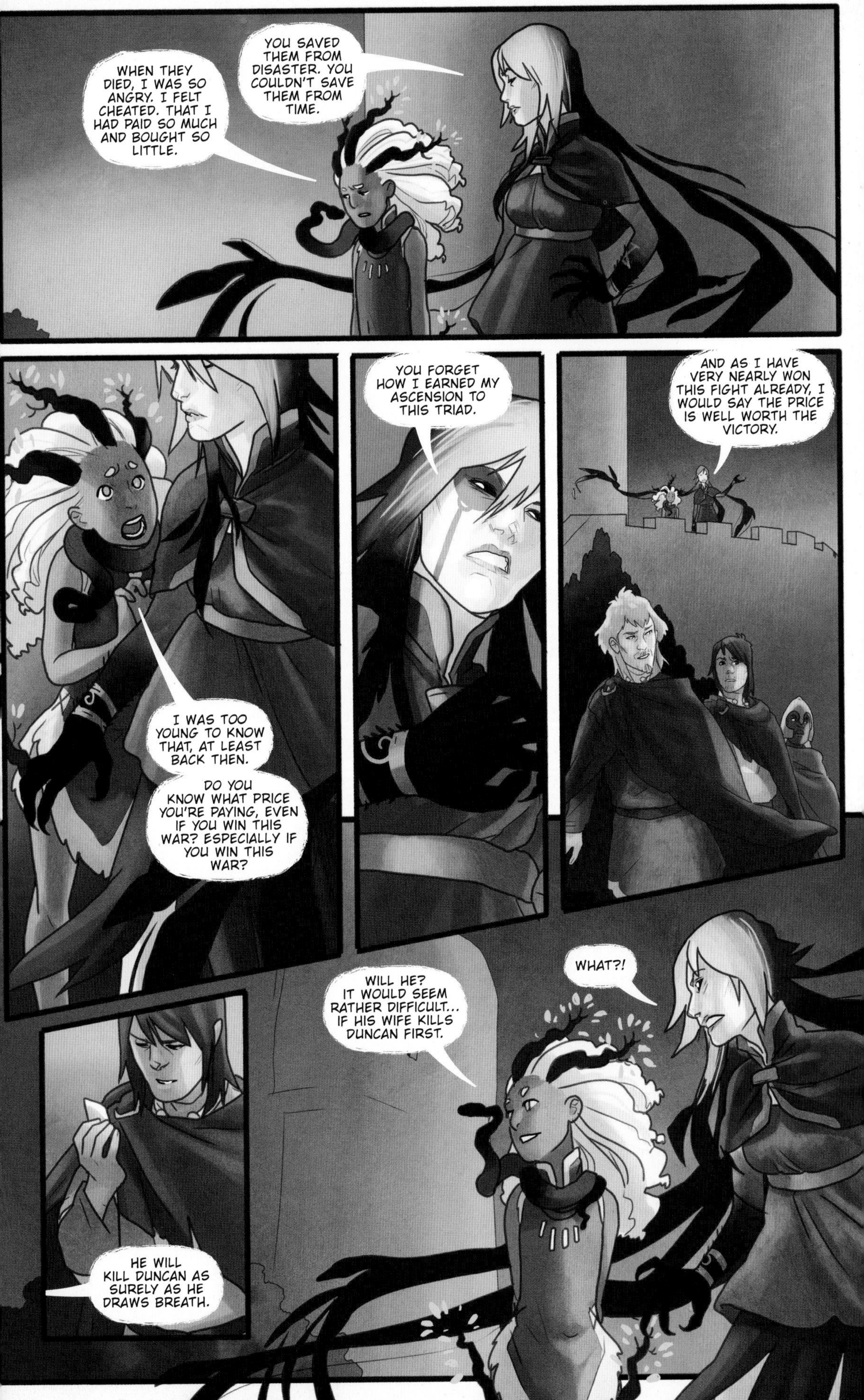
WHEN THEY DIED, I WAS SO ANGRY. I FELT CHEATED. THAT I HAD PAID SO MUCH AND BOUGHT SO LITTLE.
YOU SAVED THEM FROM DISASTER. YOU COULDN'T SAVE THEM FROM TIME.
I WAS TOO YOUNG TO KNOW THAT, AT LEAST BACK THEN.
DO YOU KNOW WHAT PRICE YOU'RE PAYING, EVEN IF YOU WIN THIS WAR? ESPECIALLY IF YOU WIN THIS WAR?
YOU FORGET HOW I EARNED MY ASCENSION TO THIS TRIAD.
AND AS I HAVE VERY NEARLY WON THIS FIGHT ALREADY, I WOULD SAY THE PRICE IS WELL WORTH THE VICTORY.
HE WILL KILL DUNCAN AS SURELY AS HE DRAWS BREATH.
WILL HE? IT WOULD SEEM RATHER DIFFICULT... IF HIS WIFE KILLS DUNCAN FIRST.
WHAT?!

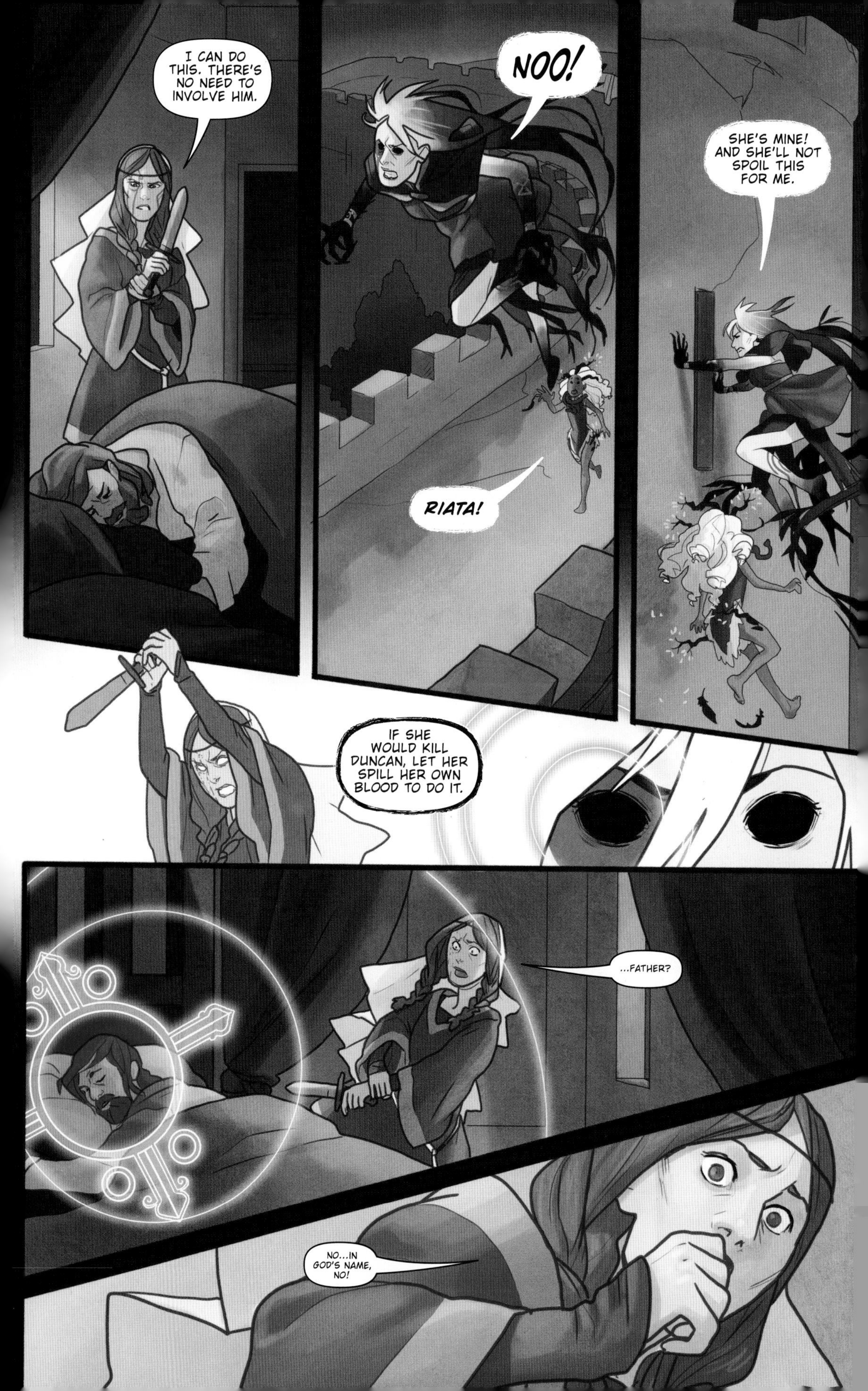
I CAN DO THIS. THERE'S NO NEED TO INVOLVE HIM.
NOO!
RIATA!
SHE'S MINE! AND SHE'LL NOT SPOIL THIS FOR ME.
IF SHE WOULD KILL DUNCAN, LET HER SPILL HER OWN BLOOD TO DO IT.
...FATHER?
NO...IN GOD'S NAME, NO!

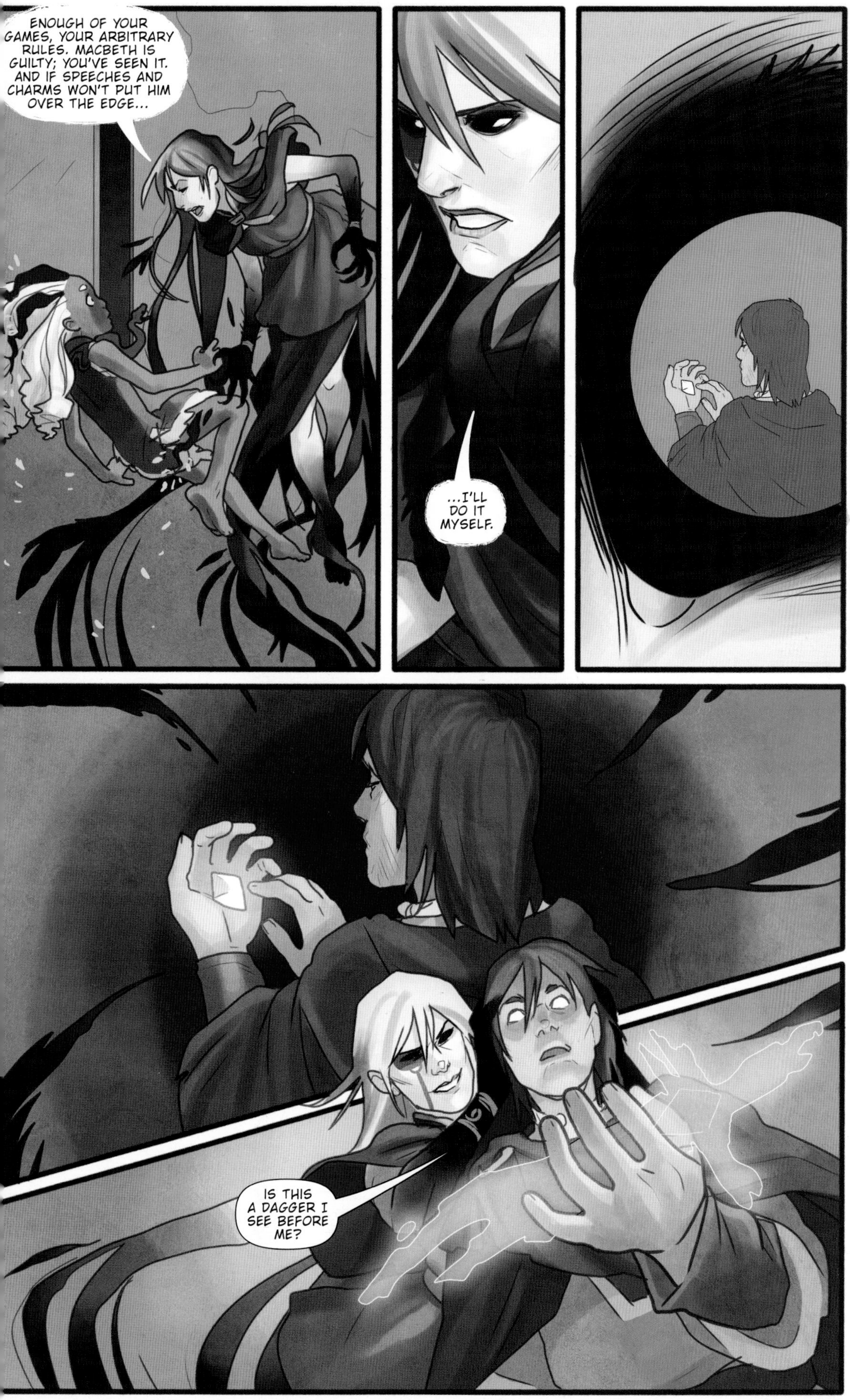
ENOUGH OF YOUR GAMES, YOUR ARBITRARY RULES. MACBETH IS GUILTY; YOU'VE SEEN IT. AND IF SPEECHES AND CHARMS WON'T PUT HIM OVER THE EDGE...
...I'LL DO IT MYSELF.
IS THIS A DAGGER I SEE BEFORE ME?

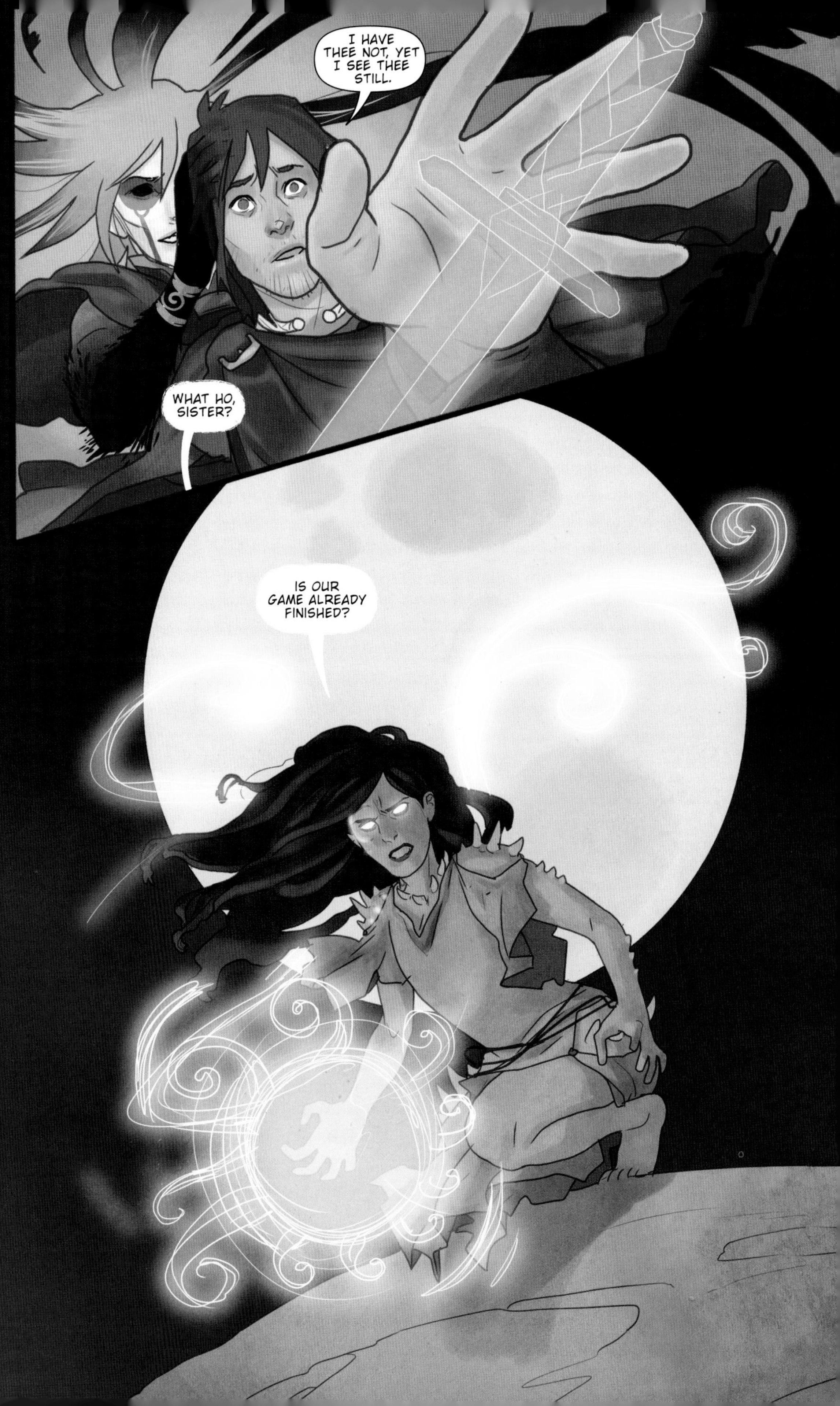
I HAVE THEE NOT, YET I SEE THEE STILL.
WHAT HO, SISTER?
IS OUR GAME ALREADY FINISHED?

Act Five

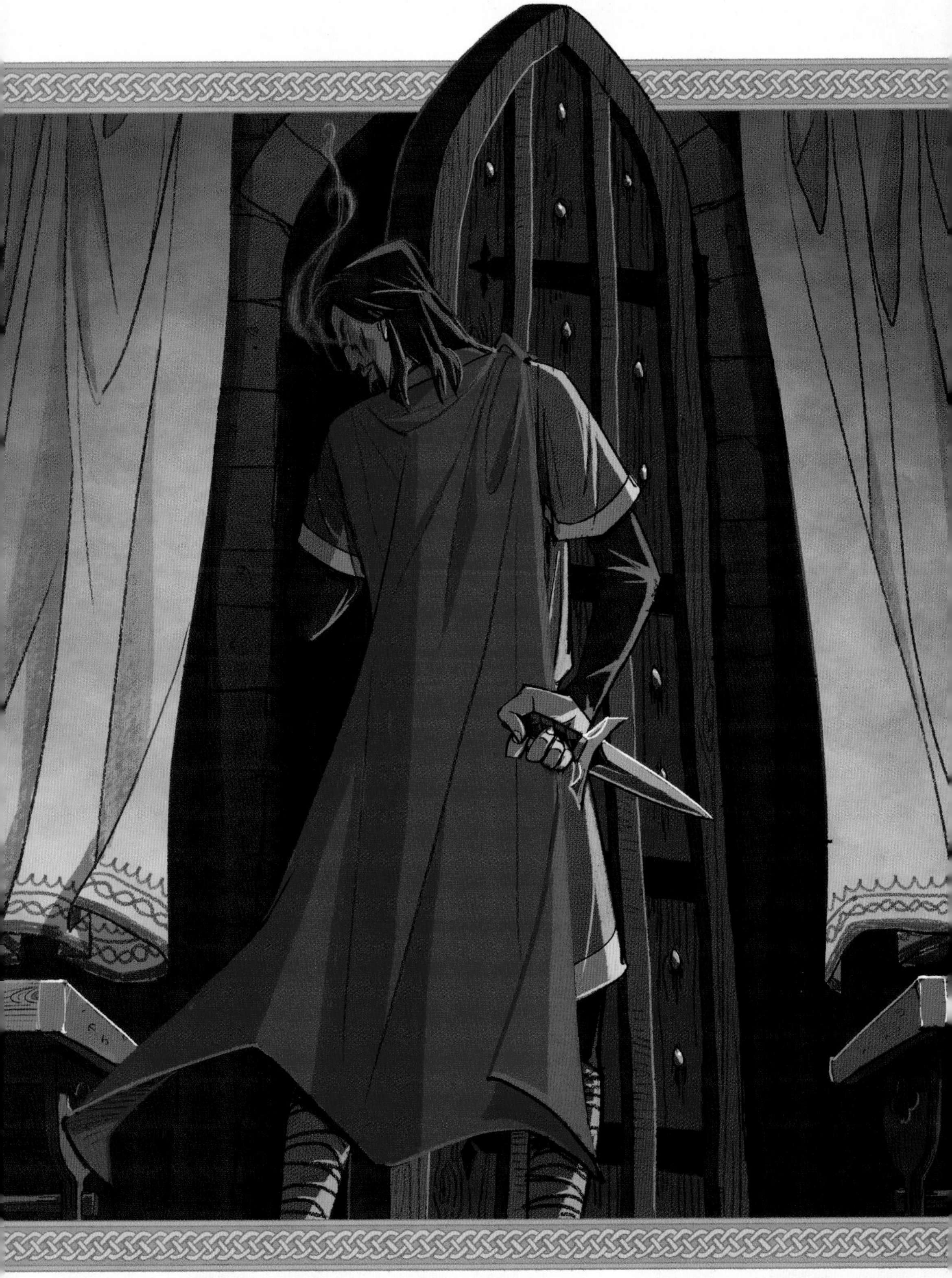

Issue Five Cover by Kyla Vanderklugt

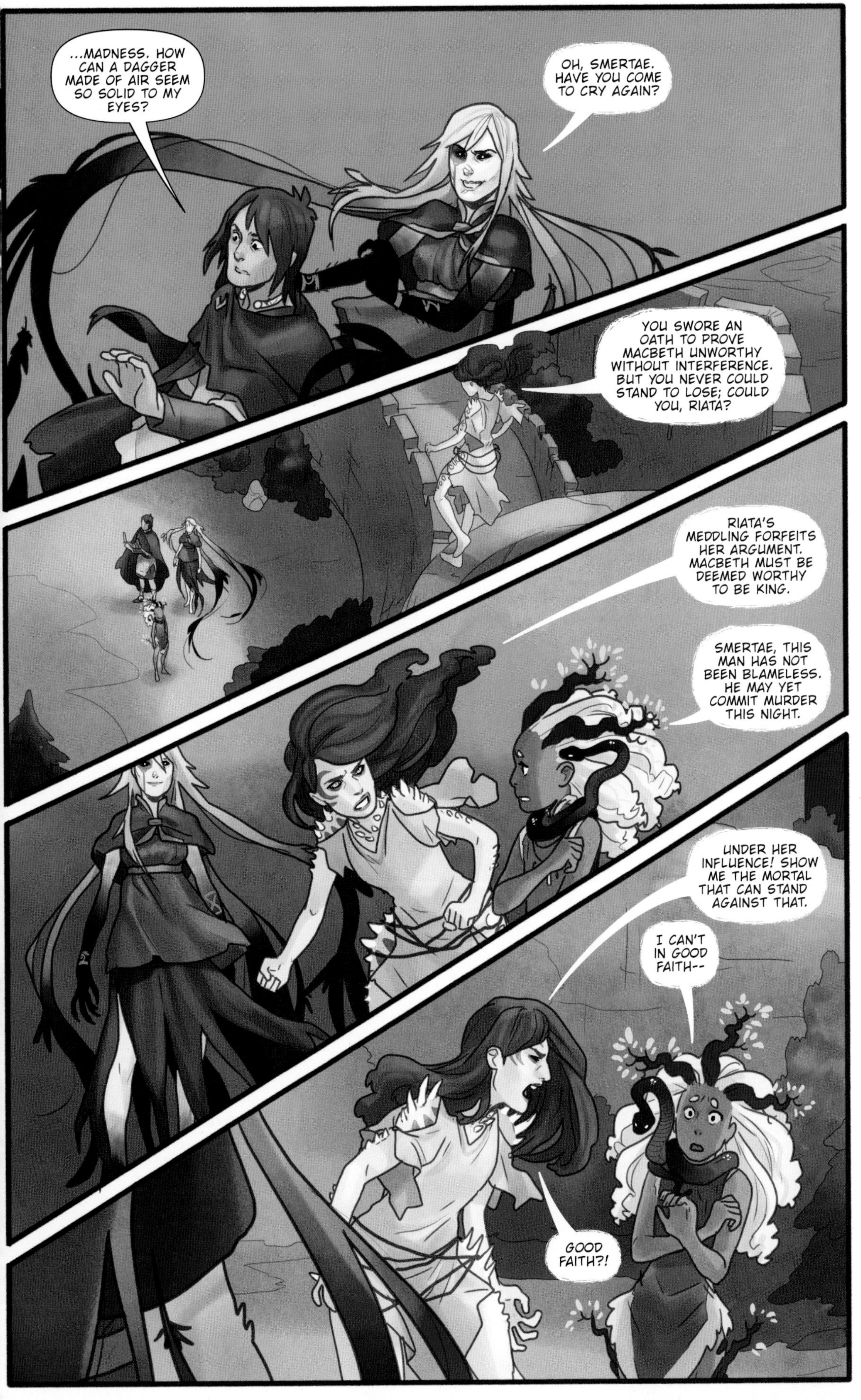
...MADNESS. HOW CAN A DAGGER MADE OF AIR SEEM SO SOLID TO MY EYES?
OH, SMERTAE. HAVE YOU COME TO CRY AGAIN?
YOU SWORE AN OATH TO PROVE MACBETH UNWORTHY WITHOUT INTERFERENCE. BUT YOU NEVER COULD STAND TO LOSE; COULD YOU, RIATA?
RIATA'S MEDDLING FORFEITS HER ARGUMENT. MACBETH MUST BE DEEMED WORTHY TO BE KING.
SMERTAE, THIS MAN HAS NOT BEEN BLAMELESS. HE MAY YET COMMIT MURDER THIS NIGHT.
UNDER HER INFLUENCE! SHOW ME THE MORTAL THAT CAN STAND AGAINST THAT.
I CAN'T IN GOOD FAITH--
GOOD FAITH?!

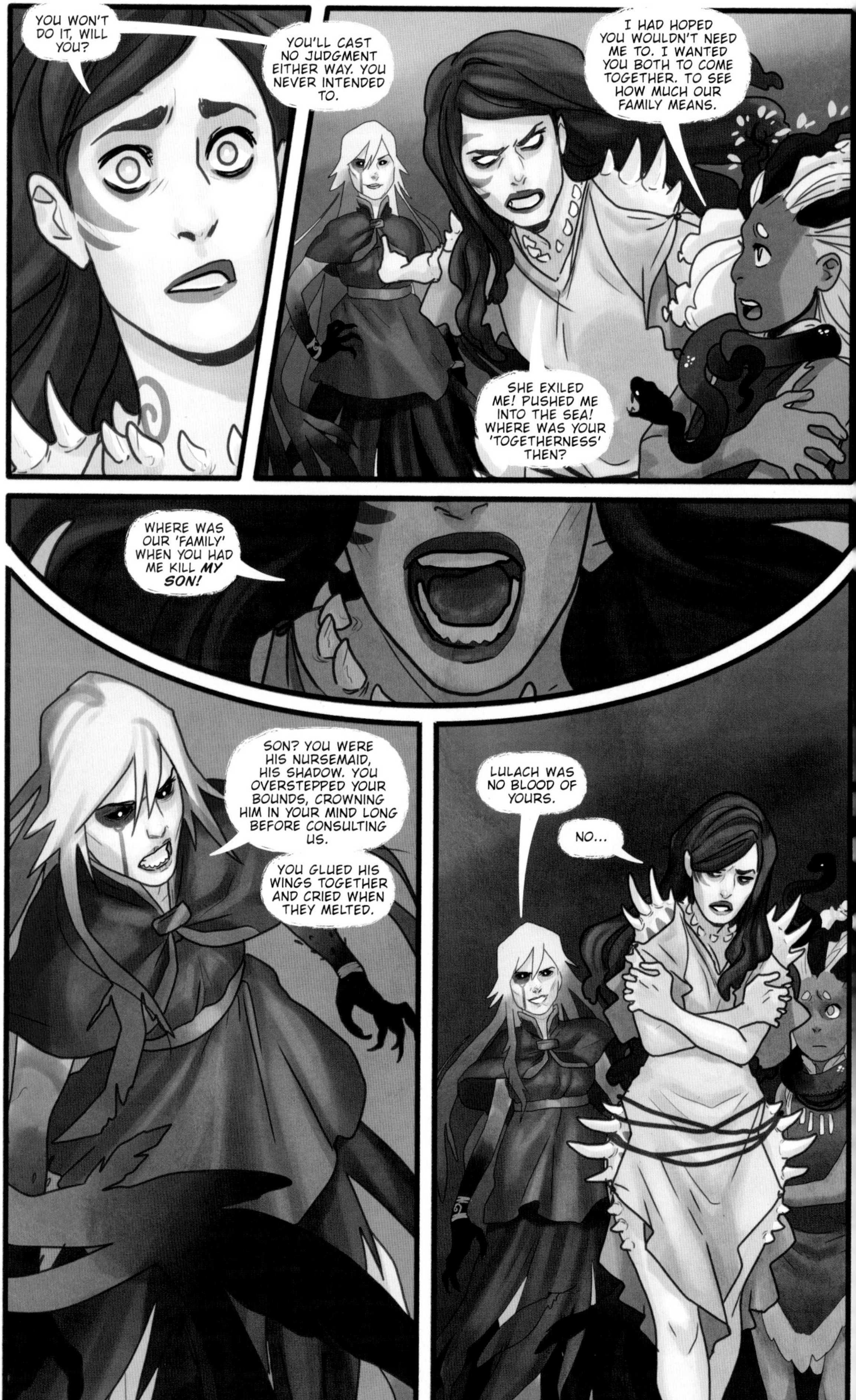
YOU WON'T DO IT, WILL YOU?
YOU'LL CAST NO JUDGMENT EITHER WAY. YOU NEVER INTENDED TO.
I HAD HOPED YOU WOULDN'T NEED ME TO. I WANTED YOU BOTH TO COME TOGETHER. TO SEE HOW MUCH OUR FAMILY MEANS.
SHE EXILED ME! PUSHED ME INTO THE SEA! WHERE WAS YOUR 'TOGETHERNESS' THEN?
WHERE WAS OUR 'FAMILY' WHEN YOU HAD ME KILL ***MY SON!***
SON? YOU WERE HIS NURSEMAID, HIS SHADOW. YOU OVERSTEPPED YOUR BOUNDS, CROWNING HIM IN YOUR MIND LONG BEFORE CONSULTING US.
YOU GLUED HIS WINGS TOGETHER AND CRIED WHEN THEY MELTED.
LULACH WAS NO BLOOD OF YOURS.
NO...

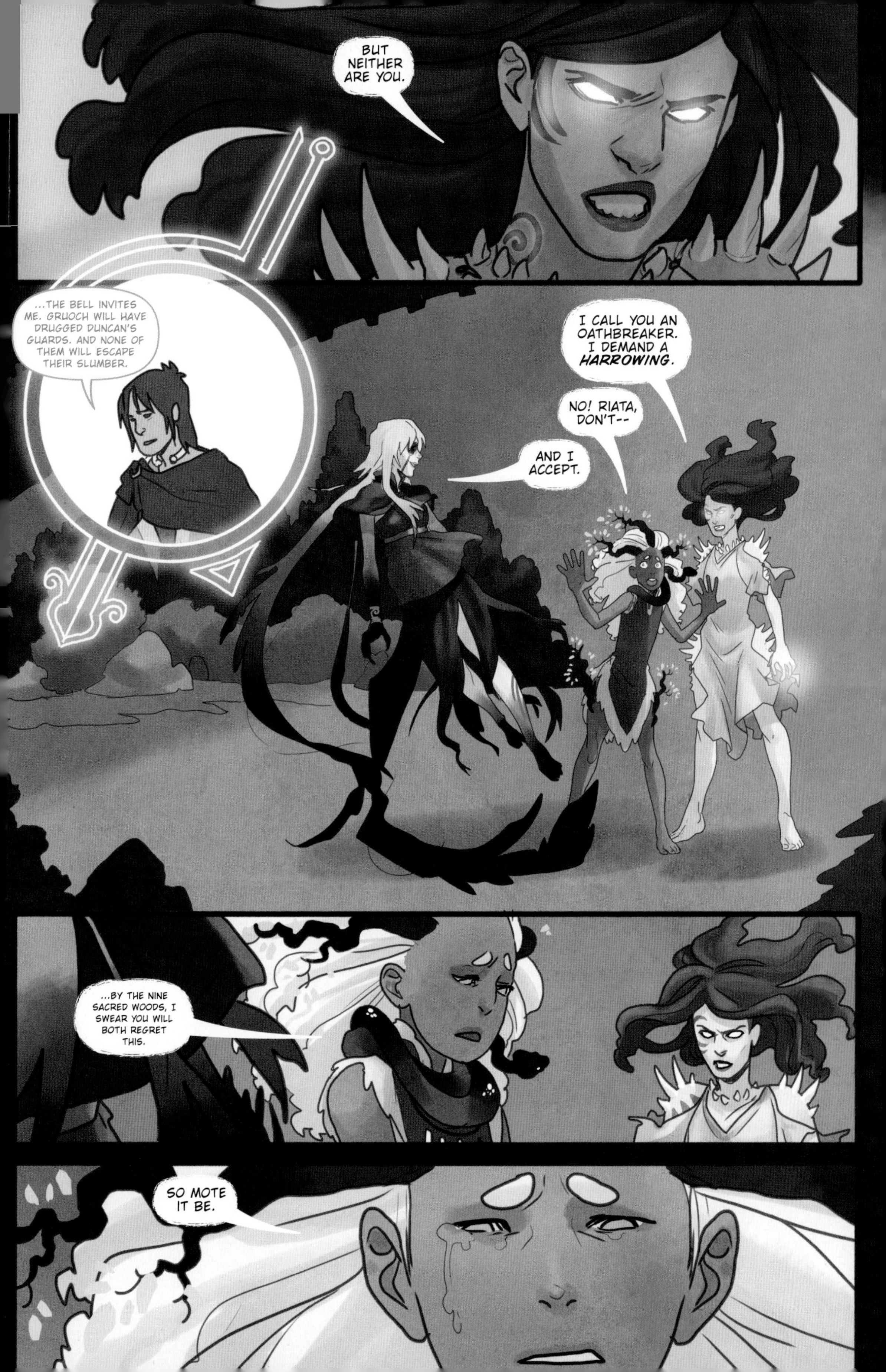
BUT NEITHER ARE YOU.
...THE BELL INVITES ME. GRUOCH WILL HAVE DRUGGED DUNCAN'S GUARDS. AND NONE OF THEM WILL ESCAPE THEIR SLUMBER.
I CALL YOU AN OATHBREAKER. I DEMAND A HARROWING.
NO! RIATA, DON'T--
AND I ACCEPT.
...BY THE NINE SACRED WOODS, I SWEAR YOU WILL BOTH REGRET THIS.
SO MOTE IT BE.

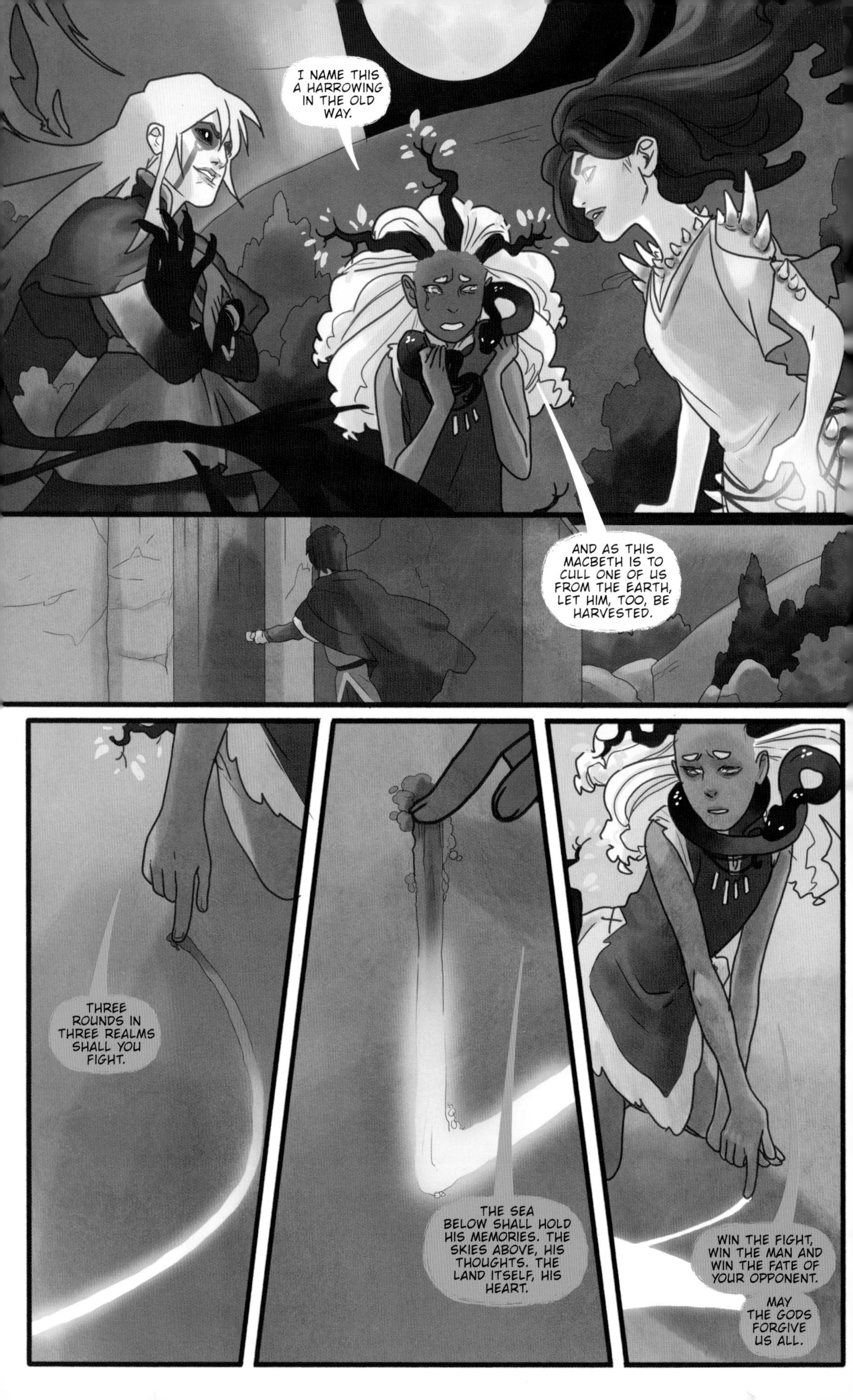
I NAME THIS A HARROWING IN THE OLD WAY.
AND AS THIS MACBETH IS TO CULL ONE OF US FROM THE EARTH, LET HIM, TOO, BE HARVESTED.
THREE ROUNDS IN THREE REALMS SHALL YOU FIGHT.
THE SEA BELOW SHALL HOLD HIS MEMORIES. THE SKIES ABOVE, HIS THOUGHTS. THE LAND ITSELF, HIS HEART.
WIN THE FIGHT, WIN THE MAN AND WIN THE FATE OF YOUR OPPONENT.
MAY THE GODS FORGIVE US ALL.

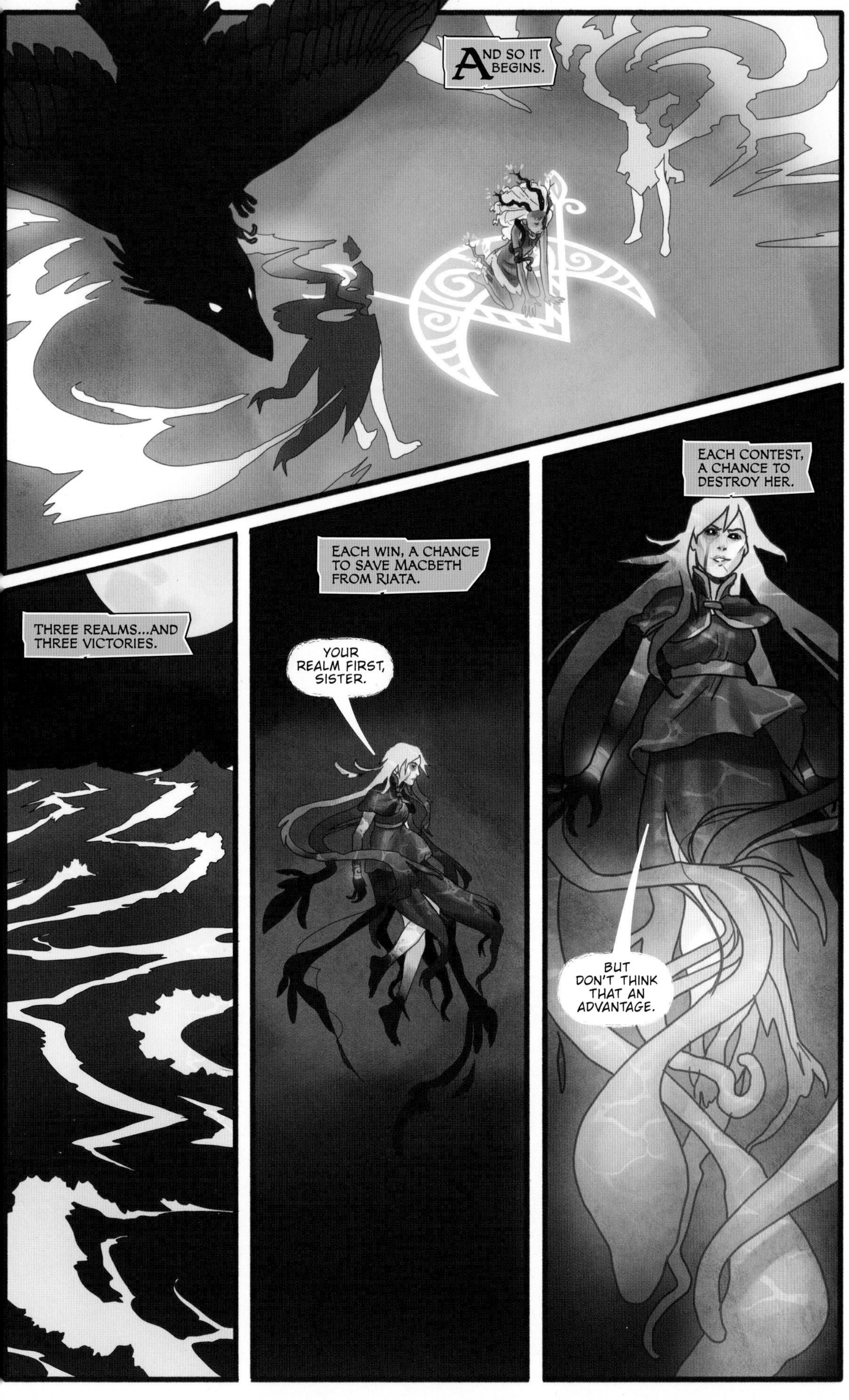
AND SO IT BEGINS.
THREE REALMS...AND THREE VICTORIES.
EACH WIN, A CHANCE TO SAVE MACBETH FROM RIATA.
YOUR REALM FIRST, SISTER.
EACH CONTEST, A CHANCE TO DESTROY HER.
BUT DON'T THINK THAT AN ADVANTAGE.

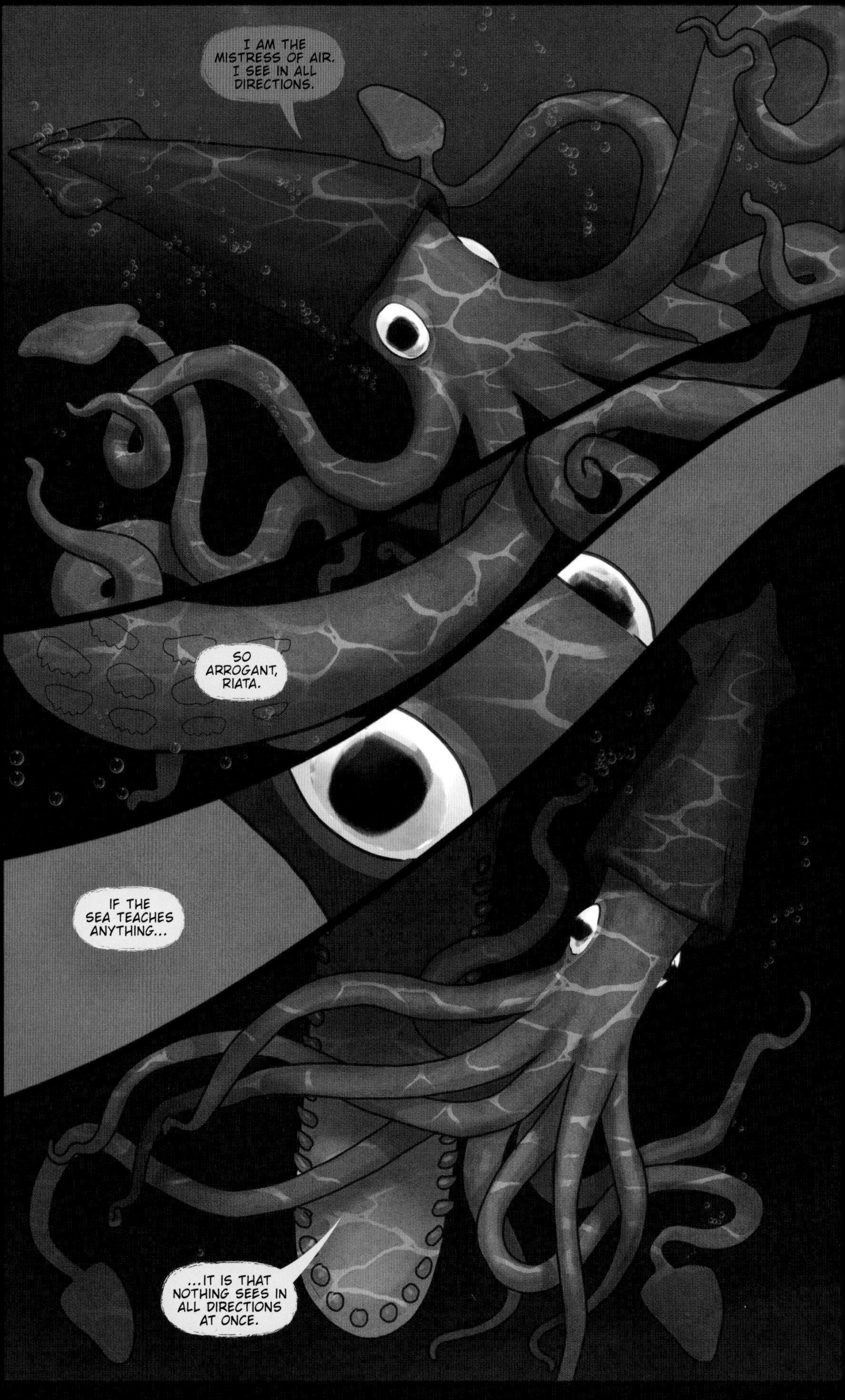
I AM THE MISTRESS OF AIR. I SEE IN ALL DIRECTIONS.
SO ARROGANT, RIATA.
IF THE SEA TEACHES ANYTHING...
...IT IS THAT NOTHING SEES IN ALL DIRECTIONS AT ONCE.

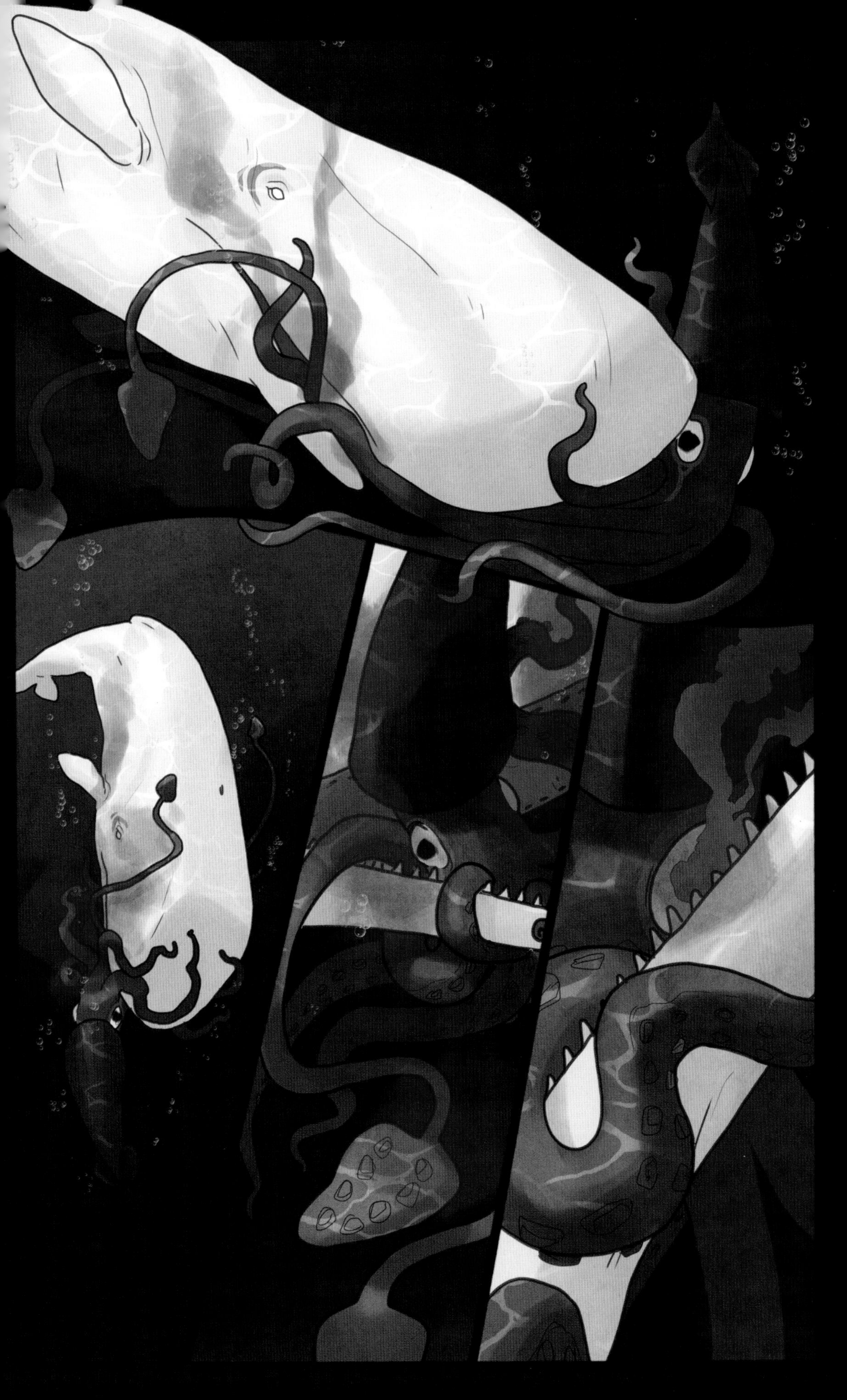

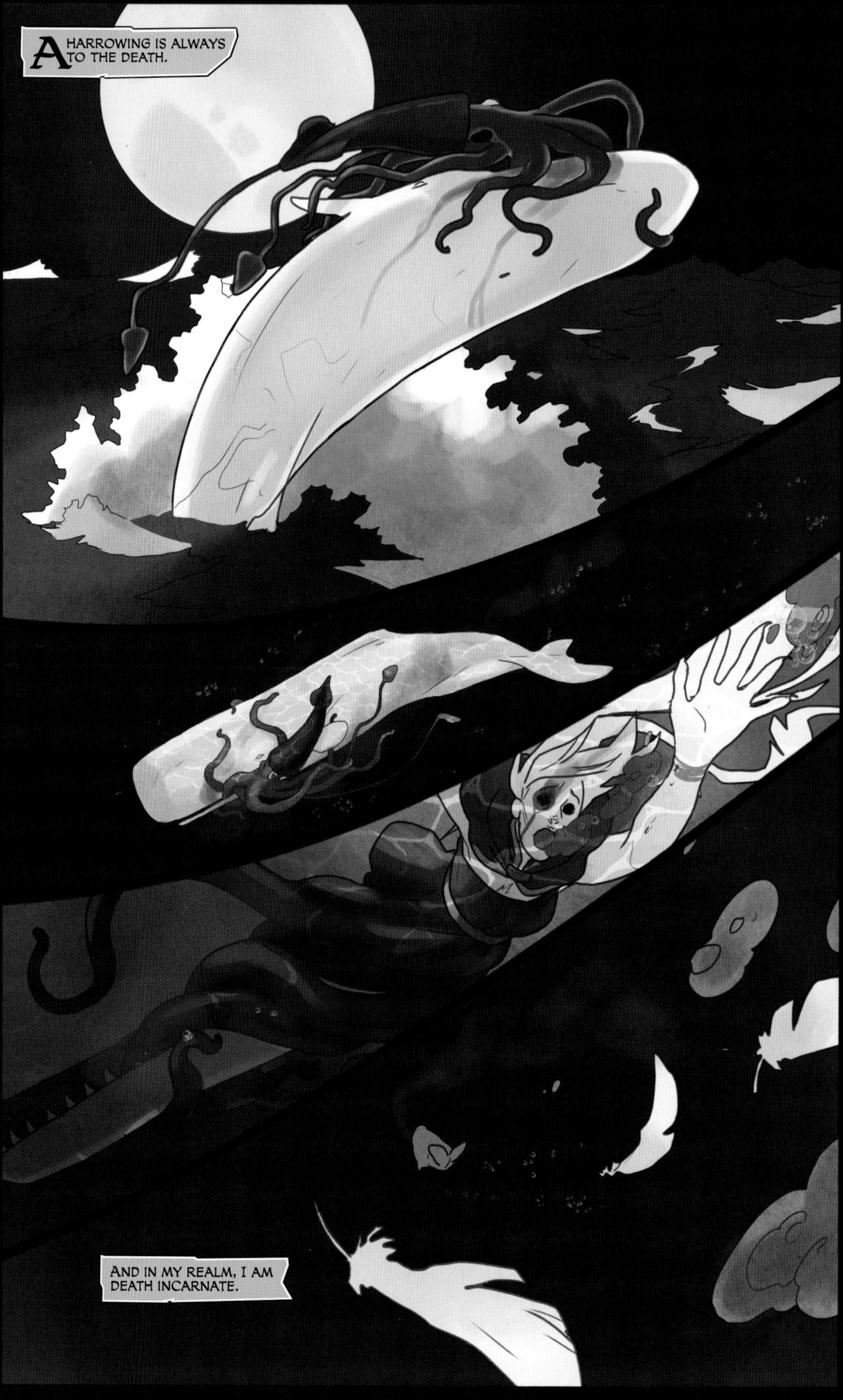
A HARROWING IS ALWAYS TO THE DEATH.
AND IN MY REALM, I AM DEATH INCARNATE.

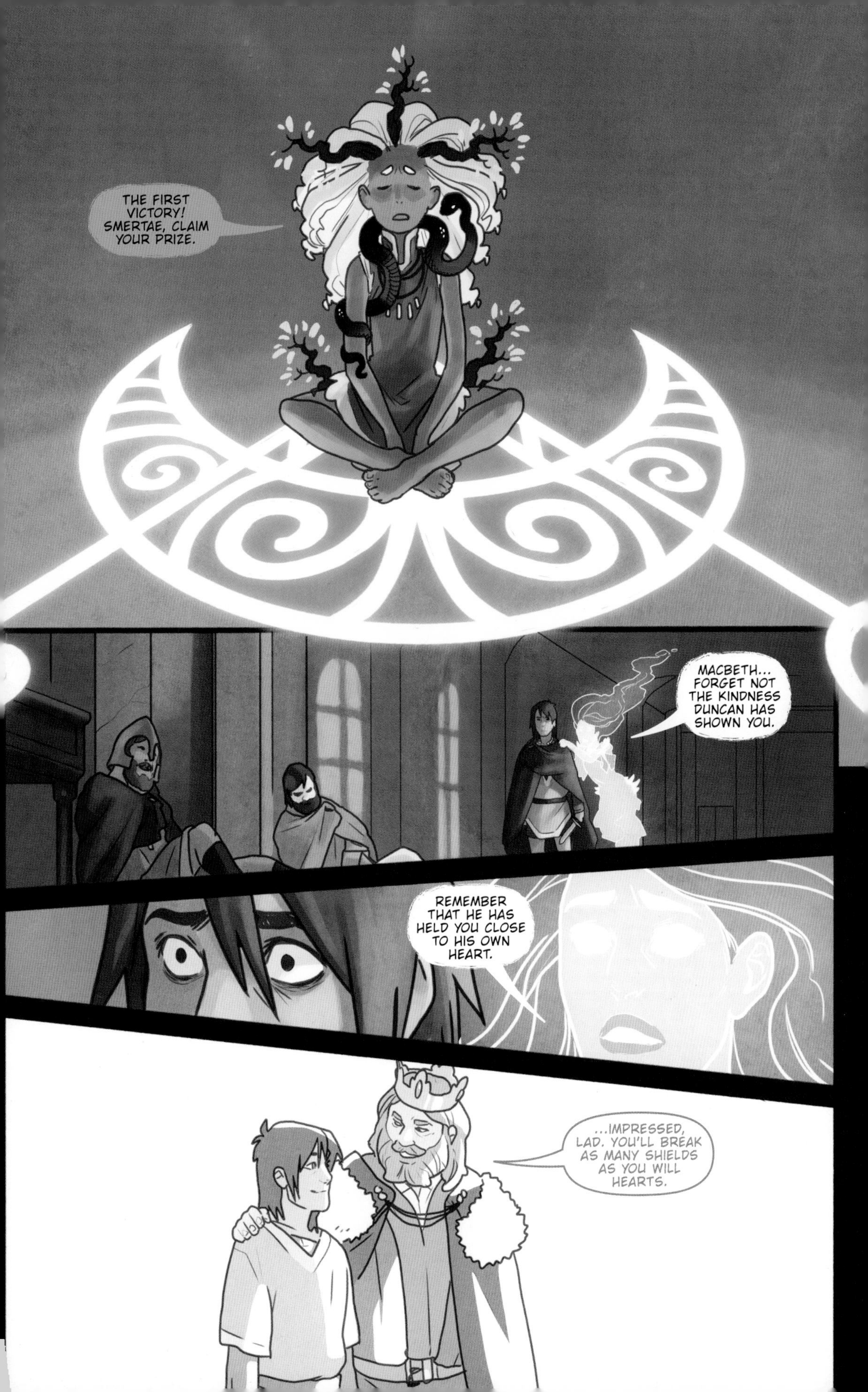
THE FIRST VICTORY! SMERTAE, CLAIM YOUR PRIZE.
MACBETH... FORGET NOT THE KINDNESS DUNCAN HAS SHOWN YOU.
REMEMBER THAT HE HAS HELD YOU CLOSE TO HIS OWN HEART.
...IMPRESSED, LAD. YOU'LL BREAK AS MANY SHIELDS AS YOU WILL HEARTS.

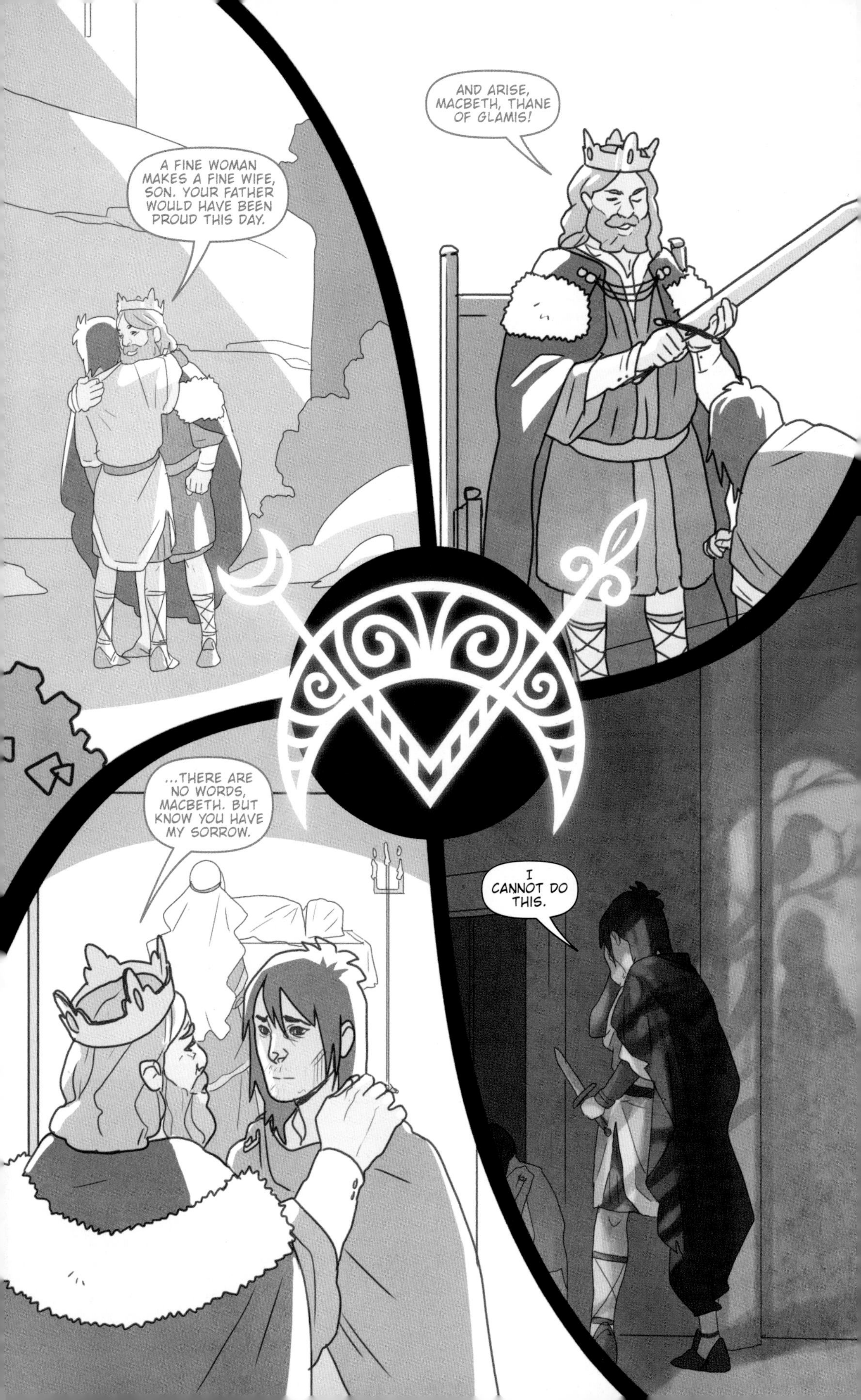
A FINE WOMAN MAKES A FINE WIFE, SON. YOUR FATHER WOULD HAVE BEEN PROUD THIS DAY.
AND ARISE, MACBETH, THANE OF GLAMIS!
...THERE ARE NO WORDS, MACBETH. BUT KNOW YOU HAVE MY SORROW.
I CANNOT DO THIS.

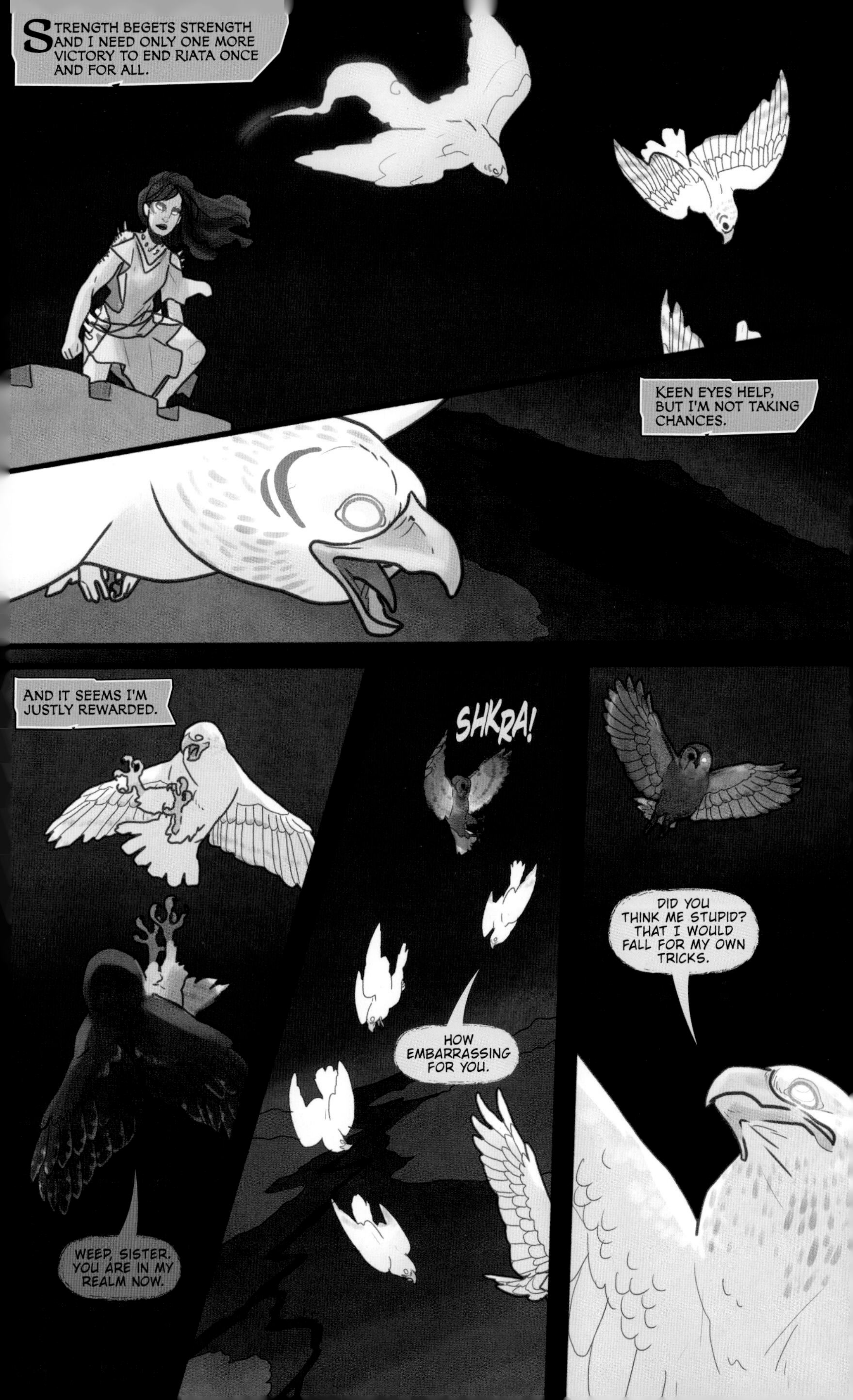
STRENGTH BEGETS STRENGTH AND I NEED ONLY ONE MORE VICTORY TO END RIATA ONCE AND FOR ALL.
KEEN EYES HELP, BUT I'M NOT TAKING CHANCES.
AND IT SEEMS I'M JUSTLY REWARDED.
WEEP, SISTER. YOU ARE IN MY REALM NOW.
SHKRA!
HOW EMBARRASSING FOR YOU.
DID YOU THINK ME STUPID? THAT I WOULD FALL FOR MY OWN TRICKS.

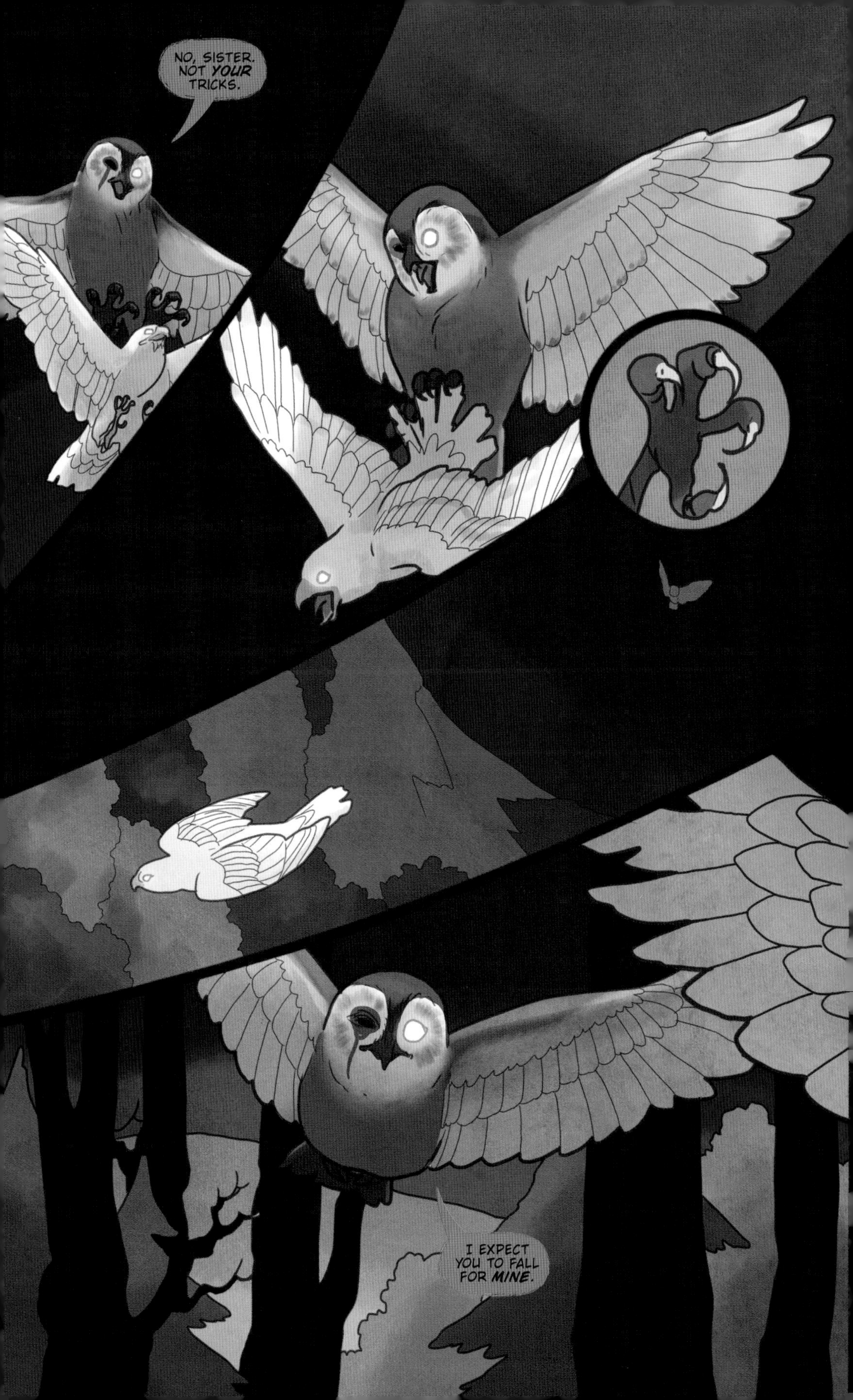
NO, SISTER. NOT *YOUR* TRICKS.
I EXPECT YOU TO FALL FOR *MINE*.

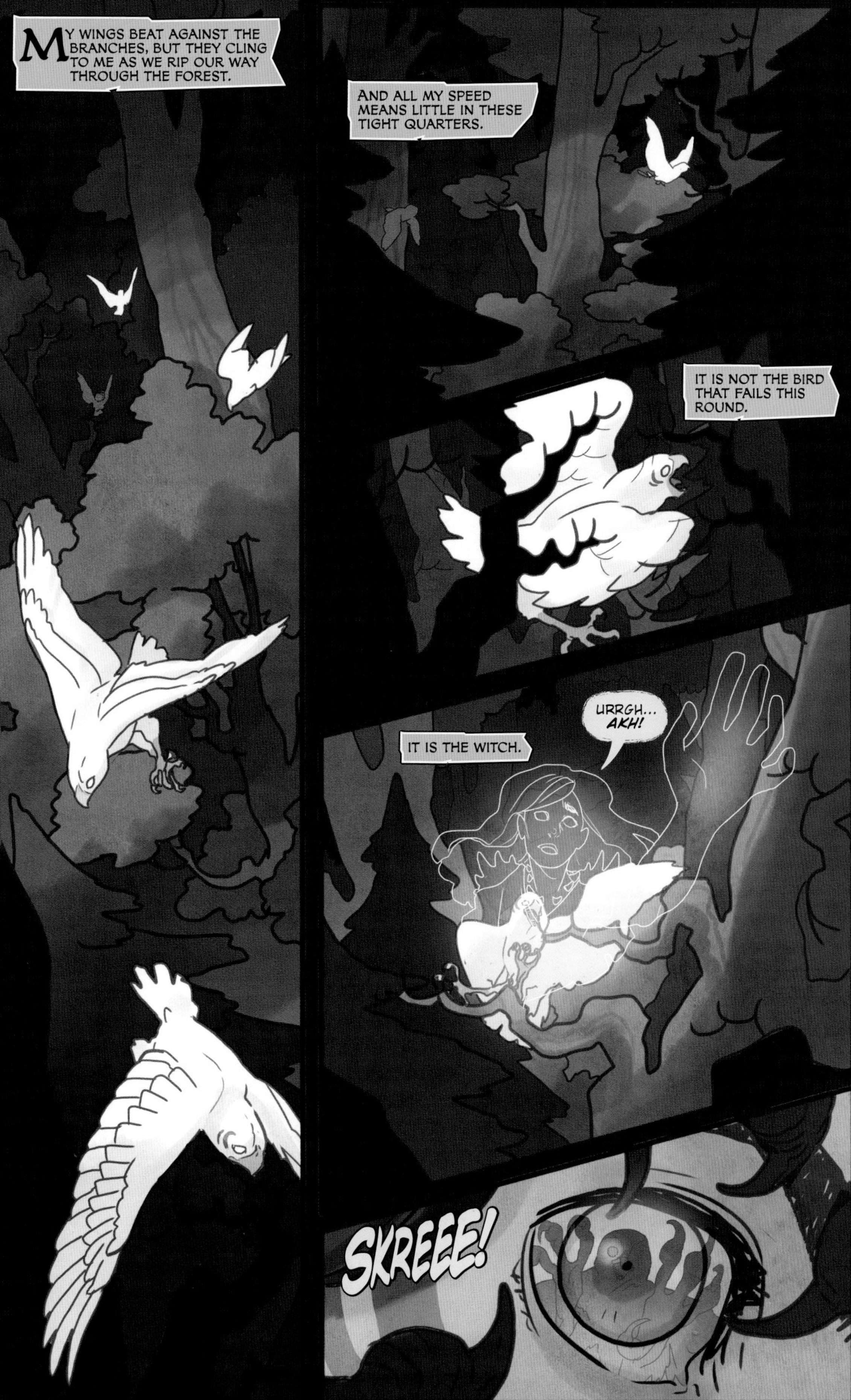
MY WINGS BEAT AGAINST THE BRANCHES, BUT THEY CLING TO ME AS WE RIP OUR WAY THROUGH THE FOREST.
AND ALL MY SPEED MEANS LITTLE IN THESE TIGHT QUARTERS.
IT IS NOT THE BIRD THAT FAILS THIS ROUND.
IT IS THE WITCH.
URRGH... AKH!
SKREEE!

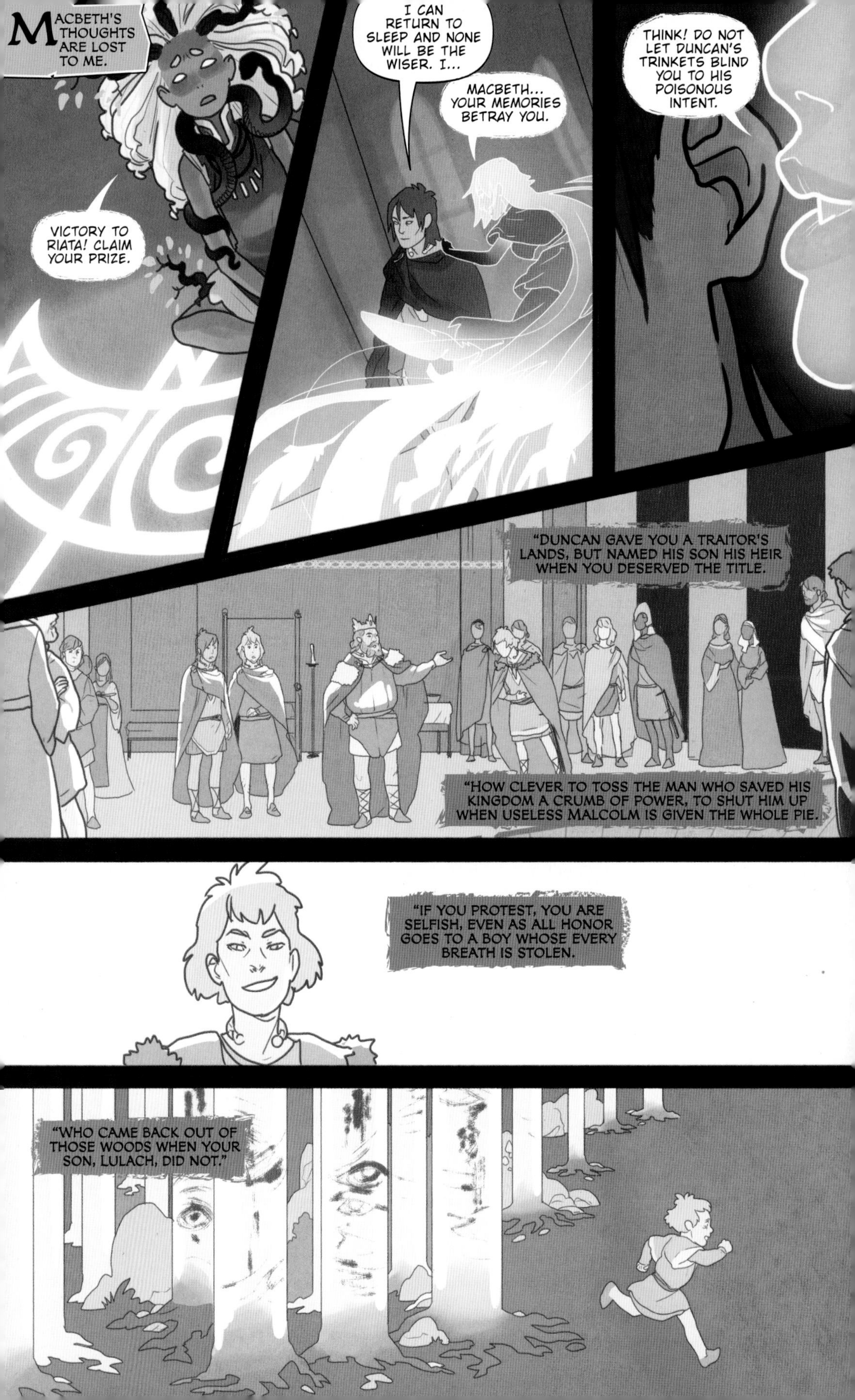
MACBETH'S THOUGHTS ARE LOST TO ME.
VICTORY TO RIATA! CLAIM YOUR PRIZE.
I CAN RETURN TO SLEEP AND NONE WILL BE THE WISER. I...
MACBETH... YOUR MEMORIES BETRAY YOU.
THINK! DO NOT LET DUNCAN'S TRINKETS BLIND YOU TO HIS POISONOUS INTENT.
"DUNCAN GAVE YOU A TRAITOR'S LANDS, BUT NAMED HIS SON HIS HEIR WHEN YOU DESERVED THE TITLE.
"HOW CLEVER TO TOSS THE MAN WHO SAVED HIS KINGDOM A CRUMB OF POWER, TO SHUT HIM UP WHEN USELESS MALCOLM IS GIVEN THE WHOLE PIE.
"IF YOU PROTEST, YOU ARE SELFISH, EVEN AS ALL HONOR GOES TO A BOY WHOSE EVERY BREATH IS STOLEN.
"WHO CAME BACK OUT OF THOSE WOODS WHEN YOUR SON, LULACH, DID NOT."

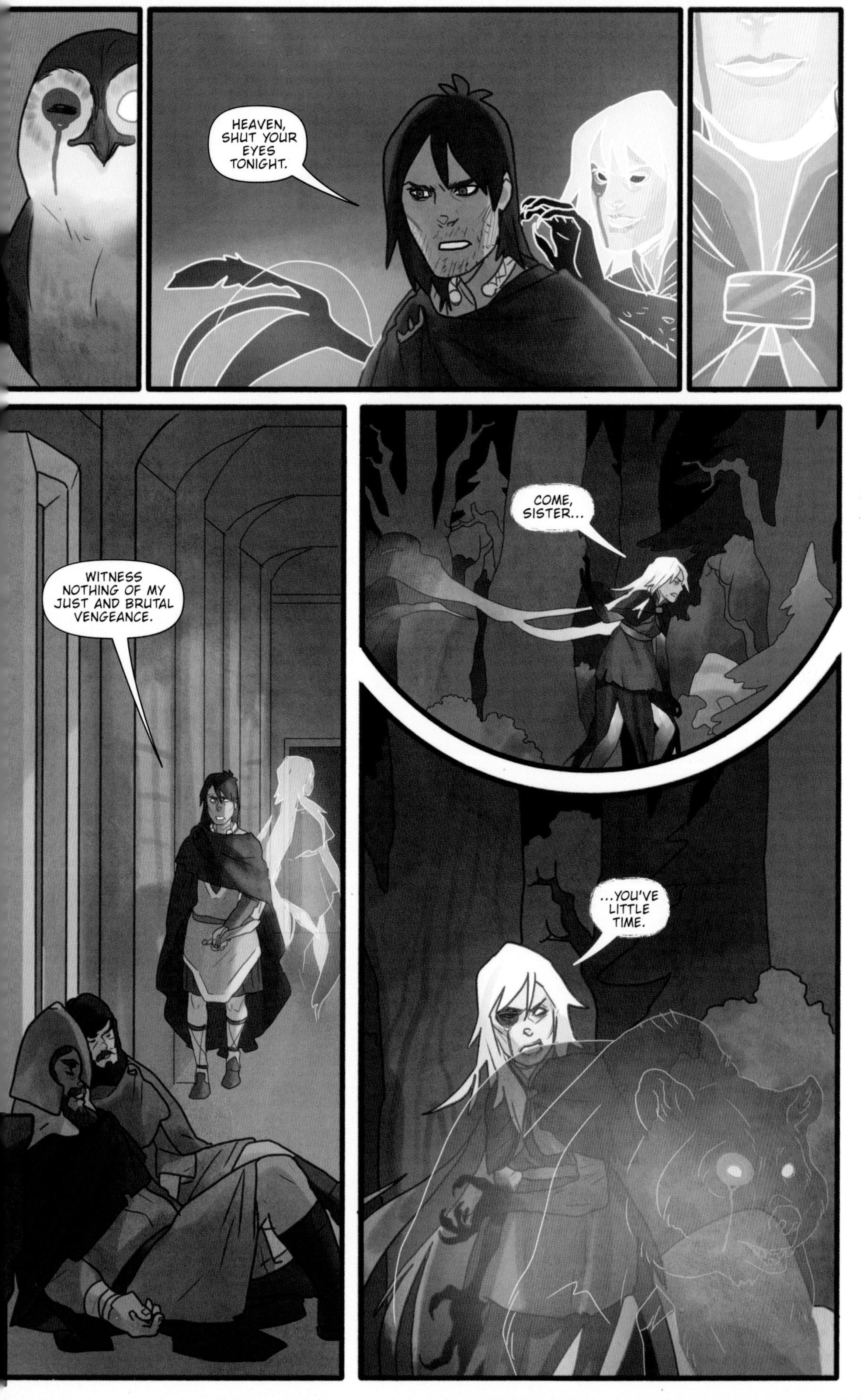
HEAVEN, SHUT YOUR EYES TONIGHT.
WITNESS NOTHING OF MY JUST AND BRUTAL VENGEANCE.
COME, SISTER...
...YOU'VE LITTLE TIME.

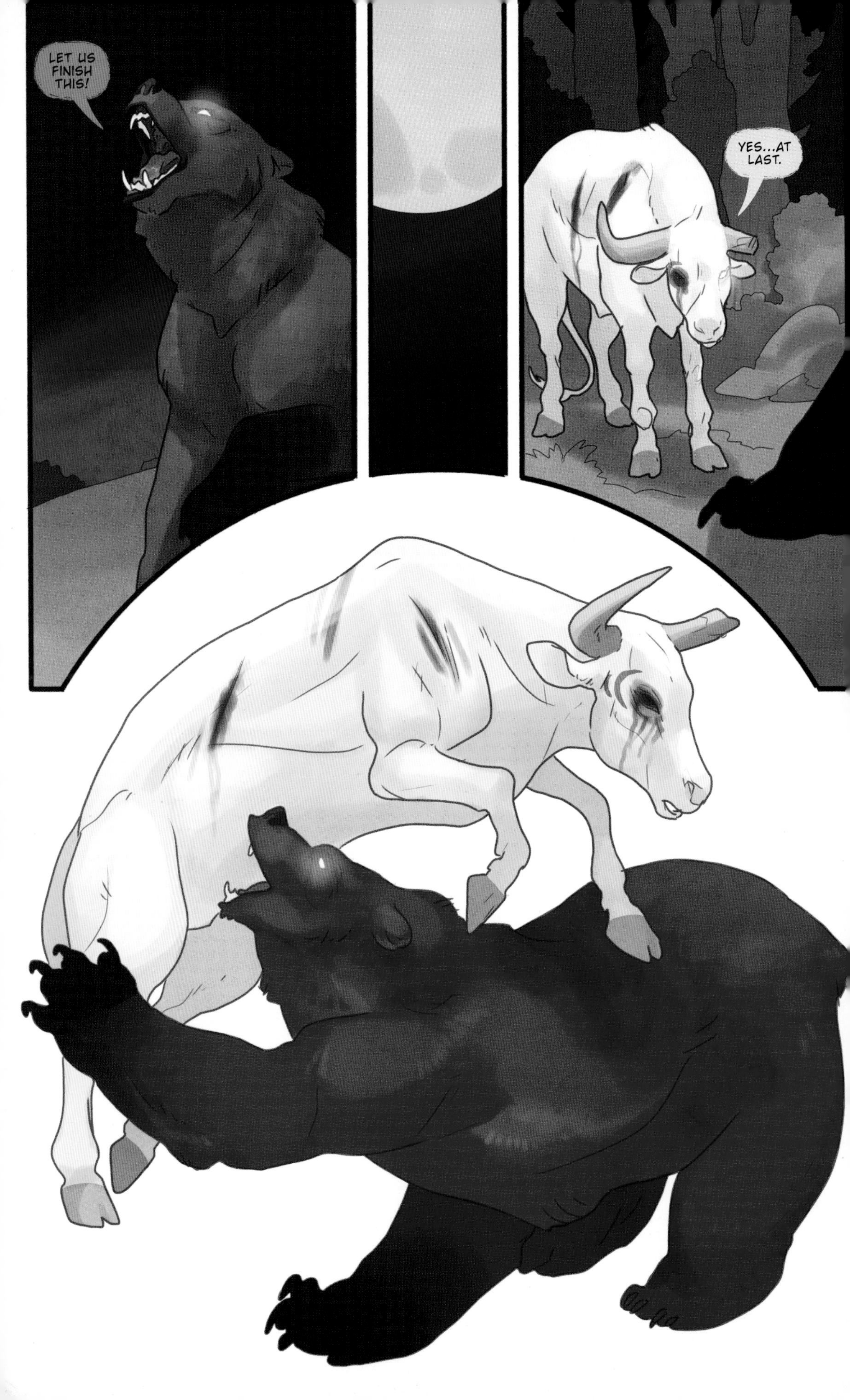
LET US FINISH THIS!
YES...AT LAST.

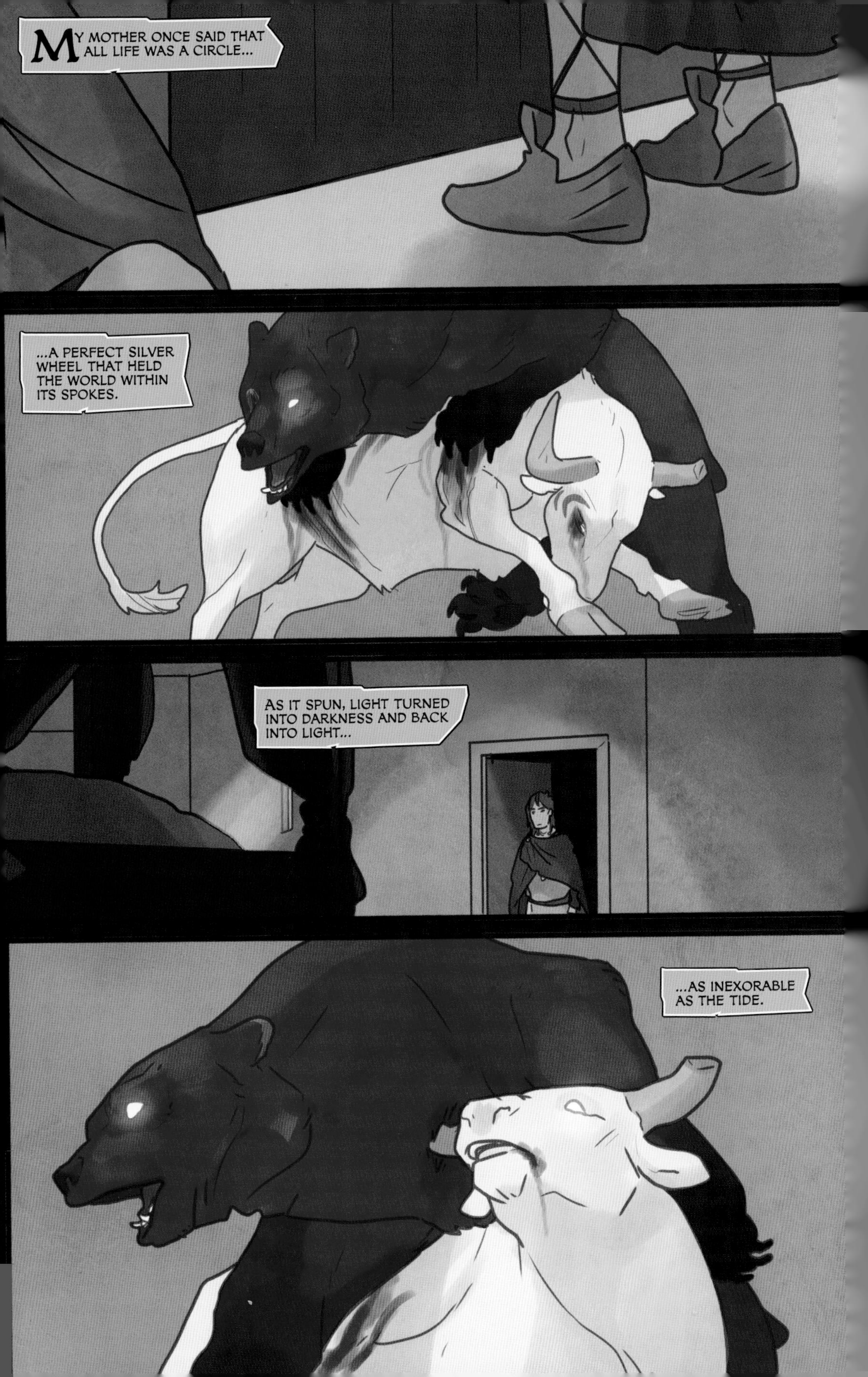
MY MOTHER ONCE SAID THAT ALL LIFE WAS A CIRCLE...
...A PERFECT SILVER WHEEL THAT HELD THE WORLD WITHIN ITS SPOKES.
AS IT SPUN, LIGHT TURNED INTO DARKNESS AND BACK INTO LIGHT...
...AS INEXORABLE AS THE TIDE.

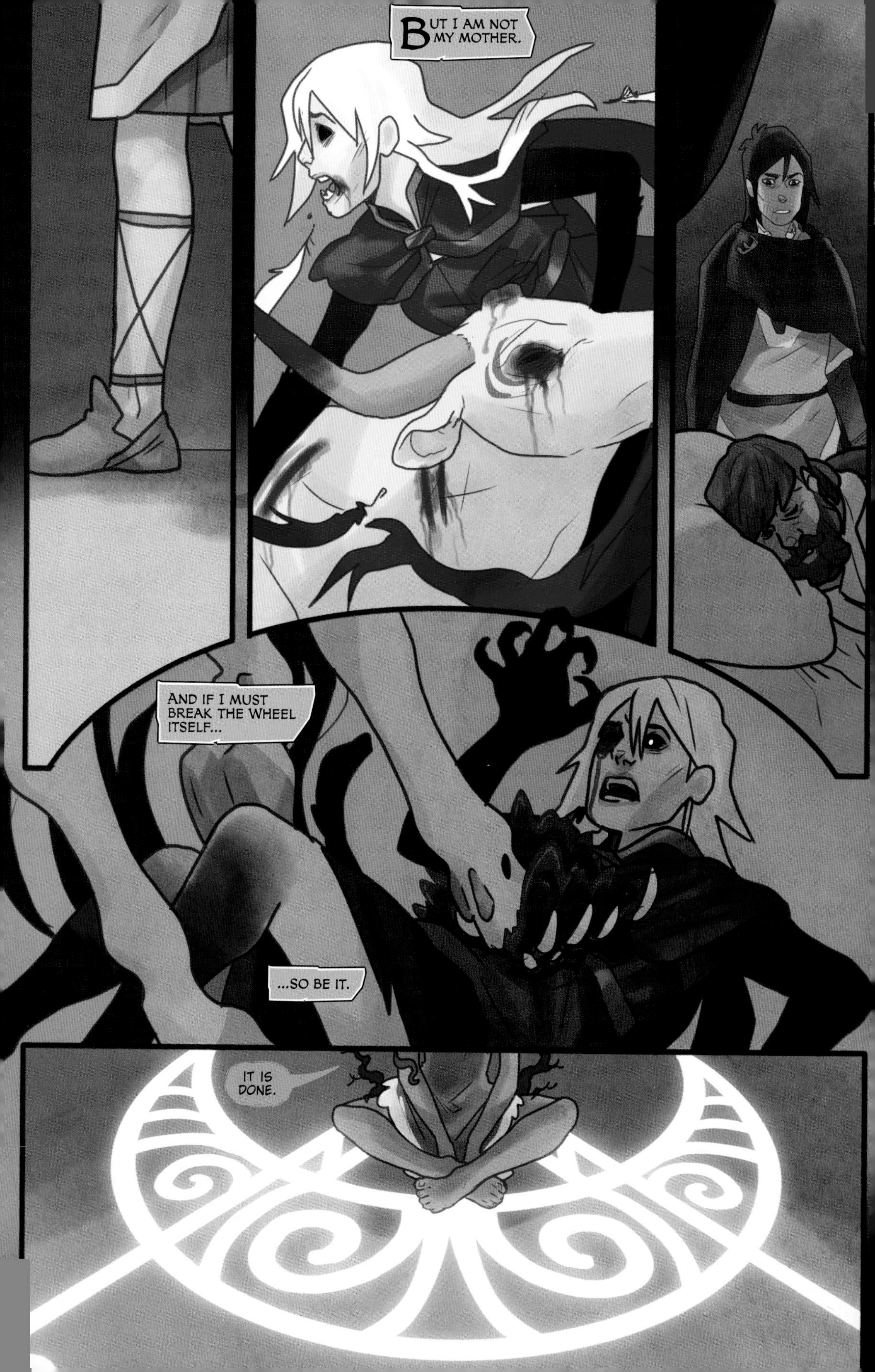
BUT I AM NOT MY MOTHER.
AND IF I MUST BREAK THE WHEEL ITSELF...
...SO BE IT.
IT IS DONE.

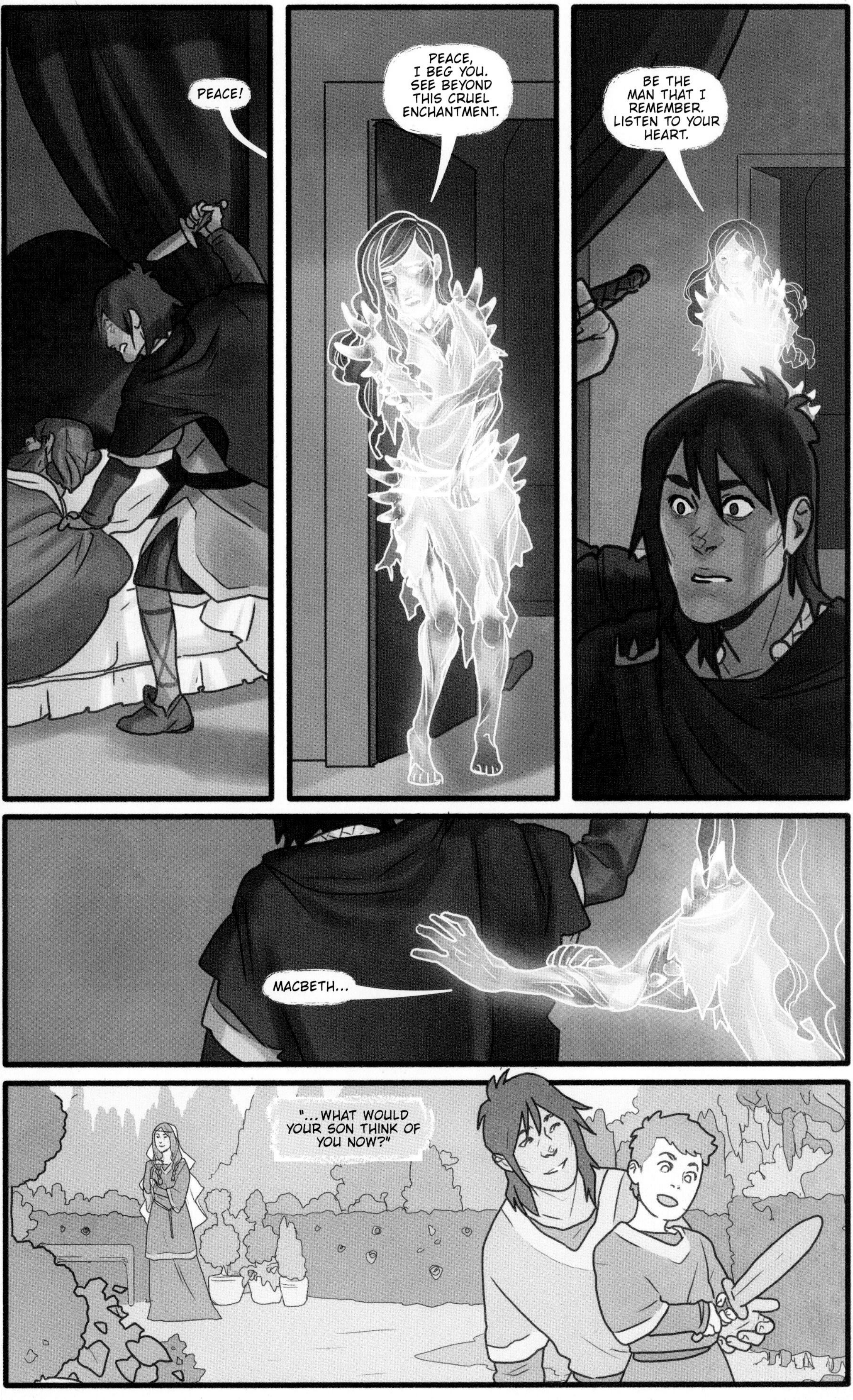
PEACE!
PEACE, I BEG YOU. SEE BEYOND THIS CRUEL ENCHANTMENT.
BE THE MAN THAT I REMEMBER. LISTEN TO YOUR HEART.
MACBETH...
"...WHAT WOULD YOUR SON THINK OF YOU NOW?"

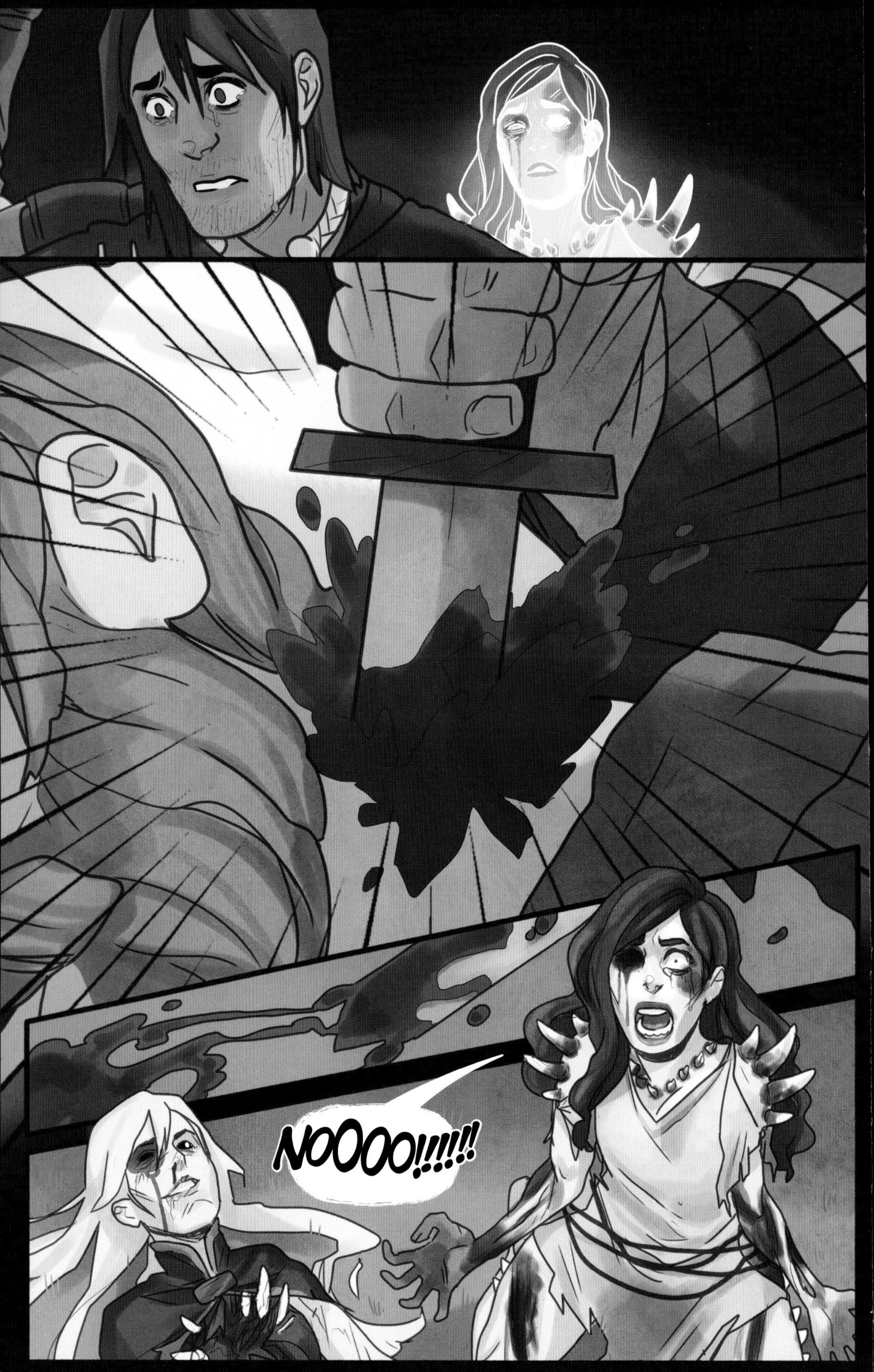
NOOOO!!!!!!

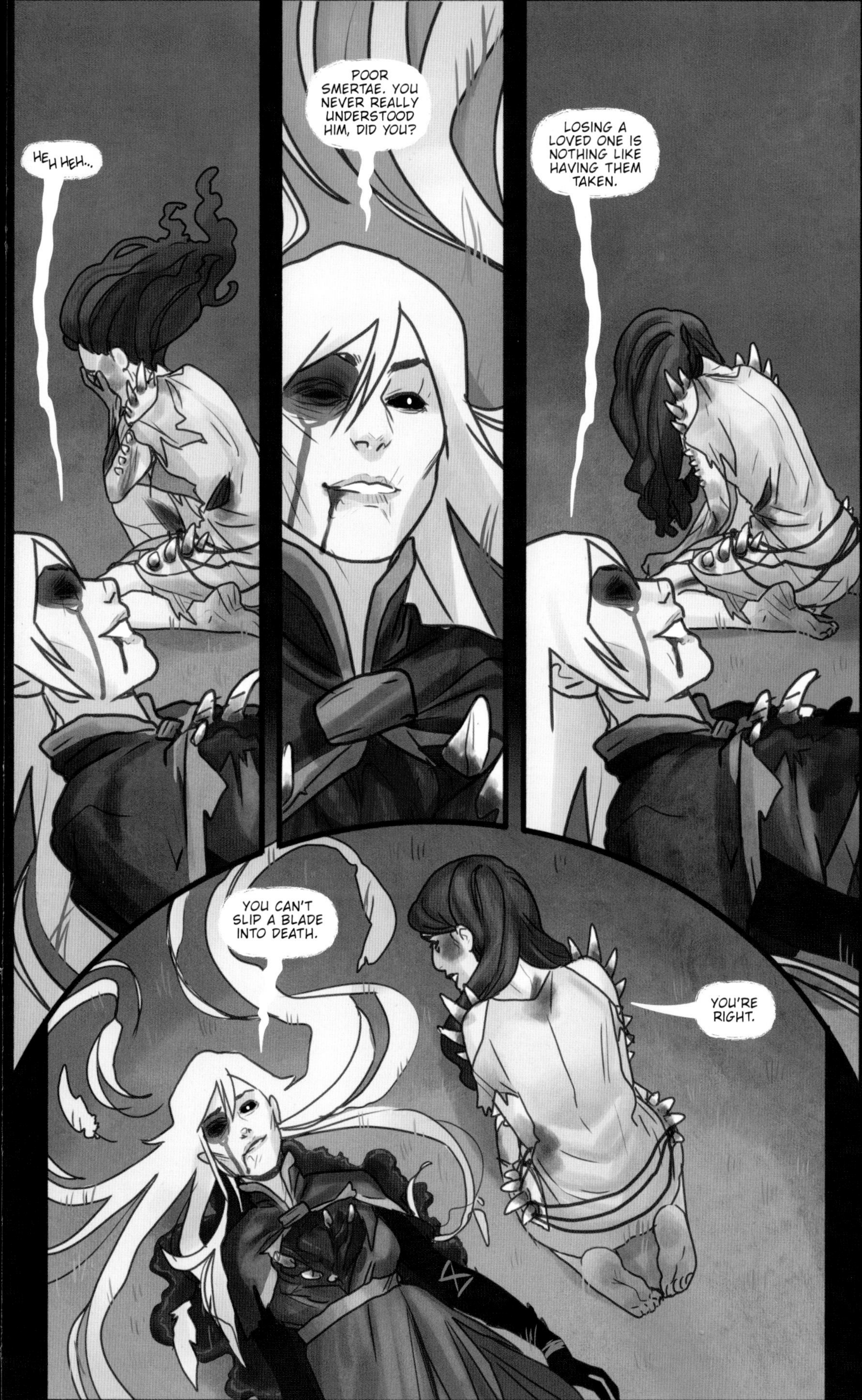
HEH HEH...
POOR SMERTAE. YOU NEVER REALLY UNDERSTOOD HIM, DID YOU?
LOSING A LOVED ONE IS NOTHING LIKE HAVING THEM TAKEN.
YOU CAN'T SLIP A BLADE INTO DEATH.
YOU'RE RIGHT.

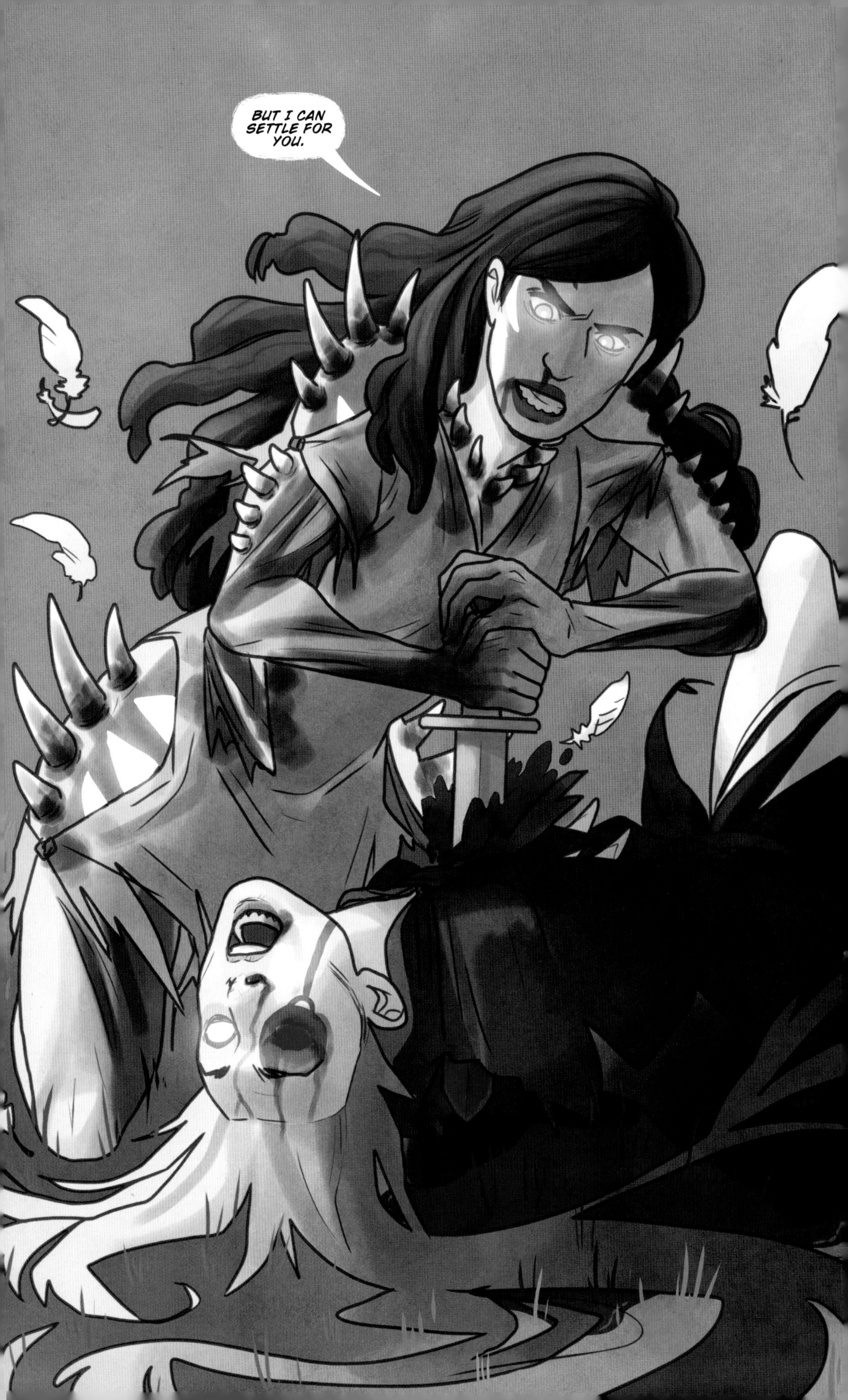
BUT I CAN SETTLE FOR YOU.

Act Six

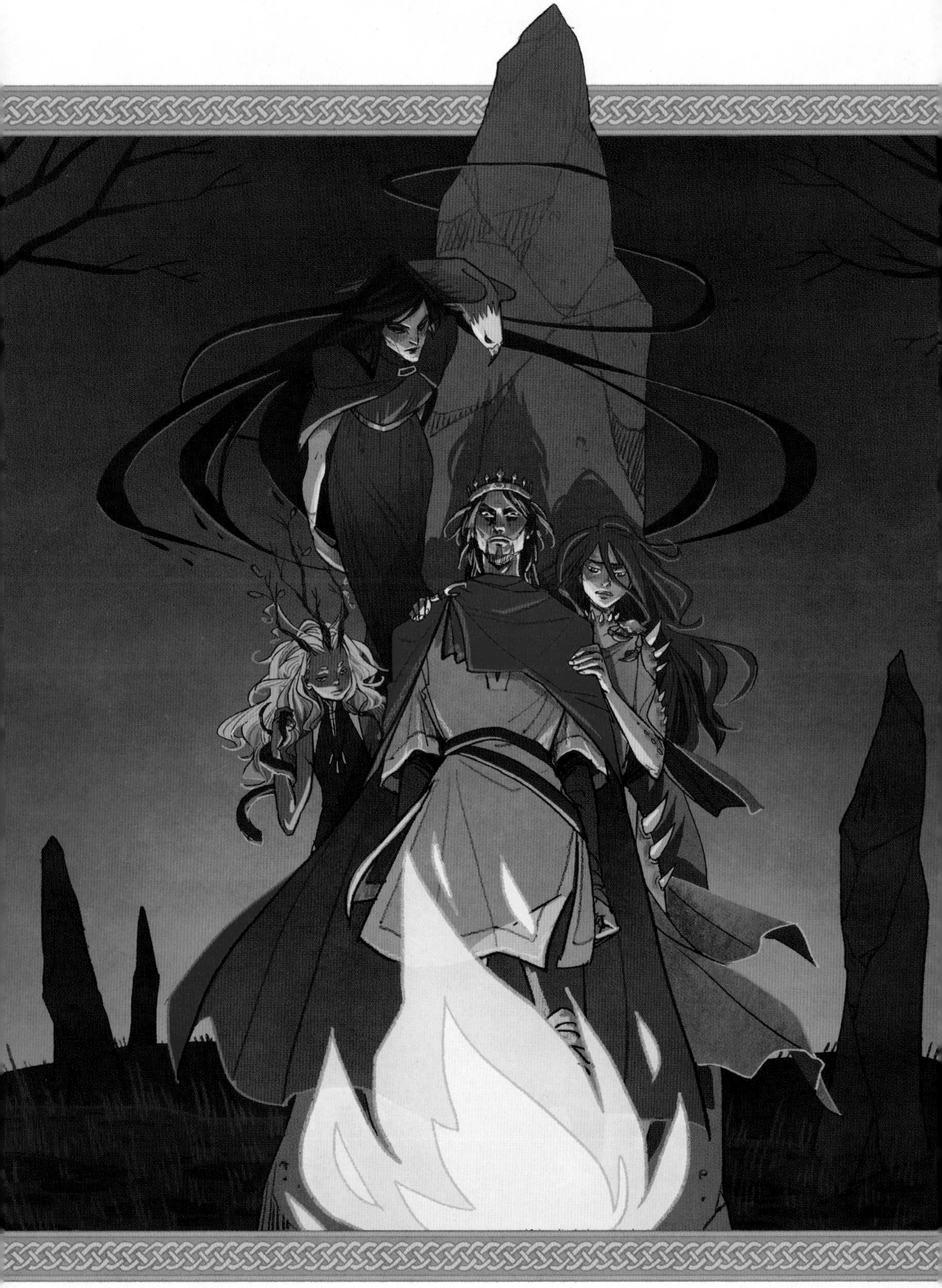

Issue Six Cover by Kyla Vanderklugt

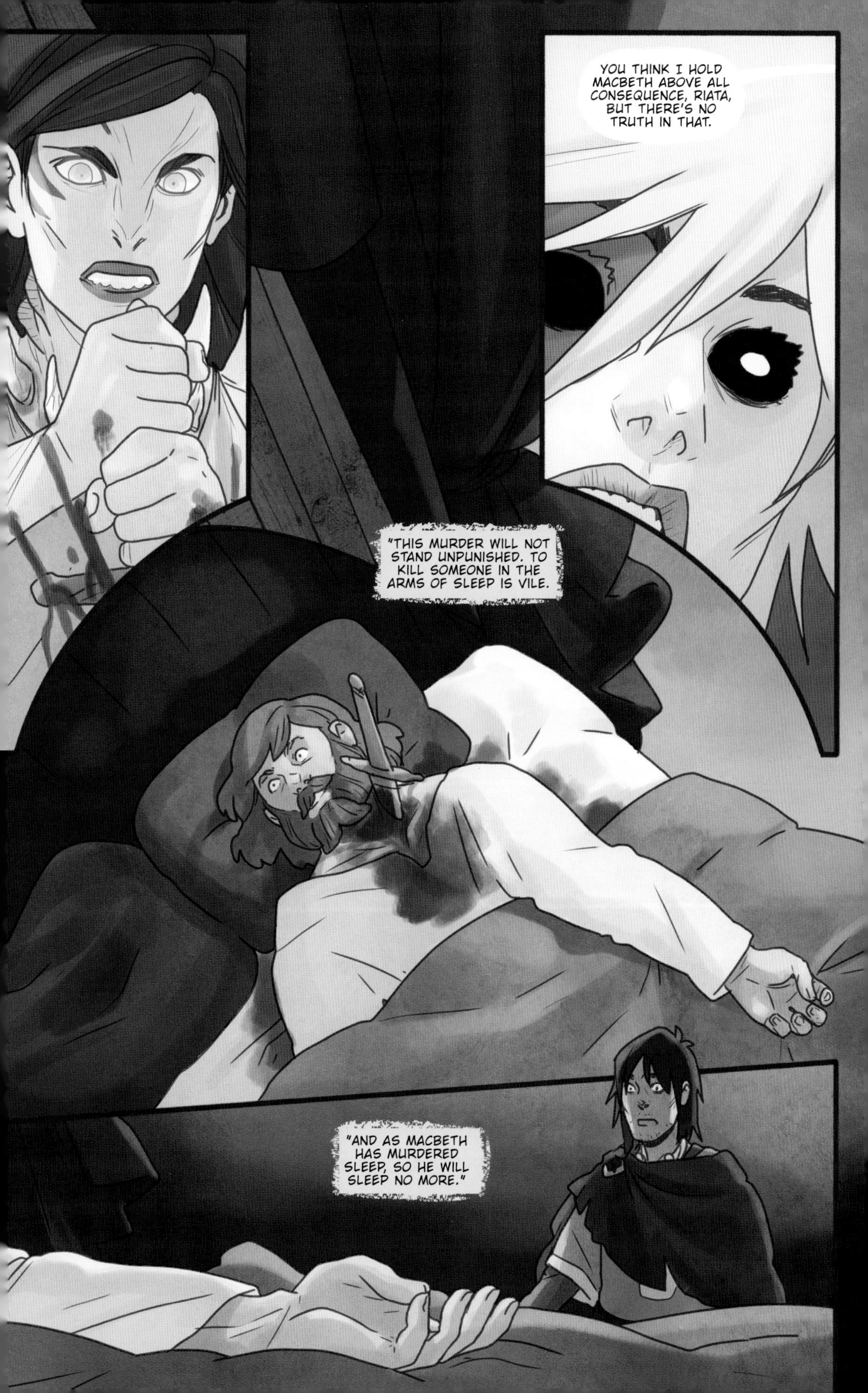
YOU THINK I HOLD MACBETH ABOVE ALL CONSEQUENCE, RIATA, BUT THERE'S NO TRUTH IN THAT.
"THIS MURDER WILL NOT STAND UNPUNISHED. TO KILL SOMEONE IN THE ARMS OF SLEEP IS VILE.
"AND AS MACBETH HAS MURDERED SLEEP, SO HE WILL SLEEP NO MORE."

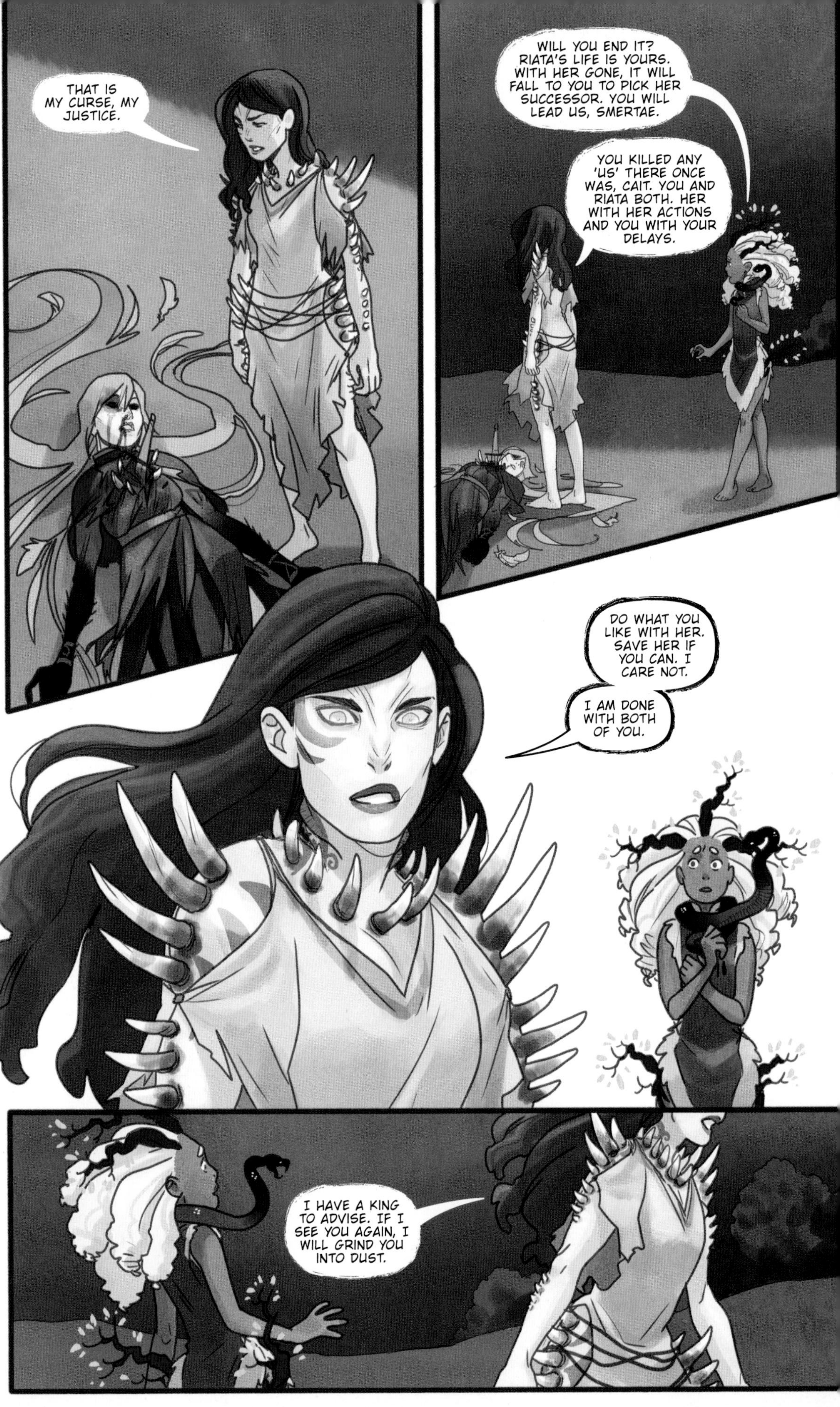
THAT IS MY CURSE, MY JUSTICE.
WILL YOU END IT? RIATA'S LIFE IS YOURS. WITH HER GONE, IT WILL FALL TO YOU TO PICK HER SUCCESSOR. YOU WILL LEAD US, SMERTAE.
YOU KILLED ANY 'US' THERE ONCE WAS, CAIT. YOU AND RIATA BOTH. HER WITH HER ACTIONS AND YOU WITH YOUR DELAYS.
DO WHAT YOU LIKE WITH HER. SAVE HER IF YOU CAN. I CARE NOT.
I AM DONE WITH BOTH OF YOU.
I HAVE A KING TO ADVISE. IF I SEE YOU AGAIN, I WILL GRIND YOU INTO DUST.

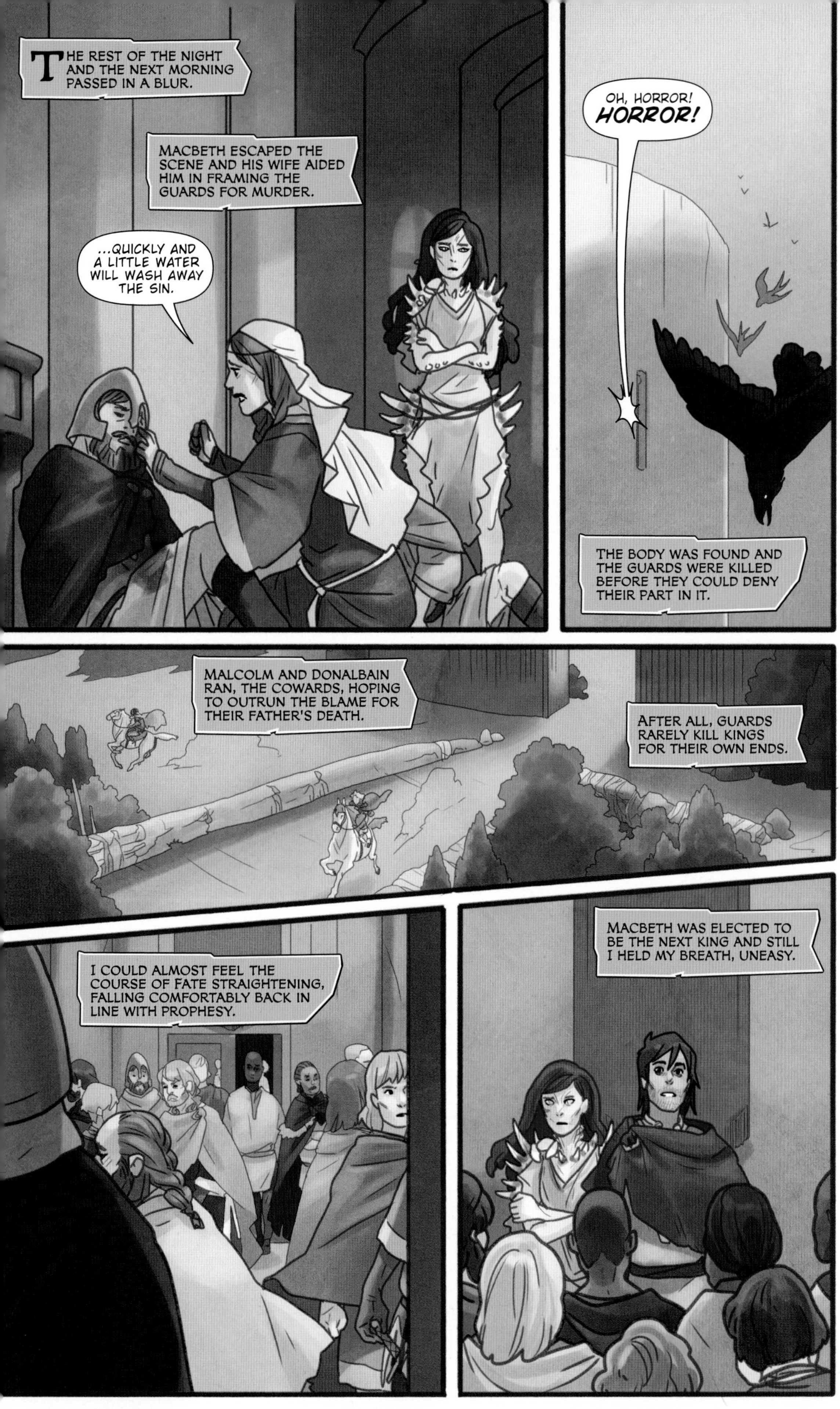
THE REST OF THE NIGHT AND THE NEXT MORNING PASSED IN A BLUR.
MACBETH ESCAPED THE SCENE AND HIS WIFE AIDED HIM IN FRAMING THE GUARDS FOR MURDER.
...QUICKLY AND A LITTLE WATER WILL WASH AWAY THE SIN.
OH, HORROR! HORROR!
THE BODY WAS FOUND AND THE GUARDS WERE KILLED BEFORE THEY COULD DENY THEIR PART IN IT.
MALCOLM AND DONALBAIN RAN, THE COWARDS, HOPING TO OUTRUN THE BLAME FOR THEIR FATHER'S DEATH.
AFTER ALL, GUARDS RARELY KILL KINGS FOR THEIR OWN ENDS.
I COULD ALMOST FEEL THE COURSE OF FATE STRAIGHTENING, FALLING COMFORTABLY BACK IN LINE WITH PROPHESY.
MACBETH WAS ELECTED TO BE THE NEXT KING AND STILL I HELD MY BREATH, UNEASY.

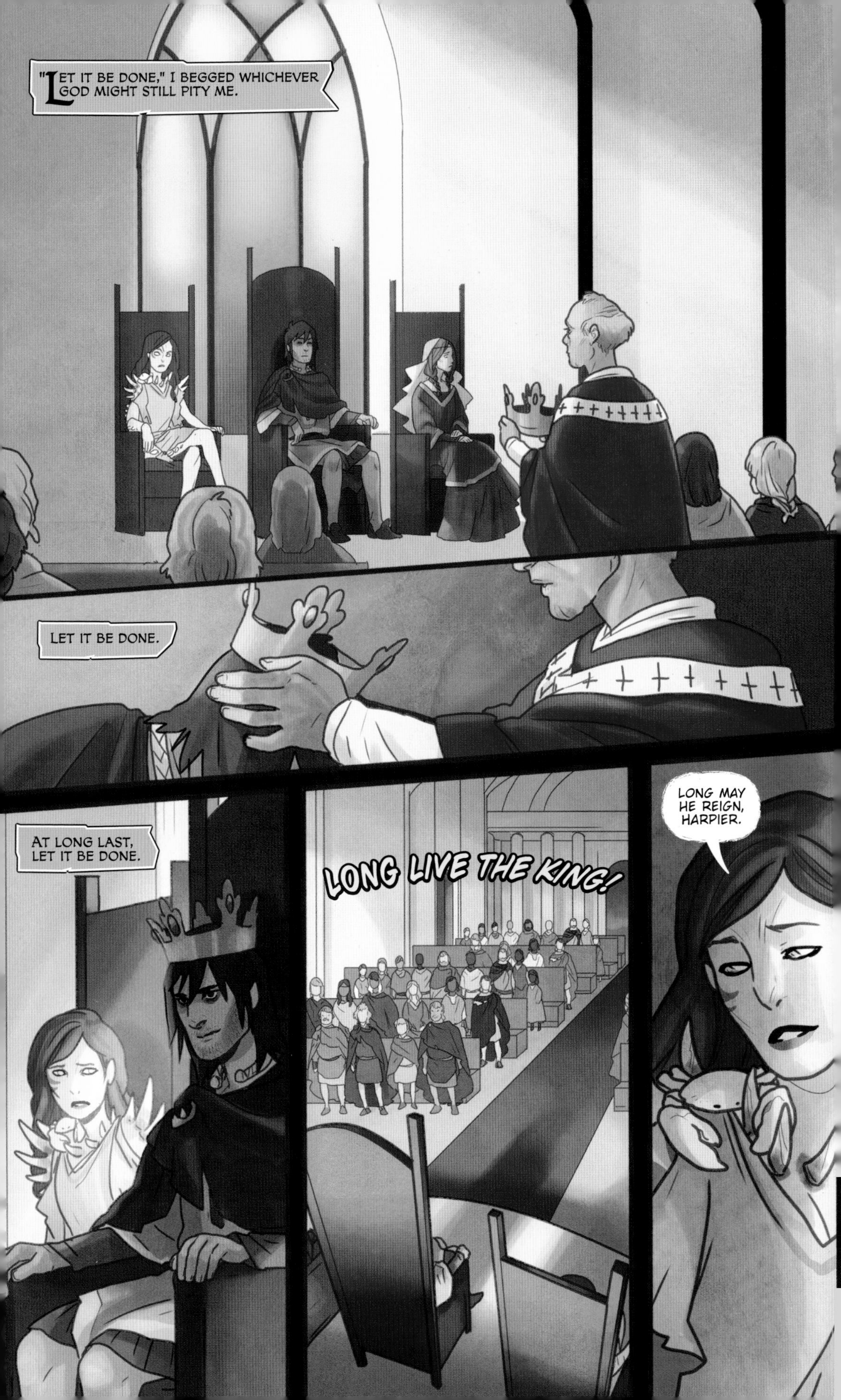
"LET IT BE DONE," I BEGGED WHICHEVER GOD MIGHT STILL PITY ME.
LET IT BE DONE.
AT LONG LAST, LET IT BE DONE.
LONG LIVE THE KING!
LONG MAY HE REIGN, HARPIER.

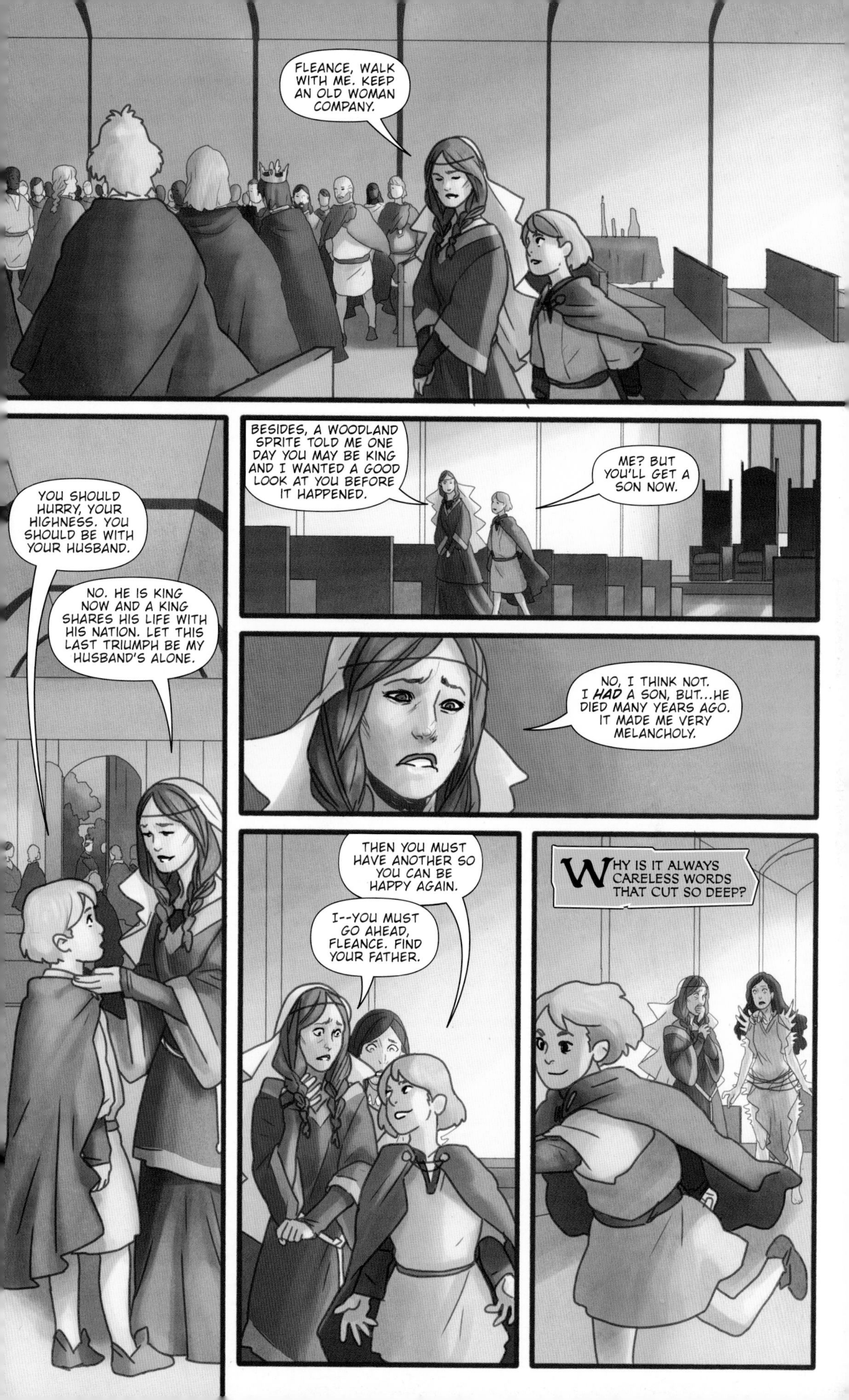
FLEANCE, WALK WITH ME. KEEP AN OLD WOMAN COMPANY.
YOU SHOULD HURRY, YOUR HIGHNESS. YOU SHOULD BE WITH YOUR HUSBAND.
NO. HE IS KING NOW AND A KING SHARES HIS LIFE WITH HIS NATION. LET THIS LAST TRIUMPH BE MY HUSBAND'S ALONE.
BESIDES, A WOODLAND SPRITE TOLD ME ONE DAY YOU MAY BE KING AND I WANTED A GOOD LOOK AT YOU BEFORE IT HAPPENED.
ME? BUT YOU'LL GET A SON NOW.
NO, I THINK NOT. I *HAD* A SON, BUT...HE DIED MANY YEARS AGO. IT MADE ME VERY MELANCHOLY.
THEN YOU MUST HAVE ANOTHER SO YOU CAN BE HAPPY AGAIN.
I--YOU MUST GO AHEAD, FLEANCE. FIND YOUR FATHER.
WHY IS IT ALWAYS CARELESS WORDS THAT CUT SO DEEP?

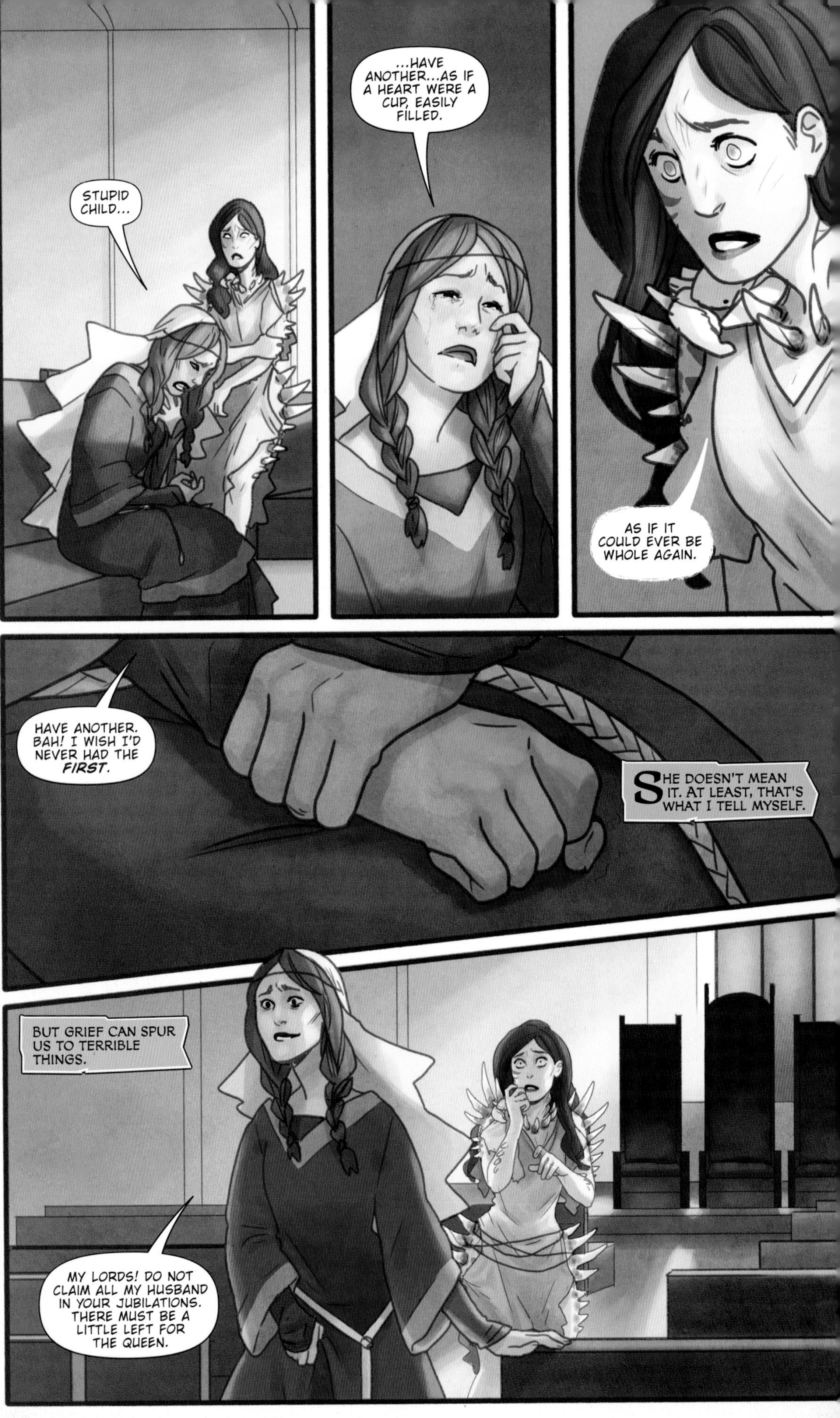
STUPID CHILD...
...HAVE ANOTHER...AS IF A HEART WERE A CUP, EASILY FILLED.
AS IF IT COULD EVER BE WHOLE AGAIN.
HAVE ANOTHER. BAH! I WISH I'D NEVER HAD THE FIRST.
SHE DOESN'T MEAN IT. AT LEAST, THAT'S WHAT I TELL MYSELF.
BUT GRIEF CAN SPUR US TO TERRIBLE THINGS.
MY LORDS! DO NOT CLAIM ALL MY HUSBAND IN YOUR JUBILATIONS. THERE MUST BE A LITTLE LEFT FOR THE QUEEN.

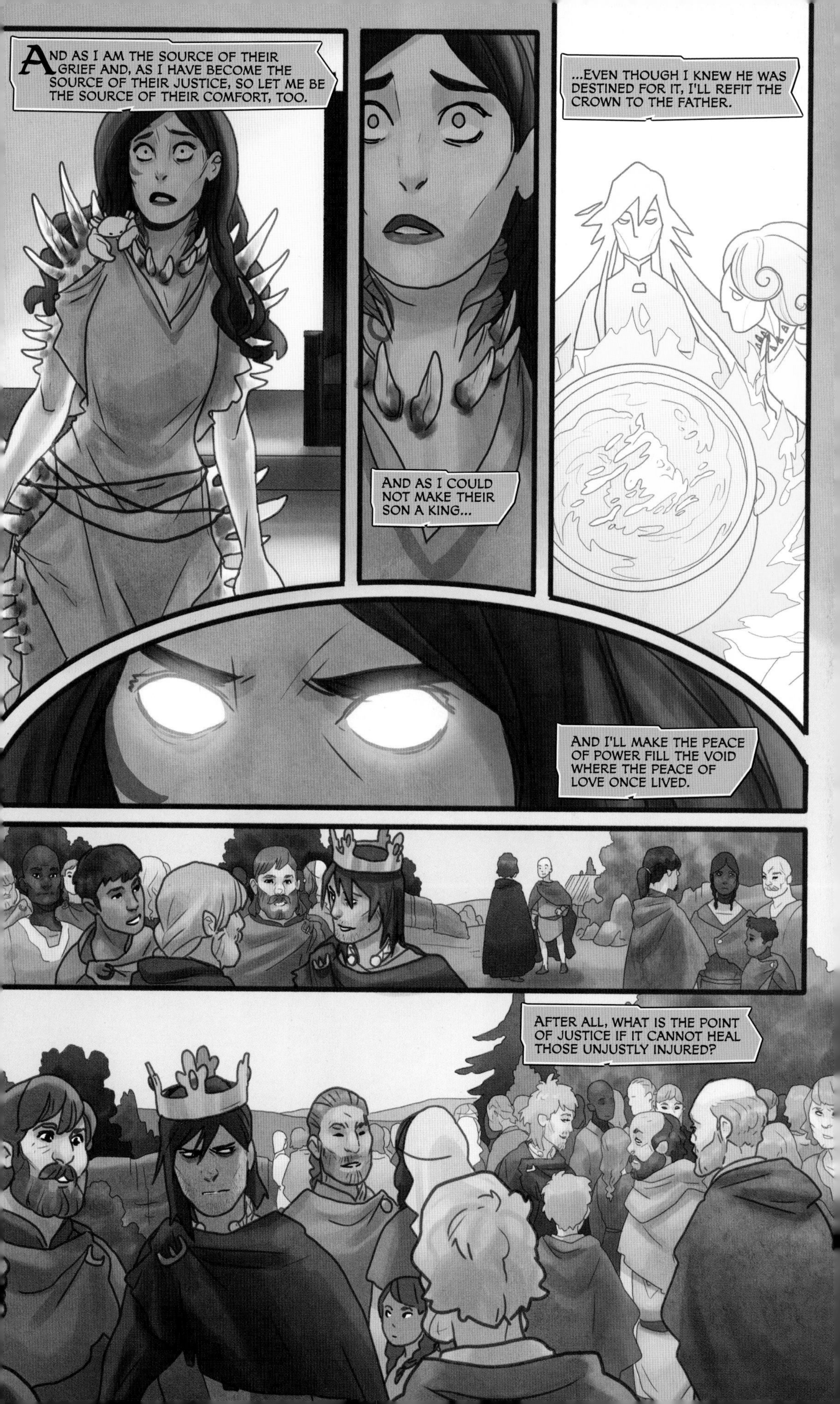
And as I am the source of their grief and, as I have become the source of their justice, so let me be the source of their comfort, too.
And as I could not make their son a king...
...Even though I knew he was destined for it, I'll refit the crown to the father.
And I'll make the peace of power fill the void where the peace of love once lived.
After all, what is the point of justice if it cannot heal those unjustly injured?

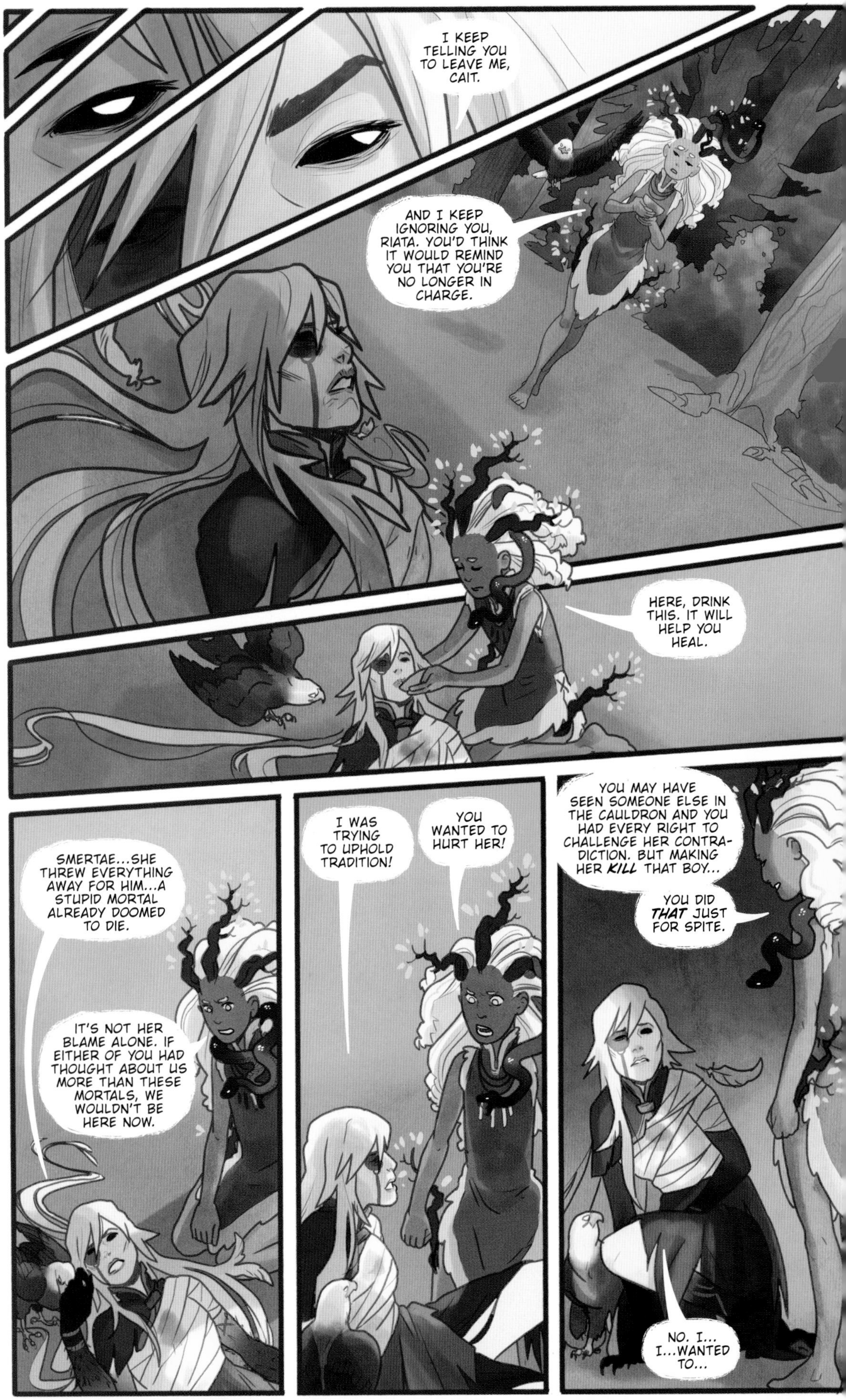
I KEEP TELLING YOU TO LEAVE ME, CAIT.
AND I KEEP IGNORING YOU, RIATA. YOU'D THINK IT WOULD REMIND YOU THAT YOU'RE NO LONGER IN CHARGE.
HERE, DRINK THIS. IT WILL HELP YOU HEAL.
SMERTAE...SHE THREW EVERYTHING AWAY FOR HIM...A STUPID MORTAL ALREADY DOOMED TO DIE.
IT'S NOT HER BLAME ALONE. IF EITHER OF YOU HAD THOUGHT ABOUT US MORE THAN THESE MORTALS, WE WOULDN'T BE HERE NOW.
I WAS TRYING TO UPHOLD TRADITION!
YOU WANTED TO HURT HER!
YOU MAY HAVE SEEN SOMEONE ELSE IN THE CAULDRON AND YOU HAD EVERY RIGHT TO CHALLENGE HER CONTRADICTION. BUT MAKING HER KILL THAT BOY...
YOU DID THAT JUST FOR SPITE.
NO. I... I...WANTED TO...

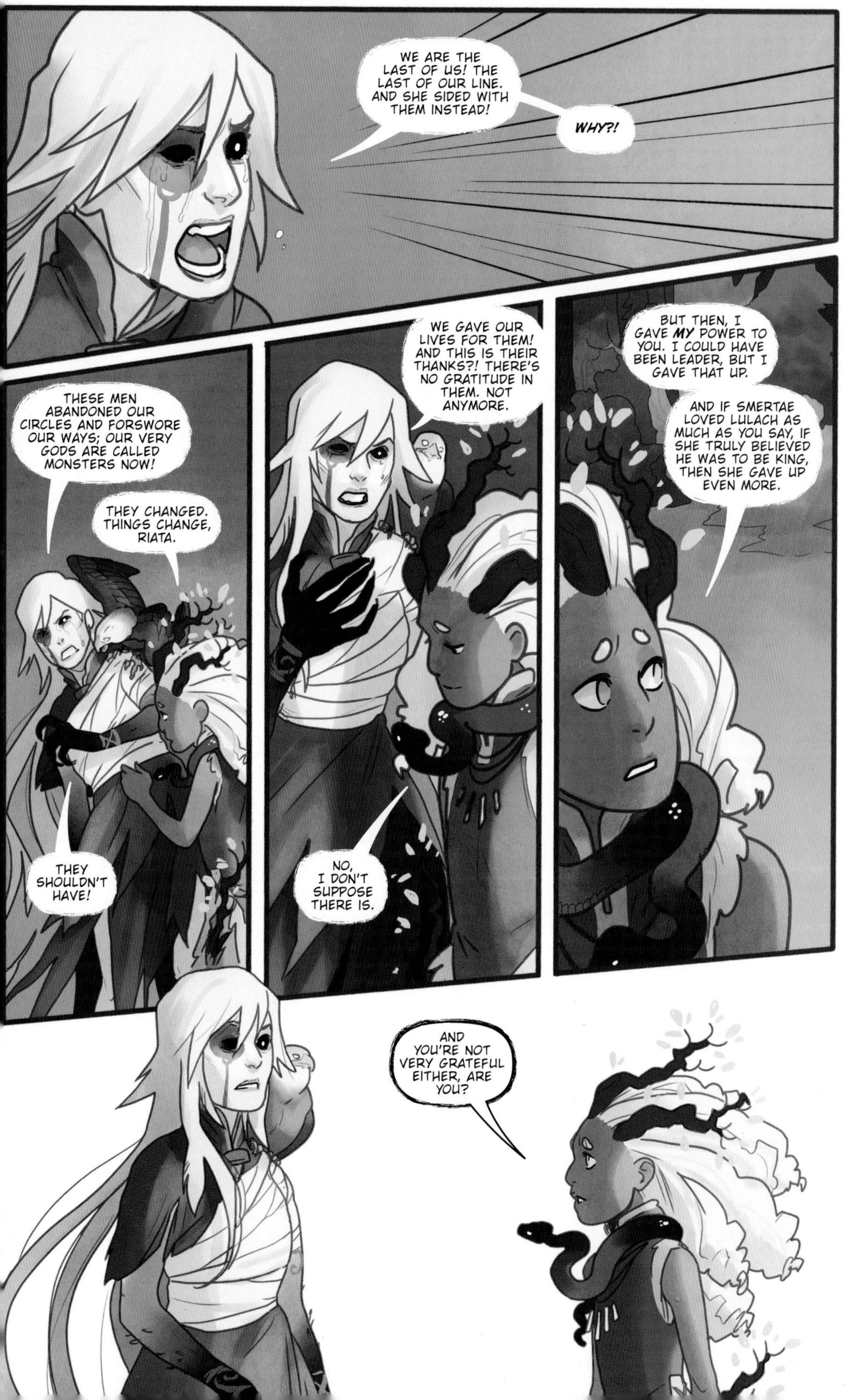
WE ARE THE LAST OF US! THE LAST OF OUR LINE. AND SHE SIDED WITH THEM INSTEAD!
WHY?!
THESE MEN ABANDONED OUR CIRCLES AND FORSWORE OUR WAYS; OUR VERY GODS ARE CALLED MONSTERS NOW!
THEY CHANGED. THINGS CHANGE, RIATA.
THEY SHOULDN'T HAVE!
WE GAVE OUR LIVES FOR THEM! AND THIS IS THEIR THANKS?! THERE'S NO GRATITUDE IN THEM. NOT ANYMORE.
NO, I DON'T SUPPOSE THERE IS.
BUT THEN, I GAVE MY POWER TO YOU. I COULD HAVE BEEN LEADER, BUT I GAVE THAT UP.
AND IF SMERTAE LOVED LULACH AS MUCH AS YOU SAY, IF SHE TRULY BELIEVED HE WAS TO BE KING, THEN SHE GAVE UP EVEN MORE.
AND YOU'RE NOT VERY GRATEFUL EITHER, ARE YOU?

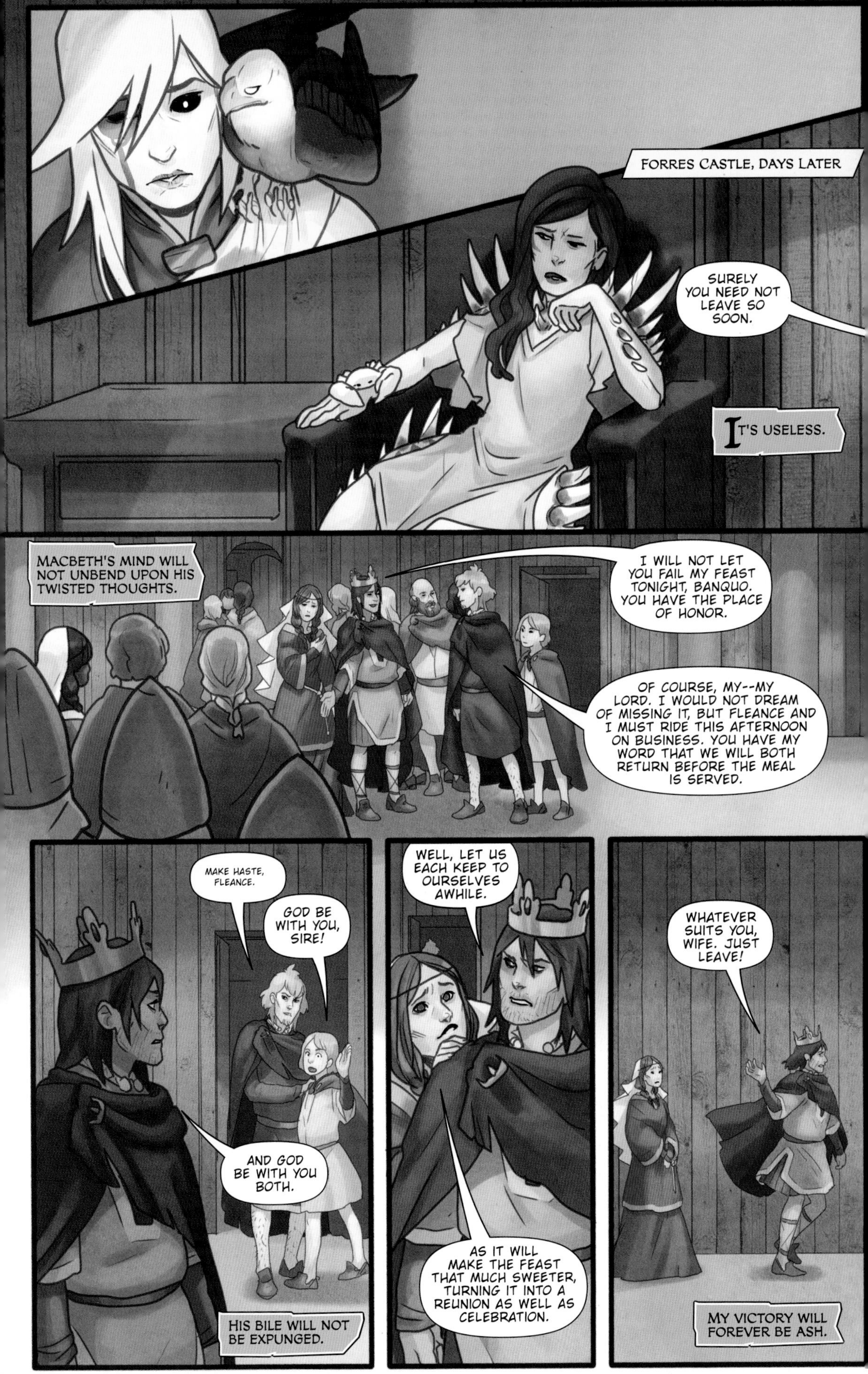
FORRES CASTLE, DAYS LATER
SURELY YOU NEED NOT LEAVE SO SOON.
IT'S USELESS.
MACBETH'S MIND WILL NOT UNBEND UPON HIS TWISTED THOUGHTS.
I WILL NOT LET YOU FAIL MY FEAST TONIGHT, BANQUO. YOU HAVE THE PLACE OF HONOR.
OF COURSE, MY--MY LORD. I WOULD NOT DREAM OF MISSING IT, BUT FLEANCE AND I MUST RIDE THIS AFTERNOON ON BUSINESS. YOU HAVE MY WORD THAT WE WILL BOTH RETURN BEFORE THE MEAL IS SERVED.
MAKE HASTE, FLEANCE.
GOD BE WITH YOU, SIRE!
AND GOD BE WITH YOU BOTH.
HIS BILE WILL NOT BE EXPUNGED.
WELL, LET US EACH KEEP TO OURSELVES AWHILE.
AS IT WILL MAKE THE FEAST THAT MUCH SWEETER, TURNING IT INTO A REUNION AS WELL AS CELEBRATION.
WHATEVER SUITS YOU, WIFE. JUST LEAVE!
MY VICTORY WILL FOREVER BE ASH.

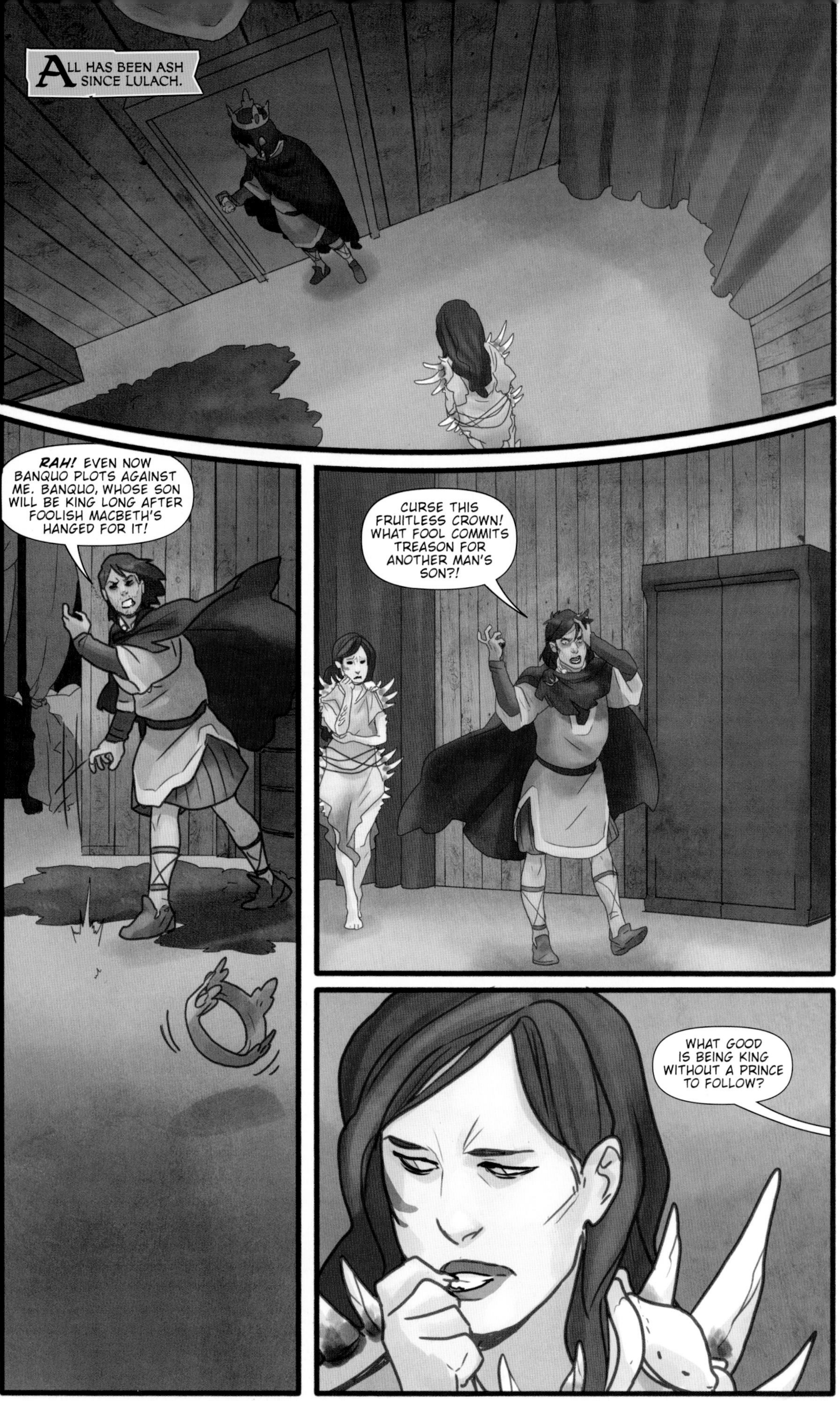
ALL HAS BEEN ASH SINCE LULACH.
RAH! EVEN NOW BANQUO PLOTS AGAINST ME. BANQUO, WHOSE SON WILL BE KING LONG AFTER FOOLISH MACBETH'S HANGED FOR IT!
CURSE THIS FRUITLESS CROWN! WHAT FOOL COMMITS TREASON FOR ANOTHER MAN'S SON?!
WHAT GOOD IS BEING KING WITHOUT A PRINCE TO FOLLOW?

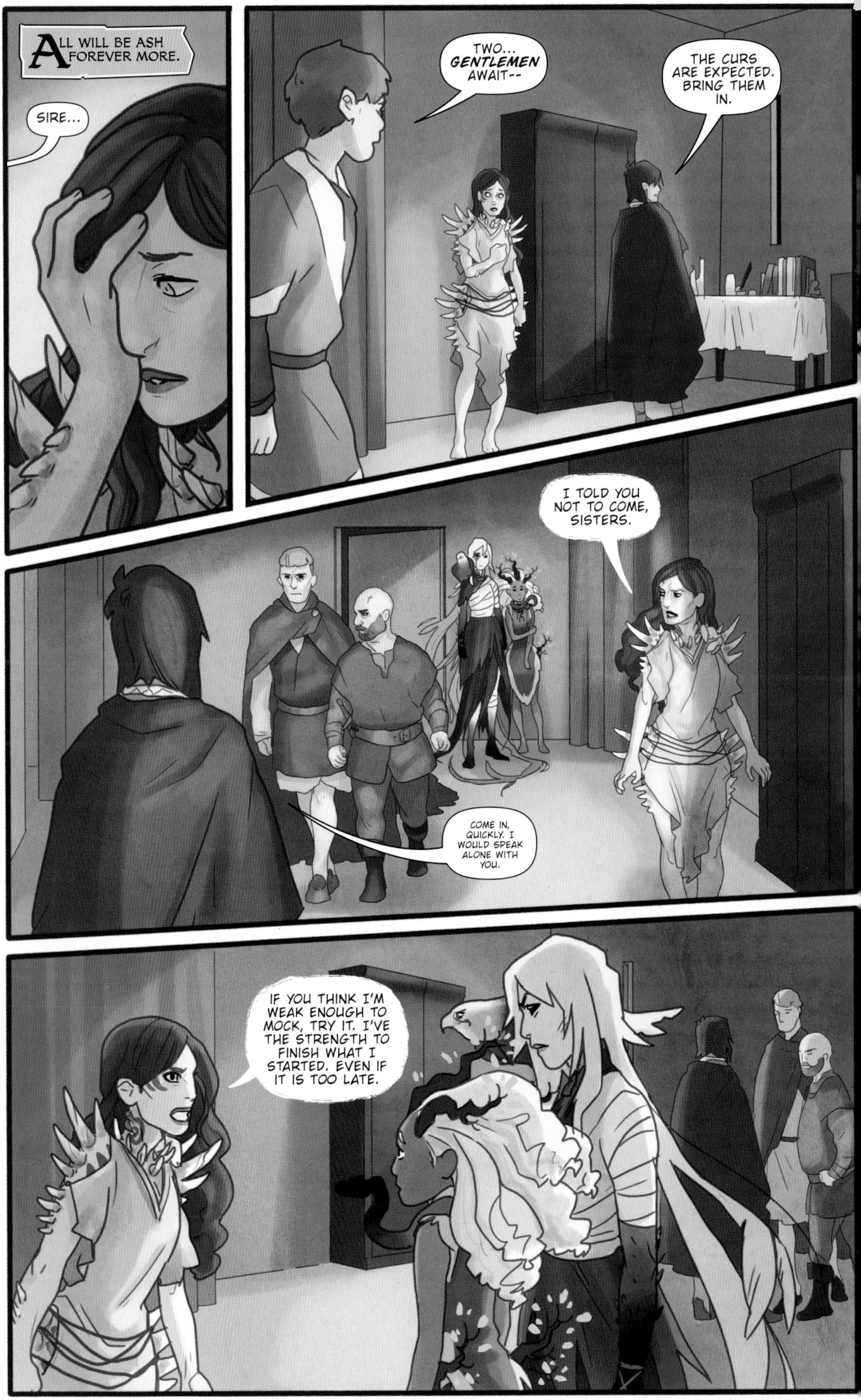
ALL WILL BE ASH FOREVER MORE.
SIRE...
TWO... **GENTLEMEN** AWAIT--
THE CURS ARE EXPECTED. BRING THEM IN.
I TOLD YOU NOT TO COME, SISTERS.
COME IN, QUICKLY. I WOULD SPEAK ALONE WITH YOU.
IF YOU THINK I'M WEAK ENOUGH TO MOCK, TRY IT. I'VE THE STRENGTH TO FINISH WHAT I STARTED. EVEN IF IT IS TOO LATE.

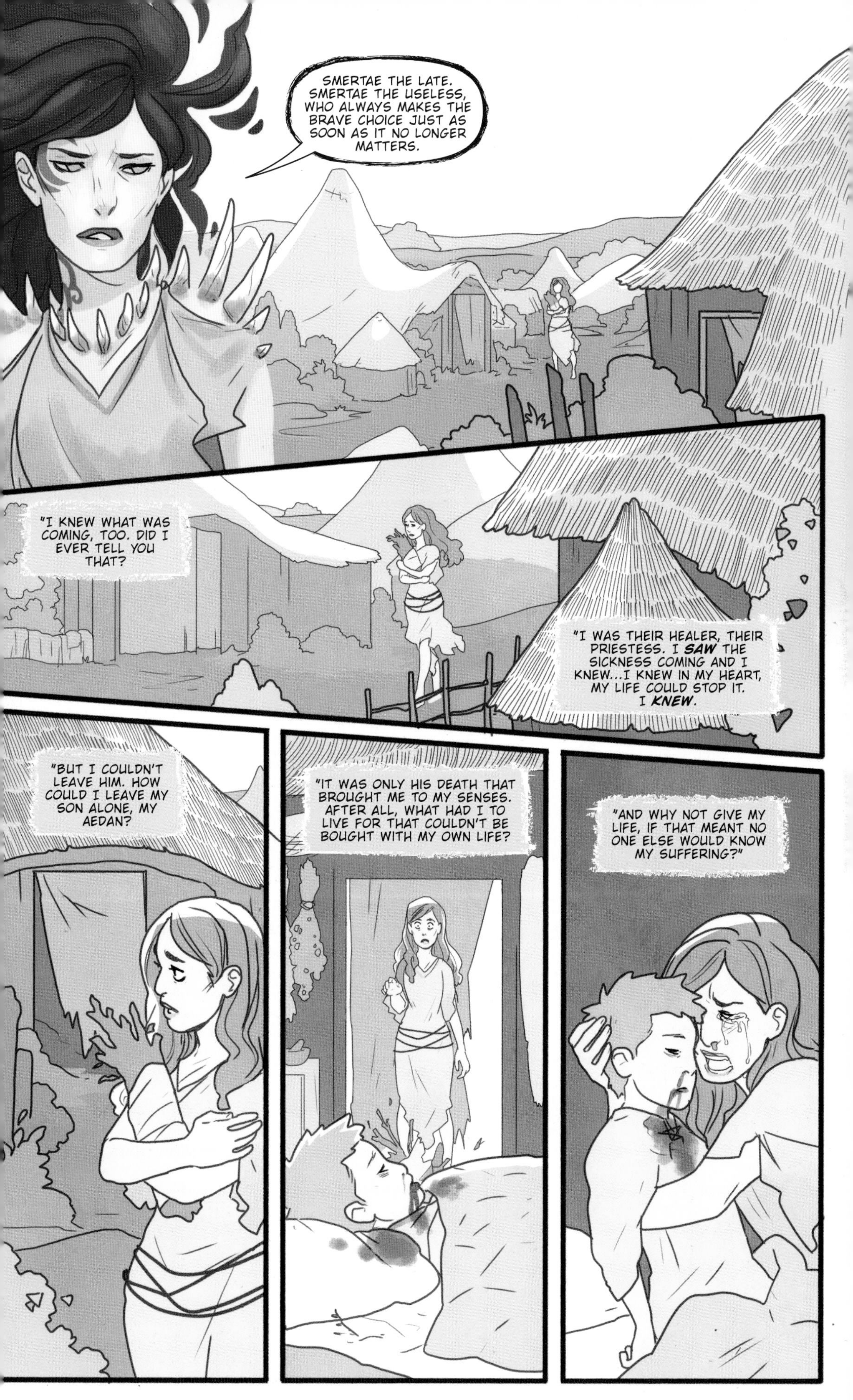
SMERTAE THE LATE. SMERTAE THE USELESS, WHO ALWAYS MAKES THE BRAVE CHOICE JUST AS SOON AS IT NO LONGER MATTERS.
"I KNEW WHAT WAS COMING, TOO. DID I EVER TELL YOU THAT?
"I WAS THEIR HEALER, THEIR PRIESTESS. I *SAW* THE SICKNESS COMING AND I KNEW...I KNEW IN MY HEART, MY LIFE COULD STOP IT. I *KNEW*.
"BUT I COULDN'T LEAVE HIM. HOW COULD I LEAVE MY SON ALONE, MY AEDAN?
"IT WAS ONLY HIS DEATH THAT BROUGHT ME TO MY SENSES. AFTER ALL, WHAT HAD I TO LIVE FOR THAT COULDN'T BE BOUGHT WITH MY OWN LIFE?
"AND WHY NOT GIVE MY LIFE, IF THAT MEANT NO ONE ELSE WOULD KNOW MY SUFFERING?"

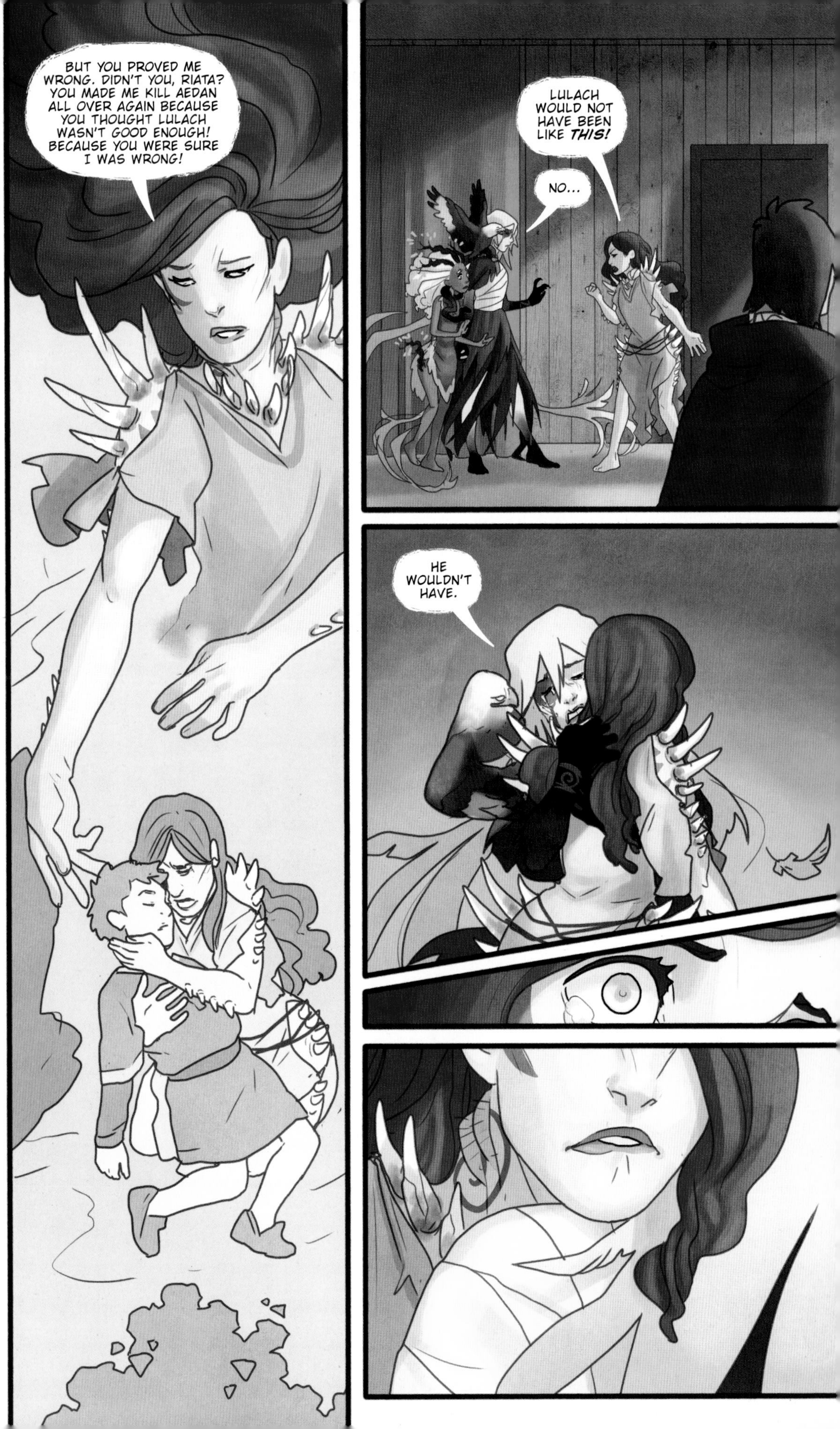
BUT YOU PROVED ME WRONG. DIDN'T YOU, RIATA? YOU MADE ME KILL AEDAN ALL OVER AGAIN BECAUSE YOU THOUGHT LULACH WASN'T GOOD ENOUGH! BECAUSE YOU WERE SURE I WAS WRONG!
LULACH WOULD NOT HAVE BEEN LIKE *THIS!*
NO...
HE WOULDN'T HAVE.

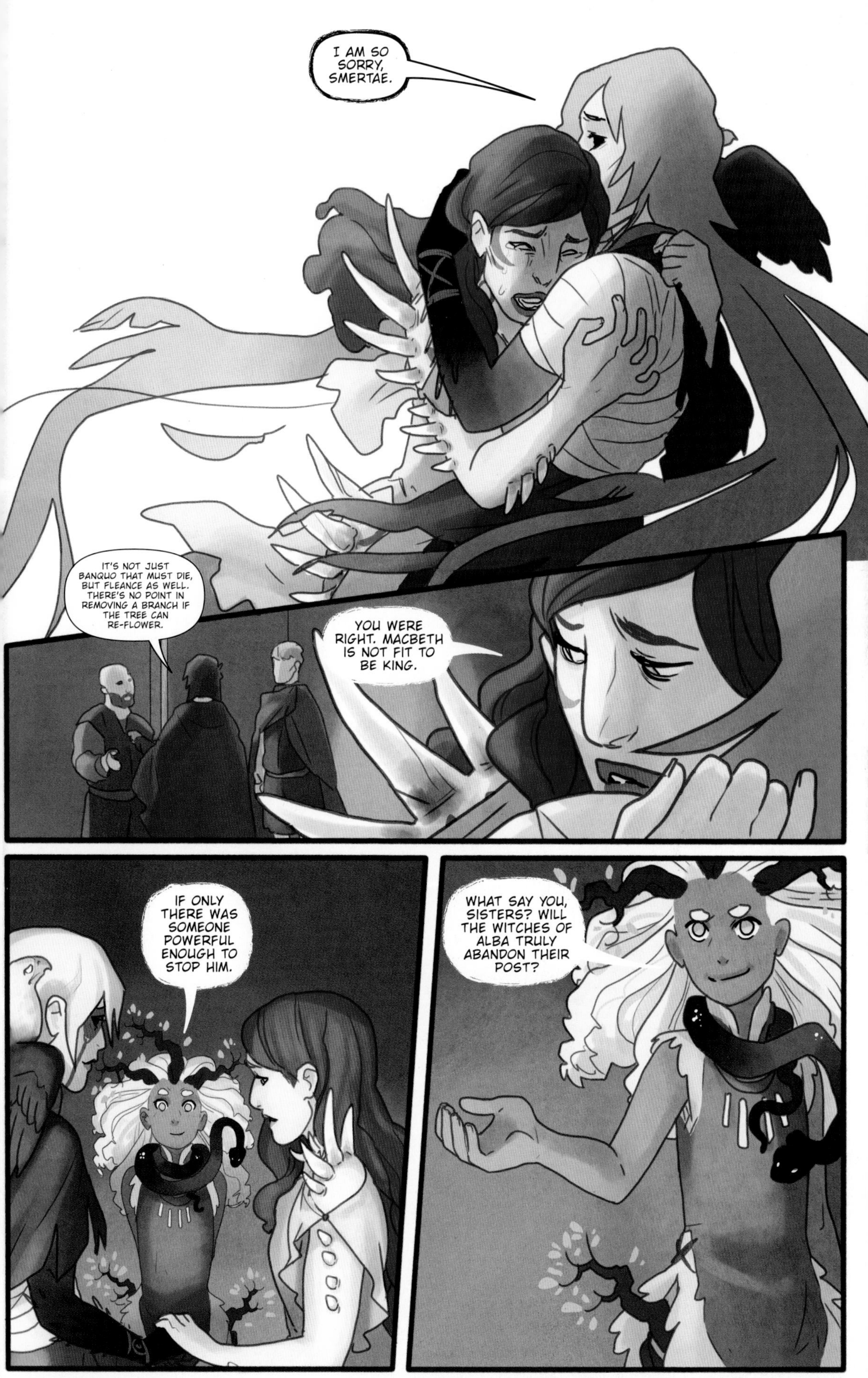
I AM SO SORRY, SMERTAE.
IT'S NOT JUST BANQUO THAT MUST DIE, BUT FLEANCE AS WELL. THERE'S NO POINT IN REMOVING A BRANCH IF THE TREE CAN RE-FLOWER.
YOU WERE RIGHT. MACBETH IS NOT FIT TO BE KING.
IF ONLY THERE WAS SOMEONE POWERFUL ENOUGH TO STOP HIM.
WHAT SAY YOU, SISTERS? WILL THE WITCHES OF ALBA TRULY ABANDON THEIR POST?

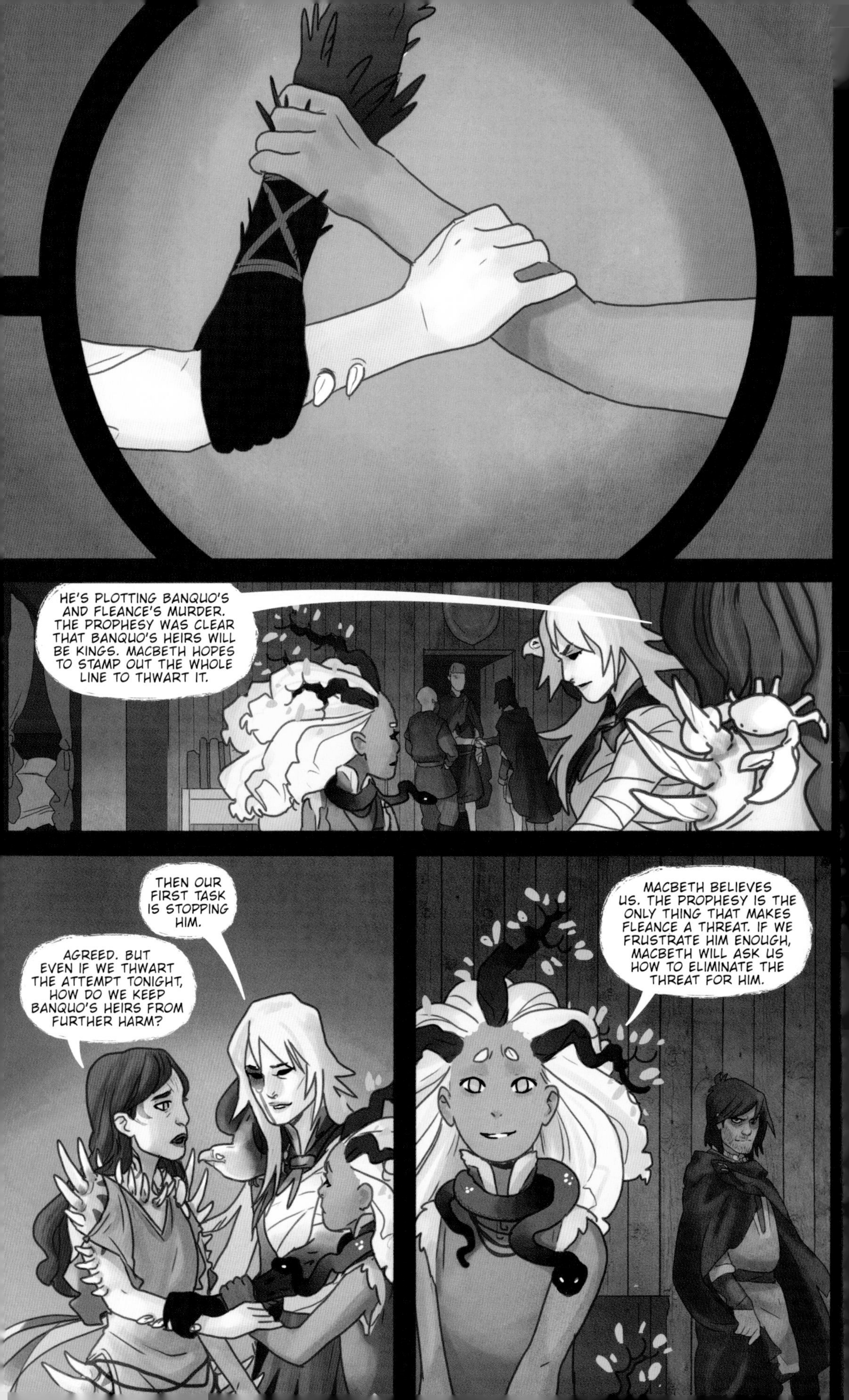
HE'S PLOTTING BANQUO'S AND FLEANCE'S MURDER. THE PROPHESY WAS CLEAR THAT BANQUO'S HEIRS WILL BE KINGS. MACBETH HOPES TO STAMP OUT THE WHOLE LINE TO THWART IT.
THEN OUR FIRST TASK IS STOPPING HIM.
AGREED. BUT EVEN IF WE THWART THE ATTEMPT TONIGHT, HOW DO WE KEEP BANQUO'S HEIRS FROM FURTHER HARM?
MACBETH BELIEVES US. THE PROPHESY IS THE ONLY THING THAT MAKES FLEANCE A THREAT. IF WE FRUSTRATE HIM ENOUGH, MACBETH WILL ASK US HOW TO ELIMINATE THE THREAT FOR HIM.

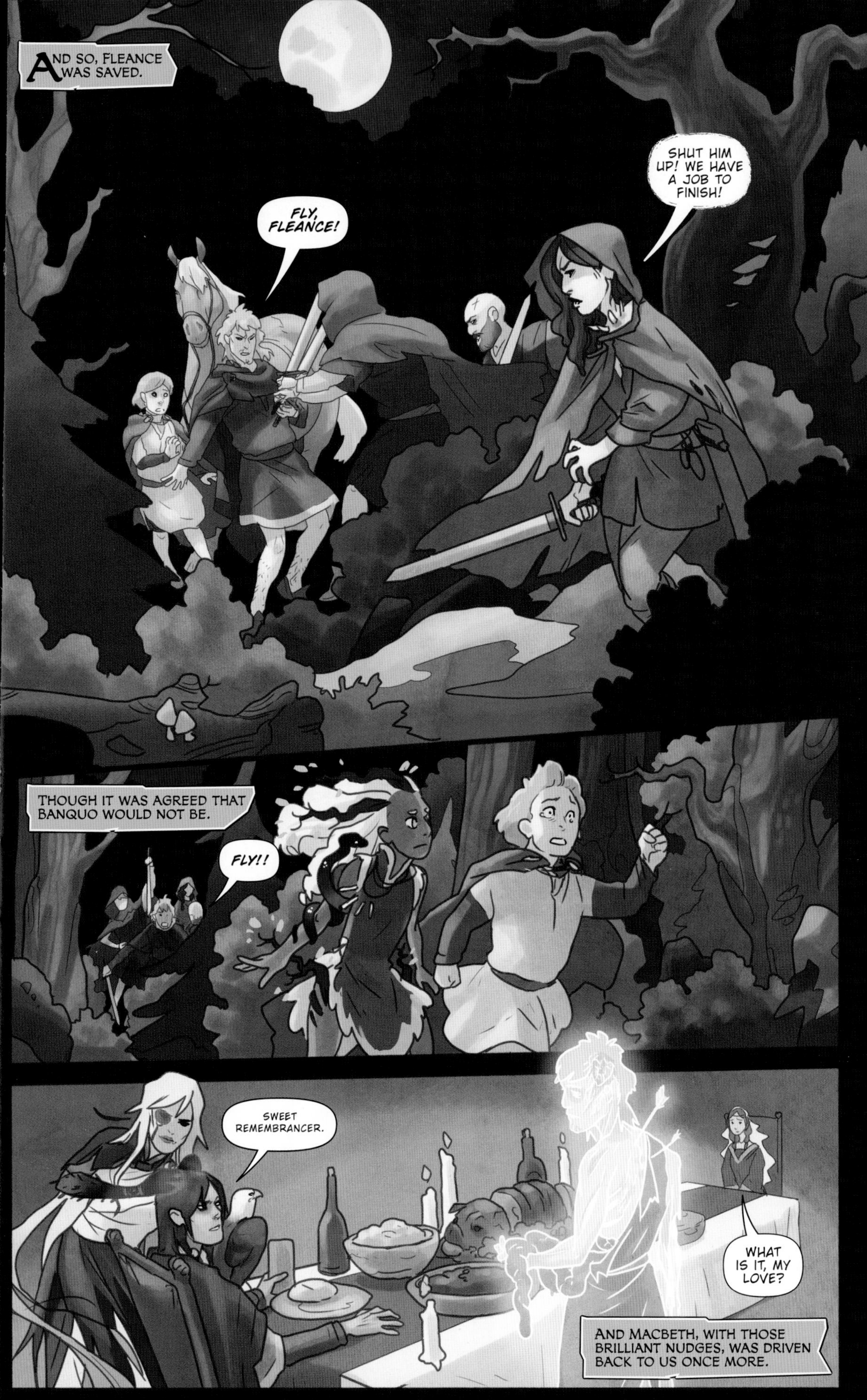

AND SO, FLEANCE WAS SAVED.
FLY, FLEANCE!
SHUT HIM UP! WE HAVE A JOB TO FINISH!
THOUGH IT WAS AGREED THAT BANQUO WOULD NOT BE.
FLY!!
SWEET REMEMBRANCER.
WHAT IS IT, MY LOVE?
AND MACBETH, WITH THOSE BRILLIANT NUDGES, WAS DRIVEN BACK TO US ONCE MORE.

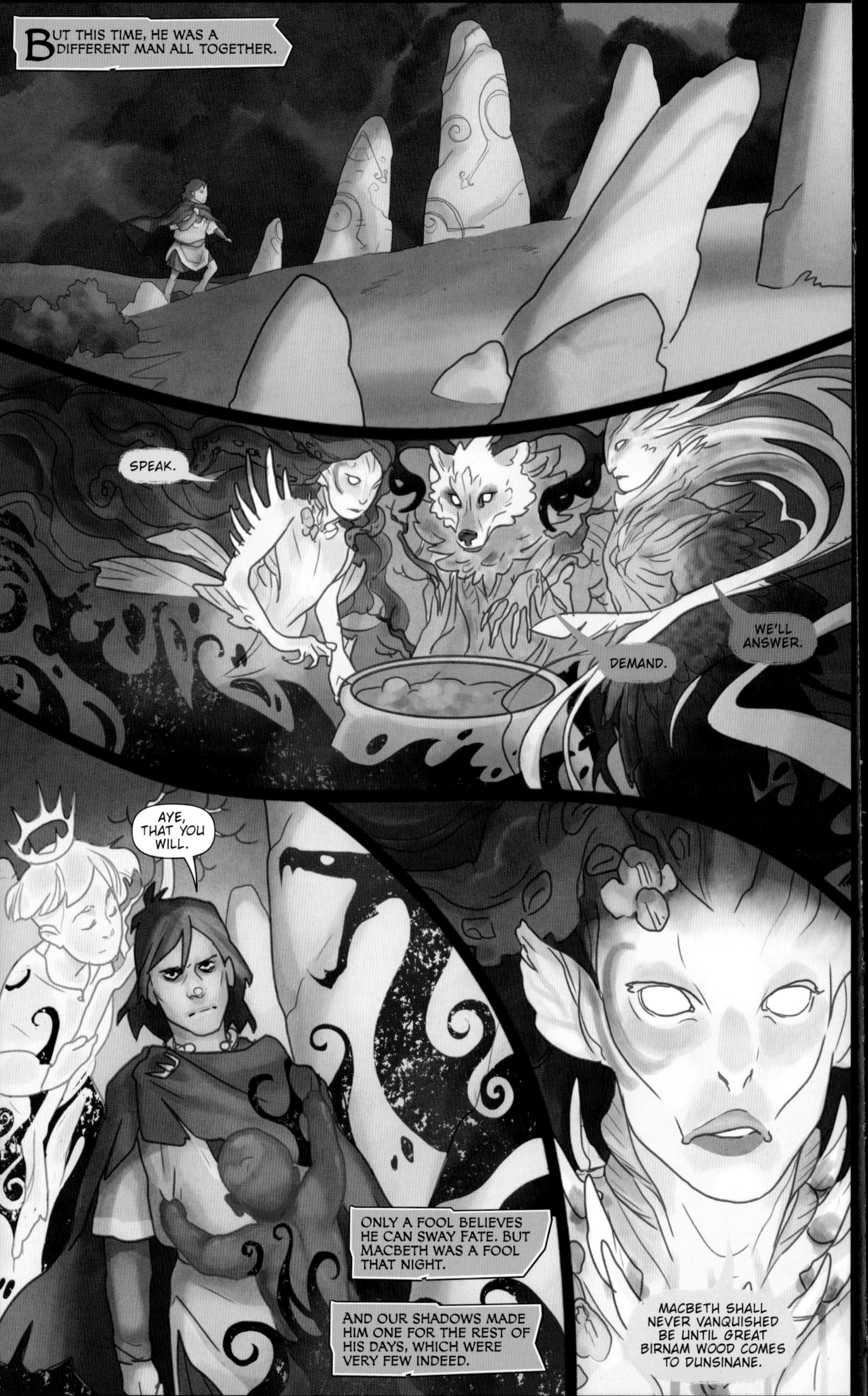
BUT THIS TIME, HE WAS A DIFFERENT MAN ALL TOGETHER.
SPEAK.
DEMAND.
WE'LL ANSWER.
AYE, THAT YOU WILL.
ONLY A FOOL BELIEVES HE CAN SWAY FATE. BUT MACBETH WAS A FOOL THAT NIGHT.
AND OUR SHADOWS MADE HIM ONE FOR THE REST OF HIS DAYS, WHICH WERE VERY FEW INDEED.
MACBETH SHALL NEVER VANQUISHED BE UNTIL GREAT BIRNAM WOOD COMES TO DUNSINANE.

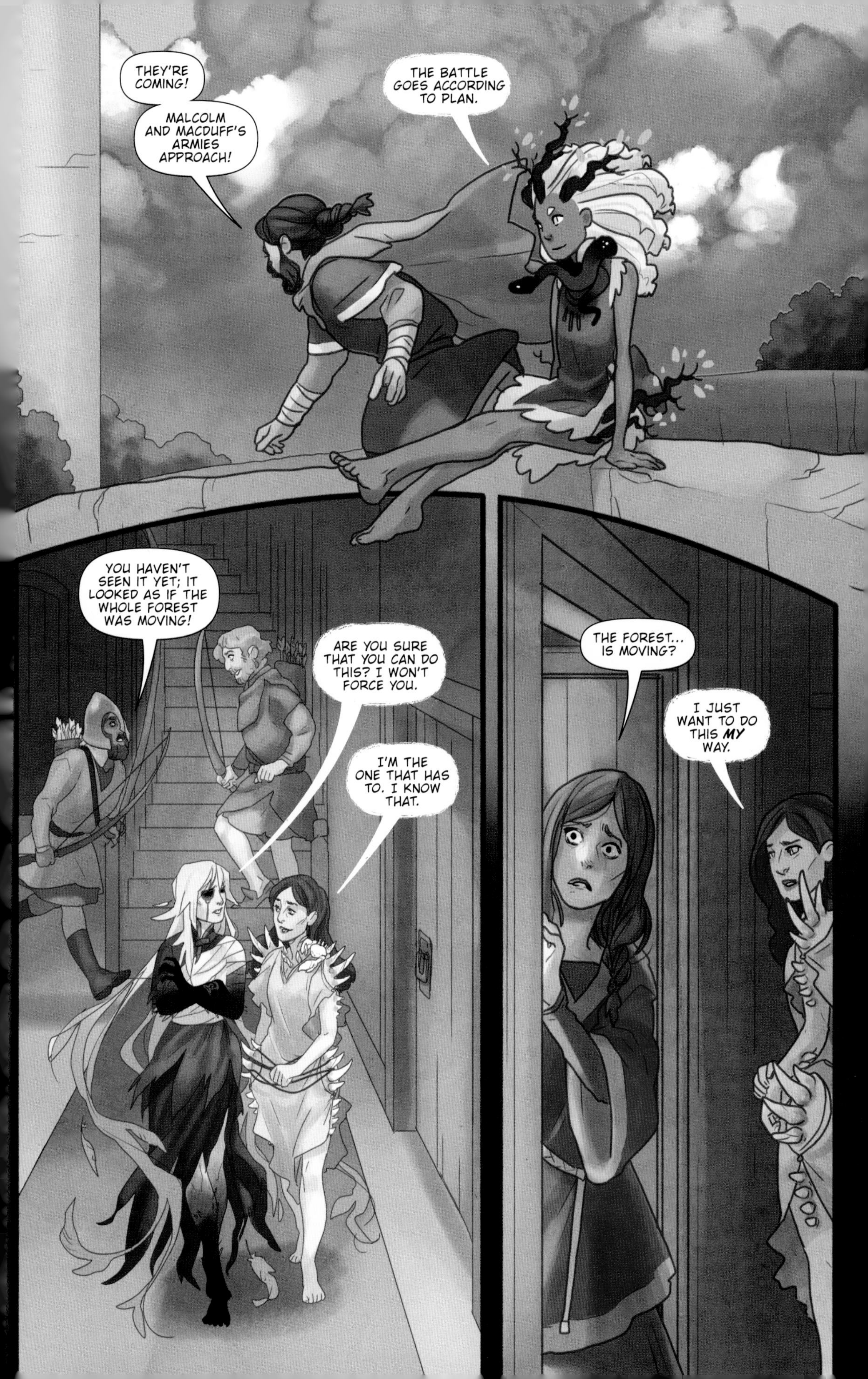
THEY'RE COMING!
MALCOLM AND MACDUFF'S ARMIES APPROACH!
THE BATTLE GOES ACCORDING TO PLAN.
YOU HAVEN'T SEEN IT YET; IT LOOKED AS IF THE WHOLE FOREST WAS MOVING!
ARE YOU SURE THAT YOU CAN DO THIS? I WON'T FORCE YOU.
I'M THE ONE THAT HAS TO. I KNOW THAT.
THE FOREST... IS MOVING?
I JUST WANT TO DO THIS ***MY*** WAY.

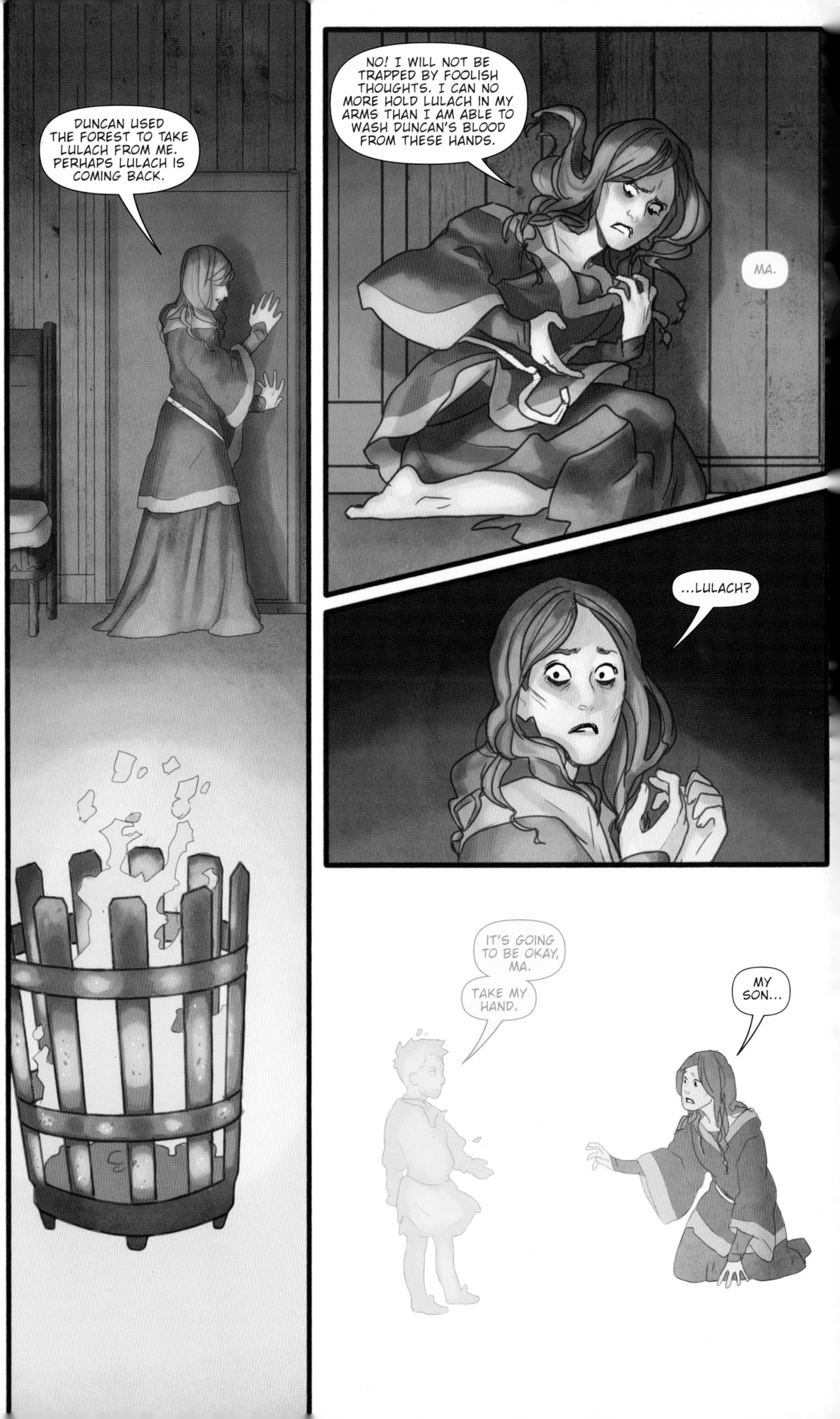
DUNCAN USED THE FOREST TO TAKE LULACH FROM ME. PERHAPS LULACH IS COMING BACK.
NO! I WILL NOT BE TRAPPED BY FOOLISH THOUGHTS. I CAN NO MORE HOLD LULACH IN MY ARMS THAN I AM ABLE TO WASH DUNCAN'S BLOOD FROM THESE HANDS.
MA.
...LULACH?
IT'S GOING TO BE OKAY, MA.
TAKE MY HAND.
MY SON...

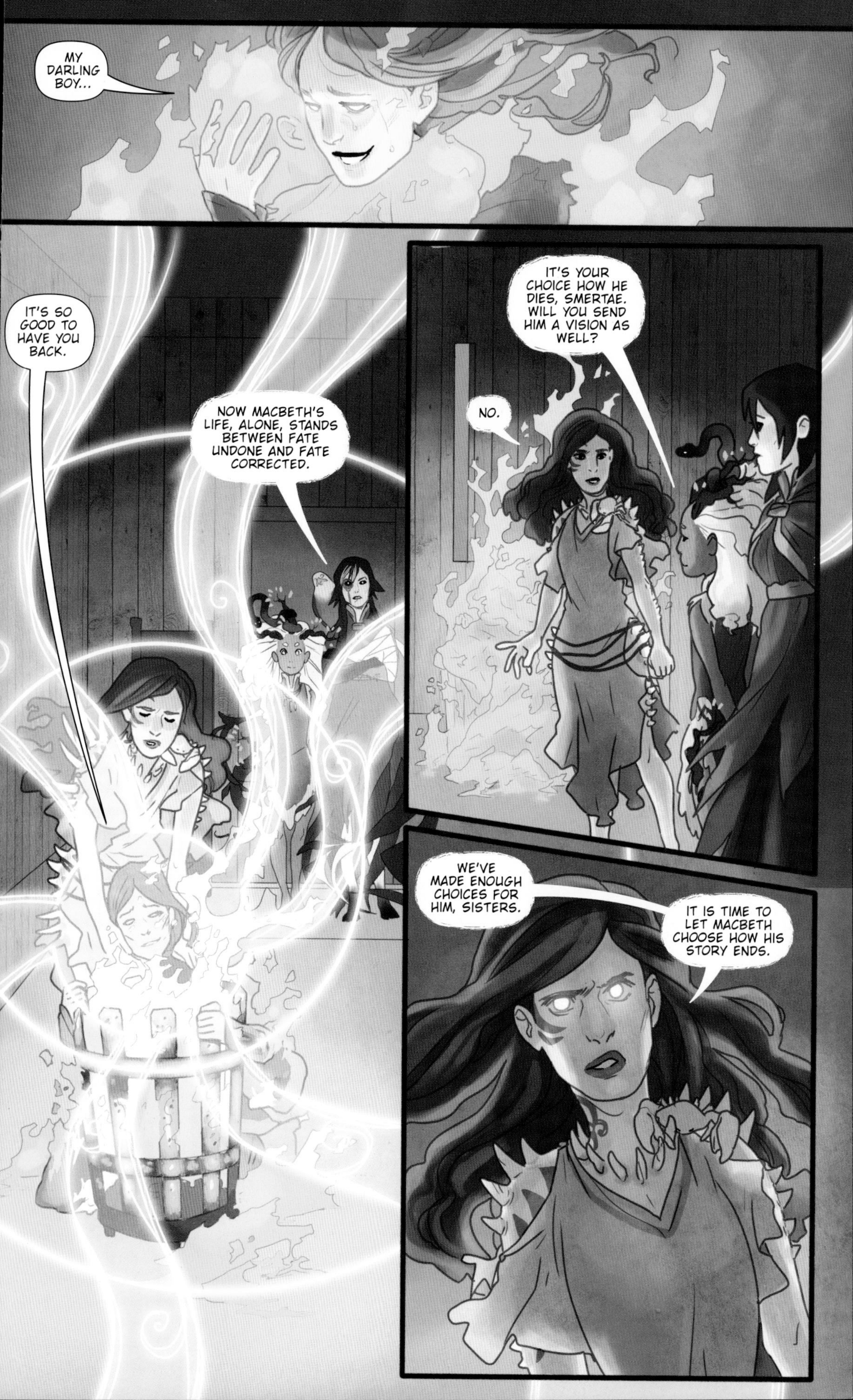
MY DARLING BOY...
IT'S SO GOOD TO HAVE YOU BACK.
NOW MACBETH'S LIFE, ALONE, STANDS BETWEEN FATE UNDONE AND FATE CORRECTED.
IT'S YOUR CHOICE HOW HE DIES, SMERTAE. WILL YOU SEND HIM A VISION AS WELL?
NO.
WE'VE MADE ENOUGH CHOICES FOR HIM, SISTERS.
IT IS TIME TO LET MACBETH CHOOSE HOW HIS STORY ENDS.

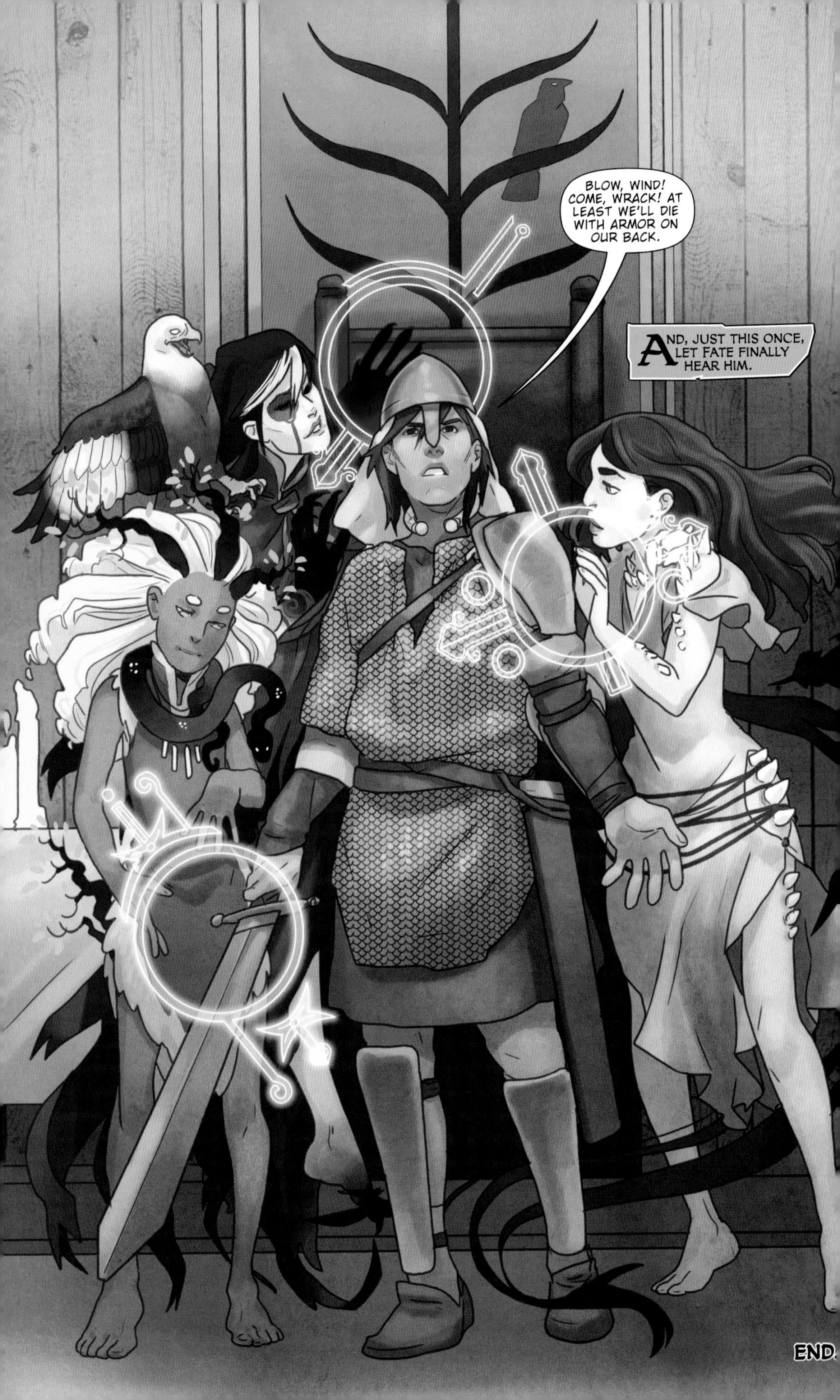
BLOW, WIND! COME, WRACK! AT LEAST WE'LL DIE WITH ARMOR ON OUR BACK.
AND, JUST THIS ONCE, LET FATE FINALLY HEAR HIM.
END.

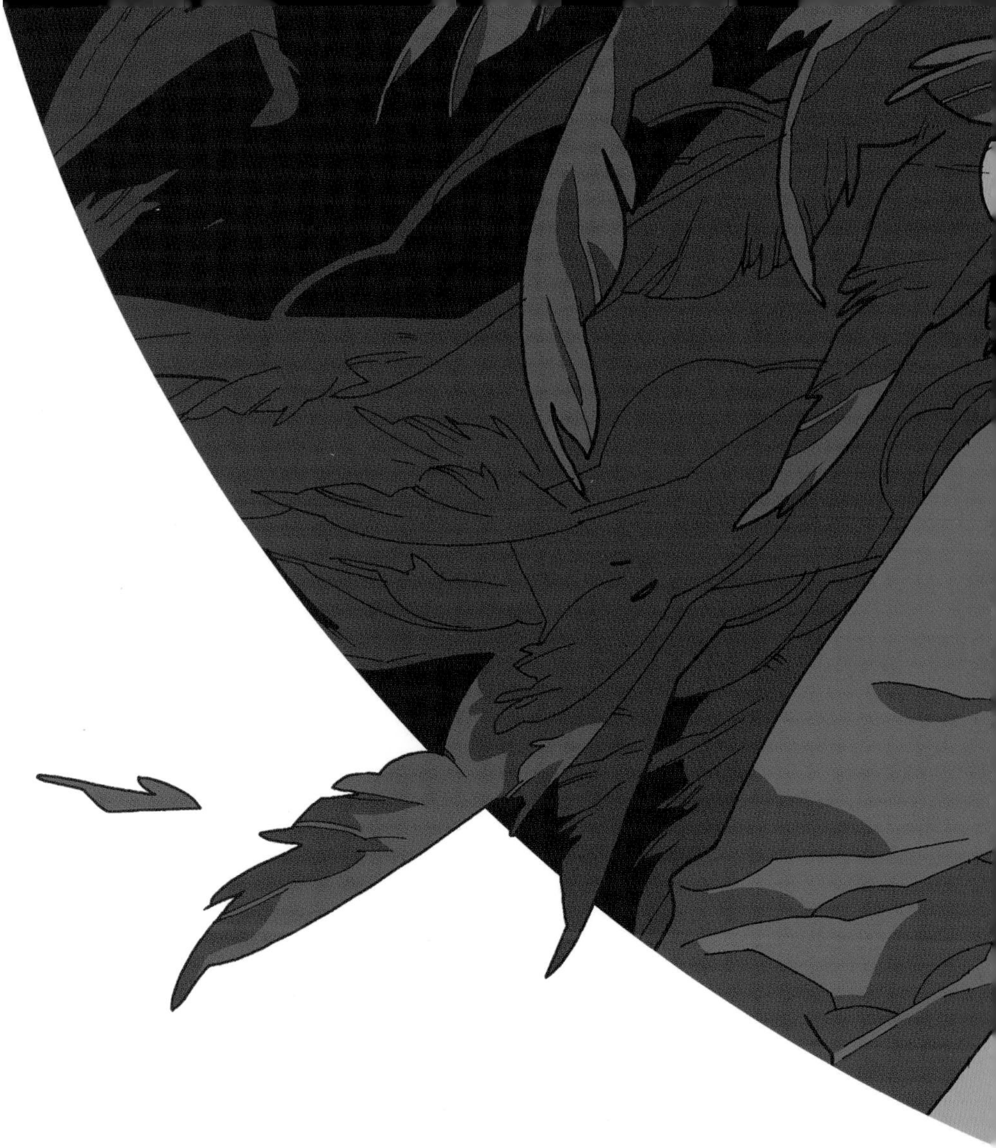

BOOM! Ten Years Anniversary Cover by Meredith McClaren

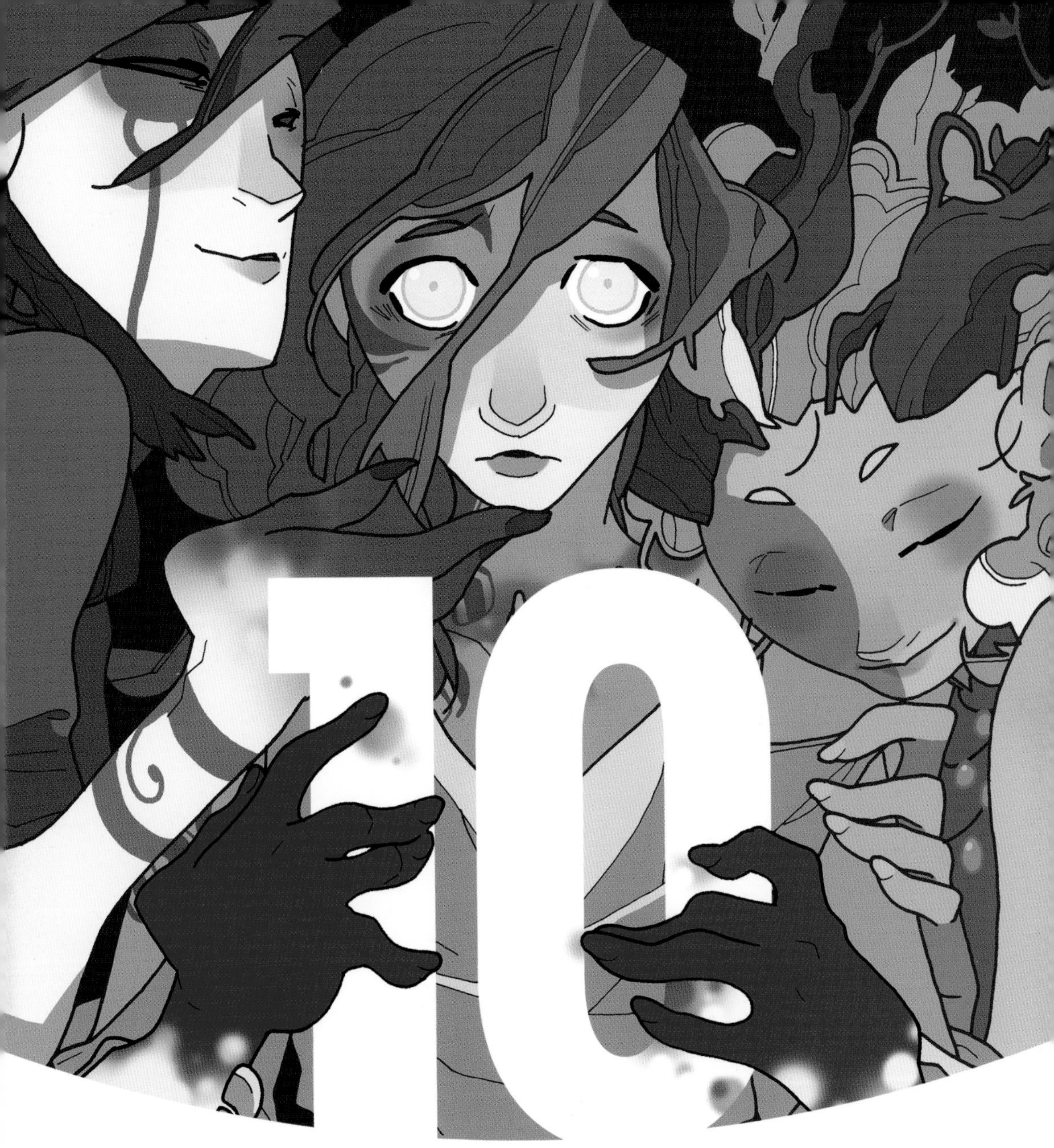
10

Variant Cover by Haemi Jang

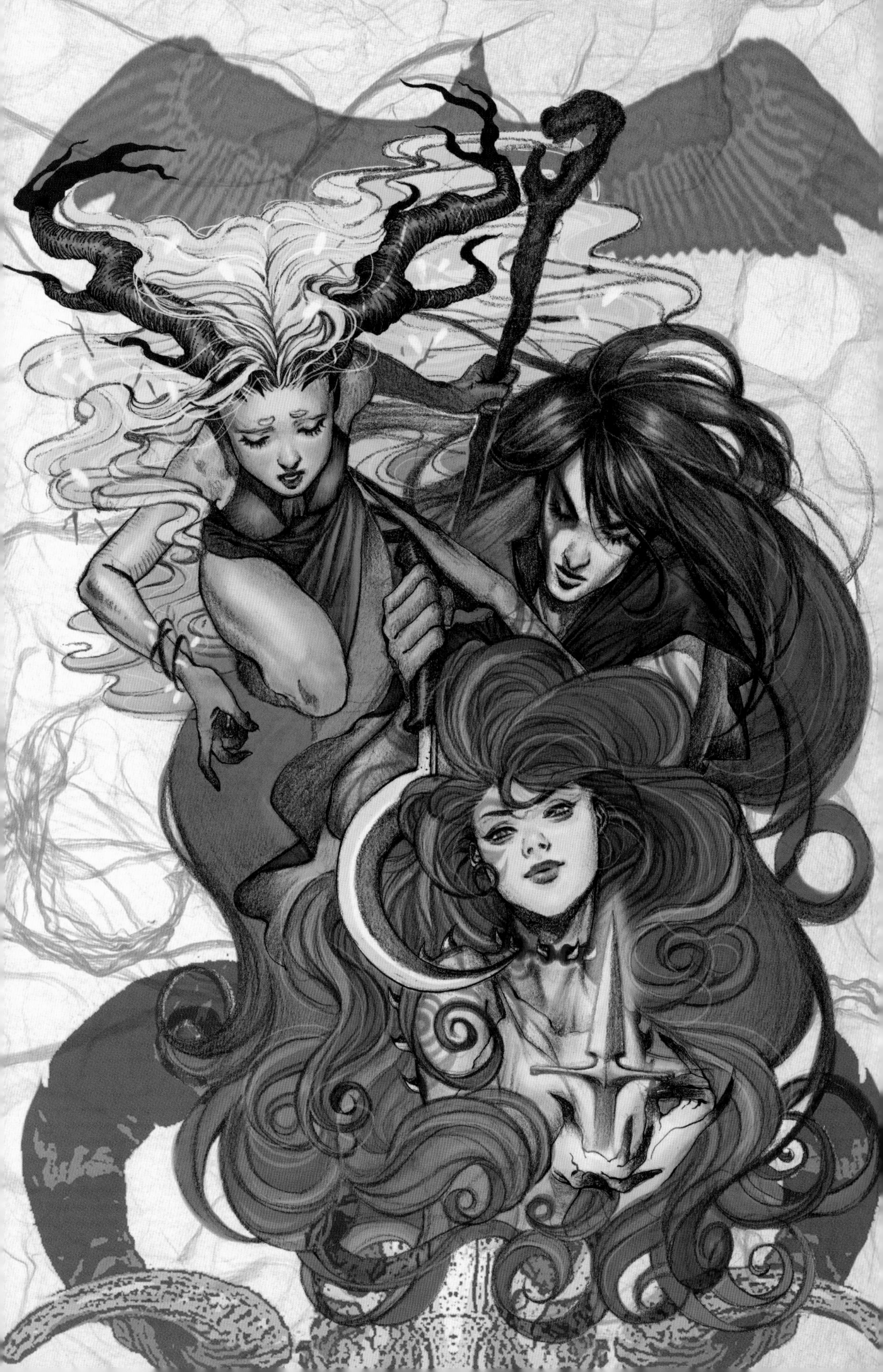

SIGNIFYING NOTHING

A Summary, Exploration and Examination of Toil and Trouble
By Mairghread Scott

I love William Shakespeare. I grew up with a very pro-Shakespeare family: I watched Kenneth Branagh's *Henry V* when I was way too young for it and my father still calls every St. Crispin's Day to read King Henry's famous 'we few' speech. We went on every school trip to Stratford's Shakespeare festival in Canada and I was encouraged to see Shakespeare as an accessible, exciting and adaptable author. He's not a perfect writer. *The Merry Wives of Windsor* is basically Falstaff fanfiction. *Henry IV* probably would have been better as one play instead of two. But the bulk of his work is brilliant in its humanity and its timelessness.

However, the Bard is not without his hurtles. My high school English teachers struggled mightily to get kids to see beyond the language barrier, but no one laughed at the hilarious "Do you bite your thumb at me?" bit in *Romeo and Juliet*. Low-grade performances tend to drag on forever, as if watching something performed at half-speed makes it more dramatic. My college professors were more interested in trying to ferret out Shakespeare's personal life (Was Bill gay?) than they were about exploring the work itself.

For a 'friend of Bill' this will not stand. I don't just love Shakespeare, I stubbornly insist everyone else love his work as well—and I love *Macbeth* most of all. I'm Scottish in ancestry (you may have noticed by my last name) and the fact that *Macbeth* is so Scottish its nickname is "The Scottish Play" made it instantly important to my family. Like the character Macduff, who foils Macbeth's prophesy that no man of woman born can defeat him, I was born via C-section. You really haven't had a birthday until your father spends it reminding you that you were also "a bloody child" in his best 'old hag' voice. Suffice it to say, there are a lot of parallels.

But I love *Macbeth* most because it's Shakespeare's most evocative work. Epic battles, supernatural events, magic, treason, and murder are all over this story. Characters drop bombshells about their past and move on without blinking an eye. Not every aspect is neatly explained or wrapped up. If there's any story in Shakespeare's canon that's actually underwritten (though delightfully so), it's this one. And that's where *Toil and Trouble* comes in.

How *Toil and Trouble* Was Written

"Better a witty fool, than a foolish wit."
-Twelfth Night, *Act 1, Scene 5*

It gives me no pleasure to say that this story originally came from a mistake on my part. My freshman year of college, a professor assigned us to write a five-page adaptation of *Macbeth*. Of course, the musical *Wicked* (an adaptation of *The Wizard of Oz*) was in full force and I assumed she meant the kind of adaptation where the story is expanded and explained. While everyone else moved the play forward in time, or changed the characters' roles and ages, I wrote my adaptation to be the scene before the play actually starts and I wrote it to answer one of the nagging questions *Macbeth* leaves behind. What the heck is up with the witches?

In *Macbeth*, three witches decide to tempt a man to murder and launch a kingdom into war, but we never learn why they do it. Why expend all this effort just to yank some random mortal's chain? It bugged me for years. The witches in the play clearly aren't mechanical specters that spit out prophesy whenever someone walks by. You see them chat with each other and joke with each other in their 'off-hours.' It's gallows humor, to be sure, but it proves that the witches are clearly 'human' enough to have some independence.

So, I started to think of Fate as their jobs. But what kind of woman picks "Hand of Fate" as a career path? How would that happen? And how heart-breaking must it be to tell someone a prophesy you know they will misunderstand. Or to see an unjust future ahead of a good person? And is there anything...anything that could make you want to bend the rules? To break them? Can the Hand of Fate rebel against Fate itself? This weird little thought-spiral consumed me and the more I thought about it, the more it became a story I had to tell.

But I only had five pages. So I wrote the very first scene exploring the idea that the three witches tempt Macbeth and test Macbeth because they are agents of Fate, even slaves to it. The scene was well received, even though no one could figure out why I'd picked the most obscure form of adaptation to work with, and I went on my merry way. But those witches and their motives wouldn't let me go. Ten years, two cities, a failed movie script, and four artists later, *Toil and Trouble* was born. It's a story as much in contrast with its source material as it is in keeping with it and the most beautiful mistake I've ever made.

What is *Macbeth*? How are We Different?

"That is a step on which I must fall down, or else o'erleap, for it lies in my way."
-Macbeth, *Act 1, Scene 4*

Shakespeare's *Macbeth* is the story of the Scottish lord (thane), Macbeth, who meets a group of witches who say that he will one day become king (and that the children of his friend, Banquo, will one day become kings). The only problem is that the king of Scotland, Duncan, is alive and promptly names his son, Malcolm, his heir. Tempted by the witches' promise, Macbeth and his wife struggle and argue over whether or not to kill King Duncan when he comes for a visit. Lady Macbeth is all for it, as it will fulfill the prophecy. But Macbeth waffles between thinking she's right and thinking he should leave the whole matter up to Fate.

In the end, Macbeth does kill Duncan and frames Malcolm and his brother Donalbain for the murder. The princes flee and Macbeth is named king in their absence. However, Macbeth does not rest easy in his power. He becomes cruel, punishing any perceived disloyalty in the extreme. He's also obsessed with the fear that Banquo's sons will become king afterward. Macbeth has Banquo killed to stop that part of the prophecy, but fails to kill his son, Fleance.

Macbeth even returns to the witches in search of a way to ensure his continued reign. The witches' prophecy tricks Macbeth and when an army of soldiers (lead by Malcolm and several of the thanes Macbeth mistreated) arrives, Macbeth's faith in the prophecies makes him feel invincible right up to the end. The witches say that no man born of woman can kill him. But Macduff, the man that does kill him, was cut out of his mother's body and therefore, not born. Macbeth is undone and killed. Peace, at last, restored.

The central theme of *Macbeth* is ambition and greed. The witches never force Macbeth to kill Duncan, they merely tempt him. In the end, his friend's misplaced encouragement, his wife's expectations, and his own ambition drive Macbeth to murder. But what is stolen can be stolen again and we see Macbeth descend to near madness as he lashes out at anything that might take away his ill-gotten crown. It's a cautionary tale about how much power is like water, the tighter you hold it, the less you have of it. Macbeth kills out of greed and a lust for power, and it is greed that destroys him.

Toil and Trouble has Macbeth in it, but it's not Macbeth's story. It is about the witch Smertae and her sisters. More than anything our theme is not ambition, but loss, specifically the failure to adapt and move on from it. The witches are literally women from earlier ages of history. Their cultures, their people, even their values are lost. They struggle to adapt to their more modern surroundings and the people in them. Macbeth loses his son, Lulach, in a terrible accident caused by Smertae. Smertae feels this loss just as deeply, because she thought Lulach would be king next. She loses the future she was so sure would come to pass. In a way, the prophecy that destroys Macbeth in *Macbeth* destroys the sisters in *Toil and Trouble* as well. It's the catalyst that pushes Macbeth over the edge and it's the anchor that drags the sisters away from each other, plunging them into war.

We end up with a lot of characters who are trying to fix the unfixable. Smertae tries to fix her lost prophesy, forcing Macbeth to fulfill Lulach's destiny. Riata tries to enforce outdated social norms. Cait tries to browbeat people into being family. Lady Macbeth is still looking for the justice she feels was long denied her after the death of her son. And Macbeth stands at the center of it all, struggling the most to move on from his grief and wanting the most to give in to the idea that he has been wronged. After all, it would be so much easier to hurt Duncan if the king had wronged Macbeth; it would be justice instead of just regicide. *Toil and Trouble* is a story about letting go: who can do it, who can't, and the pain inherent when we try to force pieces back together that just don't fit anymore.

Topics and Aspects for Discussion

"We know what we are, but know not what we may be."
-Hamlet, *Act 4, Scene 5*

There are a number of aspects of *Toil and Trouble* that provide the opportunity to compare and contrast it with the play and explore the history of the real Macbeth and 11th century Scotland. Here are some topics to discuss:

. . . .

There is only one moment in *Macbeth* that suggests Lady Macbeth had a child. But Lulach's life and death are a major turning point in *Toil and Trouble*. In fact, there are many moments in *Toil and Trouble* that are only briefly mentioned in the

original text. Can you root out which moments of this graphic novel come directly from the play *Macbeth*? Do these moments have a different context in the graphic novel? Discuss how.

. . . .

Much effort was given to make *Toil and Trouble* as historically accurate as possible. Each of the witches is from a specific time period. Riata is the most recent (from the 2nd century CE), having been part of the rebellion that drove the Romans from the Antonine Wall. Smertae is second, and is tied

to the Bronze Age. Cait is from a Mesolithic coastal settlement that was destroyed by the last Storegga Slide (the massive earthquake/tsunami that sank what was left of Doggerland in the 6000s BCE). We attempted to portray their lives as best we could, Cait's being the hardest. In flashbacks her village is actually based on the Neolithic UNESCO World Heritage Site Skara Brae, which was constructed much later than Cait's village would have been, but was the earliest example of a settlement anywhere near Scotland that I could find.

Similarly, Cait's clothing is based on the earliest European clothing I could locate, found on Ötzi—the roughly 3,300 BCE mummy discovered in the Ötzal Alps. Strangely, his outfit bore a striking resemblance to traditional Inuit outfits, which were also used in Cait's clothing design. Her headdress comes from several Mesolithic burial excavations that show various animal parts adorning human bodies (therefore her red deer antlers came from the time when she died).

Examine the costumes, architecture, and furniture within this comic and determine what time period and cultural influences were considered when establishing this world. Much like Cait, characters like Riata, Smertae, Macbeth, and Banquo were intended to visually correspond to the look and feel of their time period and region. What other historical examples can you find in *Toil And Trouble*? Where did we miss the mark? And how important is it for a work of fiction to be accurate to the time period it's trying to depict?

· ·

You might have noticed that there are a lot more racially diverse people in *Toil and Trouble* than you'd expect in 11th century Scotland. Discuss the interaction between Scotland and other cultures (the Romans, the Norse) and how accurate this depiction may or may not be.

· ·

Notably absent in *Toil and Trouble* is the Greek goddess of magic and the crossroads, Hecate, who is in most published versions of *Macbeth* as the boss of the three witches. She is not in *Toil and Trouble* because most modern scholars do not think Hecate is original to the play. In fact, chunks of her dialog appear to have been lifted from Thomas Middleton's 17th century play *The Witch*. But her presence can still be felt in this book in the appearance of a corvid throughout the story. Discuss the role of Fate in both *Toil and Trouble* and *Macbeth* and see if there are any other indications that Hecate might still be around.

· ·

Family and family-like ties are a major theme explored in both *Toil and Trouble* and *Macbeth*. How are these ties helpful and hurtful in each of these stories? Are the relationships between characters (Lady Macbeth and her husband, Banquo and Macbeth, Macbeth and Duncan) different in the comic versus the play? If so, how?

· ·

Many of the events and visuals we see in *Toil and Trouble* would be difficult or impossible to stage in a live production like *Macbeth*. Discuss the advantages and disadvantages of telling this story as a graphic novel instead of another medium. Discuss other adaptations of *Macbeth* (in film, novels, etc) and how each medium effects the storytelling experience.

AUTHOR'S NOTE: The following two pages are a good example of several character interactions and show you where some of our research actually came into play. They'll also show you how a story changes from script to final comic book page.

PANEL 1: MACDONWALD approaches a NORWEGIAN CAPTAIN. Macdonwald holds his arms out like he's seeing an old friend. Smertae stands behind them. Harpier sits in her hand, agitated.

NORWEGIAN CAPTAIN: We shall see, my thane. If we can take Kinloss by sundown, I think we have a chance. But I fear the Scottish forces will not go quietly.

MACDONWALD: You forget, we have Scottish forces of our own. Men eager to fight for me and my cause. The name Macdonwald still carries weight here.

HARPIER: !!! <angry squiggles>

SMERTAE: Don't snap, Harpier. Just get me to the circle.

AUTHOR'S NOTE: The ship designs and costumes/armor are based on known designs from the 11th century. The shoreline is based on Google map views of the east coast of Scotland.

AUTHOR'S NOTE: Harpier is an albino brown crab, which are native to Scotland.

ARTISTS' NOTES: This will always be a memorable page for us, where we could first show the magical world of the witches and the physical world of the mortals and how they interact.

PANEL 2: The Norwegian Captain gestures out to the ships in the harbor. Harpier's form stretches and morphs as he begins to transform.

SMERTAE: We'll paint the stones with their blood soon enough.

MACDONWALD: Once King Duncan's been defeated, the others will fall in line. Get me to Forres and Norway will trade a bitter enemy for a welcome ally.

PANEL 3: Macdonwald gazes admiringly at the ships, confident, proud. Harpier is now a white horse. Smertae mounts him.

CAPTION: No king has ever ruled this land without our consent.

NORWEGIAN CAPTAIN: Then by your leave, I'll see your camp. My men can not fight while still a'ship.

PANEL 4: Smertae and Harpier take off into the forest. A carrion crow watches in one of the trees.

CAPTION: And even Riata would not put this fool, Macdonwald, on the throne.

AUTHOR'S NOTE: This crow appears in every issue of the Toil and Trouble comics.

ARTISTS' NOTE: Ahh the crow. You will see it in every issue...but this one! See that text box on this page? Yeah, the crow's under there. At some point between us finishing the pages and the comic going to print he got covered up.

EDITOR'S NOTE: We changed this for the collection, our bad issue #1!

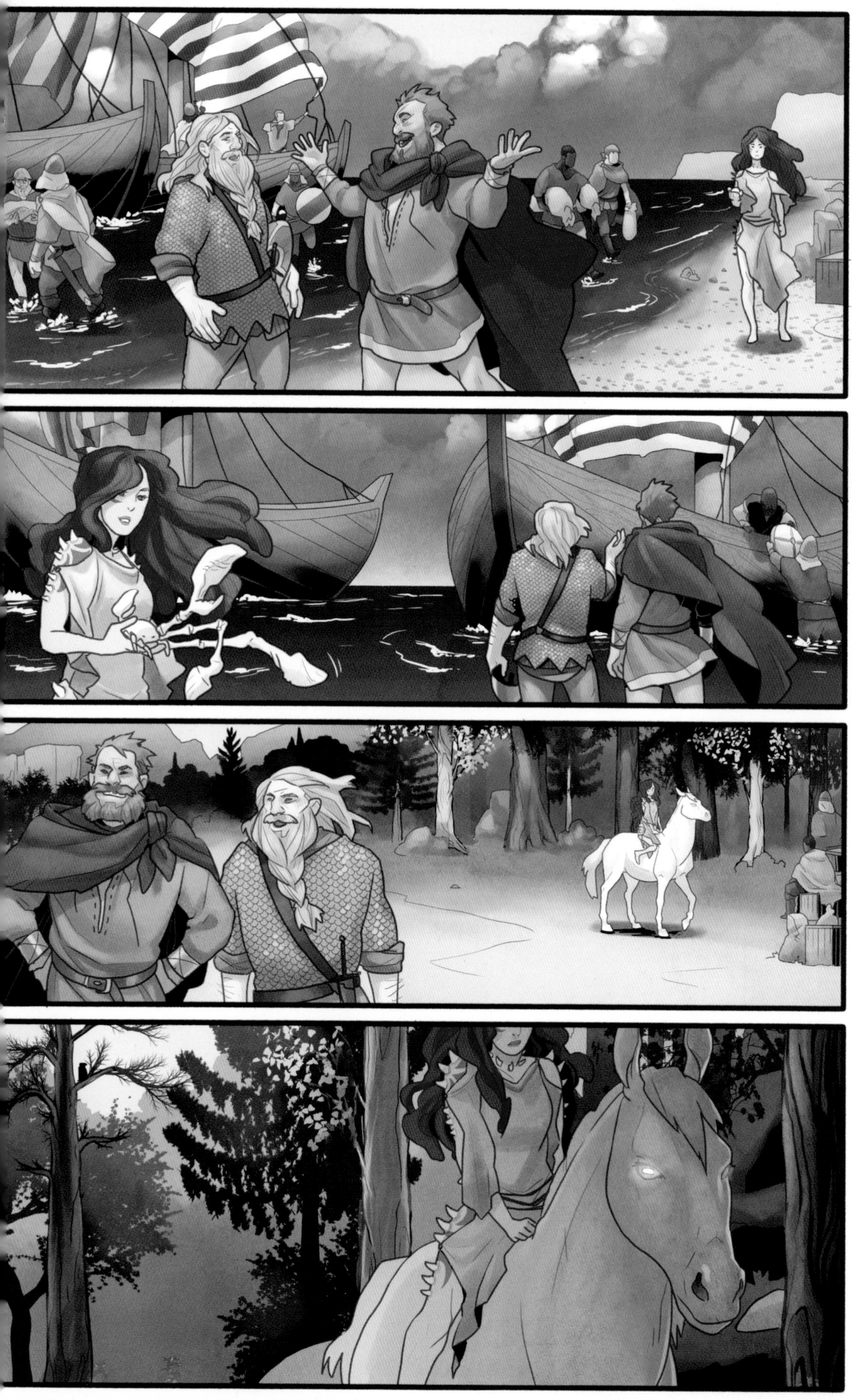

PANEL 1: Smertae and Harpier (horse) ride through a dense forest. In the foreground is the skull of a red deer stag, scraps of flesh clinging to it.

> *CAPTION:* Three witches rule Scotland, the land called Alba by those who remember.

> *CAPTION:* Three witches have ruled it since before the ice returned. Before Doggerland fell into the sea.

AUTHOR'S NOTE: Red deer are native to Scotland.

AUTHOR'S NOTE: Doggerland is a landmass that originally connected Great Britain to Europe. Its final collapse was cause by a Norwegian tsunami so large there's evidence of flooding on Scotland's coastline. This same tsunami is the wave in Cait's flashback later in the book.

ARTISTS' NOTES: The decomposing stag was a good lead in (at least for us) to the amount of gore that would eventually show up later on, both on mortal battlefields and immortal showdowns.

PANEL 2: Smertae and Harpier ride through a lush meadow. In the foreground is a young red deer stag, strong and healthy.

> *CAPTION:* We guide it to its full potential. We guard it from its enemies.

AUTHOR'S NOTE: Note the language choice here, which implies that Smertae sees herself as a needed and active part in helping Fate along. She guides Scotland's fate instead of just 'seeing' it, 'recording' it, or 'witnessing' it.

PANEL 3: Smertae and Harpier ride across a barren moor, a stone circle is ahead of them, sitting on top of a ridge.

> *CAPTION:* We lead it on the path the Gods decree.

AUTHOR'S NOTE: Some of the designs on these stones come from real life examples I found on a trip I took to Edinburgh, Inverness, and Orkney to research this book. In fact, this panel eventually came out reminding me a lot of the train trip from Inverness to Thurso. The highlands have a lot of this kind of extreme elevation change and 'see for miles' view.

ARTISTS' NOTES: Bringing to life the magic of *Toil and Trouble* was arguably what excited us the most about working on this project. Magic was such a large part of the story, both in how the witches used it on others and how it, in turn, punished the triad for misusing it. It was important for us to come to a visual style that incorporated the symbols on the stones into the witches' magic spells, with specific ones calling back to specific witches.

PANEL 4: Smertae and Harpier reach the circle, standing at its center is a bonfire that casts weird shadows from it. But no one else is there.

> *CAPTION:* The Norns fall silent and the Moirai fade into their own weave, but the witches of Alba endure.

AUTHOR'S NOTE: The Norns and Moirai are examples of other Fate-associated beings from different cultures. This line (and a few later) are meant to show that different groups of 'witches' could be working toward different fates. It also shows that our witches could be in danger of 'fading' (i.e. death) and it reveals the stakes when the witches later go to war.

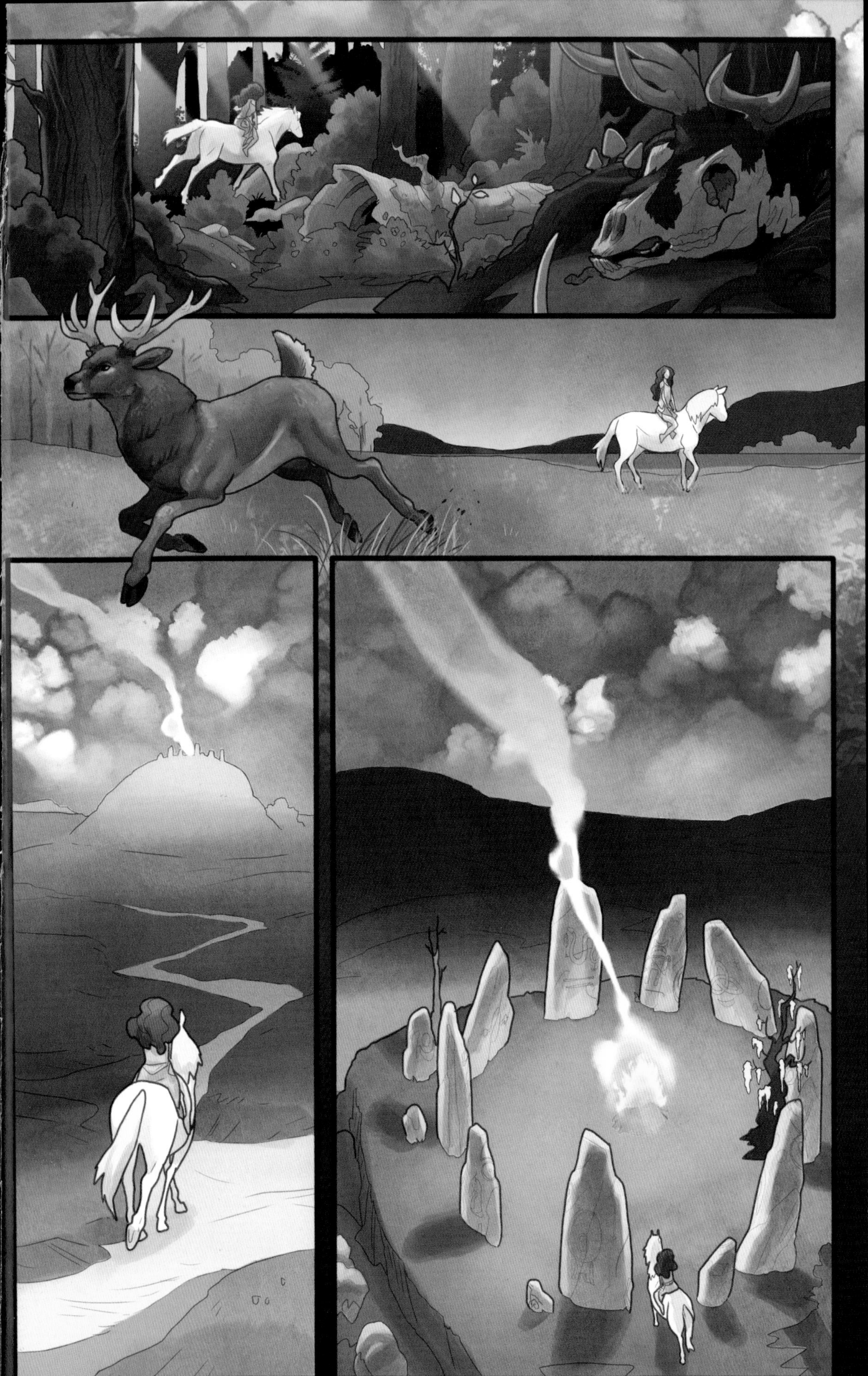